Selected Readings in 20ᵀᴴ Century American Literature
20世纪美国文学选读

陶 洁 主编

编者 陶 洁 程朝翔 刘建华 刘树森 张世耘
陈法春 林 斌 沈建青 李 晋

图书在版编目(CIP)数据

20 世纪美国文学选读 /陶洁主编. —北京：北京大学出版社，2006.8
(21 世纪外国文学系列教材)
ISBN 978-7-301-11015-7

Ⅰ.2… Ⅱ.陶… Ⅲ.①英语-阅读教学-高等学校-教材②文学-作品-简介-美国-20 世纪 Ⅳ.H319.4:I

中国版本图书馆 CIP 数据核字(2006)第 100596 号

书　　　名：20 世纪美国文学选读
著作责任者：陶　洁　主编
组稿编辑：张　冰
责任编辑：刘　强
标准书号：ISBN 978-7-301-11015-7/H·1676
出版发行：北京大学出版社
地　　　址：北京市海淀区成府路 205 号　100871
网　　　址：http://www.pup.cn
电　　　话：邮购部 62752015　发行部 62750672　编辑部 62767347　出版部 62754962
电子邮箱：landwok@163.com
印　刷　者：北京宏伟双华印刷有限公司
经　销　者：新华书店
　　　　　　787 毫米×1092 毫米　16 开本　24.75 印张　526 千字
　　　　　　2006 年 8 月第 1 版　2007 年 7 月第 2 次印刷
定　　　价：32.00 元

未经许可，不得以任何方式复制或抄袭本书之部分或全部内容。
版权所有，侵权必究　举报电话：010-62752024
　　　　　　　　　　电子邮箱：fd@pup.pku.edu.cn

前　言

近年来,我国读者对美国文学的兴趣越来越大。各大专院校的英语系纷纷设立美国文学选读和有关美国文学的课程。不过,许多选读课本常常从 19 世纪或更早一些的时期说起,而美国文学是在 20 世纪,尤其是在第一次世界大战后走向世界并称霸世界文坛的。为此,我们决定单独编一本 20 世纪美国文学选读,供有兴趣的教师做选修课教材,也便于高年级学生或研究生了解现当代美国文学和美国社会与文化发展的脉络,在增长知识的同时提高对文学的鉴赏能力,培养他们分析问题、研究问题的能力,为撰写毕业论文打下基础。

在编写过程中我们遵循以下几条原则:

首先,在作家的取舍方面,凡是已经成为经典的我们仍然收入,如海明威、福克纳和菲茨杰拉德等小说家和庞德、威廉斯、史蒂文斯等诗人。但我们增加了斯坦贝克,一方面因为他是 1930 年代关心政治的左翼作家;另一方面因为 1980 年代以来关于他的传记和评论大量出版,他在美国已经成为仅次于马克·吐温的最受欢迎的作家。

其次,考虑到美国文学的多元化发展,我们所选的作家不仅在文学史上占有一定的地位,而且在主题、手法、文体风格或种族、性别等方面有一定的代表性。所选篇目必须是该作家的经典作品。例如,我们不仅有白人、黑人和犹太裔作家,还增加了华裔和墨西哥裔作家,不仅有现实主义作家也有采用试验手法的诗人和小说家。我们还在选材上除了戏剧和个别小说家如托妮·莫里森外尽量使用独立完整的文本,并且尽量选用既有代表性又不是大家研究熟悉的材料。

第三,我们认为一本好的教科书不能面面俱到,包办一切,而是应该起引导作用,给教师和学生留有充分的思考空间和余地。因此,我们只有简明扼要的作者简介和赏析却提供了进一步阅读的篇目和一些参考书。为此,虽然此选读供一学期 18 周使用,但我们提供了 19 个单元,诗歌方面介绍的诗人就更多一些,目的在于教师和学生可以有所选择,发挥自己的主观能动性。

我们的编写者均对所介绍的作家有一定的研究,具体分工如下:陶洁:前言、绪论;程朝翔:第6、12、18 单元;张世耘:第2、3、8 单元;刘建华:第4、14 单元;刘树森:第 11 单元(其中三位诗人除外);陈法春:第7、13 单元和第 5 单元的 Hughes 及第 11 单元的 Hayden;沈建青:第1、15、16 单元;李晋:第 9 单元和第 17 单元的 Pinsky, Dove 及 Bly;林斌:第10、19 单元和第 11 单元的 Bishop 以及第 17 单元的 Warren, Ashbery 及 Soto。

虽然我们做了努力,但这本教材肯定尚未达到完美无缺的水平。我们衷心希望老师和学生以及所有的读者会对我们提出宝贵的意见。

绪论：20 世纪美国文学概述 ·· 1

I 1900—1945

第一单元 ··· 3
John Steinbeck (1902—1968) 约翰·斯坦贝克 ················ 3
The Chrysanthemums ··· 4

第二单元 ··· 16
F. Scott Fitzgerald (1896—1940) 弗·斯科特·菲茨杰拉德 ······ 16
Winter Dreams ··· 17

第三单元 ··· 40
Ernest Hemingway (1899—1961) 厄内斯特·海明威 ·········· 40
Hills Like White Elephants ······································ 41

第四单元 ··· 48
William Faulkner (1897—1962) 威廉·福克纳 ················ 48
Barn Burning ··· 49

第五单元 ··· 68
Ezra Pound (1885—1972) 艾兹拉·庞德 ······················ 68
A Girl ·· 68
Wallace Stevens (1879—1955) 华莱士·史蒂文斯 ············· 71
The Snow Man ··· 71
William Carlos Williams (1883—1963) 威廉·卡洛斯·威廉斯 ····· 74
The Uses of Poetry ··· 74
Robert Frost (1874—1963) 罗伯特·弗罗斯特 ················ 77
Love and A Question ·· 77
E. E. Cummings (1894—1962) E. E. 肯明斯 ················ 80
Humanity i love you ·· 80

Langston Hughes (1902—1967) 兰斯顿·休斯 …………………………… 83
    The Weary Blues ………………………………………………………… 84

第六单元 ……………………………………………………………………… 87
Eugene Gladstone O'Neill (1888—1953) 尤金·格拉斯通·奥尼尔 … 87
    Long Day's Journey into Night ………………………………………… 88

II 1945—2000

第七单元 ……………………………………………………………………… 125
Ralph (Waldo) Ellison (1914—1994) 拉尔夫·埃里森 ………………… 125
    King of the Bingo Game ………………………………………………… 126

第八单元 ……………………………………………………………………… 138
John Updike (1932—   ) 约翰·厄普代克 ……………………………… 138
    Separating ………………………………………………………………… 139

第九单元 ……………………………………………………………………… 152
Saul Bellow (1915—2005) 索尔·贝娄 ………………………………… 152
    A Silver Dish ……………………………………………………………… 153

第十单元 ……………………………………………………………………… 182
Flannery O'Connor (1925—1964) 弗兰纳里·奥康纳 ………………… 182
    A Good Man Is Hard to Find (1953) …………………………………… 183

第十一单元 …………………………………………………………………… 201
Allen Ginsberg (1926—1997) 艾伦·金斯堡 …………………………… 201
    On the Conduct of the World Seeking Beauty Against Government … 202
Robert Lowell (1917—1977) 罗伯特·洛威尔 ………………………… 205
    Man and Wife ……………………………………………………………… 205
Elizabeth Bishop (1911—1979) 伊丽莎白·毕晓普 …………………… 208
    Sestina ……………………………………………………………………… 208
Robert Creeley (1926—2005) 罗伯特·克里莱 ………………………… 212
    Water Music ……………………………………………………………… 212
Robert Hayden (1913—1980) 罗伯特·海登 …………………………… 215
    Those Winter Sundays …………………………………………………… 216

Sylvia Plath (1932—1963) 西尔维娅·普拉斯 ·················· 219
Last Words ·················· 219

第十二单元 ·················· 222
Edward Franklin Albee (1928—) 爱德华·富兰克林·阿尔比 ··· 222
Who's Afraid of Virginia Woolf? ·················· 223

第十三单元 ·················· 239
Toni Morrison (1931—) 托妮·莫里森 ·················· 239
Beloved ·················· 240

第十四单元 ·················· 249
Thomas Pynchon (1937—) 托马斯·品钦 ·················· 249
Entropy ·················· 250

第十五单元 ·················· 266
Maxine Hong Kingston (1940—) 汤亭亭 ·················· 266
A Song for a Barbarian Reed Pipe ·················· 266

第十六单元 ·················· 285
Leslie Marmon Silko (1948—) 莱丝莉·摩门·西尔柯 ·················· 285
Lullaby ·················· 286

第十七单元 ·················· 296
Robert Penn Warren (1905—1989) 罗伯特·潘·沃伦 ·················· 296
Evening Hawk ·················· 297

John Ashbery (1927—) 约翰·阿什贝利 ·················· 300
And Ut Pictura Poesis Is Her Name ·················· 301

Robert Pinsky (1940—) 罗伯特·平斯基 ·················· 304
To Television ·················· 305

Rita Dove (1952—) 丽塔·达夫 ·················· 308
My Mother Enters the Work Force ·················· 309

Robert Bly (1926—) 罗伯特·布莱 ·················· 312
The Buried Train ·················· 313

Gary Soto (1952—) 加里·索托 ·················· 315
Mexicans Begin Jogging ·················· 315
How Things Work ·················· 316

Adrienne Rich (1929—) 艾德里安娜·里奇 ·············· 319
Diving into the Wreck ·· 320

第十八单元 ·· 325

David Alan Mamet (1947—) 大卫·艾伦·马麦特 ·············· 325
Oleanna ·· 326

第十九单元 ·· 349

Joyce Carol Oates (1938—) 乔伊斯·卡洛尔·欧茨 ·············· 349
Where Are You Going, Where Have You Been? ·············· 350

绪论：20世纪美国文学概述

美国立国以后，尤其是在19世纪，各方面飞速发展，到20世纪初已经完成了从农业社会到工业社会的转化。与此同时，美国作家也通过各自的作品确立了关于美国的各种神话，譬如，爱默生和惠特曼等强调的美国自我的神话——美国人可以凭借个人独立自主的信心和奋斗精神获得成功，摆脱英国的影响，成为跟英国或欧洲完全不同的民族和国家。当然还有关于美国民主、美国充满机遇、美国人是上帝的特选子民、上帝派他们到新大陆来建设人间伊甸园等等。美国梦的主题、少年成长的叙述形式也逐渐形成，虽然美国因为历史不长而有些自卑，但由于这些神话，美国作家常常表现出强烈的反叛和批判意识，寻找新的手法和技巧，甚至富有美国特色的语言来建立美国独特的民族文学。这些神话至今还影响着美国和美国人民。美国文学也一直沿袭那反对权威、不断试验的传统。美国神话在第一次世界大战中受到强烈冲击，但其在文学中的反映却使得美国文学走向世界。

一、第一次世界大战后的"反叛"与试验

美国文学在20世纪初，尤其是第一次世界大战以后到20年代进一步发展成熟，开始对欧洲文化产生影响，并被称为"第二次文艺复兴"，用以区别19世纪中叶浪漫主义文学时期的"第一次文艺复兴"。

1914年，第一次世界大战爆发。1917年4月，美国向德国宣战。为了动员人民，当时的威尔逊总统提出了十分动听的口号，强调美国是"为民主而战"，"为世界的最终和平和世界人民的解放"而战。年轻人，尤其是一些文学青年，为了保卫祖国的荣誉，也为了见识世面，纷纷报名参军，甚至未到服役年龄便自愿加入英国、法国等外国军队。如海明威主动去了意大利战场做救护车队司机；肯明斯(E. E. Cummings)与约翰·多斯·帕索斯(John Dos Passos)加入了法国战地救护队；福克纳去加拿大的皇家空军接受训练。

美国参战一年半以后，战争就结束了。战后，美国进入经济繁荣时期。科技革新加速了钢铁、建筑工业、玻璃制造业的发展。尤其是汽车制造业，1900年的年产量仅为4000辆，1929年上升到480万辆。无线电、电话和电影的发明，家用电器的出现，迅速改变了人民的生活方式。1900年全国电话数量不到140万台，1930年超过2000万台。1920年美国人第一次听到无线电广播，到了1929年，收音机已成为人们生活中不可缺少的物品。电影的发展不仅吸引了大量观众，也创造了巨大的财富。1922年，4000万人买票看电影，1929年达一亿之多。广播、电影等大众媒介开始在人们生活中起着越来越重要的作用。1928年美国人达到世界上最高的生活水平，1929年美国的产品已经占世界总产量的1/3以上。生产、消费、娱乐、享受成了20年代的一大特点。因此，这个时代有"喧嚣咆哮的时代"(the Roaring Age)的雅名，也因为对黑人文化，尤其黑人音乐的兴趣而获得了"爵士时代"(The Jazz Age)的称号。然而，歌舞升平、繁荣昌盛的景象背后是重重矛盾。政治方

面所谓的"红色恐怖"给政府趋向保守带来了借口,对罢工等进步活动采取高压政策。种族歧视重新抬头,黑社会的犯罪活动猖獗。1920年实行禁酒令,1927年无辜的意大利裔工人萨柯—樊则蒂被强行处死等事件,整个社会的右倾保守使人们,尤其是敏感的知识分子感到悲观失望。

第一次世界大战对美国年轻知识分子的影响十分巨大,他们怀着理想与梦想上前线寻求荣誉与冒险,却带着迷茫和绝望下战场;认识到战争是无意义的血腥屠杀,也看清政府宣传的虚伪与蒙蔽性,他们对政府和权威失去了信心。他们经历了一场噩梦,回到美国,发现祖国依然保守落后,人们的思想依然狭隘自私,生活依然富裕而平庸。他们对国家、社会、个人前途悲观失望,对传统和价值观念,包括宗教失去信念。于是在20年代初,大批年轻人涌向欧洲,特别是巴黎,像无根之木到处漂泊,在寻欢作乐中消磨时光,有些人用文学形式来描写战争带来的痛苦与烦恼,表现他们的失落与绝望,形成了斯泰因(Gertrude Stein)称之为"迷惘的一代"的文学流派。他们几乎都以自己的经历为素材,如海明威的《太阳照样升起》、《永别了,武器》和以尼克·亚当斯为主人公的短篇小说,菲茨杰拉德的《人间天堂》和《夜色温柔》。这些自传性作品悲天悯人,对当代世界悲观失望,甚至厌恶愤慨。但它们的作者却成为20世纪20年代美国文学的"第二次文艺复兴"的中坚力量。许多优秀作品都是在美国国外写成的,这也许是这个时期美国文学的一个奇怪的特点。

这时期美国文学的一大特点是反叛、试验。所谓"反叛"首先是对美国社会、道德以及文化传统的批判,这从上个世纪末就已经开始。哲学家乔治·桑塔亚那(George Santayana)继承了19世纪的反叛传统,明确提出反"斯文传统"的口号,批评因循守旧、恪守传统、反对创新的保守势力;评论家门肯在德莱塞由于发表了描写乡下女孩进城后靠做有钱男人的情妇成功的《嘉莉妹妹》而大受批评的时候就坚决维护他,现在则大声疾呼,反对清教精神。在许多人看来,清教主义思想渗透了整个"斯文阶层",是"美国生活中一切枯燥乏味的令人感到压抑扫兴和不痛快的东西的总称",而"斯文阶层"就是门肯所抨击的对一切"真诚有趣、富有想像力和进取精神"的东西无动于衷的"有教养的、丧失了人的天性的高雅之士和上层人物"①。年轻一代的作家中,多斯·帕索斯也挺身而出,在《反对美国文学》一文中严厉质问:"难道我们还要永远死水一潭停滞不前……永远支持赞扬其他国家的文学,我们这个无数种族混杂在一起的国家难道除了钢铁、石油和粮食以外就不可能生产别的东西?"②

反叛的一大重点是拒绝把乡村小镇描绘成完美无缺的田园风光,而是努力表现乡村和小镇的平庸与乏味、传统观念和习惯势力对人性的压抑。辛克莱·刘易斯是这一主题最成功的小说家。他一生写过20多部长篇小说,但真正出色的还是20年代出版的《大街》(Main Street, 1920)、《巴比特》(Babbitt, 1922)等。这些作品多半以中西部的小镇为背景,揭露市镇生活的闭塞和保守、居民的愚昧狭隘和对新鲜事物的偏见与抵制。《大街》抨击他称之为"乡村毒菌"的习惯势力,使这个小镇成了美国社会保守生活的代名词;《巴比

---

① 丹尼尔·艾伦:《文坛状况与文学运动》,见埃默里·埃利奥特主编:《哥伦比亚美国文学史》,哥伦比亚大学出版社,1988年,第736页。

② 约翰·多斯·帕索斯:《反对美国文学》,见《新共和》第八期(1916年10月14日),第269页。

特》对一个追求享受的房地产捐客刻画得入木三分,从而使主人公的名字"巴比特"进入美国英语的词汇,成为庸俗市侩的同义词。刘易斯的成功使他在1930年成为第一个获得诺贝尔文学奖的美国作家。今天看来,刘易斯其实很欣赏他讽刺挖苦的人物和他所抨击的生活,他的作品的艺术性也并不很高,他的成功在于他诉说了当时人们反叛的心声。

  这一时期文学的另一个特点"试验性"其实跟反叛性不可分割。反叛并不只表现在思想意识方面,也还表现在努力摆脱文学艺术传统的束缚和限制。要做到这一点,就需要革新,需要试验新的手法、风格和技巧,甚至要寻找一种民族的语言来建设真正的美国文学。为此他们渴望了解外国,借鉴世界上,尤其是欧洲在文学艺术等文化领域和哲学思潮方面的成就与经验。于是,弗洛伊德在1909年被请到美国做演讲,他的关于梦和无意识的心理学和性理论在20年代被大量翻译介绍到美国,为作家们的试验创新提供理论依据。同样,尼采的超人哲学和悲剧理论、弗雷泽的神话、柏格森关于"持续时间"和直觉的观点以及马克思的阶级论等等都得到宣传和介绍,也都产生了影响。1913年,纽约举行了著名的阿默里国际艺术展,介绍了塞尚、马蒂斯和毕加索等先锋派艺术家以及达达主义(Dadaism)、立体主义(Cubism)等多种多样的先锋派绘画和雕塑品。这个展览在美国文艺界引起了极大的轰动,预示现代主义运动即将开始。

  在试验革新运动中,小杂志起了很大的作用。首先,一向受冷落的诗歌有了自己的刊物:1912年在从来不是文学中心的芝加哥出现的《诗刊》(Poetry: A Magazine of Verse)。主编门罗(Harriet Monroe)在创刊号中宣称,这本杂志"将是海洋中一个绿色的岛屿,在那里,'美'可以种植她的花园,而'真',那欢乐与悲哀、隐藏的喜悦与绝望的一丝不苟的揭示者可以无所畏惧地进行她勇敢的追求"①。应门罗的邀请,已在英国参与领导意象派新诗歌运动的庞德(Ezra Pound)成为这杂志的驻外编辑。庞德答应向读者时刻提供有关英国、法国和其他任何地方的信息,主张只进口"比国内生产的作品要好的作品,最好的外国作品"②。他还呼吁美国出现新的"文艺复兴",认为美国文学的一场"大觉醒"可能使"意大利的文艺复兴看上去不过是茶壶里的风暴"③。正是《诗刊》发表了艾略特(T. S. Eliot)的《普罗弗洛克的情歌》(The Love Song of J. Alfred Prufrock)以及日后成为大家的弗罗斯特(Robert Frost)、威廉斯(William Carlos Williams)、史蒂文斯(Wallace Stevens)和芝加哥诗人林赛(Vachel Lindsay)、埃德加·李·马斯特斯(Edgar Lee Masters)等人的早期作品。其他的小杂志应运而生,比较著名的还有试验性很强的《小评论》(The Little Review, 1914)、《他者》(Others, 1915)、《七艺》(The Seven Arts, 1916)等。在它们的影响下,即便一些老杂志也改变了编辑方针,如19世纪80年代创刊的《日晷》(The Dial)就在1922年刊登了艾略特的《荒原》。1922年在南方田纳西州纳希维尔创办的小杂志《逃亡者》(The Fugitive Magazine)成为南方作家如兰塞姆(John Crowe Ransom)、泰特(Allen Tate)和沃伦(Robert Penn Warren)等人发表作品的重要阵地,跟1921年也在南方出现的《两面人》(The Double Dealer)等其他小杂志一起为南方文学的兴起发挥了极大的作用。尽管许多小杂志维持的时间很短,但它们为作家的创新和试验提供发表园地,在介绍新

---

① 哈丽特·门罗:"编后语",见《诗刊》第一期,1912年,第28页。
② 见 D. D. 佩奇编:《庞德书信选:1907—1941》中给门罗的信,纽约:Harcout Brace 出版社,1950年,第10—11页。
③ 庞德:《文艺复兴》,见 T.S.艾略特编:《文学论文集》,伦敦:费伯出版社,1954年,第224页。

的诗歌理论、发现和扶植新秀、培养与提高读者的审美情趣,尤其为造就美国最繁荣丰富的诗歌时代和发展现代主义诗歌起了不可磨灭的作用。可以说,没有当年的小杂志也就没有20年代繁荣的美国现代派文学,尤其是现代派诗歌。

反叛与试验的一个结果是培养了一大批理论家。美国在历史上并没有什么出色的文学理论家。现在情况不同了,小杂志要宣传办刊方针和宗旨,作家们要谈论自己的创作原则,都需要理论;对旧文学传统的批评,对国外新流派新理论的介绍,对新文学的评价也都需要理论。于是,理论家们便应运而生。从反清教传统的门肯(H. L. Mencken)和凡·维克·布鲁克斯(Van Wyck Brooks)到宣传马克思主义文学理论的卡尔维登(V. F. Calverton),从做杂志编辑的埃德蒙·威尔逊(Edmund Wilson)到庞德、艾略特等诗人,他们的理论对美国文学理论的发展都起了很大的影响。《逃亡者》更是对创建30年代后期到50年代主宰美国文坛的新批评派起了不可磨灭的作用。

反叛与试验的最大成就是导致20年代现代主义文学的大繁荣。当时现代主义在文化艺术领域里是一个世界性的潮流,例如未来主义是在意大利首先诞生,而达达主义最早出现在苏黎世。至于法国,尤其是巴黎,更是一切先锋派艺术的发源地和文化中心。定居在巴黎的斯泰因的家就是欧洲艺术家和美国作家舍伍德·安德森(Sherwood Anderson)、海明威、菲茨杰拉德等人讨论文学艺术的聚会场所。美国作家从朝气蓬勃的世界文艺浪潮中汲取大量的营养。他们认为自己是世界文化的继承人,可以自由地运用各国的文化。庞德吸收罗马帝国和中国的文化,艾略特在《荒原》里使用各国的语言和神话。文学家们接受了文学等同于艺术的观点,开始高度重视形式和技巧问题,努力向艺术家学习,要在诗歌小说中创造绘画的效果。威廉斯的一些诗歌就像一幅幅绘画,海明威的小说看得出立体派绘画的痕迹。他们反对现实主义,但并不反对现实,只是在表现手法上突破传统的框框,从传统的时空顺序转到跳跃式的、不受空间限制的来回颠倒的时序,从反映外部现实转到关心人物的内心世界和意识、无意识对外界事物的流动式的反应,甚至同时表现几个人物的意识,不断转换视角来反映他们对世界的感受。总之,作家们个个标新立异,迫使社会注意他们的存在。

现代主义作家在手法上标新立异,在作品内容方面却有愤世嫉俗的共性,因为现代主义是对第一次世界大战后的社会现状的一种抗议。他们认为过去支撑人类生活的各种体系制度,无论是社会、政治,还是宗教、艺术方面的,都已经被摧毁或被证明是虚假的,因而需要革新,手法上的不连贯性等等都是为了表现这个支离破碎的社会观。换言之,他们猛烈抨击社会正说明他们认为自己的责任重大,努力想用艺术来拯救社会,为世界创造新的秩序。海明威的"压力下的优雅"就是一种处世为人的方式。诗人史蒂文斯说:"在一个没有信念的时代里……要由诗人用自己的方式、自己的风格来提供信念的快乐。"①美国的现代主义文学是从诗歌开始,以庞德领导的意象派和旋涡派诗歌为开端。美国诗人不仅学习20世纪的流派,还深受19世纪法国象征派诗人,17世纪英国玄学派诗人,以及19世纪本国诗人如惠特曼、迪金森等人的影响。这时期的诗歌可以说是百花齐放,诗人们有意识地对诗歌的传统风格、表现形式和技巧进行革新,纷纷寻找十分个性化的

---

① 史蒂文斯:《诗歌素材》,见弗兰克·科墨德与琼·理查逊编:《史蒂文斯诗歌与散文集》,"美国文库",1997年,第916页。

语言和手法来表现自己对社会、世界、人生的看法。例如,许多诗人用自由诗体而不大喜欢格律音步十分严谨的传统诗体。在语言方面,他们反对传统的高雅诗歌语言,采用日常生活的口语体。当然,诗人们也各不相同,威廉斯的自由诗体跟艾略特和庞德的风格就大不一样。威廉斯更强调视觉效果,而艾略特则看重音步和节奏的音乐性。他们都主张用口语,但弗罗斯特采用新英格兰地区农民的语言,林赛和桑德堡(Carl Sandburg)使用中西部老百姓的语言,而艾略特的诗歌虽然有口语的味道,他却认为有些思想感情用其他风格也许能表现得更好。诗人们深切感到现代生活非常复杂,充满了矛盾和冲突,他们的诗歌就是要表现这种不协调。于是,他们大量采用幽默与反讽。桑德堡和林赛依靠西部幽默,在高度夸张中达到挖苦的目的,弗罗斯特则突出新英格兰地区不露感情的冷漠式的讽刺,而艾略特、威廉斯和史蒂文斯等人的反讽就更为含蓄和深沉。艾略特运用"想像力的逻辑",在《荒原》中抛弃一般诗歌中的过渡、概括、论述等手法,把不同的意象并列在一起,用支离破碎的形象反映社会的问题。在这个"第二次鲜花盛开的时期"(the Second Flowering,意为文学高度繁荣的时期),出现了大量现在被认为是经典的诗集,诗人们还常常提出自己的文学主张。他们的理论,如庞德的"要日新月异"的口号和对意象派诗歌的定义等理论、艾略特的"客观对应物"、"感受的分化"、"想像力的逻辑"、"作家不能脱离传统但要像催化剂那样使传统起变化",以及威廉斯的"不表现观念,只描写事物"和史蒂文斯关于客观现实和想像力的关系等理论不仅在当时起作用,还对后来的诗歌有很大的影响。

美国的戏剧由于清教主义的影响一向不很发达,但一次大战后情况却有了很大的变化。德国的表现主义戏剧、瑞典表现主义戏剧家斯特林堡(August Strindberg)、挪威的易卜生(Henrik Ibsen)、意大利的皮兰德娄(Luigi Pirandello)、英国的肖伯纳(Bernard Shaw)等开始影响美国戏剧界。另一方面,由戏剧艺术爱好者组成的试验性的小剧院开始出现,对百老汇等商业剧院进行了有力的挑战。最为著名的是"华盛顿广场剧院"(战后改名为"剧院协会")、普罗文斯敦剧社和以哈佛大学的47号工作室为代表的学员剧团。这些小剧场或戏剧团体几乎都有自己的剧作家。他们一反陈腐的俗套,努力表现当前的美国生活,抨击各种社会问题。尤其是奥尼尔(Eugene O'Neill),他运用各种创作方法来揭露社会问题:表现残酷的现实如何粉碎普通家庭的生活理想等有现实意义的主题。剧作家们还大量试验各种手法与技巧。如埃尔默·赖斯(Elmer Rice)用表现主义手法写了《加算器》,而在《街景》(1929)中则采用现实主义手法。奥尼尔不仅采用传统的手法还在作品里试验了表现主义、象征主义等手法,甚至在一部作品中兼有现实主义、表现主义和象征主义等多种技巧。奥尼尔的天才与哲学思想使他成为20世纪美国戏剧的重要人物。

跟"新诗"运动和"新戏剧"运动相比,小说也在不断革新。从1914年开始到20年代末,斯泰因、凯瑟(Willa Cather)、安德森、德莱塞等老一代作家的许多优秀作品就是在这段时间里问世的。战后成长起来的年轻一代作家,如多斯·帕索斯、菲茨杰拉德、海明威、福克纳以及黑人作家吉因·图默(Jean Toomer)等人开始在文学舞台上各领风骚,都通过小说批评工业化和物质主义的恶果、战争对人的精神伤害、贫富不均和种族歧视造成的悲剧。

小说在技巧方面的试验并不落后于诗歌和戏剧。作为"现代主义文学运动巨人之一"

的斯泰因对语言和标点符号进行试验以捕捉流动不定的生活现实。安德森对小说形式进行试验,在《俄亥俄州的温斯堡镇》中用具有同一个背景、同一个主人公和同一种气氛的一系列短篇故事来加强这些故事作为整体的总主题。海明威在故事里穿插新闻报道,多斯·帕索斯在小说中插入电影、新闻片、报纸,甚至流行歌曲的片段。总之,作家们不断破坏故事的叙述线索以表现世界的混乱和社会的失控。当然,这时期传统的手法并没有消失。德莱塞、刘易斯采用文献式描写和细节堆积等自然主义手法;凯瑟、菲茨杰拉德却十分注意对细节的取舍,更看重故事的氛围,因而使他们的作品富有诗意。海明威试验用小词、短句,多对话,少描述,他的"冰山理论"确实开创了新的文风。跟他相反,福克纳用繁复的长句和晦涩的语言来表现世界的复杂。可以说,跟戏剧、诗歌一样,小说文体风格的多样性也是这个时代文学的一个特点。

二、美国的"左翼"文学

美国在第一次世界大战后的繁荣在 20 世纪 20 年代末走到了尽头。1929 年,纽约股票市场崩溃,引发了美国历史上前所未有的经济危机。一时间,银行倒闭,投资者破产,80%的钢铁工厂倒闭,无数工人失业。与此同时,1930 年开始的持续干旱使大萧条雪上加霜,沙尘暴几乎横扫美国中部和东部地区,破坏了大量农田,迫使农民背井离乡,向西部迁移去寻找生路。这场危机波及面广,延续时间很长,几乎使整个国家都处于风雨飘摇之中。到 1933 年,美国的国民生产总值下降了 29%,失业率上升到 24.9%。罗斯福 1933 年就任总统时全国几乎所有的银行都已关闭,三千多万家庭没有正常收入,数以百万计的人生活在极度的贫困之中,更有成千上万的人失去家园,在铁路线上颠沛流离,妄图找到可以糊口的工作。与此同时,经济危机加剧了劳资矛盾,罢工运动四起。1931 年,煤矿工人在宾州等五六个州举行罢工。1932 年,亨利·福特命令警察向他在底特律汽车工厂的罢工工人开枪造成的死伤事件震惊全国。同年,两千多名参加过第一次世界大战的退伍军人聚集在华盛顿。他们因生计无着落而要求政府提前支付原答应在 1945 年支付的补助。然而,麦克阿瑟将军却用刺刀和催泪弹,甚至子弹驱散了这群老兵,制造了另一起骇人听闻的事件,也使政府的信誉一落千丈。

在这种形势下,"左翼"文学或"无产阶级文学"一度成为 30 年代颇有影响的主流文学,使 30 年代有"红色十年"之称。作家和艺术家们关注社会问题和经济形势,开始发表有明确阶级意识的作品,描写经济萧条对工人、农民,甚至中产阶级的影响。其实,社会主义思想一直在美国有一定的力量。1877 年纽约的德裔移民成立社会主义劳工党,宣传马克思的思想,企图通过竞选取得政权以进行改革。1898 年又出现社会主义民主党,1901 年两党合并成为社会主义党。十月革命后,相当一部分成员认为他们应该放弃改良主义立场,立即行动起来,推翻资本主义在美国的统治。在《震撼世界的十日》的作者约翰·里德(John Reed)的帮助下,他们于 1919 年成立了美国共产党。左翼作家如迈克尔·高尔德(Michael Gold)、约瑟夫·弗里曼(Joseph Freeman)、麦克斯·伊斯特曼(Max Eastman)等人还创办了一些进步刊物,比较重要的有《群众》(*The Masses*, 1913—1926)、《解放者》(*The Liberator*, 1918—1924),尤其是标志美国激进文学重要里程碑的、后来成为共产党喉舌的《新群众》(*The New Masses*, 1926—1948)等杂志。它们介绍十月革命后的苏联,研究马克思主义理论,讨论作家的责任和文艺的方向。早在1921年,迈克尔·高尔德就在《走向无产阶级艺术》中强调艺术家应该来自工人,跟人民群众紧密团结,通过社会革命创造"新的更真实的艺术"①。1925年,著名作家厄普顿·辛克莱(Upton Sinclair)、评论家凡·维克·布鲁克斯等都是一个无产阶级作家联盟的执行委员会的委员。

30年代的经济危机使作家们更加政治化,出现了更多的左翼文化团体,如"约翰·里德俱乐部"、"工人戏剧联盟"等,也出现了一些新的如《铁砧》、《工人联盟》等左翼杂志。甚至一些有影响的自由派杂志如《新共和》(The New Republic)、《民族》(The Nation)等也都向左转。作家们把社会主义的苏联看成是希望的曙光,从老一代的德莱塞、新闻记者麦克斯·伊斯特曼到年轻的黑人诗人兰斯顿·休斯和评论家埃德蒙·威尔逊等都前往苏联进行访问,公开提出社会主义才是美国的出路。1931年德莱塞访苏回国后说:"对于世界问题,尤其是美国的问题,我的解决办法是共产主义。"②出于作家的责任感,无论中间派还是自由派都向共产党靠拢,参加或支持它的活动。1932年52位知名人士,包括老一代作家舍伍德·安德森和年轻的"迷惘的一代"作家约翰·多斯·帕索斯、麦尔科姆·考利(Malcolm Cowley)以及休斯、威尔逊等联名签署公开信,支持共产党参加竞选总统的活动。作家们还到动乱或罢工地区进行调查,撰写文章,揭露真相。德莱塞考察了宾州和肯塔基的煤矿罢工后在《悲剧的美国》(1932)里愤怒地抨击美国资本主义。威尔逊也认为他对象征主义和现代主义的研究已经过时,当前国家的经济形势更值得探讨。于是,他前往底特律、芝加哥和南方肯塔基等一些动乱地区考察,为《新共和》写文章,报道这些地方的贫困和罢工情况以及公司领导和资本家对工人的残忍与仇恨,并在1932年以《美国恐慌》(1958年修订版改名为《美国地震》)为题结集出版。评论家认为这些文章是"1932年美国的最客观的画面","是一个走到'外面'的人在亲眼目睹了取代繁荣十年的经济萧条情景后所作的新观察和新评述"③。威尔逊还大力研究马克思和列宁的著作,积极去苏联访问,并且陆续发表他的研究心得和访问观感,这些文章后来在1940年结集出版,以原彼得堡的一个地名为标题,叫《去芬兰车站》。直到晚年,威尔逊仍然认为这本书"基本上可靠地报道了革命家们认为他们为建立一个'更好的世界'所做的事情"④威尔逊可以说是转向政治的自由派作家的典型代表。诗人威廉·卡洛斯·威廉斯并不认为文学要为政治服务,但仍然表示欢迎共产主义,说"伟大的诗歌无不出自共产主义思想"⑤。由此可见左翼文学在30年代美国的影响。1935年在"约翰·里德俱乐部"的倡议下,作家们在纽约召开了第一次美国作家代表大会,成立了"美国作家同盟",接受国际革命作家联盟的领导,从此把"分散的、无党派的自由主义人士的力量全部吸收到一个统一的反法西斯主义'联合阵线'中来"⑥。

---

① 丹尼尔·艾伦:《左翼作家》,牛津大学出版社,1961、1977年,第88页。
② 同上书,第178页。
③ 这是马修·约瑟夫的话。引自里昂·伊德尔为埃德蒙·威尔逊的《30年代》所作的"注释",见埃德蒙·威尔逊:《30年代》,法拉·斯特劳斯·古罗可斯出版社,1980年,第51—52页。
④ 同上书,第xxiv页。
⑤ 威廉·卡洛斯·威廉斯:《评论》,《联系杂志》第一卷,第三期(1934年2月),转引自《激进的陈述:美国无产阶级文学中的政治与形式,1929—1941》,芭芭拉·弗雷著,杜克大学出版社,1993年,第132—133页。
⑥ 丹尼尔·艾伦:《文坛状况与文学运动》,见埃默里·埃利奥特主编:《哥伦比亚美国文学史》,哥伦比亚大学出版社,1988年,朱通伯等翻译,四川辞书出版社,1994年,第615页。

同年,罗斯福为了对付经济衰退实行新政,设立公共事业振兴署,为失业者提供就业机会。该署也为困难的作家、艺术家们设立了联邦艺术、联邦作家、联邦戏剧等项目。其中,联邦作家项目资助了已经成名的作家,如诗人康拉德·艾肯(Conrad Aiken)、剧作家埃尔默·赖斯、黑人诗人克劳德·麦克凯(Claude McKay)等以及日后成为名家的犹太小说家索尔·贝娄、剧作家阿瑟·米勒、女作家尤多拉·韦尔蒂(Eudora Welty)、黑人作家理查德·赖特(Richard Wright)和拉尔夫·埃里森、黑人女作家佐拉·尼尔·赫斯顿(Zora Neale Hurston)等。这些作家中有不少人比较激进,尽管也有中间派或思想保守的人士。因此,评论家认为30年代也许是"美国激进人士最后一次参加政府的项目,希望能够藉此让广大人民了解他们对国家的看法"①。对政府来说,这些项目是要保持与提高人民对国家的信心,树立美国是一个包容所有人的多元文化国家的形象。他们组织作家们编写各州旅游指南,同时也资助赖特、赫斯顿、埃里森等黑人作家发掘黑人文化,撰写黑人历史,反映他们的苦难生活。当然,由于是政府资助的项目,作家们不可避免地受到一定的限制,但他们还是发表了一些比较进步的作品,如在编写指南时把重点放在普通劳动人民而不是知名人士上。赖特在芝加哥、埃里森在纽约收集的有关黑人的材料对他们后来写《土生子》和《看不见的人》都起了一定的作用。赫斯顿收集整理的民间故事集《骡与人》就是联邦作家项目的一个课题。当时联邦戏剧项目创造了一种特殊的戏剧形式——"活报剧",中心人物总是一个对当前某个问题不明白的普通老百姓,通过他对问题的探究把全剧串起来,把作家的意图向观众进行交代。根据辛克莱·刘易斯小说改编的反法西斯剧作《它不可能在这里发生》(1936)同时在全国22个城市上演,造成很大的声势。但正是由于他们演出的思想内容都比较进步,国会怀疑他们是由共产党控制的,1939年,国会停止资助该项目。

30年代,在美国共产党和《新群众》的组织下,左翼作家对什么是无产阶级文学这一问题,从作家的出身、读者对象、作品的思想内容和形式、作家的观点立场、文学是艺术还是宣传等重要问题进行讨论。许多作家、评论家,如美国共产党在文学方面的主要发言人高尔德、约瑟夫·弗里曼、格兰维尔·希克斯(Granville Hicks)、范·弗·卡尔弗顿等都积极参加讨论,高尔德在《新群众》和《工人日报》上的评论、弗里曼为《美国无产阶级文学选集》写的序言、希克斯的《革命与小说》(1934)、《马克思主义批评的发展》(1935)、卡尔弗顿的《美国文学的解放》(1932)等都是这方面的重要文章。在讨论中,他们批评过艾略特的"神秘主义和经院哲学"、福克纳繁琐艰涩的语言;赖特还批评赫斯顿的《他们眼望上苍》只关注女主人公的个人发展,因而"没有主题、没有寓意、没有思想"②。

当然,左翼作家激情洋溢的话语并不是文坛上唯一的声音。当时,尤其在30年代后期,也有一些保守的作家出来批评左翼文学。艾伦·泰特和罗伯特·佩恩·沃伦本来想给他们在1930年发表的《我要表明我的立场》加一个"宣传反对共产主义的文章"的副标题。泰特在1933年批评左翼共产主义文学是"把人类困境过分简单化……是逃避现实"。沃

---

① 劳拉·布劳德尔:《唤醒民族:萧条时期美国的激进文化》,麻省大学出版社,1998年,第177页。
② 芭芭拉·弗雷:《激进的陈述:美国无产阶级文学中的政治与形式,1929—1941》,杜克大学出版社,1993年,第115页。

伦在1936年说无产阶级文学失败了,因为它"把文学政治化"①。30年代后期,由于经济情况的好转,右翼势力重新抬头,过去同情左翼文学的作家和知识分子开始跟美共分裂,对左翼文学的批评也越来越尖锐。政府对联邦艺术项目的限制也起了分化作用。当时,伊斯特曼的《穿制服的艺术家》(1934)批评前苏联的文艺政策;威尔逊发表《马克思主义与文学》等批评文章,强调文学不是武器,"文学中的党派路线无聊透顶"。影响最大的恐怕是《新群众》和《党派评论》的大论战。1937年,后者公开脱离党的领导,它周围的作家们纷纷撰文攻击美共及左翼文学。詹姆斯·T.法雷尔(James T. Farrell)的《论文学批评》激烈抨击《新群众》和高尔德所代表的左翼文学。菲利普·拉夫在许多文章,尤其是《无产阶级文学:政治剖析》中攻击无产阶级文学是把"一个党派的文学伪装成一个阶级的文学"②。此后,1939年苏联与德国签订《德苏互不侵犯条约》,加剧了左翼作家的思想混乱,许多人退党。左翼力量从此大大削弱。但他们仍然在活动,1937年召开了第二次全国作家大会,海明威以记者身份访问西班牙,并在会上发言斥责法西斯主义。一些作家参加林肯支队支援反佛朗哥法西斯政府的斗争。海明威的剧本《第五纵队》(1938)和《丧钟为谁而鸣》(1940)、斯坦贝克的《月落》(1942)、麦克利什(Archbald MacLeash)的诗剧《城市的陷落》(1937)、丽莲·海尔曼(Lilian Hellman)的《守望莱茵河》(1941)等都是当年优秀的反法西斯文学作品。

多年来,美国文学界一直贬低左翼文学,认为左翼作家受命于前苏联,为共产党所控制,过于强调文学与政治的关系,因此创作水平低,没有文学价值。但近年来,随着政治批评在美国的兴起,评论家开始重新评价30年代的左翼文学,在指出他们问题的同时,也对他们进行了充分的肯定。例如,劳拉·布劳德尔指出,30年代是美国历史上"激进作家最后一次感到他们受大家欢迎并参与讨论什么是美国这个更重要的问题,也是激进作家最后一次努力探索如何创造一个从政治思想到手法技巧都比较老练高超而又能吸引广大群众的文学",而且这种对"美国本质特性的争论、对美国历史的再认识……是用歌曲、舞蹈、文学、戏剧和电影来表现的"③。她以约翰·多斯·帕索斯在1930—1933年发表的《北纬四十二度》(1930)、《一九一九年》(1932)、《赚大钱》(1933)为例说明左翼文学实际上既有传统的现实主义的文献式写实手法又有现代主义的意识流、不连贯性等技巧。里塔·巴纳德等评论家们还注意到30年代为了争取读者,作家们往往主动采用通俗小说的手法。巴纳德认为,在30年代严肃艺术与大众文化的界限变得模糊了,因为当时人们可以随时通过无线电广播倾听高雅音乐,参观凡高或塞尚等名家的画展或购买他们的作品,高雅艺术本身已成为一种大众文化。当时无产阶级文学"努力要创立一种新的激进文化,既非高雅也不低俗,既不是由一群孤立的艺术家创造的也不是自上而下由媒体巨头产生的"④。此外,有些作家努力把大众文化的语言运用到他们的写作之中。兰斯顿·休斯、克利福德·奥德兹(Clifford Odets, 1906—1963)都是马克思主义者,也都是严肃作家,但休斯写

---

① 芭芭拉·弗雷:《激进的陈述:美国无产阶级文学中的政治与形式,1929—1941》,杜克大学出版社,1993年,第4—5页。
② 同上书,第16—17页。
③ 劳拉·布劳德尔:《唤醒民族:萧条时期美国的激进文化》,麻省大学出版社,1998年,第14,174页。
④ 里塔·巴纳德:《大萧条与富裕文化:肯尼思·费尔林、纳撒尼尔·韦斯特与30年代的大众文化》,剑桥大学出版社,1995年,第6—7页。

诗歌颂爵士音乐,他在剧本《难道你不想自由?》里采用了布鲁斯、爵士和其他通俗音乐的节奏来宣传他对美国黑人历史的进步观点。剧作家克利福德·奥德兹甚至想去好莱坞把电影"变成为人民大众的真正的艺术形式"①。他的表现纽约汽车工人罢工斗争的《等待"老左"》(1934)是在百老汇上演的最激进的无产阶级戏剧,其充满激情的语言和结尾处的"罢工!罢工!"口号非常有煽动性,但它那基本没有舞台布景和打破舞台与观众界限的做法又是一种创新,对后来的剧作家有很大的影响。20世纪90年代,奥德兹的《醒来歌唱》(1935)、《金孩子》(1937)和《发向月球的火箭》(1938)等又重新上演并受到好评,说明奥德兹的剧作并不仅仅是政治宣传,还是富有艺术魅力的。左翼文学也许有种种缺点,但它并没有从实用主义角度出发牺牲文学使之为政治宣传服务。斯坦贝克表现流动农工悲惨生活的《愤怒的葡萄》(1939)、《人鼠之间》(1937),亨利·罗思(Henry Roth,1907—1995)的《称它为睡觉》(1934),迈克尔·高尔德的《没有钱的犹太人》等都是30年代出色的文学作品。

即使并未积极参加左翼活动的作家也更有意识地关心社会现实,福克纳的《圣殿》(1931)、《八月之光》(1932)都直接反映当时的社会问题。另一位南方作家凯瑟琳·安·波特(Katherine Anne Porter)虽然主要描写南方社会与家族,但也为《民族》、《新共和》等左翼杂志撰稿。尽管奥尼尔的《卖冰的人来了》(1934)要在1946年才上演,但这个剧本还是多少折射出他在30年代的心态。

从30年代到第二次世界大战前,一些作家出版了他们极为优秀的作品,福克纳的约克那帕塔法系列小说的主要作品除了《喧哗与骚动》外,基本上都是在这阶段发表的。华莱士·史蒂文斯的《在基韦斯特形成的秩序观念》(1934)、《带蓝吉他的人》(1937)最终确定了他在美国诗歌中的地位。虽然弗罗斯特与艾略特已是成名作家,但前者的《诗选》(1930)和《更广阔的领域》为他赢得了更大的声誉,而后者的《四个四重奏》(1943)则是他诗歌生涯中的又一部力作。至于南方诗人的兴起,不但发扬了艾略特的传统,还为美国文学带来了自己的批评理论。

三、从"平静"到动荡——第二次世界大战后的美国文学

1945年8月美国在日本广岛和长崎投下的原子弹,震惊全世界。第二次世界大战刚一结束,冷战就拉开了序幕。从此,美国以头号强国的面目出现于世界。

作为在大战中获益最大而损失最小的国家,战后美国进入了空前的繁荣、发达和扩张的时期并充满信心地致力于发展社会、经济、科技和提高人民生活水平等问题。1950年末美国已经开始使用核反应堆发电,1951年电视信号能够横跨东西大陆,发射到全国各地,1952年底第一颗氢弹爆炸成功,1956年州际高速公路开始建造,跨越大西洋的电话线也已经铺设,1958年第一颗卫星发射成功,民航开始使用喷气式飞机,1959年它的疆土增加了阿拉斯加和夏威夷两个州。五六十年代还是美国人口爆炸的时期,从大战结束时的大约一亿五千万人口,10年增加了18.5%。人民生活水平大幅度提高,仅从1948到1958年的10年之间,美国建造了1300万家庭住宅,从此出现了住在郊区的中产阶级,并促使超级市场、购物中心和汽车旅馆或汽车电影院等设施的发展。1954年底特律

---

① 劳拉·布劳德尔:《唤醒民族:萧条时期美国的激进文化》,第7页。

建成第一个现代化的大型购物中心。为了方便生活,家用电器日新月异,1948年洗衣机的销售量便超过400万台。1950年电视机的销售量高达700多万台,90%以上的家庭拥有电视机。汽车成为人们生活中的必需品。1950年美国生产的汽车占全世界总产量的65%,到1955年,一年之内的销售量达到近800万辆,1960年全国60%的家庭拥有汽车。大战前不到2%的旅客乘飞机旅行,但在1956年,坐火车和乘飞机出行的旅客人数已经相当。

然而,这也是两极分化十分严重的时期,在中产阶级收入不断提高、人们乐观向上的同时,处于社会底层的20%的人民看不到希望。贫富之间、白人与少数族裔之间、郊区居民与城市贫民区居民之间的差距日益扩大,为60年代的社会动荡埋下了不安定因素。

这时期美国政治和社会趋向保守。表现之一是人们重新强调宗教的作用,性别角色也十分明确,在家庭中父亲永远是权威,母亲则应该呆在家中养儿育女、伺候丈夫,甚至女孩也只玩代表女性美的芭比娃娃(Barbie doll)①。当然,在政治上,这是个反共冷战的时期。苏联、中国等社会主义国家与共产党都被认为是"红色恐怖",是美国的敌人。一时间,政府雇员要宣誓忠诚于政府,科学家奥本海默(Charles Oppenheim)对过分发展热核武器提出质疑而受到怀疑,不少好莱坞的剧作家上了黑名单。1950年2月,参议员麦卡锡(Joseph McCarthy)声称共产主义分子已经渗入美国国务院,后来又不断强调他们甚至打入了军队和政府的高层机构,从而开始了一场全国性的政治迫害运动。最典型的例子是1953年罗森堡夫妇被以间谍罪判处死刑。

美国乐观自信的时代精神在1963年11月22日随着肯尼迪总统的遇刺事件而烟消云散。从此,美国进入了动荡不安的多事之秋。一方面在国际上冷战加剧,如1960年前苏联击落美国U2飞机的事件、1961年企图颠覆古巴卡斯特罗政府的猪湾事件、1962年由于前苏联企图运输导弹到古巴而引起的冲突,当然更重要的是1965—1973年的越南战争。美国的冷战政策及扩张行动在国内受到人民的反对。60年代,争取自由平等的黑人民权运动,反对校园内政治压制、争取言论自由的学生运动以及反对越南战争的罢课示威、贫民区的骚动等事件此起彼伏,加上自50年代末期开始的嬉皮士反文化运动,对美国社会和政治产生了深刻的影响。黑人运动促使印第安人看到自己面临的困境,也开始了他们的抗议和示威。妇女领袖如贝蒂·弗里丹(Betty Friedan)和格萝莉亚·斯坦能姆(Gloria Steinem)开始质疑妇女的不平等地位,发动了妇女解放运动。人们对政府普遍失望与不信任,抛弃旧的信念和追求,对一切权威体系和价值观念进行挑战,强调个人在追求幸福时有采取自己方式的自由,在性观念、性行为,甚至毒品观念等方面都产生了激烈的变化。这一切有其积极的效果,如民权运动结束了种族隔离的制度,改变了美国的种族关系和南方的面貌。但反文化生活方式造成的性自由及吸毒等负面影响也为社会带来了很多后遗症。所有这一切政治和社会等领域中发生的问题都在这时期的美国文学中有比较真实的反映。不过,动荡不安的60年代文学跟平静保守的50年代文学还是有一定的不同的。

二战后,在小说方面,老一代作家如福克纳、海明威和斯坦贝克等仍在继续写作。尽

---

① 这是50年代在美国十分流行的一个洋娃娃,她身材的三围非常标准,模仿当时流行的时尚服饰。

管他们都先后获得诺贝尔文学奖①,但功力已经不如以前。海明威的《过河入林》(1950)刚出版就受到评论家的严厉批评。福克纳的情况好一些,但他本人常常怀疑自己是否已经耗尽才华。大战结束后,战争小说很自然地流行起来。年轻一代中参加过战争的作家开始在40年代末发表关于第二次世界大战的作品,如诺曼·梅勒的《裸者与死者》(1948)、欧文·肖(Irving Shaw)的《幼狮》(1948)、詹姆斯·琼斯(James Jones)的《从这里到永恒》(1951)、威廉·斯泰隆(William Styron)的《漫长的行军》(1952)等。虽然当时的政治形势要求作家反映民主的胜利和法西斯的失败,但他们往往受30年代和第一次世界大战后战争文学的影响,更多的是质疑军事组织的权力和军官阶层的残酷与没有人性。② 约瑟夫·海勒(Joseph Heller)的《第22条军规》(1961)不仅跟其他战争小说一样,揭露战争的恐怖、军队的官僚主义以及军事与工业组织如何左右人们的生活、摧残人的精神,它还在技巧上有所发展,大量采用象征手段和超现实主义手法,使整个故事荒诞不经却又寓意深刻,开创了"黑色幽默"的先河。

随着冷战与麦卡锡主义的加剧,美国作家开始反思美国价值的真实内涵、考虑个人是否应该顺应时势和社会规范。50年代作家普遍批评郊区中产阶级对物质生活的追求和企业、公司对人的个性的压抑。甚至连社会学家大卫·莱斯曼和经济学家约翰·肯尼思·盖尔布来思都撰写论著对社会过于强求一致而扼杀个性表示忧虑。③ 但影响最大的著作可能是塞林格(J.D. Salinger)的《麦田里的守望者》(1951)和金斯堡(Allen Ginsberg)的长诗《嚎叫》(1956)。前者对读者起了振聋发聩的"神化"④作用。小说刚一出版就成为畅销书,其魅力经久不衰,多年来一直是大中学生心爱的读物。小说讲述中学生霍尔顿在纽约的几天经历,他的苦闷、寂寞和最终的精神崩溃反映了50年代青少年的心态与精神世界,"通过把天真理想和罪恶现实的冲突具体化和戏剧化,使人们重新评价美国梦"⑤。为此,塞林格被誉为"50年代青少年的目标与价值观念的代言人"。由于这本小说所抨击的种种丑恶现象至今仍然存在,由于它"很真实地表现了当今(20世纪末)青年的问题"⑥,因而今天仍是美国中学生的阅读书目之一。

至于金斯堡,他和凯鲁亚克(Jack Kerouac)、巴勒斯(William Burroughs)、劳伦斯·佛林盖逊(Lawrence Ferlinghetti)等人形成了声势浩大的反文化的"垮掉一代"⑦。他们抽大

---

① 福克纳在1950年获得1949年的诺贝尔文学奖;海明威于1954年而斯坦贝克则在1962年得奖。
② 林达·瓦格纳—马丁:《世纪中期的美国小说:1935—1966》中的第二章"各种各样的战争",纽约:特维恩出版社,1997年,第53—72页。
③ 莱斯曼写了《孤独的人群》;盖尔布来思的著作为《富裕的社会》。
④ 伊哈布·哈桑:《极端的天真》,普林斯顿大学出版社,1961年,第61页。
⑤ 同上书,第259页。
⑥ 见罗伯特·戴维斯编:《当代文学批评》第56卷,底特律:盖尔研究出版社,第317—318页。
⑦ The Beat Generation 在中文里常常译为"垮掉的一代",但创造这名称的凯鲁亚克在1959年的《垮掉的一代的起源》中称:"'beat'一词原意为贫穷、穷愁潦倒、过流浪生活、悲哀的、在地铁睡觉的。由于此词正在成为一个正式的名词,它正在被扩展到包括那些不在地铁睡觉但有一种新的姿态、或新的态度(我只能描绘为)一种新的道德态度。'垮掉的一代'已经成为美国在生活方式方面的一场革命的口号或标签。"见A.罗伯特·李编:《垮掉的一代作家》,伦敦:柏拉图出版社,1996年,第1页。但"beat"一词还相当于诗歌或音乐的"节奏",从社会学、心理学意义上说,它有"被打垮、被异化、被边缘化"的含义,代表从边缘看社会,拒绝社会的规范与行为准则的一种态度;由于这些诗人或作家相信禅宗佛教,它又有"纯真、福祉"等意思。

麻，过放荡不羁的生活，以持不同政见的文化战士自居，通过诗歌和小说来揭露中产阶级的美国和官方政治，冲击传统的观念、习俗，甚至生活方式。他们的出现受到欢迎，也引起恐惧和攻击。经过几乎半个世纪的争论，现在的共识是："垮掉一代"的诗人和作家在嬉笑怒骂的背后是对生存危机的严肃关注。他们企图通过嘲弄调侃来颠覆已有的秩序，惊醒读者，解放受各种压抑，包括性压抑的年轻人，使他们考虑建立新秩序和重建一个新的美国。

"垮掉一代"作家更大的贡献在于对文体的试验和改革。金斯堡直抒胸臆而又激情澎湃的长句一反艾略特的非个性诗歌理论，冲破新批评派为诗歌规定的种种束缚，掀起一场新诗歌革命。当时已经成名的老诗人威廉斯把金斯堡给他的信件收入长诗《佩特森》。金斯堡1955年在旧金山朗诵了他的代表作《嚎叫》，他的朗诵震撼了罗伯特·洛威尔——一位紧跟新批评规范的诗人，迫使他改变诗风，采用个人化的话语，反映个人的情感与心态，从而在年轻人中间造就了一批诸如西尔维娅·普拉斯和安·塞克斯顿(Ann Sexton)等自白派诗人。凯鲁亚克一气呵成的小说《在路上》综合多种文学体裁和表现手法。它既是游记小说又是一个青少年成长的故事，既刻画人物流动的心理意识又描述具体的游历过程。它通过主人公一路追寻而又始终未能实现梦想的经历嘲弄了美国梦和西部理想天堂等美国神话。凯鲁亚克的"自发散文"把写作过程和游历过程高度统一，迫使读者分享他的经验和感受。这种试验文体虽然模仿者不多，却启发作家在手法和技巧方面进行多种探索和实验。

50年代的作家不但重新审视美国社会，也不断反省自我，探讨人的本质、人与社会、人与人、人的内心矛盾和冲突。作家们各自以不同的方式进行探索和表现。贝娄的《奥吉·玛琪历险记》(1953)、《雨王汉德逊》(1959)、《只争朝夕》(1956)和马拉默德的《天生运动员》(又译《呆头呆脑的人》, 1952)、《店员》(1957)等以犹太人的心路历程为主题，也使犹太文学形成了美国文学中比较独立的一支力量。南方作家奥康纳的《慧血》(又译《智血》, 1952)与短篇小说集《好人难寻》(1955)，甚至海明威的《老人与海》(1952)关注的也都是人性这个大主题。但最出色的恐怕是黑人作家拉尔夫·埃里森的《看不见的人》(1952)，虽然作家在小说中描写了一个黑人少年的成长过程，反映了黑人与白人之间的种族矛盾，但他更关心的是西方现代人具有共性的命运问题。50年代并不重视黑人作家，但《看不见的人》使埃里森成为第一个获得国家图书奖的黑人作家(1953)。1965年，200位作家、评论家和编辑一致推荐该书为"最近20年来出版的最为出色的一本书"，主要原因不是因为小说把现实主义和超现实主义巧妙地结合起来，也不是因为作者充分运用黑人的语言、民间传说或音乐舞蹈和宗教仪式等手法，而是因为小说引起了读者的强烈共鸣。无论白人还是黑人，他们都从主人公只有转入地下才能保持他的思想和灵魂的经历中发现他们共同面临的社会压力和对生存意义的困惑。

在戏剧方面，第二次世界大战以后美国戏剧家跟小说家一样，也表现战争及其后果，如托马斯·赫根(Thomas Hogan)和乔西亚·洛根(Joshua Logan)根据小说改编的喜剧《罗伯茨先生》讽刺一位暴君般的海军指挥官。但影响更大的恐怕是根据《安妮·弗兰克的日记》改编的戏剧。此剧1956年开始上演，反映法西斯对犹太人的迫害。虽然当时社会日趋保守，但剧作家还是用戏剧表现政治权力的腐败作用，如1956年根据罗伯特·潘·沃伦的

《国王的人马》改编的戏剧和戈尔·维达尔(Gore Vidal)的《最佳人选》(1960)等。

这时期奥尼尔虽已去世,但1956年上演的《漫长的一天到黑夜》使他重新引起人们的注意,证明他不愧为一位出色的有创新性的戏剧家。阿瑟·米勒、田纳西·威廉斯(Tennessee Williams)和黑人女剧作家洛兰·汉斯贝里(Lorraine Hansberry)等都有新的建树。米勒的《推销员之死》(1949)再一次刻画了以金钱和成功为重要内容的美国梦的幻灭,以一首失败者的挽歌迫使千百万普通美国人从主人公的悲剧联想到自己的命运,产生了恐惧。这出戏是对美国文化的十分深刻的批评。

总之,50年代的美国社会虽然在很多方面强求一律,没有给人们多少自由的余地;但这却在文学方面造成一个相当繁荣的局面。随着动荡不安的60年代的到来,这种局面有了进一步的发展。作家们积极投身政治,参加反对越南战争、支持民权运动等政治活动并在文学作品中加以反映。例如,梅勒(Norman Mailer)的《黑夜的军队》(又译《夜幕下的大军》,1968)就是描写1967年向华盛顿的五角大楼进军的示威活动。哈伯·李(Harper Lee, 1926—)的《杀死一只模仿鸟》(又译《杀死一只知更鸟》,1960)描写南方一个小镇中的种族矛盾。小说出版后引起空前的轰动,一年之内发行250万册,第二年获普利策奖并被改编成电影。这一事实说明不仅作家关心社会问题,读者的阅读兴趣也转向政治题材。同时,贝蒂·弗里丹的《女性的奥秘》(1963)、蒂莉·奥尔逊(Tillie Olsen)探讨女作家缘何为数极少的讲演稿和文集《沉默》①拉开了妇女解放运动的序幕。肯·凯西(Ken Kesey)不仅在小说《飞越疯人院》(1962)里揭露冷酷无情的社会对自由的束缚和对人的个性的压抑,而且身体力行地推动反对社会体制的反文化运动。1964年6月他和一群志同道合的朋友自称为"快乐的捣蛋鬼",驾驶一辆油漆得五颜六色的公共汽车,一边抽大麻、吸麻醉药品,一边发表演说、进行演唱,从西向东漫游全国,到纽约跟"垮掉一代"作家金斯堡与凯鲁亚克会晤,又继续东上去联系其他的嬉皮士,从而把一场反文化运动推向整个美国。

这时期文学的一个重要特点是作家们在越来越关注社会政治问题的同时也不断在手法技巧方面加以创新。如特鲁门·卡波特(1924—1984)在1966年发表的《残杀》(又译《冷血》)既报道了一场残酷的谋杀案,又仿佛是一本侦探小说,把虚构成分和事实相结合。汤姆·沃尔夫(Tom Wolf)在对肯·凯西反文化的全国漫游的报道《电动冷饮剂酸性试验》(1968)中把新闻报道的手法和小说技巧相结合,把事实重新安排并加上作者的主观想像使之更富有戏剧性,形成了所谓的"新新闻主义"。另一些作家用黑色幽默的手法表现荒诞的没有理性的世界,如约瑟夫·海勒、托马斯·品钦(Thomas Pynchon)、唐纳德·巴塞尔姆(Donald Barthelme)等都在60年代开始发表小说②。

50年代后期,剧作家不满越来越商业化的百老汇剧院,认为那里上演的剧目并没有真正反映美国现实,因此外百老汇等小剧场开始兴起。在这里上演的剧目无论在主题内

---

① 此书是奥尔逊的一系列的讲话发言稿,在1978年正式出版,但早在1961年她就已经在拉德克利夫女子学院第一次发表关于女作家因社会、经济等原因而无法从事写作的讲话。第二年这篇讲话以"沉默"为题在《哈珀氏》杂志正式发表,引起轰动。

② 品钦在1963年发表《V.》、1966年出版《拍卖第四十九批》;巴思在1966年发表《牧童贾尔斯》,巴塞尔姆的第一部短篇小说集《回来,加利盖里大夫》是在1964年出版的。

容还是手法技巧方面都可以说是百老汇的对立面。60年代影响最大的戏剧家爱德华·阿尔比(Edward Albee)认为大部分所谓"现实主义"的、在百老汇上演的戏剧"讨好公众,满足他们自我庆幸和自我安慰的需要,为我们自己提供了一张虚假的图画",而所谓的"荒诞派戏剧"才是真正的当代戏剧,迫使观众"面对真实的人类景况"①。阿尔比身体力行,不断在作品中揭露人们采用的各种使他们可以忍受现实的幻想。为此,他大胆革新,采用不完整的阐述、模棱两可的结局和语言游戏等荒诞派手法。评论家们认为,阿尔比的《动物园的故事》和杰克·理查德逊(Jack Richardson, 1935—)的《浪子》、杰克·盖尔博(Jack Gilboa, 1932—)的《关系》等三部戏在1959至1960年的演出给美国戏剧界带来了清新的空气,宣告了美国战后年代的结束。②

50年代妇女和少数族裔作家,除个别人如埃里森外,影响都不大。但在60年代,随着民权运动和女权运动的兴起,他们也开始有了自己的呼声。黑人作家詹姆斯·鲍德温(James Baldwin, 1924—1987)从多年居住的法国回到美国参加民权运动,并在60年代发表了批评美国种族歧视的散文集《没有人知道我的名字》(1961)和《下一次将是烈火》(1963)。他的小说《告诉我火车开走多久了》(1968)也是一本战斗性很强的作品,他甚至还撰写戏剧,但成就不如小说与散文。黑人诗人、剧作家勒鲁伊·琼斯(Leroi Jones, 1934—)原来是"垮掉一代"作家,后来为了表示决心献身黑人解放事业,在1965年改信伊斯兰教,放弃原来的名字,改为伊玛穆·阿米利·巴拉卡(Imamui Amiri Baraka),跟白人妻子离婚,并且搬到黑人贫民窟去居住。他的诗集如《黑人艺术》(1966)赞扬黑人艺术和文化,他反映种族冲突的剧本《荷兰人》(1964)在外百老汇小剧院演出时大受欢迎。他还在纽约黑人居住区哈莱姆建立"黑人艺术宝库剧院",为发扬黑人文化而努力。

另一方面,女作家(无论白人还是黑人)也开始在文坛上占有一席之地。例如,普拉斯的小说《钟瓮》(1963)和诗歌《爹爹》(1962)、《拉扎罗斯夫人》(1962)等以及女诗人阿德里安·里奇(Adrienne Rich, 1929—)的诗集《一个儿媳妇的快照》(1963)都有明显的女性意识。黑人女作家玛格丽特·沃克·亚历山大(Margaret Walker Alexander, 1915—1998)的小说《欢乐》(1966)和诗集《新日子的预言家》(1970)、诗人玛雅·安吉罗(Maya Angelou, 1928—)的自传《我知道笼中鸟为什么会唱歌》(1968)、洛兰·汉斯贝里的戏剧《阳光下的葡萄干》(1959)等把种族与性别元素纳入文学题材的范围之中,使黑人文学登上了美国文坛,成为美国文学的一个引人注目的分支。所有这一切预示着在70年代会出现一个新的文学繁荣时期。

四、20世纪70年代以来的美国文学

20世纪从70年代开始,美国和世界的形势都有很大的变化。在世界方面,70年代的大事是尼克松访华,中美恢复邦交;80年代是东西德统一,柏林墙被拆除;90年代则是前苏联的瓦解。世界不再是两个超级大国对峙的局面。冷战似乎结束了,但美国却越来越多

---

① 爱德华·阿尔比:《哪个戏剧才是荒诞的?》,见霍尔斯特·弗棱茨编:《美国戏剧家论戏剧》,纽约:希尔与王出版社,1965年,第169—170页。
② 托马斯·艾德勒:《美国戏剧批评史:1940—1960》,"特维恩美国戏剧批评史丛书",波士顿:特维恩出版社,1994年,第202页。

地扮演世界警察的角色,不断干预第三世界的政治,甚至出动武力,尽管它总是争取联合国或欧洲国家的支持。

在美国方面,70年代延续了60年代的学生运动和民权运动,社会仍然动荡不安,游行示威成了家常便饭。人们上街可以是为了抗议越南战争或争取种族与男女平等,也可以是反对试验核武器;可以是批评政府腐败,也可以是抗议警察的暴虐。当时影响最大的是妇女解放运动。尽管争取宪法增加平等法案的努力始终没有成功,但妇女的地位确实有所提高。她们开始到过去只收男生的高等院校就读,在过去属于男人的领域里工作,甚至进入高校和企事业机构的领导阶层。1975年全国有175个妇女研究中心,学校课程开始注意包括妇女问题。总的来说,美国社会的混乱局面一直到1975年美国从越南撤军以后才有所缓和。但是,1972年尼克松卷入水门事件,1973年副总统因受贿而被迫辞职,1974年尼克松辞职和福特上台后对他无条件宽恕,这一切使得人们对政府和政治更加失望。1980年代表共和党极右势力的里根当选总统,整个美国社会再度趋向保守。80年代被称为"我,我,我"的时代,至今并未有太多变化。人们一心向往的是金钱和地位,对政治不再关心。1996年克林顿竞选连任时,只有不到一半的选民投票。虽然美国在海湾战争(1990—1991)、瓦解海地军事政变(1993年)和轰炸南斯拉夫(1999年)等国际事件中都扮演重要角色,但都没有引起美国人民的太多关注。

然而,所有这一切都在文学与文化中有所反映,甚至人们的语言也受到影响。历史学家罗斯(Donald Ross)说:"20世纪最后30年,哲学、美学和政治争论的中心常常是语言跟世界的关系。"① 过去美国被称为"大熔炉",因为移民都希望被同化,但现在强调多元文化,人们更强调美国像"马赛克",更看重如何保持各自的民族文化及传统特色。为了尊重妇女地位的变化,人们注意用不突出性别的中性名词,所谓"政治准确"的语言,尽管这受到思想保守人士的反对。

70年代以来美国文学的一大特点是很多过去壁垒分明的界限变得模糊。比如60年代嬉皮士的服装与发式是为了表示他们对社会的不满而有意跟传统不一样,它们一直被视为"另类"的文化现象,但现在被社会接受了。同样,在文学方面,主流文学与边缘文学的区别也渐渐地不太明显。一些过去处于边缘的少数族裔文学,如黑人文学、亚裔文学、妇女文学开始进入文学主流。其中,黑人文学的成就最大。七八十年代,黑人文学作品,如阿历克斯·哈利(Alex Haley)的《根》(1976)、艾丽斯·沃克(Alice Walker)的《紫颜色》(1982)、托妮·莫里森的《宝贝儿》(又译《爱娃》、《娇女》、《宠儿》,1987)等不仅登上畅销书名单而且被改编成电影。1993年托尼·莫里森获得诺贝尔文学奖一事进一步提高了黑人文学在美国文坛的地位。更值得注意的是,现在的黑人文学不再以抗议为主要主题、以现实主义为主要手法、以白人读者为主要受众,而是在语言、技巧、主题方面都有了新的突破。例如莫里森对意识流、多视角、象征等手法的运用,她对黑人文化、民族神话和传说的借鉴使她继承并超越了黑人文学和白人文学的优秀传统。沃克的成就也许不如莫里森,但她的诗歌和小说打破了黑人文学的禁区,面向黑人来探索黑人男女之间的关系、提倡妇女主义和肯定女人的才能和出路,为黑人文学和妇女解放运动及女性主义文学做出新的贡献。其他出色的黑人作家还有1993—1995年担任美国桂冠诗人的丽塔·达夫、曾在

---

① 唐纳德·罗斯:《美国历史与文化:从探险者到有线电视》,纽约:彼得·朗出版社,2000年,第544页。

克林顿就职仪式上朗诵诗歌的玛雅·安吉罗、得过两次普利策奖的剧作家奥古斯特·威尔逊（August Wilson）以及小说家伊什梅尔·里德（Ishmael Reed）、约翰·埃德加·韦德曼（1941—　）和格罗莉亚·内勒（Gloria Nailor）等。有意思的是他们中间很多人是大学英语系的教授。这说明黑人文学在美国的影响，预示着黑人文学更加光明的未来。

在美国，亚裔人口占总人口的 2.9%，其中绝大部分是华裔。但长期以来，他们没有形成自己的文学，即使有亚裔作家，他们也并未受到重视。这种情形一直到 80 年代后期才有所改变。1974 年赵健秀（Frank Chin）与人合作编撰的包括华裔、日裔和菲裔美国作家文选《哎——咿！》出版，被评论家称作"亚裔美国文艺复兴的宣言"，是亚裔美国人"思想和语言的独立宣言"。1976 年汤亭亭发表《女勇士》，引起轰动。1982 年金惠经（Elaine Kim）出版第一本关于亚裔美国文学的专著：《亚裔美国文学：有关作品和社会背景的介绍》。从此，亚裔（主要是华裔）美国文学作品走进美国大学课堂，成为大学教材，例如强调多元文化的《希思美国文学选读》（初版 1989 年）就收有 10 位亚裔美国作家的作品。这些作家基本上是在美国出生的。他们的写作有明确的目的，要回忆过去，诉说长期受忽略的族群的历史和心声，更要纠正主流社会对他们的误解和陈腐的看法，肯定他们自己是美国社会中合法的一部分。他们表现自己族裔特殊的种族、文化、性别、阶级等问题，也反映如越南战争、民权运动和妇女解放运动以及环保等美国作家所共同关心的问题。现在美国文坛上比较著名的亚裔作家有华裔小说家汤亭亭、谭恩美（Amy Tan）、任碧莲（Gish Jen），诗人、剧作家、小说家赵健秀，剧作家黄哲伦（David Henry Hwang）等，以及兼有韩裔和华裔血统的诗人宋凯蒂（Cathy Song）等。他们采用的如超现实主义的时空换位、现代拼贴、多视角多叙述者以及模棱两可的开放性结局等手法也说明他们在艺术技巧方面已经相当成熟了。

早在美国立国以前，印第安人就是美洲大陆的土著居民。但他们的早期文学（主要是部落口头文学）长期以来一直被忽视。然而，1968 年印第安诗人、小说家斯科特·莫马迪（N. Scott Momaday）的小说《黎明之屋》的出版及获奖改变了印第安文学默默无闻的状况，预示了印第安文学进入主流文坛的可能性。

即便是以白人作家为主的主流文学在这几十年内也产生了很大的变化。在小说方面，约翰·厄普代克、乔伊斯·卡洛尔·欧茨以及贝娄、马拉默德（Bernard Malamud）等老作家继续用现实主义手法探索美国社会和美国价值观念，表现那些失去精神支柱、对现代社会并不满足的人的痛苦与困惑。但也有相当一部分作家认为面对已经变得光怪陆离、充满暴力、犹如梦魇的现实生活，传统的手法已经不能发挥作用，文学也已经不可能起到教育的作用，作家不可能也没有责任为读者指出生活的道路或前进的方向。于是他们下工夫在语言文字和手法技巧等方面进行试验。库特·冯纳古特（Kurt Vonnegut）延续并发展了 60 年代海勒式的黑色幽默。菲利普·罗思（Philip Roth）、埃·劳·道克托罗（E. L. Doctorow）和罗伯特·库佛（Robert Coover）等利用历史"事实"来创造新的小说形式，把历史上的真人真事和虚构的人物与匪夷所思的情节巧妙地糅合在一起，从而在嬉笑之余无情地揭露美国政治的虚伪性，迫使读者或者怀疑美国"光辉"历史的真实性，或者明白过去的不光彩的历史在今天也还是有可能重复的。在语言与形式的试验方面最为成功的作家是托马斯·品钦，他运用混乱而不相关的事物、不知所终的故事情节以及语言上的重

复、不关联等手法说明科技进步造成的信息过剩正在形成对现代生活的威胁。

在品钦等作家倾心于构建规模庞杂的寓言式元小说的时候,另外一些作家却在试验完全不同的小说形式。80年代出现了"简约派"小说,代表作家为诗人、小说家雷蒙德·卡佛(Raymond Carver)。这类作家常常描写普通人日常生活中发生的小事情以及他们的失意与绝望。他们对文字很吝啬,绝对不使用多余的话或可能影响读者的文字。他们只是用最简单的语言把生活中一个个特定的时刻或事件告诉读者。作品中没有一个全能的、无所不知的、起主宰作用的叙述者,一切均由读者自己来做各种层次的分析。

由于试验小说的文体、结构比故事更重要,由于作家们力图扩大读者与情节或人物之间的距离,他们的作品常常给读者造成阅读上的困难,因此也就常常失去读者。80年代以后,随着整个社会渐趋保守,作家们也逐渐放弃试验,回归到现实主义手法。当然,这并非传统的现实主义,而是有所变革、有所不同。尽管冯纳古特在《囚鸟》(1979)和《神枪手迪克》(1982)中并没有放弃黑色幽默,但他不再使用试验手法,也不如过去尖刻激烈。曾经极力主张革新的巴思在《信件》(1979)和《休假》(1982)中也采用了比较传统的写作手法。

在戏剧方面,由于电视、电影和录像机的发展,也由于剧院票价的不断上涨,去剧院的人少了,戏剧失去越来越多的观众,但它作为叙述的一种方式,仍然被人们阅读。另一方面,自60年代开始,演员扮演角色而观众被动地观看的传统戏剧方式受到质疑,一些打破生活与艺术、演员与剧作家、演员与观众界限的试验剧场,如外百老汇、外外百老汇剧场和一些地方小剧场迅速兴起并且发展得很快。1998年,戏剧发展基金会和剧院与制作人联盟对纽约所有剧院观众的调查报告说明,去外百老汇或外外百老汇剧场看戏的观众是百老汇剧院观众人数的两倍,前者平均一年要看10次以上的演出,而后者只看5次。由此可以看出小剧场的旺盛的生命力。这些剧场上演的剧目往往是电视电影为了票房价值所不愿意触及的颠覆性很强的试验题材,因此是表现美国社会现实问题的先锋和主力军。这时期戏剧的总体情况正如华裔戏剧家黄哲伦所说:"美国戏剧正在开始发现美国人。(有了)黑人戏剧、妇女戏剧、同性恋戏剧、亚裔美国人戏剧、西班牙裔美国人戏剧。"[①] 确实,妇女戏剧家的出现可能是个典型的例子。70年代,在美国上演的所有剧目中,只有7%是妇女写的,6%是妇女导演的。1978年,女导演朱莉亚·迈尔斯创办了妇女戏剧与演出工程来帮助女作家撰写剧本并协助她们找机会演出。1986年,这工程成为美国最大也是历史最悠久的、专门上演妇女写的剧本的独立妇女剧院和剧团。23年来,它已上演了110个剧本,举办了400多次剧本朗读。1992年,迈尔斯说:"现在有了一个强大的妇女戏剧作家的核心组织。她们既写关于妇女问题的戏剧也写关于公共问题的戏剧。她们写作的目的是为了探索人的价值以及超越自我的愿望……她们希望观众能分享她们写进剧本里的想法、感受及梦想……"[②] 这工程每年举行活动,奖励有卓越成就的妇女,从朗诵活动、研究小组和大众读者寄来的500到800部稿子里选出三到四个剧本,请著名的演员、导演和舞台设计家组织演出,还把优秀剧作结集出版了七卷妇女戏剧选,为

---

① 鲁比·科恩:《20世纪戏剧:1945—目前》,见埃默里·埃利奥特主编:《哥伦比亚美国文学史》,哥伦比亚大学出版社,1988年,第1112页。

② 朱莉亚·迈尔斯:"前言",见朱莉亚·迈尔斯编:《写戏剧的妇女:选自妇女戏剧工程的7个剧本》,海尼曼出版社,1993年,第9页。

国内外演出提供方便。为了后继有人,她们甚至在全国两千多所学校进行妇女写作戏剧的教育项目。所有这一切大大促进了妇女戏剧的发展。

在美国历史上,由于清教主义的影响,戏剧一向不受重视,一直到奥尼尔的出现,这种情况才有所改变。20世纪的最后几十年内涌现出一大批出色的戏剧家,如引起人们注意的华裔作家赵健秀和黄哲伦,以《晚安,母亲》(1982)而一举成名并连连获奖的女作家玛莎·诺曼(Marsha Norman),连续获得两个普利策戏剧奖的黑人作家奥古斯特·威尔逊,以及既是戏剧家又是导演、既在舞台上又在银幕上获得成功,然而由于专写男人世界而不断引起争议的大卫·马麦特等。更有意思的是,美国现代语言学会的会刊 *PMLA* 和颇具权威性的《美国文学》杂志改变以往做法,开始刊登有关戏剧的文章,出版《美国文学》的杜克大学还决定推出一本新的杂志《戏剧》。也许临近世纪末年,人们开始怀旧,纽约剧院重新上演了米勒的《推销员之死》、威廉斯的《并非关于夜莺》和奥尼尔的《卖冰的人来了》,并且大获成功。① 这一切都说明,戏剧已经是美国文学不可忽略的一部分。

诗歌跟戏剧、小说一样,70年代一方面继续60年代的反叛及在诗行长短、节奏、遣词造句方面的试验与革新,另一方面由于大学的写作课程和各种诗歌朗诵活动的兴起而变得大众化。诗人们根据他们对诗歌的看法而分成了各种派别。金斯堡与里奇相信诗歌可以改变现实,约翰·阿什贝利则认为人们生活在一个荒诞的世界里,他们的思想和感情跟外部现实只有一种任意的、非逻辑性的联系。查尔斯·奥尔森(Charles Olsen)认为诗歌是认识和感觉的过程;罗伯特·布莱却相信诗歌表现诗人刚开始想的,甚至还没有开始想的思想。但无论他们的见解如何不同,他们都企图寻找能够更直接表现个人经历的最佳方式。80年代,自白派诗歌和超现实主义的"深层意象"派诗歌开始受到读者和诗人的质疑,影响有所减弱。与此同时,新现实主义诗歌开始兴起,并渐渐成为主流。诗人们从自身经历出发既反映个人与社会问题也探讨历史、思想观念、个人与社会责任等哲理问题。另一方面,60年代一些激进的左派诗人,尤其是"深层意象"派诗人在突破诗歌传统中起了很大的作用。今天他们继续对诗歌形式进行各种试验,一心解构和颠覆"官方诗歌文化",可惜他们把试验、语言、理论看得比生活和诗歌本身更重要,结果他们的"语言诗歌"不免有些曲高和寡。在诗歌走向大众化时,还有些比较保守的诗人却努力想恢复它过去高雅的、为少数人所掌握或欣赏的文化。他们模仿四五十年代后期现代主义诗歌,强调严谨的格律和反讽、象征等技巧,追求完美的形式,因而他们的作品被称为新形式主义诗歌。80年代语言诗派和新形式主义派曾互相攻击,前者说后者是"落伍的造句者",以"填满平庸杂志的空白和奖项"为目的,而后者说前者"不过是在填补学院论文之空白而已……"②进入90年代以后,诗歌发展仍然是多元化,或者按思想体系(如女性主义、同性恋、族裔),或者按地区(纽约派、爱荷华市超现实主义等)③分门别类。正是各种不同的流派和各种不同族裔的诗人使20世纪后期的诗歌变得十分丰富多彩。1985年美国国会通过一个法案,把过去的国会图书馆"诗歌顾问"正式改名为"桂冠诗人",充分说明从政府到公

---

① 詹姆斯·J.马丁尼:《戏剧》,见大卫·J.诺德洛主编:《美国文学研究:1998》,达勒姆:杜克大学出版社,2000年,第391页。

② 周伟驰:《美国当代诗坛》,见《世界文学》2001年第5期,第305页。

③ 詹姆斯、E.B.布雷斯林:《20世纪诗歌:1945—目前》,见埃默里·埃利奥特主编:《哥伦比亚美国文学史》,哥伦比亚大学出版社,1988年,第1100页。

众社会对诗歌发展的重视。

20世纪最后的几十年中还有一个值得注意的现象是文学批评理论的兴起。由于几乎主宰60年代整个社会的反传统反主流的思想行为，在文学批评方面曾经占主导地位的新批评开始衰落,70年代以后欧洲大陆，尤其是法国的各种新思潮新观念大量涌入美国，学者们在接受这些理论之余还努力用它们来审视自己的文学，构建可以应用于美国文学的批评理论。跟其他文学现象一样,这时期的理论也是百花齐放,有多元化的特点。不仅如此,文学批评理论已经发展成为一个独立的学科,成为一种独立的专业。

20世纪后几十年还有一个变化是严肃文学和通俗文学的界限越来越模糊。严肃文学也可以上畅销书榜，也可以被拍成电影，成为大众文化的一部分。① 严肃作家也喜欢采用通俗小说的格局，冯纳古特在很长的时间里一直被认为是科幻小说家，品钦的作品就像侦探小说，主人公千方百计要破奥秘，只是永远不得所求。另一方面，通俗文学并不是完全没有政治含义的。如汤姆·克兰西(Tom Clancy)的间谍小说就跟前苏联没有解体以前的冷战有关。迈克尔·克莱顿(Michael Crichton)的高科技惊险小说跟科技的突飞猛进有着密切的联系。当人们为高离婚率带来的后果所困扰，对爱情的追求产生疑惑时，他们希望从西德尼·谢尔顿(Sidney Sheldon)或埃里克·西格尔(Erich Segal)等人的爱情小说中得到安慰。暴露小说一直在美国有市场，20世纪初就有过"专门报道丑事"的作品。70年代以来，腐败事件层出不穷，这方面的作品就成为最受欢迎的通俗小说类别之一。最著名的作家是90年代崛起的、专写司法界腐败的约翰·格里森姆(John Grisham)。通俗小说家中间有些人的作品发行量常常在100万册以上。当前，美国学术界和思想界对通俗文学日益重视的现象应该引起我们的注意。

这30年还是电视、录像机、手机、个人电脑迅速发展的时代。90年代更是电子时代。1992年万维网的诞生改变了人们的生活方式，人们可以在网上进行通讯、购物、做生意、寻找信息，甚至阅读电子书籍。据统计,1998年美国有一亿以上的人使用互联网。这一切正在改变人们的生活和思维方式，也一定会在文学中有所表现，但恐怕要到21世纪中期才能看清眉目和结果。

---

① 例如，尤多拉·韦尔蒂、托尼·莫里森，甚至托马斯·品钦等严肃作家的小说都曾上过畅销书榜。肯·凯西的《飞越疯人院》、艾丽斯·沃克的《紫颜色》、道克托罗的《雷格泰姆音乐》等都曾被改编为电影。

I

1900—1945

第一单元
John Steinbeck
(1902—1968)

约翰·斯坦贝克

作者简介

约翰·斯坦贝克,小说家,生于加利福尼亚州的一个中产阶级家庭。受母亲的熏陶,很早就接触欧洲古典文学作品。1919年,进入斯坦福大学并开始写作。他当过筑路工人、农场季节工、饭店侍者、报馆采访员等等,熟悉社会底层的人们,他的许多作品都以他们为主人公,表现他们善良、质朴的品格,创造了"斯坦贝克式的英雄"形象。

斯坦贝克一生的创作大致可分为三个时期。第一个时期是30年代前后。1935年小说《煎饼坪》(Tortilla Flat)出版,得到出版界和评论界的关注。作者以幽默的笔调描写了自己家乡蒙特雷的一批退伍士兵。他们尽管失业流浪,但仍珍视友情,帮助弱者。类似的题材在作者后来的作品中不断出现。1937年出版的《人与鼠》(Of Mice and Men)描写的是两个流离失所的农业工人的故事。1939年出版的《愤怒的葡萄》(The Grapes of Wrath)是关于美国30年代大萧条时期的一部史诗,也是20世纪美国文学的经典。小说所反映的社会问题引起了强烈的反响,1940年获普利策小说奖。这一时期,他还创作了不少短篇小说并汇集在《长谷》(The Long Valley,1938)中出版。第二个时期是40年代。主要作品包括反法西斯的《月落》(The Moon Is Down,1942)以及探讨金钱和人性问题的《珍珠》(The Pearl,1947)、《任性的公共汽车》(The Wayward Bus,1947)等。50年代到60年代初是斯坦贝克创作的第三个时期,主要作品包括长篇小说《伊甸园以东》(East of Eden,1952)和《烦恼的冬天》(The Winter of Our Discontent,1961),前者用写实和象征手法描绘了善与恶的斗争,后者描写了社会道德的沦丧,表现了作家对美国精神危机的忧虑,博得评论家的好评。

斯坦贝克一生写了17部作品,显示了卓越的小说创作才能。福克纳曾把他列入美国现代"五大小说家"。他的许多作品先后被改编为电影。由于"通过现实主义的、富于想象的创作,表现出富于同情的幽默和对社会的敏感的观察",他于1962年获得了诺贝尔文学奖。在上个世纪,斯坦贝克的作品由于所反映的政治倾向一度受到美国学术界的冷落;不过,20世纪90年代以来,他的作品又开始受到重视,出现了新的斯坦贝克研究热。

The Chrysanthemums

The high grey-flannel fog of winter closed off the Salinas Valley[①] from the sky and from all the rest of the world. On every side it sat like a lid on the mountains and made of the great valley a closed pot. On the broad, level land floor the gang ploughs bit deep and left the black earth shining like metal where the shares had cut. On the foot-hill ranches across the Salinas River, the yellow stubble fields seemed to be bathed in pale cold sunshine, but there was no sunshine in the valley now in December. The thick willow scrub along the river flamed with sharp and positive yellow leaves.

It was a time of quiet and of waiting. The air was cold and tender. A light wind blew up from the southwest so that the farmers were mildly hopeful of a good rain before long; but fog and rain do not go together.

Across the river, on Henry Allen's foot-hill ranch there was little work to be done, for the hay was cut and stored and the orchards were ploughed up to receive the rain deeply when it should come. The cattle on the higher slopes were becoming shaggy and rough-coated.

Elisa Allen, working in her flower garden, looked down across the yard and saw Henry, her husband, talking to two men in business suits. The three of them stood by the tractor-shed, each man with one foot on the side of the little Fordson. They smoked cigarettes and studied the machine as they talked.

Elisa watched them for a moment and then went back to her work. She was thirty-five. Her face was lean and strong and her eyes were as clear as water. Her figure looked blocked and heavy in her gardening costume, a man's black hat pulled low down over her eyes, clod-hopper shoes, a figured print dress almost-completely covered by a big corduroy apron with four big pockets to hold the snips, the trowel and scratcher, the seeds and the knife she worked with. She wore heavy leather gloves to protect her hands while she worked.

She was cutting down the old year's chrysanthemum stalks with a pair of short and powerful scissors. She looked down toward the men by the tractor-shed

---

① the Salinas Valley：萨利纳斯山谷，位于美国加利福尼亚州西部。

now and then. Her face was eager and mature and handsome; even her work with the scissors was overeager, over-powerful. The chrysanthemum stems seemed too small and easy for her energy.

She brushed a cloud of hair out of her eyes with the back of her glove, and left a smudge of earth on her cheek in doing it. Behind her stood the neat white farmhouse with red geraniums close-banked around it as high as the windows. It was a hard-swept-looking little house, with hard-polished windows, and a clean mud-mat on the front steps.

Elisa cast another glance toward the tractor-shed. The strangers were getting into their Ford coupé①. She took off a glove and put her strong fingers down into the forest of new green chrysanthemum sprouts that were growing around the old roots. She spread the leaves and looked down among the close-growing stems. No aphids were there, no sow bugs or snails or cut-worms. Her terrier fingers destroyed such pests before they could get started.

Elisa started at the sound of her husband's voice. He had come near quietly, and he leaned over the wire fence that protected her flower garden from cattle and dogs and chickens.

"At it again," he said. "You've got a strong new crop coming."

Elisa straightened her back and pulled on the gardening glove again. "Yes. They'll be strong this coming year." In her tone and on her face there was a little smugness.

"'You've got a gift with things," Henry observed. "Some of those yellow chrysanthemums you had this year were ten inches across. I wish you'd work out in the orchard and raise some apples that big."

Her eyes sharpened. "Maybe I could do it, too. I've a gift with things, all right. My mother had it. She could stick anything in the ground and make it grow. She said it was having planters' hands that knew how to do it."

"Well, it sure works with flowers," he said.

"Henry, who were those men you were talking to?"

"Why, sure, that's what I came to tell you. They were from the Western Meat Company. I sold those thirty head of three-year-old steers. Got nearly my own price, too."

"Good," she said. "Good for you."

---

① Ford coupé：福特牌双门箱式小客车。

"And I thought," he continued, "I thought how it's Saturday afternoon, and we might go into Salinas for dinner at a restaurant, and then to a picture show—to celebrate, you see."

"Good," she repeated. "Oh, yes. That will be good."

Henry put on his joking tone. "There's fights tonight. How'd you like to go to the fights?"

"Oh, no," she said breathlessly. "No, I wouldn't like fights."

"Just fooling, Elisa. We'll go to a movie. Let's see. It's two now. I'm going to take Scotty and bring down those steers from the hill. It'll take us maybe two hours. We'll go in town about five and have dinner at the Cominos Hotel. Like that?"

"Of course I'll like it. It's good to eat away from home."

"All right, then. I'll go get up a couple of horses."

She said: "I'll have plenty of time to transplant some of these sets, guess."

She heard her husband calling Scotty down by the barn. And a little later she saw the two men ride up the pale yellow hillside in search of the steers.

There was a little square sandy bed kept for rooting the chrysanthemums. With her trowel she turned the soil over and over, and smoothed it and patted it firm. Then she dug ten parallel trenches to receive the sets. Back at the chrysanthemum bed she pulled out the little crisp shoots, trimmed off the leaves of each one with her scissors and laid it on a small orderly pile.

A squeak of wheels and plod of hoofs came from the road. Elisa looked up. The country road ran along the dense bank of willows and cottonwoods that bordered the river, and up this road came a curious vehicle, curiously drawn. It was an old spring-wagon, with a round canvas top on it like the cover of a prairie schooner. It was drawn by an old bay horse and a little grey-and-white burro. A big stubble-bearded man sat between the cover flaps and drove the crawling team. Underneath the wagon, between the hind wheels, a lean and rangy mongrel dog walked sedately. Words were painted on the canvas, in clumsy, crooked letters. "Pots, pans, knives, sisors①, lawn mores, Fixed." Two rows of articles, and the triumphantly definitive "Fixed" below. The black paint had run down in little sharp points beneath each letter.

Elisa, squatting on the ground, watched to see the crazy, loose-jointed wagon

---

① sisors: scissors.

pass by.　But it didn't pass.　It turned into the farm road in front of her house, crooked old wheels skirling and squeaking.　The rangy dog darted from between the wheels and ran ahead. Instantly the two ranch shepherds flew out at him. Then all three stopped, and with stiff and quivering tails, with taut straight legs, with ambassadorial dignity, they slowly circled, sniffing daintily. The caravan pulled up to Elisa's wire fence and stopped. Now the newcomer dog, feeling out-numbered, lowered his tail and retired under the wagon with raised hackles and bared teeth.

　　The man on the wagon seat called out: "That's a bad dog in a fight when he gets started."

　　Elisa laughed. "I see he is. How soon does he generally get started?"

　　The man caught up her laughter and echoed it heartily. "Sometimes not for weeks and weeks," he said. He climbed stiffly down, over the wheel. The horse and the donkey drooped like unwatered flowers.

　　Elisa saw that he was a very big man.　Although his hair and beard were greying,　he did not look old.　His worn black suit was wrinkled and spotted with grease.　The laughter had disappeared from his face and eyes the moment his laughing voice ceased. His eyes were dark, and they were full of the brooding that gets in the eyes of teamsters and of sailors.　The calloused hands he rested on the wire fence were cracked,　and every crack was a black line.　He took off his battered hat.

　　"I'm off my general road, ma'am," he said. "Does this dirt road cut over across the river to the Los Angeles highway?"

　　Elisa stood up and shoved the thick scissors in her apron pocket. "Well, yes, it does, but it winds around and then fords the river. I don't think your team could pull through the sand."

　　He replied with some asperity: "It might surprise you what them beasts can pull through."

　　"When they get started?" she asked.

　　He smiled for a second. "Yes. When they get started."

　　"Well," said Elisa, "I think you'll save time if you go back to the Salinas road and pick up the highway there."

　　He drew a big finger down the chicken wire and made it sing.　"I ain't[①] in any hurry, ma'am. I go from Seattle to San Diego and back every year. Takes all

---

① ain't: am not; is not; are not; have not; has not.

my time. About six months each way. I aim① to follow nice weather."

Elisa took off her gloves and stuffed them in the apron pocket with the scissors. She touched the under edge of her man's hat, searching for fugitive hairs. "That sounds like a nice kind of way to live," she said.

He leaned confidentially over the fence. "Maybe you noticed the writing on my wagon. I mend pots and sharpen knives and scissors. You got any of them things to do?"

"Oh, no," she said quickly. "Nothing like that." Her eyes hardened with resistance.

"Scissors is the worst thing," he explained. "Most people just ruin scissors trying to sharpen 'em②, but I know how. I got a special tool. It's a little bobbit kind of thing, and patented. But it sure does the trick."

"No. My scissors are all sharp."

"All right, then. Take a pot," he continued earnestly, "a bent pot, or a pot with a hole. I can make it like new so you don't have to buy no new ones. That's a saving for you."

"No," she said shortly. "I tell you I have nothing like that for you to do."

His face fell to an exaggerated sadness. His voice took on a whining undertone. "I ain't had a thing to do today. Maybe I won't have no supper tonight. You see I'm off my regular road. I know folks on the highway clear from Seattle to San Diego. They save their things for me to sharpen up because they know I do it so good and save them money."

"I'm sorry," Elisa said irritably. "I haven't anything for you to do."

His eyes left her face and fell to searching the ground. They roamed about until they came to the chrysanthemum bed where she had been working. "What's them plants, ma'am?"

The irritation and resistance melted from Elisa's face. "Oh, those are chrysanthemums, giant whites and yellows. I raise them every year, bigger than anybody around here."

"Kind of a long-stemmed flower? Looks like a quick puff of colored smoke?" he asked.

"That's it. What a nice way to describe them."

"They smell kind of nasty till you get used to them," he said.

---

① I aim: I am.

② 'em: them.

"It's a good bitter smell," she retorted, "not nasty at all."

He changed his tone quickly. "I like the smell myself."

"I had ten-inch blooms this year," she said.

The man leaned farther over the fence. "Look. I know a lady down the road a piece, has got the nicest garden you ever seen. Got nearly every kind of flower but no chrysanthemums. Last time I was mending a copper-bottom washtub for her (that's a hard job but I do it good), she said to me: 'If you ever run acrost① some nice chrysanthemums I wish you'd try to get me a few seeds.' That's what she told me."

Elisa's eyes grew alert and eager. "She couldn't have known much about chrysanthemums. You *can* raise them from seed, but it's much easier to root the little sprouts you see here."

"Oh," he said. "I s'pose② I can' take none to her, then."

"Why yes you can," Elisa cried. "I can put some in damp sand, and you can carry them right along with you. They'll take root in the pot if you keep them damp. And then she can transplant them."

"She'd sure like to have some, ma'am. You say they're nice ones?"

"Beautiful," she said. "Oh, beautiful." Her eyes shone. She tore off the battered hat and shook out her dark pretty hair. "I'll put them in a flowerpot, and you can take them right with you. Come into the yard."

While the man came through the picket gate Elisa ran excitedly along the geranium-bordered path to the back of the house. And she returned carrying a big red flower-pot. The gloves were forgotten now. She knelt on the ground by the starting bed and dug up the sandy soil with her fingers and scooped it into the bright new flower-pot. Then she picked up the little pile of shoots she had prepared. With her strong fingers she pressed them into the sand and tamped around them with her knuckles. The man stood over her. "I'll tell you what to do," she said. "You remember so you can tell the lady."

"Yes, I'll try to remember."

"Well, look. These will take root in about a month. Then she must set them out, about a foot apart in good rich earth like this, see?" She lifted a handful of dark soil for him to look at. "They'll grow fast and tall. Now remember this: In July tell her to cut them down, about eight inches from the ground."

---

① acrost: across.

② I s'pose: I suppose.

"Before they bloom?" he asked.

"Yes, before they bloom." Her face was tight with eagerness. "They'll grow right up again. About the last of September the buds will start."

She stopped and seemed perplexed. "It's the budding that takes the most care," she said hesitantly. "I don't know how to tell you." She looked deep into his eyes, searchingly. Her mouth opened a little, and she seemed to be listening. "I'll try to tell you," she said. "Did you ever hear of planting hands?"

"Can't say I have, ma'am."

"Well, I can only tell you what it feels like. It's when you're picking off the buds you don't want. Everything goes right down into your fingertips. You watch your fingers work. They do it themselves. You can feel how it is. They pick and pick the buds. They never make a mistake. They're with the plant. Do you see? Your fingers and the plant. You can feel that, right up your arm. They know. They never make a mistake. You can feel it. When you're like that you can't do anything wrong. Do you see that? Can you understand that?"

She was kneeling on the ground looking up at him. Her breast swelled passionately.

The man's eyes narrowed. He looked away self-consciously.

"Maybe I know," he said. "Sometimes in the night in the wagon there—"

Elisa's voice grew husky. She broke in on him: "I've never lived as you do, but I know what you mean. When the night is dark—why, the stars are sharp-pointed, and there's quiet. Why, you rise up and up! Every pointed star gets driven into your body. It's like that. Hot and sharp and—lovely."

Kneeling there, her hand went out toward his legs in the greasy black trousers. Her hesitant fingers almost touched the cloth. Then her hand dropped to the ground. She crouched low like a fawning dog.

He said: "It's nice, just like you say. Only when you don't have no dinner[①], it ain't."

She stood up then, very straight, and her face was ashamed. She held the flower-pot out to him and placed it gently in his arms. "Here. Put it in your wagon, on the seat, where you can watch it. Maybe I can find something for you to do."

At the back of the house she dug in the can pile and found two old and bat-

---

① only when you don't have no dinner：这里的双重否定仍然表示否定的意思。句中的 no 意为 any。

tered aluminum saucepans. She carried them back and gave them to him. "Here, maybe you can fix these."

His manner changed. He became professional. "Good as new I can fix them." At the back of his wagon he set a little anvil, and out of an oily tool-box dug a small machine hammer. Elisa came through the gate to watch him while he pounded out the dents in the kettles. His mouth grew sure and knowing. At a difficult part of the work he sucked his underlip.

"You sleep right in the wagon?" Elisa asked.

"Right in the wagon, ma'am. Rain or shine I'm dry as a cow in there."

"It must be nice," she said. "It must be very nice. I wish women could do such things."

"It ain't the right kind of a life for a woman."

Her upper lip raised a little, showing her teeth. "How do you know? How can you tell?" she said.

"I don't know, ma'am," he protested. "Of course I don't know. Now here's your kettles, done①. You don't have to buy no new ones."

"How much?"

"Oh, fifty cents'll do. I keep my prices down and my work good. That's why I have all them satisfied customers up and down the highway."

Elisa brought him a fifty-cent piece from the house and dropped it in his hand. "You might be surprised to have a rival some time. I can sharpen scissors, too. And I can beat the dents out of little pots. I could show you what a woman might do."

He put his hammer back in the oily box and shoved the little anvil out of sight. "It would be a lonely life for a woman, ma'am, and a scarey life, too, with animals creeping under the wagon all night." He climbed over the single-tree, steadying himself with a hand on the burro's white rump. He settled himself in the seat, picked up the lines. "Thank you kindly ma'am," he said. "I'll do like you told me; I'll go back and catch the Salinas road."

"Mind," she called, "if you're long in getting there, keep the sand damp."

"Sand, ma'am? ... Sand? Oh, sure. You mean around the chrysanthemums. Sure I will." He clucked his tongue. The beasts leaned luxuriously into their collars. The mongrel dog took his place between the back wheels. The wagon turned

---

① done：完成了。

and crawled out the entrance road and back the way it had come, along the river.

Elisa stood in front of her wire fence watching the slow progress of the caravan. Her shoulders were straight, her head thrown back, her eyes half-closed, so that the scene came vaguely into them. Her lips moved silently, forming the words "Good-bye—good-bye." Then she whispered: "That's a bright direction. There's a glowing there." The sound of her whisper startled her. She shook herself free and looked about to see whether anyone had been listening. Only the dogs had heard. They lifted their heads toward her from their sleeping in the dust, and then stretched out their chins and settled asleep again. Elisa turned and ran hurriedly into the house.

In the kitchen she reached behind the stove and felt the water tank. It was full of hot water from the noonday cooking. In the bathroom she tore off her soiled clothes and flung them into the corner. And then she scrubbed herself with a little block of pumice, legs and thighs, loins and chest and arms, until her skin was scratched and red. When she had dried herself she stood in front of a mirror in her bedroom and looked at her body. She tightened her stomach and threw out her chest. She turned and looked over her shoulders at her back.

After a while she began to dress, slowly. She put on her newest underclothing and her nicest stockings and the dress which was the symbol of her prettiness. She worked carefully on her hair, pencilled her eyebrows and roughed her lips.

Before she was finished she heard the little thunder of hoofs and the shouts of Henry and his helper as they drove the red steers into the corral. She heard the gate bang shut and set herself for Henry's arrival.

His step sounded on the porch. He entered the house calling: "Elisa, where are you?"

"In my room, dressing. I'm not ready. There's hot water for your bath. Hurry up. It's getting late."

When she head him splashing in the tub, Elisa laid his dark suit on the bed, and shirt and socks and tie beside it. She stood his polished shoes on the floor beside the bed. Then she went to the porch and sat primly and stiffly down. She looked toward the river road where the willow-line was still yellow with frosted leaves so that under the high grey fog they seemed a thin band of sunshine. This was the only color in the grey afternoon. She sat unmoving for a long time. Her eyes blinked rarely.

Henry came banging out of the door, shoving his tie inside his vest as he came. Elisa stiffened and her face grew tight. Henry stopped short and looked at her. "Why—why, Elisa. You look so nice!"

"Nice? You think I look nice? What do you mean 'nice'?"

Henry blundered on. "I don't know. I mean you look different, strong and happy."

"I am strong? Yes, strong. What do you mean 'strong'?"

He looked bewildered. "You're playing some kind of a game," he said helplessly. "It's a kind of a play. You look strong enough to break a calf over your knee, happy enough to eat it like a watermelon."

For a second she lost her rigidity. "Henry! Don't talk like that. You didn't know what you said." She grew complete again. "I'm strong," she boasted. "I never knew before how strong."

Henry looked down toward the tractor-shed, and when he brought his eyes back to her, they were his own again. "I'll get out the car. You can put on your coat while I'm starting."

Elisa went into the house. She heard him drive to the gate and idle down his motor, and then she took a long time to put on her hat. She pulled it here and pressed it there. When Henry turned the motor off she slipped into her coat and went out.

The little roadster bounced along on the dirt road by the river, raising the birds and driving the rabbits into the brush. Two cranes flapped heavily over the willow-line and dropped into the river-bed.

Far ahead on the road Elisa saw a dark speck. She knew.

She tried not to look as they passed it, but her eyes would not obey. She whispered to herself sadly: "He might have thrown them off the road. That wouldn't have been much trouble, not very much. But he kept the pot," she explained. "He had to keep the pot. That's why he couldn't get them off the road."

The roadster turned a bend and she saw the caravan ahead. She swung full around toward her husband so she could not see the little covered wagon and the mis-matched team as the car passed them.

In a moment it was over. The thing was done. She did not look back.

She said loudly, to be heard above the motor: "It will be good, tonight, a good dinner."

"Now you've changed again," Henry complained. He took one hand from the wheel and patted her knee. "I ought to take you in to dinner oftener. It would be good for both of us. We get so heavy out on the ranch."

"Henry," she asked, "could we have wine at dinner?"

"Sure we could. Say! That will be fine."

She was silent for a while; then she said: "Henry, at those prizefights, do the men hurt each other very much?"

"Sometimes a little, not often. Why?"

"Well, I've read how they break noses, and blood runs down their chests. I've read how the fighting gloves get heavy and soggy with blood."

He looked around at her. "What's the matter, Elisa? I didn't know you read things like that." He brought the car to a stop, then turned to the right over the Salinas River bridge.

"Do any women ever go to the fights?" she asked.

"Oh, sure, some. What's the matter, Elisa? Do you want to go? I don't think you'd like it, but I'll take you if you really want to go."

She relaxed limply in the seat. "Oh, no. No. I don't want to go. I'm sure I don't." Her face was turned away from him. "It will be enough if we can have wine. It will be plenty." She turned up her coat collar so he could not see that she was crying weakly—like an old woman.

作品赏析

《菊花》选自约翰·斯坦贝克的短篇小说集《长谷》是作者关注女性生活、描写女性内心世界及其变化的一篇名著,被评论家誉为斯坦贝克在艺术上最成功的短篇小说。故事发生在加利福尼亚萨利纳斯山谷一个偏僻的农场。女主人公伊莉莎在花园里精心修剪菊花。丈夫亨利谈完生意后路过花园,夸她的菊花种得大,但又表示她要是能把苹果培育得像菊花那样大就好了;亨利还说晚上要带她去城里吃饭,庆祝他谈了一笔好生意。显然,亨利占据着话语权,他对妻子心爱的菊花并不感兴趣。交谈中,伊莉莎虽然表现出对自己种花手艺的自豪,但她不时重复或附和丈夫的话,语言有些呆板。作家寥寥几笔,勾勒出女主人公生活环境的封闭和压抑,以及婚姻和家庭生活的单调乏味。亨利走后,来了一个补锅匠,表示想找点挣钱的活干,伊莉莎拒绝了;但当补锅匠假装欣赏她种的菊花时,她好像完全变了一个人,她不仅慷慨地付了补锅的工钱,而且热情地挑选菊花苗送给他,甚至激动地告诉他自己种花的经验和体会。交谈中,她还流露出对他那种自由生活的羡慕。女主人公的语言这时变得丰富而生动,与先前大不相同。补锅匠带着那盆菊花苗走后,伊莉莎兴奋地梳洗打扮,穿上最漂亮的衣服。补锅匠对她的菊花表现出的赏识,使她产生了对自我价值的新认识和对未来生活的憧憬。不过,亨利回来后,她的心理发生了微妙变化,语言和神情又变得呆板起来。尤其是,当她发现那盆菊花苗被当作一钱不值的东西扔弃在路上时,她的精神被击垮了。故事以女主人公暗自饮泣结束。该作品以菊花为线索,以理想与现实的冲突为主题,通过环境烘托、人物对话、心理描写以及对照和象征等艺术手法的运用,用洗练的文笔刻画了一个向往独立和自由、渴望实现自我价值而屡屡受挫的孤独无奈的女性形象,反映了美国20世纪30年代普通家庭妇女的困顿和苦闷,表现了作家对女性的深切同情。

思考题

1. How would you describe Elisa? What textual information compels you to have that "mental picture" of this central character?

2. What kind of man is Henry? What specific clues does Steinbeck provide us in order to form our impression of Elisa's husband?

3. How does the tinker manipulate Elisa to give him some work, overcoming her initial resistance? What does this action suggest about his character?

4. What is the significance of Elisa's bathing and admiring herself in the mirror after her encounter with the tinker?

5. How do events at the end of the story—particularly her seeing the flowers discarded in the road—alter the characterization of Elisa? What changes, both in thought and action, does this event cause in her?

推荐作品

Of Mice and Men (1937)
The Grapes of Wrath (1939)
The Winter of Our Discontent (1961)

参考资料

Benson, Jackson, ed. *The Short Novels of John Steinbeck: Critical Essays with a Checklist to Steinbeck Criticism.* Durbam & London: Duke UP, 1990.

French, Warren G., *Steinbeck's Fiction Revisited.* New York: Twaybne Publishers, 1994.

Hayashi, Tetsumaro, ed. *A New Study Guide to Steinbeck's Major Works, with Critical Explications.* New Jersey: The Scarecrow Press, Inc., 1993.

第二单元
F. Scott Fitzgerald
(1896—1940)
弗·斯科特·菲茨杰拉德

✎ 作者简介

弗·斯科特·菲茨杰拉德,小说家,生于明尼苏达州一个破落士绅家庭。他在圣保罗学院和普林斯顿大学上学主要依靠母亲娘家资助。1917年,美国宣布对德作战,他辍学参军。1918年夏,他在训练驻地与当地的富家女泽尔达·塞尔(Zelda Sayre)订婚。1919年他退役后,泽尔达因他没有成功的事业而与他解除婚约。1920年3月他出版了小说《人间天堂》(*This Side of Paradise*)。他因此一鸣惊人,名利双收。同年4月,他与泽尔达结婚。他们婚后的生活奢华,恰成美国战后的享乐风潮的写照。这期间他发表了短篇小说集《姑娘们与哲学家们》(*Flappers and Philosophers*, 1920)和小说《漂亮的冤家》(*The Beautiful and Damned*, 1922)和《爵士乐时代的故事》(*Tales of the Jazz Age*, 1922)。1924年,他来到巴黎,结识了斯泰因、庞德、海明威等一批"迷惘的一代"的旅欧美国作家并创作了《了不起的盖茨比》(*The Great Gatsby*, 1925)。1934年,他的另一部重要小说《夜色温柔》(*Tender Is the Night*)出版,但并没有获得预期的成功。1940年他死于心脏病。他的好友、文学评论家爱德蒙·威尔逊把他的散文结集出版,题名为《崩溃》(*The Crack-Up*, 1945)。菲茨杰拉德的创作活跃时期适值美国一战后的所谓"喧嚣的20年代"和"爵士乐时代"。他的作品深入刻画了注重金钱和享乐的时代潮流,一方面他自己随波逐流,沉湎于物质享乐,另一方面却又能客观审视自身的矛盾心态,以冷静批判的笔触反思社会现实和浮华表面下蕴藏的精神危机和"美国梦"的追求和幻灭,因而他的作品被看作是这个时代风貌的真实写照。菲茨杰拉德曾在给女儿的信中谈到,"我想我骨子里是个道德家,总想以一种可以接受的方式向人们说教,而不是娱乐大众。"

菲茨杰拉德在20世纪50年代前已失去公众的关注,但在威尔逊和其他评论家的推动下,菲茨杰拉德的声誉重上新的台阶。一些调查结果显示,菲茨杰拉德作为经典作家和明星人物对美国公众的魅力在20世纪末仍未减弱,人们普遍认为他是20世纪最重要的美国作家之一。菲茨杰拉德曾对电影的表现能力表示羡慕,而大概不会想到他的经典作品《了不起的盖茨比》被四次改编成影视作品(1926年默片版,1949年版,1974年版,2001年电视版等),2002年的电影《G》也是根据其主题摄制,而他的《夜色温柔》也被多次搬上影视屏幕(2006年还将有新改编版发行)。2001年摄制的"美国大师"系列记录片《弗·斯科特·菲茨杰拉德:冬天的梦》再现了主人公的生活和创作经历。

Winter Dreams

Some of the caddies were poor as sin and lived in one-room houses with a neurasthenic cow in the front yard, but Dexter Green's father owned the second best grocery-store in Black Bear—the best one was "The Hub," patronized by the wealthy people from Sherry Island—and Dexter caddied only for pocket-money.

In the fall when the days became crisp and gray, and the long Minnesota winter shut down like the white lid of a box, Dexter's skis moved over the snow that hid the fairways of the golf course. At these times the country gave him a feeling of profound melancholy—it offended him that the links should lie in enforced fallowness, haunted by ragged sparrows for the long season. It was dreary, too, that on the tees where the gay colors fluttered in summer there were now only the desolate sand-boxes knee-deep in crusted ice. When he crossed the hills the wind blew cold as misery, and if the sun was out he tramped with his eyes squinted up against the hard dimensionless glare.

In April the winter ceased abruptly. The snow ran down into Black Bear Lake scarcely tarrying for the early golfers to brave the season with red and black balls. Without elation, without an interval of moist glory, the cold was gone.

Dexter knew that there was something dismal about this Northern spring, just as he knew there was something gorgeous about the fall. Fall made him clinch his hands and tremble and repeat idiotic sentences to himself, and make brisk abrupt gestures of command to imaginary audiences and armies. October filled him with hope which November raised to a sort of ecstatic triumph, and in this mood the fleeting brilliant impressions of the summer at Sherry Island were ready grist to his mill①. He became a golf champion and defeated Mr. T. A. Hedrick in a marvellous match played a hundred times over the fairways of his imagination, a match each detail of which he changed about untiringly—sometimes he won with almost laughable ease, sometimes he came up magnificently from behind②.

---

① grist to his mill：可供他想象发挥的素材。
② come up... from behind：从落后的局面反超。

Again, stepping from a Pierce-Arrow① automobile, like Mr. Mortimer Jones, he strolled frigidly into the lounge of the Sherry Island Golf Club② — or perhaps, surrounded by an admiring crowd, he gave an exhibition of fancy diving from the spring-board of the club raft... Among those who watched him in open-mouthed wonder was Mr. Mortimer Jones.

And one day it came to pass that Mr. Jones—himself and not his ghost③ — came up to Dexter with tears in his eyes and said that Dexter was the—best caddy in the club, and wouldn't he decide not to quit if Mr. Jones made it worth his while, because every other—caddy in the club lost one ball a hole for him—regularly—

"No, sir," said Dexter decisively, "I don't want to caddy any more." Then, after a pause: "I'm too old."

"You're not more than fourteen. Why the devil did you decide just this morning that you wanted to quit? You promised that next week you'd go over to the State tournament with me."

"I decided I was too old."

Dexter handed in his "A Class" badge, collected what money was due him from the caddy master, and walked home to Black Bear Village.

"The best—caddy I ever saw," shouted Mr. Mortimer Jones over a drink that afternoon. "Never lost a ball! Willing! Intelligent! Quiet! Honest! Grateful!"

The little girl who had done this④ was eleven—beautifully ugly as little girls are apt to be who are destined after a few years to be inexpressibly lovely and bring no end of misery to a great number of men. The spark, however, was perceptible. There was a general ungodliness in the way her lips twisted down at the corners when she smiled, and in the—Heaven help us! —in the almost passionate quality of her eyes. Vitality is born in such women. It was utterly in evidence now, shining through her thin frame in a sort of glow.

She had come eagerly out on to the course at nine o'clock with a white linen nurse and five small new golf-clubs in a white canvas bag which the nurse was carrying. When Dexter first saw her she was standing by the caddy house, rather ill at ease and trying to conceal the fact by engaging her nurse in an obviously

---

① Pierce-Arrow：20 世纪初美国一款豪华车品牌。
② golf club：高尔夫球俱乐部往往是财富的象征，俱乐部会员一般都是社会名流和富人。
③ himself and not his ghost：是他本人而不是梦中幻影。
④ The little girl who had done this：使他作出决定的小姑娘。

unnatural conversation graced by startling and irrelevant grimaces from herself.

"Well, it's certainly a nice day, Hilda," Dexter heard her say. She drew down the corners of her mouth, smiled, and glanced furtively around, her eyes in transit falling for an instant on Dexter.

Then to the nurse:

"Well, I guess there aren't very many people out here this morning, are there?"

The smile again—radiant, blatantly artificial—convincing.

"I don't know what we're supposed to do now," said the nurse, looking nowhere in particular.

"Oh, that's all right. I'll fix it up."

Dexter stood perfectly still, his mouth slightly ajar. He knew that if he moved forward a step his stare would be in her line of vision—if he moved backward he would lose his full view of her face. For a moment he had not realized how young she was. Now he remembered having seen her several times the year before—in bloomers.

Suddenly, involuntarily, he laughed, a short abrupt laugh—then, startled by himself, he turned and began to walk quickly away.

"Boy!"

Dexter stopped.

"Boy—"

Beyond question he was addressed. Not only that, but he was treated to that absurd smile, that preposterous smile—the memory of which at least a dozen men were to carry into middle age.

"Boy, do you know where the golf teacher is?"

"He's giving a lesson."

"Well, do you know where the caddy-master is?"

"He isn't here yet this morning."

"Oh." For a moment this baffled her. She stood alternately on her right and left foot.

"We'd like to get a caddy," said the nurse. "Mrs. Mortimer Jones sent us out to play golf, and we don't know how without we get a caddy[①]."

Here she was stopped by an ominous glance from Miss Jones, followed im-

---

① we don't know how without we get a caddy.：没有球童管理员，我们不知道怎么找到球童。

mediately by the smile.

"There aren't any caddies here except me," said Dexter to the nurse, "and I got to stay here in charge until the caddy-master gets here."

"Oh."

Miss Jones and her retinue now withdrew, and at a proper distance from Dexter became involved in a heated conversation, which was concluded by Miss Jones taking one of the clubs and hitting it on the ground with violence. For further emphasis she raised it again and was about to bring it down smartly upon the nurse's bosom, when the nurse seized the club and twisted it from her hands.

"You damn little mean old *thing*!" cried Miss Jones wildly.

Another argument ensued. Realizing that the elements of comedy were implied in the scene, Dexter several times began to laugh, but each time restrained the laugh before it reached audibility. He could not resist the monstrous conviction that the little girl was justified in beating the nurse.

The situation was resolved by the fortuitous appearance of the caddy-master, who was appealed to immediately by the nurse.

"Miss Jones is to have a little caddy, and this one says he can't go."

"Mr. McKenna said I was to wait here till you came," said Dexter quickly.

"Well, he's here now." Miss Jones smiled cheerfully at the caddy-master. Then she dropped her bag and set off at a haughty mince toward the first tee.

"Well?" The caddy-master turned to Dexter. "What you standing there like a dummy for? Go pick up the young lady's clubs."

"I don't think I'll go out to-day," said Dexter.

"You don't—"

"I think I'll quit."

The enormity of his decision frightened him. He was a favorite caddy, and the thirty dollars a month he earned through the summer were not to be made elsewhere around the lake. But he had received a strong emotional shock, and his perturbation required a violent and immediate outlet.

It was not so simple as that, either. As so frequently would be the case in the future, Dexter was unconsciously dictated to by his winter dreams.

II

Now, of course, the quality and the reasonability of these winter dreams varied, but the stuff of them remained. They persuaded Dexter several years later to pass up a business course at the State university—his father, prospering now, would have paid his way—for the precarious advantage of attending an older and more famous university in the East, where he was bothered by his scanty funds. But do not get the impression, because his winter dreams happened to be concerned at first with musings on the rich, that there was anything merely snobbish in the boy. He wanted not association with glittering things and glittering people—he wanted the glittering things themselves. Often he reached out for the best without knowing why he wanted it—and sometimes he ran up against the mysterious denials and prohibitions in which life indulges. It is with one of those denials and not with his career as a whole that this story deals.

He made money. It was rather amazing. After college he went to the city from which Black Bear Lake draws its wealthy patrons. When he was only twenty-three and had been there not quite two years, there were already people who liked to say: "Now *there's* a boy—" All about him rich men's sons were peddling bonds precariously, or investing patrimonies precariously, or plodding through the two dozen volumes of the "George Washington Commercial Course," but Dexter borrowed a thousand dollars on his college degree and his confident mouth[①], and bought a partnership in a laundry.

It was a small laundry when he went into it, but Dexter made a specialty of learning how the English washed fine woolen golf-stockings without shrinking them, and within a year he was catering to the trade that wore knickerbockers. Men were insisting that their Shetland hose and sweaters go to his laundry, just as they had insisted on a caddy who could find golf-balls. A little later he was doing their wives' lingerie as well—and running five branches in different parts of the city. Before he was twenty-seven he owned the largest string of laundries in his section of the country. It was then that he sold out and went to New York. But the part of his story that concerns us goes back to the days when he was making his first big success.

---

① on his college degree and his confident mouth：这里指主人公以他的大学学历和他自信的口才使人相信他有能力偿还借款。

When he was twenty-three Mr. Hart—one of the gray-haired men who liked to say "Now there's a boy"—gave him a guest card to the Sherry Island Golf Club for a week-end. So he signed his name one day on the register, and that afternoon played golf in a foursome with Mr. Hart and Mr. Sandwood and Mr. T. A. Hedrick. He did not consider it necessary to remark that he had once carried Mr. Hart's bag over this same links, and that he knew every trap and gully with his eyes shut—but he found himself glancing at the four caddies who trailed them, trying to catch a gleam or gesture that would remind him of himself, that would lessen the gap which lay between his present and his past.

It was a curious day, slashed abruptly with fleeting, familiar impressions. One minute he had the sense of being a trespasser—in the next he was impressed by the tremendous superiority he felt toward Mr. T. A. Hedrick, who was a bore and not even a good golfer any more.

Then, because of a ball Mr. Hart lost near the fifteenth green, an enormous thing happened. While they were searching the stiff grasses of the rough there was a clear call of "Fore!" from behind a hill in their rear. And as they all turned abruptly from their search a bright new ball sliced abruptly over the hill and caught Mr. T. A. Hedrick in the abdomen.

"By Gad!" cried Mr. T. A. Hedrick, "they ought to put some of these crazy women off the course. It's getting to be outrageous."

A head and a voice came up together over the hill:

"Do you mind if we go through?"

"You hit me in the stomach!" declared Mr. Hedrick wildly.

"Did I?" The girl approached the group of men. "I'm sorry. I yelled 'Fore!'"

Her glance fell casually on each of the men—then scanned the fairway for her ball.

"Did I bounce into the rough?"

It was impossible to determine whether this question was ingenuous or malicious. In a moment, however, she left no doubt, for as her partner came up over the hill she called cheerfully:

"Here I am! I'd have gone on the green except that I hit something."

As she took her stance for a short mashie shot, Dexter looked at her closely. She wore a blue gingham dress, rimmed at throat and shoulders with a white edging that accentuated her tan. The quality of exaggeration, of thinness, which had made her passionate eyes and down-turning mouth absurd at eleven, was gone now. She was arrestingly beautiful. The color in her cheeks was centered like the color in a picture—it was not a "high" color①, but a sort of fluctuating and feverish warmth, so shaded that it seemed at any moment it would recede and disappear. This color and the mobility of her mouth gave a continual impression of flux, of intense life, of passionate vitality—balanced only partially by the sad luxury of her eyes.

She swung her mashie impatiently and without interest, pitching the ball into a sand-pit on the other side of the green. With a quick, insincere smile and a careless "Thank you!" she went on after it.

"That Judy Jones!" remarked Mr. Hedrick on the next tee, as they waited—some moments—for her to play on ahead. "All she needs is to be turned up and spanked for six months and then to be married off to an old-fashioned cavalry captain."

"My God, she's good-looking!" said Mr. Sandwood, who was just over thirty.

"Good-looking!" cried Mr. Hedrick contemptuously, "she always looks as if she wanted to be kissed! Turning those big cow-eyes on every calf in town!"

It was doubtful if Mr. Hedrick intended a reference to the maternal instinct.

"She'd play pretty good golf if she'd try," said Mr. Sandwood.

"She has no form," said Mr. Hedrick solemnly.

"She has a nice figure," said Mr. Sandwood.

"Better thank the Lord she doesn't drive a swifter ball," said Mr. Hart, winking at Dexter.

Later in the afternoon the sun went down with a riotous swirl of gold and varying blues and scarlets, and left the dry, rustling night of Western summer. Dexter watched from the veranda of the Golf Club, watched the even overlap of the waters in the little wind, silver molasses under the harvest-moon. Then the moon held a finger to her lips and the lake became a clear pool, pale and quiet. Dexter put on his bathing-suit and swam out to the farthest raft, where he stretched dripping on the wet canvas of the springboard.

There was a fish jumping and a star shining and the lights around the lake were gleaming. Over on a dark peninsula a piano was playing the songs of last summer and of summers before that—songs from "Chin-Chin" and "The Count

---

① "high" color: 较明显的红色。

of Luxemburg" and "The Chocolate Soldier"—and because the sound of a piano over a stretch of water had always seemed beautiful to Dexter he lay perfectly quiet and listened.

The tune the piano was playing at that moment had been gay and new five years before when Dexter was a sophomore at college. They had played it at a prom once when he could not afford the luxury of proms, and he had stood outside the gymnasium and listened. The sound of the tune precipitated in him a sort of ecstasy and it was with that ecstasy he viewed what happened to him now. It was a mood of intense appreciation, a sense that, for once, he was magnificently attuned to life and that everything about him was radiating a brightness and a glamour he might never know again.

A low, pale oblong detached itself suddenly from the darkness of the Island, spitting forth the reverberated sound of a racing motor-boat. Two white streamers of cleft water rolled themselves out behind it and almost immediately the boat was beside him, drowning out the hot tinkle of the piano in the drone of its spray. Dexter raising himself on his arms was aware of a figure standing at the wheel, of two dark eyes regarding him over the lengthening space of water—then the boat had gone by and was sweeping in an immense and purposeless circle of spray round and round in the middle of the lake. With equal eccentricity one of the circles flattened out and headed back toward the raft.

"Who's that?" she called, shutting off her motor. She was so near now that Dexter could see her bathing-suit, which consisted apparently of pink rompers.

The nose of the boat bumped the raft, and as the latter tilted rakishly he was precipitated toward her. With different degrees of interest they recognized each other.

"Aren't you one of those men we played through this afternoon?" she demanded.

He was.

"Well, do you know how to drive a motor-boat? Because if you do I wish you'd drive this one so I can ride on the surf-board behind. My name is Judy Jones"—she favored him with an absurd smirk—rather, what tried to be a smirk, for, twist her mouth as she might, it was not grotesque, it was merely beautiful—"and I live in a house over there on the Island, and in that house there is a man waiting for me. When he drove up at the door I drove out of the dock because he says I'm his ideal."

There was a fish jumping and a star shining and the lights around the lake were gleaming. Dexter sat beside Judy Jones and she explained how her boat was driven. Then she was in the water, swimming to the floating surf-board with a sinuous crawl. Watching her was without effort to the eye, watching a branch waving or a sea-gull flying. Her arms, burned to butternut, moved sinuously among the dull platinum ripples, elbow appearing first, casting the forearm back with a cadence of falling water, then reaching out and down, stabbing a path ahead.

They moved out into the lake; turning. Dexter saw that she was kneeling on the low rear of the now uptilted surf-board.

"Go faster," she called, "Fast as it'll go."

Obediently he jammed the lever forward and the white spray mounted at the bow. When he looked around again the girl was standing up on the rushing board, her arms spread wide, her eyes lifted toward the moon.

"It's awful cold," she shouted. "What's your name?"

He told her.

"Well, why don't you come to dinner to-morrow night?"

His heart turned over like the fly-wheel of the boat, and, for the second time, her casual whim gave a new direction to his life.

III

Next evening while he waited for her to come down-stairs, Dexter peopled the soft deep summer room and the sun-porch that opened from it with the men who had already loved Judy Jones. He knew the sort of men they were—the men who when he first went to college had entered from the great prep schools with graceful clothes and the deep tan of healthy summers. He had seen that, in one sense, he was better than these men. He was newer and stronger. Yet in acknowledging to himself that he wished his children to be like them he was admitting that he was but the rough, strong stuff from which they eternally sprang.

When the time had come for him to wear good clothes, he had known who were the best tailors in America, and the best tailors in America had made him the suit he wore this evening. He had acquired that particular reserve peculiar to his university, that set it off from other universities. He recognized the value to him of such a mannerism and he had adopted it; he knew that to be careless in dress and manner required more confidence than to be careful. But carelessness was for his children. His mother's name had been Krimplich. She was a Bohemian of the peasant class① and she had talked broken English to the end of her days. Her son must keep to the set patterns.

At a little after seven Judy Jones came down-stairs. She wore a blue silk afternoon dress, and he was disappointed at first that she had not put on something more elaborate. This feeling was accentuated when, after a brief greeting, she went to the door of a butler's pantry and pushing it open called: "You can serve dinner, Martha." He had rather expected that a butler would announce dinner, that there would be a cocktail. Then he put these thoughts behind him as they sat down side by side on a lounge and looked at each other.

"Father and mother won't be here," she said thoughtfully.

He remembered the last time he had seen her father, and he was glad the parents were not to be here to-night—they might wonder who he was. He had been born in Keeble, a Minnesota village fifty miles farther north, and he always gave Keeble as his home instead of Black Bear Village. Country towns were well enough to come from if they weren't inconveniently in sight and used as footstools by fashionable lakes.

They talked of his university, which she had visited frequently during the past two years, and of the near-by city which supplied Sherry Island with its patrons, and whither Dexter would return next day to his prospering laundries.

During dinner she slipped into a moody depression which gave Dexter a feeling of uneasiness. Whatever petulance she uttered in her throaty voice worried him. Whatever she smiled at—at him, at a chicken liver, at nothing—it disturbed him that her smile could have no root in mirth, or even in amusement. When the scarlet corners of her lips curved down, it was less a smile than an invitation to a kiss.

Then, after dinner, she led him out on the dark sun-porch and deliberately changed the atmosphere.

"Do you mind if I weep a little?" she said.

"I'm afraid I'm boring you," he responded quickly.

"You're not. I like you. But I've just had a terrible afternoon. There was a

---

① a Bohemian of the peasant class：作者在这里表明主人公的母亲是来自中欧农民阶层的贫穷移民。

man I cared about, and this afternoon he told me out of a clear sky that he was poor as a churchmouse. He'd never even hinted it before. Does this sound horribly mundane?"

"Perhaps he was afraid to tell you."

"Suppose he was," she answered. "He didn't start right. You see, if I'd thought of him as poor—well, I've been mad about loads of poor men, and fully intended to marry them all. But in this case, I hadn't thought of him that way, and my interest in him wasn't strong enough to survive the shock. As if a girl calmly informed her fiancé that she was a widow. He might not object to widows, but—

"Let's start right," she interrupted herself suddenly. "Who are you, anyhow?"

For a moment Dexter hesitated. Then:

"I'm nobody," he announced. "My career is largely a matter of futures."

"Are you poor?"

"No," he said frankly, "I'm probably making more money than any man my age in the Northwest. I know that's an obnoxious remark, but you advised me to start right."

There was a pause. Then she smiled and the corners of her mouth drooped and an almost imperceptible sway brought her closer to him, looking up into his eyes. A lump rose in Dexter's throat, and he waited breathless for the experiment, facing the unpredictable compound that would form mysteriously from the elements of their lips. Then he saw—she communicated her excitement to him, lavishly, deeply, with kisses that were not a promise but a fulfilment. They aroused in him not hunger demanding renewal but surfeit that would demand more surfeit... kisses that were like charity, creating want by holding back nothing at all.

It did not take him many hours to decide that he had wanted Judy Jones ever since he was a proud, desirous little boy.

IV

It began like that—and continued, with varying shades of intensity, on such a note right up to the dénouement. Dexter surrendered a part of himself to the most direct and unprincipled personality with which he had ever come in contact.

Whatever Judy wanted, she went after with the full pressure of her charm. There was no divergence of method, no jockeying for position or premeditation of effects—there was a very little mental side to any of her affairs. She simply made men conscious to the highest degree of her physical loveliness. Dexter had no desire to change her. Her deficiencies were knit up with a passionate energy that transcended and justified them.

When, as Judy's head lay against his shoulder that first night, she whispered, "I don't know what's the matter with me. Last night I thought I was in love with a man and to-night I think I'm in love with you—" —it seemed to him a beautiful and romantic thing to say. It was the exquisite excitability that for the moment he controlled and owned. But a week later he was compelled to view this same quality in a different light. She took him in her roadster to a picnic supper, and after supper she disappeared, likewise in her roadster, with another man. Dexter became enormously upset and was scarcely able to be decently civil to the other people present. When she assured him that she had not kissed the other man, he knew she was lying—yet he was glad that she had taken the trouble to lie to him.

He was, as he found before the summer ended, one of a varying dozen who circulated about her. Each of them had at one time been favored above all others—about half of them still basked in the solace of occasional sentimental revivals. Whenever one showed signs of dropping out through long neglect, she granted him a brief honeyed hour, which encouraged him to tag along for a year or so longer. Judy made these forays upon the helpless and defeated without malice, indeed half unconscious that there was anything mischievous in what she did.

When a new man came to town every one dropped out—dates were automatically cancelled.

The helpless part of trying to do anything about it was that she did it all herself. She was not a girl who could be "won" in the kinetic sense—she was proof against cleverness, she was proof against charm; if any of these assailed her too strongly she would immediately resolve the affair to a physical basis, and under the magic of her physical splendor the strong as well as the brilliant played her game and not their own. She was entertained only by the gratification of her desires and by the direct exercise of her own charm. Perhaps from so much youthful love, so many youthful lovers, she had come, in self-defense, to nourish herself wholly from within.

Succeeding Dexter's first exhilaration came restlessness and dissatisfaction. The helpless ecstasy of losing himself in her was opiate rather than tonic. It was fortunate for his work during the winter that those moments of ecstasy came infrequently. Early in their acquaintance it had seemed for a while that there was a deep and spontaneous mutual attraction—that first August, for example—three days of long evenings on her dusky veranda, of strange wan kisses through the late afternoon, in shadowy alcoves or behind the protecting trellises of the garden arbors, of mornings when she was fresh as a dream and almost shy at meeting him in the clarity of the rising day. There was all the ecstasy of an engagement about it, sharpened by his realization that there was no engagement. It was during those three days that, for the first time, he had asked her to marry him. She said "maybe some day," she said "kiss me," she said "I'd like to marry you," she said "I love you" —she said—nothing.

The three days were interrupted by the arrival of a New York man who visited at her house for half September. To Dexter's agony, rumor engaged them. The man was the son of the president of a great trust company. But at the end of a month it was reported that Judy was yawning. At a dance one night she sat all evening in a motor-boat with a local beau, while the New Yorker searched the club for her frantically. She told the local beau that she was bored with her visitor, and two days later he left. She was seen with him at the station, and it was reported that he looked very mournful indeed.

On this note the summer ended. Dexter was twenty-four, and he found himself increasingly in a position to do as he wished. He joined two clubs in the city and lived at one of them. Though he was by no means an integral part of the stag-lines at these clubs, he managed to be on hand at dances where Judy Jones was likely to appear. He could have gone out socially as much as he liked—he was an eligible young man, now, and popular with down-town fathers. His confessed devotion to Judy Jones had rather solidified his position. But he had no social aspirations and rather despised the dancing men who were always on tap for the Thursday or Saturday parties and who filled in at dinners with the younger married set. Already he was playing with the idea of going East to New York. He wanted to take Judy Jones with him. No disillusion as to the world in which she had grown up could cure his illusion as to her desirability.

Remember that—for only in the light of it can what he did for her be understood.

Eighteen months after he first met Judy Jones he became engaged to another girl. Her name was Irene Scheerer, and her father was one of the men who had always believed in Dexter. Irene was light-haired and sweet and honorable, and a little stout, and she had two suitors whom she pleasantly relinquished when Dexter formally asked her to marry him.

Summer, fall, winter, spring, another summer, another fall—so much he had given of his active life to the incorrigible lips of Judy Jones. She had treated him with interest, with encouragement, with malice, with indifference, with contempt. She had inflicted on him the innumerable little slights and indignities possible in such a case—as if in revenge for having ever cared for him at all. She had beckoned him and yawned at him and beckoned him again and he had responded often with bitterness and narrowed eyes. She had brought him ecstatic happiness and intolerable agony of spirit. She had caused him untold inconvenience and not a little trouble. She had insulted him, and she had ridden over him, and she had played his interest in her against his interest in his work—for fun. She had done everything to him except to criticise him—this she had not done—it seemed to him only because it might have sullied the utter indifference she manifested and sincerely felt toward him.

When autumn had come and gone again it occurred to him that he could not have Judy Jones. He had to beat this into his mind but he convinced himself at last. He lay awake at night for a while and argued it over. He told himself the trouble and the pain she had caused him, he enumerated her glaring deficiencies as a wife. Then he said to himself that he loved her, and after a while he fell asleep. For a week, lest he imagined her husky voice over the telephone or her eyes opposite him at lunch, he worked hard and late, and at night he went to his office and plotted out his years.

At the end of a week he went to a dance and cut in on her once. For almost the first time since they had met he did not ask her to sit out with him or tell her that she was lovely. It hurt him that she did not miss these things—that was all. He was not jealous when he saw that there was a new man to-night. He had been hardened against jealousy long before.

He stayed late at the dance. He sat for an hour with Irene Scheerer and talked about books and about music. He knew very little about either. But he was beginning to be master of his own time now, and he had a rather priggish notion that he—the young and already fabulously successful Dexter Green—should know more about such things.

That was in October, when he was twenty-five. In January, Dexter and Irene became engaged. It was to be announced in June, and they were to be married three months later.

The Minnesota winter prolonged itself interminably, and it was almost May when the winds came soft and the snow ran down into Black Bear Lake at last. For the first time in over a year Dexter was enjoying a certain tranquillity of spirit. Judy Jones had been in Florida, and afterward in Hot Springs, and somewhere she had been engaged, and somewhere she had broken it off. At first, when Dexter had definitely given her up, it had made him sad that people still linked them together and asked for news of her, but when he began to be placed at dinner next to Irene Scheerer people didn't ask him about her any more—they told him about her. He ceased to be an authority on her.

May at last. Dexter walked the streets at night when the darkness was damp as rain, wondering that so soon, with so little done, so much of ecstasy had gone from him. May one year back had been marked by Judy's poignant, unforgivable, yet forgiven turbulence—it had been one of those rare times when he fancied she had grown to care for him. That old penny's worth of happiness he had spent for this bushel of content. He knew that Irene would be no more than a curtain spread behind him, a hand moving among gleaming tea-cups, a voice calling to children... fire and loveliness were gone, the magic of nights and the wonder of the varying hours and seasons... slender lips, down-turning, dropping to his lips and bearing him up into a heaven of eyes... The thing was deep in him. He was too strong and alive for it to die lightly.

In the middle of May when the weather balanced for a few days on the thin bridge that led to deep summer he turned in one night at Irene's house. Their engagement was to be announced in a week now—no one would be surprised at it. And to-night they would sit to-gether on the lounge at the University Club and look on for an hour at the dancers. It gave him a sense of solidity to go with her—she was so sturdily popular, so intensely "great."

He mounted the steps of the brownstone house and stepped inside.

"Irene," he called.

Mrs. Scheerer came out of the living-room to meet him.

"Dexter," she said, "Irene's gone up-stairs with a splitting head-ache. She wanted to go with you but I made her go to bed."

"Nothing serious, I—"

"Oh, no. She's going to play golf with you in the morning. You can spare her for just one night, can't you, Dexter?"

Her smile was kind. She and Dexter liked each other. In the living-room he talked for a moment before he said good-night.

Returning to the University Club, where he had rooms, he stood in the doorway for a moment and watched the dancers. He leaned against the doorpost, nodded at a man or two—yawned.

"Hello, darling."

The familiar voice at his elbow startled him. Judy Jones had left a man and crossed the room to him—Judy Jones, a slender enamelled doll in cloth of gold: gold in a band at her head, gold in two slipper points at her dress's hem. The fragile glow of her face seemed to blossom as she smiled at him. A breeze of warmth and light blew through the room. His hands in the pockets of his dinner-jacket tightened spasmodically. He was filled with a sudden excitement.

"When did you get back?" he asked casually.

"Come here and I'll tell you about it."

She turned and he followed her. She had been away—he could have wept at the wonder of her return. She had passed through enchanted streets, doing things that were like provocative music. All mysterious happenings, all fresh and quickening hopes, had gone away with her, come back with her now.

She turned in the doorway.

"Have you a car here? If you haven't, I have."

"I have a coupé."

In then, with a rustle of golden cloth. He slammed the door. Into so many cars she had stepped—like this—like that—her back against the leather, so—her elbow resting on the door—waiting. She would have been soiled long since had there been anything to soil her—except herself—but this was her own self outpouring.

With an effort he forced himself to start the car and back into the street. This was nothing, he must remember. She had done this before, and he had put her behind him, as he would have crossed a bad account from his books①.

He drove slowly down-town and, affecting abstraction, traversed the deserted streets of the business section, peopled here and there where a movie was giving out its crowd or where consumptive or pugilistic youth lounged in front of pool halls. The clink of glasses and the slap of hands on the bars issued from saloons, cloisters of glazed glass and dirty yellow light.

She was watching him closely and the silence was embarrassing, yet in this crisis he could find no casual word with which to profane the hour. At a convenient turning he began to zigzag back toward the University Club.

"Have you missed me?" she asked suddenly.

"Everybody missed you."

He wondered if she knew of Irene Scheerer. She had been back only a day—her absence had been almost contemporaneous with his engagement.

"What a remark!" Judy laughed sadly—without sadness. She looked at him searchingly. He became absorbed in the dashboard.

"You're handsomer than you used to be," she said thoughtfully. "Dexter, you have the most rememberable eyes."

He could have laughed at this, but he did not laugh. It was the sort of thing that was said to sophomores. Yet it stabbed at him.

"I'm awfully tired of everything, darling." She called every one darling, endowing the endearment with careless, individual comaraderie. "I wish you'd marry me."

The directness of this confused him. He should have told her now that he was going to marry another girl, but he could not tell her. He could as easily have sworn that he had never loved her.

"I think we'd get along," she continued, on the same note, "unless probably you've forgotten me and fallen in love with another girl."

Her confidence was obviously enormous. She had said, in effect, that she found such a thing impossible to believe, that if it were true he had merely committed a childish indiscretion—and probably to show off. She would forgive him, because it was not a matter of any moment but rather something to be brushed aside lightly.

"Of course you could never love anybody but me," she continued. "I like the

---

① books：这里指账簿。

way you love me. Oh, Dexter, have you forgotten last year?"

"No, I haven't forgotten."

"Neither have I!"

Was she sincerely moved—or was she carried along by the wave of her own acting?

"I wish we could be like that again," she said, and he forced himself to answer:

"I don't think we can."

"I suppose not... I hear you're giving Irene Scheerer a violent rush."

There was not the faintest emphasis on the name, yet Dexter was suddenly ashamed.

"Oh, take me home," cried Judy suddenly; "I don't want to go back to that idiotic dance—with those children."

Then, as he turned up the street that led to the residence district, Judy began to cry quietly to herself. He had never seen her cry before.

The dark street lightened, the dwellings of the rich loomed up around them, he stopped his coupé in front of the great white bulk of the Mortimer Joneses' house, somnolent, gorgeous, drenched with the splendor of the damp moonlight. Its solidity startled him. The strong walls, the steel of the girders, the breadth and beam and pomp of it were there only to bring out the contrast with the young beauty beside him. It was sturdy to accentuate her slightness—as if to show what a breeze could be generated by a butterfly's wing.

He sat perfectly quiet, his nerves in wild clamor, afraid that if he moved he would find her irresistibly in his arms. Two tears had rolled down her wet face and trembled on her upper lip.

"I'm more beautiful than anybody else," she said brokenly, "why can't I be happy?" Her moist eyes tore at his stability—her mouth turned slowly downward with an exquisite sadness: "I'd like to marry you if you'll have me, Dexter. I suppose you think I'm not worth having, but I'll be so beautiful for you, Dexter."

A million phrases of anger, pride, passion, hatred, tenderness fought on his lips. Then a perfect wave of emotion washed over him, carrying off with it a sediment of wisdom, of convention, of doubt, of honor. This was his girl who was speaking, his own, his beautiful, his pride.

"Won't you come in?" He heard her draw in her breath sharply.

Waiting.

"All right," his voice was trembling, "I'll come in."

V

It was strange that neither when it was over nor a long time afterward did he regret that night. Looking at it from the perspective of ten years, the fact that Judy's flare for him endured just one month seemed of little importance. Nor did it matter that by his yielding he subjected himself to a deeper agony in the end and gave serious hurt to Irene Scheerer and to Irene's parents, who had befriended him. There was nothing sufficiently pictorial about Irene's grief to stamp itself on his mind.

Dexter was at bottom hard-minded. The attitude of the city on his action was of no importance to him, not because he was going to leave the city, but because any outside attitude on the situation seemed superficial. He was completely indifferent to popular opinion. Nor, when he had seen that it was no use, that he did not possess in himself the power to move fundamentally or to hold Judy Jones, did he bear any malice toward her. He loved her, and he would love her until the day he was too old for loving—but he could not have her. So he tasted the deep pain that is reserved only for the strong, just as he had tasted for a little while the deep happiness.

Even the ultimate falsity of the grounds upon which Judy terminated the engagement that she did not want to "take him away" from Irene—Judy, who had wanted nothing else—did not revolt him. He was beyond any revulsion or any amusement.

He went East in February with the intention of selling out his laundries and settling in New York—but the war came to America in March and changed his plans. He returned to the West, handed over the management of the business to his partner, and went into the first officers' training-camp in late April. He was one of those young thousands who greeted the war with a certain amount of relief, welcoming the liberation from webs of tangled emotion.

VI

This story is not his biography, remember, although things creep into it which have nothing to do with those dreams he had when he was young. We are almost done with them and with him now. There is only one more incident to be related here, and it happens seven years farther on.

It took place in New York, where he had done well—so well that there were no barriers too high for him. He was thirty-two years old, and, except for one flying trip immediately after the war, he had not been West in seven years. A man named Devlin from Detroit came into his office to see him in a business way, and then and there this incident occurred, and closed out, so to speak, this particular side of his life.

"So you're from the Middle West," said the man Devlin with careless curiosity. "That's funny—I thought men like you were probably born and raised on Wall Street. You know—wife of one of my best friends in Detroit came from your city. I was an usher at the wedding."

Dexter waited with no apprehension of what was coming.

"Judy Simms," said Devlin with no particular interest; "Judy Jones she was once."

"Yes, I knew her." A dull impatience spread over him. He had heard, of course, that she was married—perhaps deliberately he had heard no more.

"Awfully nice girl," brooded Devlin meaninglessly, "I'm sort of sorry for her."

"Why?" Something in Dexter was alert, receptive, at once.

"Oh, Lud Simms has gone to pieces in a way. I don't mean he ill-uses her, but he drinks and runs around— "

"Doesn't she run around?"

"No. Stays at home with her kids."

"Oh."

"She's a little too old for him," said Devlin.

"Too old!" cried Dexter. "Why, man, she's only twenty-seven."

He was possessed with a wild notion of rushing out into the streets and taking a train to Detroit. He rose to his feet spasmodically.

"I guess you're busy," Devlin apologized quickly. "I didn't realize—"

"No, I'm not busy," said Dexter, steadying his voice. "I'm not busy at all. Not busy at all. Did you say she was—twenty-seven? No, I said she was twenty-seven."

"Yes, you did," agreed Devlin dryly.

"Go on, then. Go on."

"What do you mean?"

"About Judy Jones."

Devlin looked at him helplessly.

"Well, that's—I told you all there is to it. He treats her like the devil. Oh, they're not going to get divorced or anything. When he's particularly outrageous she forgives him. In fact, I'm inclined to think she loves him. She was a pretty girl when she first came to Detroit."

A pretty girl! The phrase struck Dexter as ludicrous

"Isn't she—a pretty girl, any more?"

"Oh, she's all right."

"Look here," said Dexter, sitting down suddenly, "I don't understand. You say she was a 'pretty girl' and now you say she's 'all right.' I don't understand what you mean—Judy Jones wasn't a pretty girl, at all. She was a great beauty. Why, I knew her, I knew her. She was—"

Devlin laughed pleasantly.

"I'm not trying to start a row," he said. "I think Judy's a nice girl and I like her. I can't understand how a man like Lud Simms could fall madly in love with her, but he did." Then he added: "Most of the women like her."

Dexter looked closely at Devlin, thinking wildly that there must be a reason for this, some insensitivity in the man or some private malice.

"Lots of women fade just like *that*," Devlin snapped his fingers. "You must have seen it happen. Perhaps I've forgotten how pretty she was at her wedding. I've seen her so much since then, you see. She has nice eyes."

A sort of dullness settled down upon Dexter. For the first time in his life he felt like getting very drunk. He knew that he was laughing loudly at something Devlin had said, but he did not know what it was or why it was funny. When, in a few minutes, Devlin went he lay down on his lounge and looked out the window at the New York sky-line into which the sun was sinking in dull lovely shades of

pink and gold.

He had thought that having nothing else to lose he was invulnerable at last—but he knew that he had just lost something more, as surely as if he had married Judy Jones and seen her fade away before his eyes.

The dream was gone. Something had been taken from him. In a sort of panic he pushed the palms of his hands into his eyes and tried to bring up a picture of the waters lapping on Sherry Island and the moonlit veranda, and gingham on the golf-links and the dry sun and the gold color of her neck's soft down. And her mouth damp to his kisses and her eyes plaintive with melancholy and her freshness like new fine linen in the morning. Why, these things were no longer in the world! They had existed and they existed no longer.

For the first time in years the tears were streaming down his face. But they were for himself now. He did not care about mouth and eyes and moving hands. He wanted to care, and he could not care. For he had gone away and he could never go back any more. The gates were closed, the sun was gone down, and there was no beauty but the gray beauty of steel that withstands all time. Even the grief he could have borne was left behind in the country of illusion, of youth, of the richness of life, where his winter dreams had flourished.

"Long ago," he said, "long ago, there was something in me, but now that thing is gone. Now that thing is gone, that thing is gone. I cannot cry. I cannot care. That thing will come back no more."

《冬天的梦》(1922)是一个穷小子爱上了富家小姐的故事,这是作者创作的一个主要题材。故事的主人公戴克斯特住在穷人区黑熊镇,在高尔夫球俱乐部作球童为来自雪利岛的富人服务。在这样的贫富反差环境下,他小小年纪就被富家小姐裘德所吸引,开始了他的追梦之旅:他"要的不仅是接近五光十色的东西和人们,而是自己拥有五光十色的东西"。从美国建国时期开始的功利主义文化变革将幸福归根于外在的善(external goods)——物欲的满足,而在作者所经历的"爵士乐时代",财富和享乐更是人们追求的目的。在裘德身上,可以看到多重性格特点:她看重财富,但她选择男人的标准又不仅仅是金钱;她追求享乐,寻求情感刺激,但她又安守并不理想的婚姻;她我行我素,将男人玩弄于股掌,而不按男人的游戏规则行事,但她又时时不能离开对男人的情感和经济依附。这就是戴克斯特的梦幻理想的矛盾混合体。而戴克斯特自身难道就没有这些特点吗?他同样崇尚财富、享乐和自我理想的追求;与艾琳的平淡比较,他更喜欢裘德带给他的情感刺激;在艾琳眼里,他的情感同样不可预测,没有原则。奎德身上的特质不仅代表了20年代的"新女性",而且代表了传统价值和功利个人主义时代价值的矛盾混合体。冬天的梦或所谓"美国梦"对个人来说可以幻灭,但它的魅力在这样的社会里却是不死的。作者以巧妙的细节描写和色彩运用创造出丰富的象征寓意,细细读来,亦有相当解读空间。

思考题

1. What are Dexter's first dreams?
2. Why does Dexter want to attend an older and more famous university in the East?
3. What does Sherry Island represent to Dexter?
4. What does Judy look for in a man?
5. Why is Dexter in tears after hearing about Judy's unhappy marriage?

推荐作品

The Great Gatsby (1925)

"*Babylon Revisited*" (1931)

Tender Is the Night (1934)

参考资料

Bruccoli, Matthew J., ed. *New Essays on The Great Gatsby*. Beijing: Peking UP; Cambridge UP, 2006.

Bryer, Jackson R., Allan Margolies, and Ruth Prigozy, eds. *F. Scott Fitzgerald: New Perspectives.* Athens: U of Gegorgia P, 2000.

Pelzer, Linda C. *Student Companion to F. Scott Fitzgerald.* West port: Greenwood Press, 2000.

Prigozy, Ruth, ed. *The Cambridge Companion to F. Scott Fitzgerald.* Cambridge: Cambridge UP, 2002.

第三单元
Ernest Hemingway
(1899—1961)
厄内斯特·海明威

作者简介

厄内斯特·海明威,小说家,出生在伊利诺伊州一个医生家庭。他从小随父亲参加捕鱼、狩猎活动,这些户外经历成为他文学创作中的重要题材。他中学毕业后成为报社记者。第一次世界大战期间,虽因视力原因无法参军,但他参加了志愿救护车队来到前线作战。这段战争经历为他的名著《永别了,武器》(*A Farewell to Arms*, 1929)等作品提供了创作素材。1925年,短篇小说集《在我们的时代里》(*In Our Time*)发表后,他凝练的文笔,不动声色的叙述风格开始引起人们的注意。1926年他的第一部长篇小说《太阳照样升起》(*The Sun Also Rises*)发表。故事描述了第一次世界大战后流落巴黎的青年,他们迷惘、空虚,靠酗酒、情爱的刺激寻求精神慰藉。主人公巴恩斯在战争中受伤,丧失了性爱能力后,仍然能够坦然面对生活。这部小说奠定了海明威在文坛的重要地位,同时成为"迷惘的一代"[①]作家代表。三年后他的另一部长篇小说《永别了,武器》出版。小说讲述了主人公亨利在一战中负伤,恋爱,但爱人却难产而死,表现了战争带来的只是心灵创伤和传统信念的破灭。1940年发表的《丧钟为谁而鸣》(*For Whom the Bell Tolls*)以西班牙内战为背景描写主人公在残酷的战斗中勇敢面对死亡。最后一部体现他人生价值和行为准则的《老人与海》(*The Old Man and the Sea*, 1952)为他赢得了1954年的诺贝尔文学奖。1961年他因病痛折磨而自杀。在他的许多作品中,男主人公们表现为可以遭遇逆境、灾难、厄运或失败,虽然他们可能会迷惘、绝望,但他们却能谈笑若定,保持优雅风度、勇气和尊严。当然,评论家曾因此较多关注海明威作品中的男性中心地位或他对女性的偏见,但随着对海明威作品中的女性视角的重新认识,评论界的看法已有所改变。[②]海明威的文风承接马克·吐温的口语体传统,文字质朴无华,生动自然,叙述简约,却蕴涵丰富。借用他本人的比喻:冰山移动的尊严在于它仅有八分之一露出水面。

[①] "迷惘的一代"(the Lost Generation)泛指第一次世界大战后的一代人,也特指一批美国作家,他们是一次大战时的青年,20世纪20年代在文坛初露头角。作家斯泰因曾对海明威说:"你们都是迷惘的一代",这句话被海明威用作小说《太阳照样升起》的卷首语。这一代人的迷惘是因为他们的传统价值观与战后的世界格格不入,加之美国受政府推行的"恢复常态"政策影响,使这些青年感到美国只关注实际利益,从而这些青年与美国在精神上疏远起来。这些作家包括海明威、菲茨杰拉德、多斯·帕索斯等许多其他作家,但他们并没有形成统一的文学流派,而各自保留着自己独立的风格。

[②] 参见本章节的作品赏析部分。

海明威独特的个人经历与他的作品之间的复杂关系使海明威的个人生活与其作品一样受到公众的关注,也一直是评论家和传记作家所争论、褒贬的焦点。海明威去世后陆续面世的手稿、通信和其他文献资料,甚至包括联邦调查局的档案使沉寂一时的海明威研究在20世纪80年代又重现高潮。2002年古巴政府和美国国会众议院议员詹姆斯·麦戈文(James McGovern)签署协议共同修复保管海明威在1939至1960年期间住在哈瓦那郊外他的"眺望农场"(Finca Vigia)时留在那里的大量文字材料,包括2000多封信件及作品草稿等。海明威研究学者宾西法尼亚州立大学英语教授Sandra Spanier认为,这些材料将填补学界研究海明威个人生活和创作过程的一些空白之处。

Hills Like White Elephants

The hills across the valley of the Ebro① were long and white. On this side there was no shade and no trees and the station was between two lines of rails in the sun②. Close against the side of the station there was the warm shadow of the building and a curtain, made of strings of bamboo beads, hung across the open door into the bar, to keep out flies. The American and the girl with him sat at a table in the shade, outside the building. It was very hot and the express from Barcelona would come in forty minutes. It stopped at this junction for two minutes and went on to Madrid.

"What should we drink?" the girl asked. She had taken off her hat and put it on the table.

"It's pretty hot," the man said.

"Let's drink beer."

"Dos cervezas③," the man said into the curtain.

"Big ones?" a woman asked from the doorway.

"Yes. Two big ones."

The woman brought two glasses of beer and two felt pads. She put the felt pads and the beer glasses on the table and looked at the man and the girl. The girl

---

① the Ebro: the Ebro River.
② 故事发生的地点是巴塞罗那至马德里铁路线上的一个车站。该地点在现实中位于埃布罗河附近的嘉塞塔镇(Caseta),从此经过的铁道北面是白色的山峦和荒野,南面是郁郁葱葱的埃布罗河岸区和山峰。南面的勃勃生机与北面的荒芜恰与围绕堕胎问题产生的冲突形成对应。
③ dos cervezas(西班牙语): two beers.

was looking off at the line of hills.　They were white in the sun and the country was brown and dry.

"They look like white elephants," she said.

"I've never seen one," the man drank his beer.

"No, you wouldn't have."

"I might have," the man said. "Just because you say I wouldn't have doesn't prove anything."

The girl looked at the bead curtain. "They've painted something on it," she said. "What does it say?"

"Anis del Toro. It's a drink."

"Could we try it?"

The man called "Listen" through the curtain. The woman came out from the bar.

"Four reales."

"We want two Anis del Toro①."

"With water?"

"Do you want it with water?"

"I don't know," the girl said. "Is it good with water?"

"It's all right."

"You want them with water?" asked the woman.

"Yes, with water."

"It tastes like licorice," the girl said and put the glass down.

"That's the way with everything."

"Yes," said the girl. "Everything tastes of licorice. Especially all the things you've waited so long for, like absinthe②."

"Oh, cut it out."

"You started it," the girl said. "I was being amused. I was having a fine time."

"Well, let's try and have a fine time."

"All right. I was trying. I said the mountains looked like white elephants. Was't that bright?"

"That was bright."

---

① Anis del Toro (西班牙语)：一种深色、甘草味的酒，西班牙语的意思是：Anis of the Bull。

② absinthe：苦艾酒，在当时大多欧洲国家，苦艾酒因可能引起不良反应已被禁止。当时的看法认为苦艾会导致幻觉和不孕。

"I wanted to try this new drink. That's all we do, isn't it—look at things and try new drinks?"

"I guess so."

The girl looked across at the hills.

"They're lovely hills," she said. "They don't really look like white elephants. I just meant the coloring of their skin through the trees."

"Should we have another drink?"

"All right."

The warm wind blew the bead curtain against the table.

"The beer's nice and cool," the man said.

"It's lovely," the girl said.

"It's really an awfully simple operation, Jig," the man said. "It's not really an operation at all."

The girl looked at the ground the table legs rested on.

"I know you wouldn't mind it, Jig. It's really not anything. It's just to let the air in①."

The girl did not say anything.

"I'll go with you and I'll stay with you all the time. They just let the air in and then it's all perfectly natural."

"Then what will we do afterward?"

"We'll be fine afterward. Just like we were before."

"What makes you think so?"

"That's the only thing that bothers us. It's the only thing that's made us unhappy."

The girl looked at the bead curtain, put her hand out and took hold of two of the strings of beads.

"And you think then we'll be all right and be happy."

"I know we will. Yon don't have to be afraid. I've known lots of people that have done it."

"So have I," said the girl. "And afterward they were all so happy."

"Well," the man said, "if you don't want to you don't have to. I wouldn't have you do it if you didn't want to. But I know it's perfectly simple."

"And you really want to?"

---

① It's just to let the air in: 这里指"简单手术"的方法。

"I think it's the best thing to do. But I don't want you to do it if you don't really want to."

"And if I do it you'll be happy and things will be like they were and you'll love me?"

"I love you now. You know I love you."

"I know. But if I do it, then it will be nice again if I say things are like white elephants, and you'll like it?"

"I'll love it. I love it now but I just can't think about it. You know how I get when I worry."

"If I do it you won't ever worry?"

"I won't worry about that because it's perfectly simple."

"Then I'll do it. Because I don't care about me."

"What do you mean?"

"I don't care about me."

"Well, I care about you."

"Oh, yes. But I don't care about me. And I'll do it and then everything will be fine."

"I don't want you to do it if you feel that way."

The girl stood up and walked to the end of the station. Across, on the other side, were fields of grain and trees along the banks of the Ebro. Far away, beyond the river, were mountains. The shadow of a cloud moved across the field of grain and she saw the river through the trees.

"And we could have all this,' she said. 'And we could have everything and every day we make it more impossible."

"What did you say?"

"I said we could have everything."

"We can have everything."

"No, we can't."

"We can have the whole world."

"No, we can't."

"We can go everywhere."

"No, we can't. It isn't ours any more."

"It's ours."

"No, it isn't. And once they take it away, you never get it back."

"But they haven't taken it away."

"We'll wait and see."

"Come on back in the shade," he said. "You mustn't feel that way."

"I don't feel any way," the girl said. "I just know things."

"I don't want you to do anything that you don't want to do—"

"Nor that isn't good for me," she said. "I know. Could we have another beer?"

"All right. But you've got to realize—"

"I realize," the girl said. "Can't we maybe stop talking?"

They sat down at the table and the girl looked across at the hills on the dry side of the valley and the man looked at her and at the table.

"You've got to realize," he said, "that I don't want you to do it if you don't want to. I'm perfectly willing to go through with it if it means anything to you."

"Doesn't it mean anything to you? We could get along."

"Of course it does. But I don't want anybody but you. I don't want any one else. And I know it's perfectly simple."

"Yes, you know it's perfectly simple."

"It's all right for you to say that, but I do know it."

"Would you do something for me now?"

"I'd do anything for you."

"Would you please please please please please please please stop talking?"

He did not say anything but looked at the bags against the wall of the station. There were labels on them from all the hotels where they had spent nights.

"But I don't want you to," he said, "I don't care anything about it."

"I'll scream," the girl said.

The woman came out through the curtains with two glasses of beer and put them down on the damp felt pads. "The train comes in five minutes," she said.

"What did she say?" asked the girl.

"That the train is coming in five minutes."

The girl smiled brightly at the woman, to thank her.

"I'd better take the bags over to the other side of the station," the man said. She smiled at him.

"All right. Then come back and we'll finish the beer."

He picked up the two heavy bags and carried them around the station to the other tracks. He looked up the tracks but could not see the train. Coming back, he walked through the barroom, where people waiting for the train were drinking.

He drank an Anis at the bar and looked at the people. They were all waiting reasonably for the train. He went out through the bead curtain. She was sitting at the table and smiled at him.

"Do you feel better?" he asked.

"I feel fine," she said. "There's nothing wrong with me. I feel fine."

《白象似的群山》(1927)的故事围绕在火车站等车的一对男女展开，他们之间的话题显然是关于一个"简单手术"。两人的谈话透露出他们之间相互冲突的看法和态度，而直至故事结尾，冲突并没有真正解决。故事的极为独特的场景以及两人对环境和事物的不同观察和反应与故事的中心题材相呼应，凸显出故事冲突的含义。女主人公吉格将群山比喻成"白象"，评论家的解读不尽相同，但大多认为，"白象"的形象与生育呼应，对两人具有对立的寓意，对一方意味着自然中的罕物珍奇，盎然生机，对另一方却意味着无用之物，荒芜死寂。故事中的对话自然、简洁，看似无意闲谈，然而其弦外之音才是水面下的"冰山"。男子实际、"理智"、情感麻木；吉格则想象丰富、感性。这里值得一提的是，传统上认为海明威作品主要突出表现了海明威式男性硬汉角色和相应的男性视角，而这自然成为了20世纪70年代兴起的女权主义文学批评的审视对象。有意思的是，新的批评视角却使得海明威一些作品中被相对忽视的一个层面——一个其他许多男性作家难于具有的敏锐的女性视角和情感体验①——得到了新的重视，从而也进一步扩展了海明威研究的视野。

另一方面，如果将故事中心题材置于具有深厚宗教传统的美国文化大背景之下，我们应了解，堕胎问题至今仍然是美国一个意见极端对立的重大公共议题，无论是基于传统基督教义的胎儿自受孕即被赋予灵魂说(ensoulment)或胎儿的独立人格权，反对一方(Pro-lifer)认为堕胎便是谋杀无辜生命；而支持一方(Pro-choicer)则强调选择自由(女性的权利)。当然，男主人公要求对方做堕胎手术自有其目的。不难理解，有评论家从故事中帘子上的珠子和主人公们相关的行为细节上推断吉格的宗教信仰②；无疑，特定文化背景强化了该题材蕴含的自然和生命与人为干预和死亡的对立。与传统故事结局不同，没有解决的故事冲突拓展了读者参与和思考的空间，而冲突本身也蕴涵了两性关系、权力结构、语言交流，不同性别对幸福，情爱和同一生活世界的不同理解等众多层面的意义。

---

① 海明威其他表现独特女性视角的作品包括：The Short Happy Life of Francis Macomber, Up in Michigan, Cat in the Rain 等。

② 天主教有以念珠记数祈祷的作法。

思考题

1. Are the two characters in the story a married couple?
2. What is the nature of their relationship?
3. Why does Jig want to scream but then soften and smile at her companion?
4. Do they communicate their thoughts and feelings effectively? Why or why not?
5. Will Jig agree to the operation?

"*Indian Camp*" (1924)

"*A Clean, Well-lighted Place*" (1932)

"*The Short Happy Life of Francis Macomber*" (1936)

参考资料

Donaldson, Scott, ed. *New Essays on A Farewell to Arms*. Beijing: Peking UP; Cambridge UP, 2006.

Smith, Paul. *A Reader's Guide to the Short Stories of Ernest Hemingway*. Boston: G. K. Hall & Co., 1989.

Smith, Paul, ed. *New Essays on Hemingway's Short Fiction*. Beijing: Peking UP; Cambridge UP, 2006.

海明威:《海明威谈创作》,董衡巽编选,北京:三联书店,1985。

第四单元
William Faulkner
(1897—1962)
威廉·福克纳

✎ 作者简介

威廉·福克纳,小说家,生于密西西比州的新奥尔巴尼(New Albany)的一没落贵族家庭,后随家迁居奥克斯福(Oxford)。中学时代迷上诗歌,经常逃课,于最后一年辍学,在就读于耶鲁大学的好友斯东(Phil Stone)的指点下,广泛阅读文学名著。1918年,在女友奥岂(Estelle Oldham)与别人订婚后,参加英国皇家空军赴加拿大受训,因一战结束而没能参战。退伍后,在密西西比大学学习一年,开始发表诗作。1924年,发表第一部诗集《大理石牧神》(The Marble Faun)后,动身去欧洲旅行,途经新奥尔良时结识了安德森(Sherwood Anderson, 1876—1941),在他的帮助下发表了第一部小说《士兵的报酬》(Soldier's Pay, 1926)。安德森建议他着力用小说体裁描写他熟悉的家乡,他便在发表了描写艺术家的《蚊群》(Mosquitoes, 1927)后,以家乡为原型虚构出约克纳帕塔法(Yoknapatawpha)县,开始创作反映内战后南方的物质与精神衰败的约克纳帕塔法系列小说,其中主要作品有《喧哗与骚动》(The Sound and the Fury, 1929)、《我弥留之际》(As I Lay Dying, 1930)《八月之光》(Light in August, 1932)、《押沙龙,押沙龙!》(Absalom, Absalom!, 1936)等。这些作品创造性地运用了意识流与多视角等叙事手法,具有复杂的结构和史诗的风格。他名下共有19部长篇小说、100多个短篇、7个诗集。他还曾把自己或他人的作品改变成电影剧本。其中被拍成电影并署有他名字的共有6部电影及1个电视剧剧本。他获得的大奖有1949年度诺贝尔文学奖、1954和1962年度普利策奖等。他去世之时,已被公认为同代人中最伟大的美国小说家。《纽约时报》头版刊登了他逝世的消息,并转引了肯尼迪总统对他的评价:"自亨利·詹姆斯以来,还没有哪位作家为繁荣的美国文学留下过这样一座不朽的丰碑。"如今,福克纳的名声有增无减。他的主要长篇小说和《献给爱米丽的一朵玫瑰花》、《干旱的九月》、《烧畜棚》、《红叶》和《夕阳》等短篇小说已经成为大学文学课上的必读作品。他也是最受研究者关注的美国作家。每年在他家乡召开的福克纳研讨会都会吸引数以百计的世界各地的学者。每年出版研究他的专著和论文有一二百种。冷战时期的读者把福克纳看作代表了个人主义和言论自由等美国价值的典范。如今的读者更重视他对美国价值的批判,包括他在揭露南方种族压迫过程中对美国的自由和平等理想的反思。

Barn Burning

The store in which the Justice of the Peace's court was sitting smelled of cheese. The boy, crouched on his nail keg at the back of the crowded room, knew he smelled cheese, and more: from where he sat he could see the ranked shelves close-packed with the solid, squat, dynamic shapes of tin cans whose labels his stomach read, not from the lettering which meant nothing to his mind but from the scarlet devils and the silver curve of fish—this, the cheese which he knew he smelled and the hermetic meat① which his intestines believed he smelled coming in intermittent gusts momentary and brief between the other constant one, the smell and sense just a little of fear because mostly of despair and grief, the old fierce pull of blood. He could not see the table where the Justice sat and before which his father and his father's enemy (*our enemy he thought in that despair; ourn*②*! mine and hisn*③ *both! He's my father!*) stood, but he could hear them, the two of them that is, because his father had said no word yet:

"But what proof have you, Mr. Harris?"

"I told you. The hog got into my corn. I caught it up and sent it back to him. The next time I put the hog in my pen. When he came to get it I gave him enough wire to patch up his pen. The next time I put the hog up and kept it. I rode down to his house and saw the wire I gave him still rolled on to the spool in his yard. I told him he could have the hog when he paid me a dollar pound fee. That evening a nigger came with the dollar and got the hog. He was a strange nigger. He said, 'He say to tell you wood and hay kin burn.' I said, 'What?' 'That whut he say to tell you,' the nigger said. 'Wood and hay kin burn.' That night my barn burned. I got the stock out but I lost the barn."

"Where is the nigger? Have you got him?"

"It was a strange nigger, I tell you. I don't know what became of him."

"But that's not proof. Don't you see that's not proof?"

"Get that boy up here. He knows." For a moment the boy thought too that

---

① hermetic meat：罐装肉。
② ourn：ours.
③ hisn：his.

the man meant his older brother until Harris said, "Not him. The little one. The boy," and, crouching, small for his age, small and wiry like his father, in patched and faded jeans even too small for him, with straight, uncombed, brown hair and eyes gray and wild as storm scud, he saw the men between himself and the table part and become a lane of grim faces, at the end of which he saw the Justice, a shabby, collarless, graying man in spectacles, beckoning him. He felt no floor under his bare feet; he seemed to walk beneath the palpable weight of the grim turning faces. His father, stiff in his black Sunday coat donned not for the trial but for the moving, did not even look at him. He aims for me to lie, he thought, again with that frantic grief and despair. *And I will have to do hit*①.

"What's your name, boy?" the Justice said.

"Colonel Sartoris② Snopes," the boy whispered.

"Hey?" the Justice said. "Talk louder. Colonel Sartoris? I reckon anybody named for Colonel Sartoris in this country can't help but tell the truth, can they?" The boy said nothing. *Enemy! Enemy!* He thought; for a moment he could not even see, could not see that the Justice's face was kindly nor discern that his voice was troubled when he spoke to the man named Harris: "Do you want me to question this boy?" But he could hear, and during those subsequent long seconds while there was absolutely no sound in the crowded little room save that of quiet and intent breathing it was as if he had swung outward at the end of a grape vine, over a ravine, and at the top of the swing had been caught in a prolonged instant of mesmerized gravity, weightless in time.

"No!" Harris said violently, explosively. "Damnation! Send him out of here!" Now time, the fluid world, rushed beneath him again, the voices coming to him again through the smell of cheese and sealed meat, the fear and despair and the old grief of blood:

"This case is closed. I can't find against you, Snopes, but I can give you advice. Leave this country and don't come back to it."

His father spoke for the first time, his voice cold and harsh, level, without emphasis: "I aim to. I don't figure to stay in a country among people who..." he said something unprintable and vile, addressed to no one.

"That'll do," the Justice said. "Take your wagon and get out of this country

---

① hit: it.

② Colonel Sartoris: 沙多里斯上校,福克纳所虚构的杰弗逊(Jefferson)镇上的名人,内战中的南军军官。穷白人斯诺普斯家族也住此镇。两个家族多次出现于福克纳的其他作品中。

before dark. Case dismissed."

His father turned, and he followed the stiff black coat, the wiry figure walking a little stiffly from where a Confederate provost's man's musket ball had taken him in the heel① on a stolen horse thirty years ago, followed the two backs now, since his older brother had appeared from somewhere in the crowd, no taller than the father but thicker, chewing tobacco steadily, between the two lines of grim-faced men and out of the store and across the worn gallery and down the sagging steps and among the dogs and half-grown boys in the mild May dust, where as he passed a voice hissed:

"Barn burner!"

Again he could not see, whirling; there was a face in a red haze, moonlike, bigger than the full moon, the owner of it half again his size②, he leaping in the red haze toward the face, feeling no blow, feeling no shock when his head struck the earth, scrabbling up and leaping again, feeling no blow this time either and tasting no blood, scrabbling up to see the other boy in full flight and himself already leaping into pursuit as his father's hand jerked him back, the harsh, cold voice speaking above him: "Go get in the wagon."

It stood in a grove of locusts and mulberries across the road. His two hulking sisters in their Sunday dresses and his mother and her sister in calico and sunbonnets were already in it, sitting on and among the sorry residue of the dozen and more movings③ which even the boy could remember—the battered stove, the broken beds and chairs, the clock inlaid with mother-of-pearl, which would not run, stopped at some fourteen minutes past two o'clock of a dead and forgotten day and time, which had been his mother's dowry. She was crying, though when she saw him she drew her sleeve across her face and began to descend from the wagon. "Get back," the father said.

"He's hurt. I got to get some water and wash his..."

"Get back in the wagon," his father said. He got in too, over the tail-gate. His father mounted to the seat where the older brother already sat and struck the gaunt mules two savage blows with the peeled willow, but without heat. It was not even sadistic; it was exactly that same quality which in later years would

---

① a Confederate provost's man's musket ball had taken him in the heel：一位南方军宪兵的滑膛枪子弹击中他的脚后跟。

② half again his size：个子比他高出一半。

③ the sorry residue of the dozen and more movings：因十多次搬迁而剩下的几样残破的家具。

cause his descendants to over-run the engine before putting a motor car into motion, striking and reining back in the same movement. The wagon went on, the store with its quiet crowd of grimly watching men dropped behind; a curve in the road hid it. *Forever* he thought. *Maybe he's done*① *satisfied now, now that he has...* stopping himself, not to say it aloud even to himself. His mother's hand touched his shoulder.

"Does hit hurt?" she said.

"Naw," he said. "Hit don't hurt. Lemme be."

"Can't you wipe some of the blood off before it dries?"

"I'll wash to-night," he said. "Lemme be, I tell you."

The wagon went on. He did not know where they were going. None of them ever did or ever asked, because it was always somewhere, always a house of sorts waiting for them a day or two days or even three days away. Likely his father had already arranged to make a crop on another farm before he... Again he had to stop himself. He (the father) always did. There was something about his wolflike independence and even courage when the advantage was at least neutral which impressed strangers, as if they got from his latent ravening ferocity not so much a sense of dependability as a feeling that his ferocious conviction in the rightness of his own actions would be of advantage to all whose interest lay with his.

That night they camped, in a grove of oaks and beeches where a spring ran. The nights were still cool and they had a fire against it, of a rail lifted from a nearby fence and cut into lengths—a small fire, neat, niggard almost, a shrewd fire; such fires were his father's habit and custom always, even in freezing weather. Older, the boy might have remarked this and wondered why not a big one; why should not a man who had not only seen the waste and extravagance of war, but who had in his blood an inherent voracious prodigality with material not his own, have burned everything in sight? Then he might have gone a step farther and thought that that was the reason: that niggard blaze was the living fruit of nights passed during those four years in the woods hiding from all men, blue or gray②, with his strings of horses (captured horses, he called them). And older still, he might have divined the true reason: that the element of fire spoke to some deep mainspring of his father's being, as the element of steel or of powder spoke to other men, as the one weapon for the preservation of integrity, else breath were

---

① done：已经。

② blue or gray：蓝色和灰色分别是内战中北军和南军的军服颜色，这里指北军和南军。

not worth the breathing, and hence to be regarded with respect and used with discretion.

But he did not think this now and he had seen those same niggard blazes all his life. He merely ate his supper beside it and was already half asleep over his iron plate when his father called him, and once more he followed the stiff back, the stiff and ruthless limp, up the slope and on to the starlit road where, turning, he could see his father against the stars but without face or depth—a shape black, flat, and bloodless as though cut from tin in the iron folds of the frockcoat which had not been made for him, the voice harsh like tin and without heat like tin:

"You were fixing① to tell them. You would have told him." He didn't answer. His father struck him with the flat of his hand on the side of the head, hard but without heat, exactly as he had struck the two mules at the store, exactly as he would strike either of them with any stick in order to kill a horse fly, his voice still without heat or anger: "You're getting to be a man. You got to learn. You got to learn to stick to your own blood or you ain't going to have any blood to stick to you. Do you think either of them, any man there this morning, would? Don't you know all they wanted was a chance to get at me because they knew I had them beat? Eh?" Later, twenty years later, he was to tell himself, "If I had said they wanted only truth, justice, he would have hit me again." But now he said nothing. He was not crying. He just stood there. "Answer me," his father said.

"Yes," he whispered. His father turned.

"Get on to bed. We'll be there tomorrow."

To-morrow they were there. In the early afternoon the wagon stopped before a paintless two-room house identical almost with the dozen others it had stopped before even in the boy's ten years, and again, as on the other dozen occasions, his mother and aunt got down and began to unload the wagon, although his two sisters and his father and brother had not moved.

"Likely hit ain't fitten for hawgs,"② one of the sisters said.

"Nevertheless, fit it will and you'll hog it and like it," his father said. "Get out of them chairs and help your Ma unload."

The two sisters got down, big, bovine, in a flutter of cheap ribbons; one of them drew from the jumbled wagon bed a battered lantern, the other a worn broom. His father handed the reins to the older son and began to climb stiffly over

---

① fixing: 打算，准备。

② Likely hit ain't fitten for hawgs: Likely it isn't fit for hogs.

the wheel. "When they get unloaded, take the team to the barn and feed them." Then he said, and at first the boy thought he was still speaking to his brother:

"Come with me."

"Me?" he said.

"Yes," his father said. "You."

"Abner," his mother said. His father paused and looked back—the harsh level stare beneath the shaggy, graying, irascible brows.

"I reckon I'll have a word with the man that aims to begin to-morrow owning me body and soul for the next eight months."

They went back up the road. A week ago—or before last night, that is—he would have asked where they were going, but not now. His father had struck him before last night but never before had he paused afterward to explain why; it was as if the blow and the following calm, outrageous voice still rang, repercussed, divulging nothing to him save the terrible handicap of being young, the light weight of his few years, just heavy enough to prevent his soaring free of the world as it seemed to be ordered but not heavy enough to keep him footed solid in it, to resist it and try to change the course of its events.

Presently he could see the grove of oaks and cedars and the other flowering trees and shrubs and where the house would be, though not the house yet. They walked beside a fence massed with honeysuckle and Cherokee roses and came to a gate swinging open between two brick pillars, and now, beyond a sweep of drive, he saw the house for the first time and at that instant he forgot his father and the terror and despair both, and even when he remembered his father again (who had not stopped) the terror and despair did not return. Because, for all the twelve movings, they had sojourned until now in a poor country, a land of small farms and fields and houses, and he had never seen a house like this before. *Hit's big as a courthouse* he thought quietly, with a surge of peace and joy whose reason he could not have thought into words, being too young for that: *They are safe from him. People whose lives are a part of this peace and dignity are beyond his touch, he no more to them than a buzzing wasp: capable of stinging for a little moment but that's all; the spell of this peace and dignity rendering even the barns and stable and cribs which belong to it impervious to the puny flames he might contrive*…this, the peace and joy, ebbing for an instant as he looked again at the stiff black back, the stiff and implacable limp of the figure which was not dwarfed by the house, for the reason that it had never looked big anywhere and which now, against the serene columned backdrop, had more than ever that impervious quality of something cut ruthlessly from tin, depthless, as though, sidewise to the sun, it would cast no shadow. Watching him, the boy remarked the absolutely undeviating course which his father held and saw the stiff foot come squarely down in a pile of fresh droppings where a horse had stood in the drive and which his father could have avoided by a simple change of stride. But it ebbed only for a moment, though he could not have thought this into words either, walking on in the spell of the house, which he could even want but without envy, without sorrow, certainly never with that ravening and jealous rage which unknown to him walked in the ironlike black coat before him: *Maybe he will feel it too. Maybe it will even change him now from what maybe he couldn't help but be.*

  They crossed the portico. Now he could hear his father's stiff foot as it came down on the boards with clocklike finality, a sound out of all proportion to the displacement of the body it bore and which was not dwarfed either by the white door before it, as though it had attained to a sort of vicious and ravening minimum not to be dwarfed by anything—the flat, wide, black hat, the formal coat of broadcloth which had once been black but which had now that friction-glazed greenish cast of the bodies of old house flies, the lifted sleeve which was too large, the lifted hand like a curled claw. The door opened so promptly that the boy knew the Negro must have been watching them all the time, an old man with neat grizzled hair, in a linen jacket, who stood barring the door with his body, saying, "Wipe yo foots, white man, fo you come in here.① Major ain't home nohow."

  "Get out of my way, nigger," his father said, without heat too, flinging the door back and the Negro also and entering, his hat still on his head. And now the boy saw the prints of the stiff foot on the doorjamb and saw them appear on the pale rug behind the machinelike deliberation of the foot which seemed to bear (or transmit) twice the weight which the body compassed. The Negro was shouting "Miss Lula! Miss Lula!" somewhere behind them, then the boy, deluged as though by a warm wave by a suave turn of carpeted stair and a pendant glitter of chandeliers and a mute gleam of gold frames, heard the swift feet and saw her too, a lady—perhaps he had never seen her like before either—in a gray, smooth gown with lace at the throat and an apron tied at the waist and the sleeves turned back,

---

① Wipe yo foots, white man, fo you come in here.: Wipe your feet, white man, before you come in here.

wiping cake or biscuit dough from her hands with a towel as she came up the hall, looking not at his father at all but at the tracks on the blond rug with an expression of incredulous amazement.

"I tried," the Negro cried. "I tole[①] him to..."

"Will you please go away?" she said in a shaking voice. "Major de Spain is not at home. Will you please go away?"

His father had not spoken again. He did not speak again. He did not even look at her. He just stood stiff in the center of the rug, in his hat, the shaggy iron-gray brows twitching slightly above the pebble-colored eyes as he appeared to examine the house with brief deliberation. Then with the same deliberation he turned; the boy watched him pivot on the good leg and saw the stiff foot drag round the arc of the turning, leaving a final long and fading smear. His father never looked at it, he never once looked down at the rug. The Negro held the door. It closed behind them, upon the hysteric and indistinguishable woman-wail. His father stopped at the top of the steps and scraped his boot clean on the edge of it. At the gate he stopped again. He stood for a moment, planted stiffly on the stiff foot, looking back at the house. "Pretty and white, ain't it?" he said. "That't sweat. Nigger sweat. Maybe it ain't white enough yet to suit him. Maybe he wants to mix some white sweat with it."

Two hours later the boy was chopping wood behind the house within which his mother and aunt and the two sisters (the mother and aunt, not the two girls, he knew that; even at this distance and muffled by walls the flat loud voices of the two girls emanated an incorrigible idle inertia) were setting up the stove to prepare a meal, when he heard the hooves and saw the linen-clad man on a fine sorrel mare, whom he recognized even before he saw the rolled rug in front of the Negro youth following on a fat bay carriage horse—a suffused, angry face vanishing, still at full gallop, beyond the corner of the house where his father and brother were sitting in the two tilted chairs; and a moment later, almost before he could have put the axe down, he heard the hooves again and watched the sorrel mare go back out of the yard, already galloping again. Then his father began to shout one of the sisters' names, who presently emerged backward from the kitchen door dragging the rolled rug along the ground by one end while the other sister walked behind it.

---

① tole: told.

"If you ain't going to tote, go on and set up the wash pot," the first said.

"You, Sarty!" the second shouted. "Set up the wash pot!" His father appeared at the door, framed against that shabbiness, as he had been against that other bland perfection, impervious to either, the mother's anxious face at his shoulder.

"Go on," the father said. "Pick it up." The two sisters stooped, broad, lethargic; stooping, they presented an incredible expanse of pale cloth and a flutter of tawdry ribbons.

"If I thought enough of a rug to have to git hit[①] all the way from France I wouldn't keep hit where folks coming in would have to tromp on hit," the first said. They raised the rug.

"Abner," the mother said. "Let me do it."

"You go back and git dinner," his father said. "I'll tend to this."

From the woodpile through the rest of the afternoon the boy watched them, the rug spread flat in the dust beside the bubbling wash-pot, the two sisters stooping over it with that profound and lethargic reluctance, while the father stood over them in turn, implacable and grim, driving them though never raising his voice again. He could smell the harsh homemade lye they were using; he saw his mother come to the door once and look toward them with an expression not anxious now but very like despair; he saw his father turn, and he fell to with the axe and saw from the corner of his eye his father raise from the ground a flattish fragment of field stone and examine it and return to the pot, and this time his mother actually spoke: "Abner. Abner. Please don't. Please, Abner."

Then he was done too. It was dusk; the whippoorwills had already begun. He could smell coffee from the room where they would presently eat the cold food remaining from the mid-afternoon meal, though when he entered the house he realized they were having coffee again probably because there was a fire on the hearth, before which the rug now lay spread over the backs of the two chairs. The tracks of his father's foot were gone. Where they had been were now long, water-cloudy scoriations resembling the sporadic course of a lilliputian[②] mowing machine.

It still hung there while they ate the cold food and then went to bed, scattered

---

① git hit: get it.
② Lilliputian: 小人国(人)的。源自英国作家斯威夫特(Jonathan Swift)所著小说《格列佛游记》(*Gulliver's Travels*, 1726)中的虚构岛国小人国(Lilliput)。此国的居民身高仅六英寸左右,他们的用品也都很小。

without order or claim up and down the two rooms, his mother in one bed, where his father would later lie, the older brother in the other, himself, the aunt, and the two sisters on pallets on the floor. But his father was not in bed yet. The last thing the boy remembered was the depthless, harsh silhouette of the hat and coat bending over the rug and it seemed to him that he had not even closed his eyes when the silhouette was standing over him, the fire almost dead behind it, the stiff foot prodding him awake. "Catch up the mule," his father said.

When he returned with the mule his father was standing in the black door, the rolled rug over his shoulder. "Ain't you going to ride?" he said.

"No. Give me your foot."

He bent his knee into his father's hand, the wiry, surprising power flowed smoothly, rising, he rising with it, on to the mule's bare back (they had owned a saddle once; the boy could remember it though not when or where) and with the same effortlessness his father swung the rug up in front of him. Now in the starlight they retraced the afternoon's path, up the dusty road rife with honeysuckle, through the gate and up the black tunnel of the drive to the lightless house, where he sat on the mule and felt the rough warp of the rug drag across his thighs and vanish.

"Don't you want me to help?" he whispered. His father did not answer and now he heard again that stiff foot striking the hollow portico with that wooden and clocklike deliberation, that outrageous overstatement of the weight it carried. The rug, hunched, not flung (the boy could tell that even in the darkness) from his father's shoulder struck the angle of wall and floor with a sound unbelievably loud, thunderous, then the foot again, unhurried and enormous; a light came on in the house and the boy sat, tense, breathing steadily and quietly and just a little fast, though the foot itself did not increase its beat at all, descending the steps now; now the boy could see him.

"Don't you want to ride now?" he whispered. "We kin① both ride now," the light within the house altering now, flaring up and sinking. *He's coming down the stairs now,* he thought. He had already ridden the mule up beside the horse block; presently his father was up behind him and he doubled the reins over and slashed the mule across the neck, but before the animal could begin to trot the hard, thin arm came round him, the hard, knotted hand jerking the mule back to a walk.

---

① kin: can.

In the first red rays of the sun they were in the lot, putting plow gear on the mules. This time the sorrel mare was in the lot before he heard it at all, the rider collarless and even bareheaded, trembling, speaking in a shaking voice as the woman in the house had done, his father merely looking up once before stooping again to the hame he was buckling, so that the man on the mare spoke to his stooping back:

"You must realize you have ruined that rug. Wasn't there anybody here, any of your women..." he ceased, shaking, the boy watching him, the older brother leaning now in the stable door, chewing, blinking slowly and steadily at nothing apparently. "It cost a hundred dollars. But you never had a hundred dollars. You never will. So I'm going to charge you twenty bushels of corn against your crop. I'll add it in your contract and when you come to the commissary you can sign it. That won't keep Mrs. de Spain quiet but maybe it will teach you to wipe your feet off before you enter her house again."

Then he was gone. The boy looked at his father, who still had not spoken or even looked up again, who was now adjusting the logger-head① in the hame.

"Pap," he said. His father looked at him—the inscrutable face, the shaggy brows beneath which the gray eyes glinted coldly. Suddenly the boy went toward him, fast, stopping as suddenly. "You done the best you could!" he cried. "If he wanted hit done different why didn't he wait and tell you how? He won't git no twenty bushels! He won't git none!② We'll gether hit and hide hit! I kin watch..."

"Did you put the cutter back in that straight stock③ like I told you?"

"No, sir," he said.

"Then go do it."

That was Wednesday. During the rest of that week he worked steadily, at what was within his scope and some which was beyond it, with an industry that did not need to be driven nor even commanded twice; he had this from his mother, with the difference that some at least of what he did he liked to do, such as splitting wood with the half-size axe which his mother and aunt had earned, or saved money somehow, to present him with at Christmas. In company with the two older women (and on one afternoon, even one of the sisters), he built pens

---

① logger-head: 马颈轭的一部分。
② He won't git no twenty bushels! He won't git none!: 这里的双重否定仍表示否定的意思。两句中的 no 与 none 意为 any。
③ straight stock: 犁。

for the shoat and the cow which were a part of his father's contract with the landlord, and one afternoon, his father being absent, gone somewhere on one of the mules, he went to the field.

They were running a middle buster① now, his brother holding the plow straight while he handled the reins, and walking beside the straining mule, the rich black soil shearing cool and damp against his bare ankles, he thought *Maybe this is the end of it. Maybe even that twenty bushels that seems hard to have to pay for just a rug will be a cheap price for him to stop forever and always from being what he used to be;* thinking, dreaming now, so that his brother had to speak sharply to him to mind the mule: *Maybe he even won't collect the twenty bushels. Maybe it will all add up and balance and vanish—corn, rug, fire; the terror and grief, the being pulled two ways like between two teams of horses—gone, done with for ever and ever.*

Then it was Saturday; he looked up from beneath the mule he was harnessing and saw his father in the black coat and hat. "Not that," his father said. "The wagon gear." And then, two hours later, sitting in the wagon bed behind his father and brother on the seat, the wagon accomplished a final curve, and he saw the weathered paintless store with its tattered tobacco-and patent-medicine posters and the tethered wagons and saddle animals below the gallery. He mounted the gnawed steps behind his father and brother, and there again was the lane of quiet, watching faces for the three of them to walk through. He saw the man in spectacles sitting at the plank table and he did not need to be told this was a Justice of the Peace; he sent one glare of fierce, exultant, partisan defiance at the man in collar and cravat now, whom he had seen but twice before in his life, and that on a galloping horse, who now wore on his face an expression not of rage but of amazed unbelief which the boy could not have known was at the incredible circumstance of being sued by one of his own tenants, and came and stood against his father and cried at the Justice: "He ain't done it! He ain't burnt..."

"Go back to the wagon," his father said.

"Burnt?" the Justice said. "Do I understand this rug was burned too?"

"Does anybody here claim it was?" his father said. "Go back to the wagon."

But he did not, he merely retreated to the rear of the room, crowded as that other had been, not to sit down this time, instead, to stand pressing among the motionless bodies, listening to the voices:

---

① middle buster: 犁的一种。

"And you claim twenty bushels of corn is too high for the damage you did to the rug?"

"He brought the rug to me and said he wanted the tracks washed out of it. I washed the tracks out and took the rug back to him."

"But you didn't carry the rug back to him in the same condition it was in before you made the tracks on it."

His father did not answer, and now for perhaps half a minute there was no sound at all save that of breathing, the faint, steady suspiration of complete and intent listening.

"You decline to answer that, Mr. Snopes?" Again his father did not answer. "I'm going to find against you, Mr. Snopes. I'm going to find that you were responsible for the injury to Major de Spain's rug and hold you liable for it. But twenty bushels of corn seems a little high for a man in your circumstances to have to pay. Major de Spain claims it cost a hundred dollars. October corn will be worth about fifty cents. I figure that if Major de Spain can stand a ninety-five-dollar loss on something he paid cash for, you can stand a five-dollar loss you haven't earned yet. I hold you in damages to Major de Spain to the amount of ten bushels of corn over and above your contract with him, to be paid to him out of your crop at gathering time. Court adjourned."

It had taken no time hardly, the morning was but half begun. He thought they would return home and perhaps back to the field, since they were late, far behind all other farmers. But instead his father passed on behind the wagon, merely indicating with his hand for the older brother to follow with it, and crossed the road toward the blacksmith shop opposite, pressing on after his father, overtaking him, speaking, whispering up at the harsh, calm face beneath the weathered hat: "He won't git no ten bushels neither. He won't git one. We'll..." until his father glanced for an instant down at him, the face absolutely calm, the grizzled eyebrows tangled above the cold eyes, the voice almost pleasant, almost gentle:

"You think so? Well, we'll wait till October anyway."

The matter of the wagon—the setting of a spoke or two and the tightening of the tires—did not take long either, the business of the tires accomplished by driving the wagon into the spring branch behind the shop and letting it stand there, the mules nuzzling into the water from time to time, and the boy on the seat with the idle reins, looking up the slope and through the sooty tunnel of the shed where the slow hammer rang and where his father sat on an upended cypress bolt, easily, either talking or listening, still sitting there when the boy brought the dripping wagon up out of the branch and halted it before the door.

"Take them on to the shade and hitch," his father said. He did so and returned. His father and the smith and a third man squatting on his heels inside the door were talking, about crops and animals; the boy, squatting too in the ammoniac dust and hoof-parings and scales of rust, heard his father tell a long and unhurried story out of the time before the birth of the older brother even when he had been a professional horsetrader. And then his father came up beside him where he stood before a tattered last year's circus poster on the other side of the store, gazing rapt and quiet at the scarlet horses, the incredible poisings and convolutions of tulle and tights and the painted leers of comedians, and said, "It's time to eat."

But not at home. Squatting beside his brother against the front wall, he watched his father emerge from the store and produce from a paper sack a segment of cheese and divide it carefully and deliberately into three with his pocket knife and produce crackers from the same sack. They all three squatted on the gallery and ate, slowly, without talking; then in the store again, they drank from a tin dipper tepid water smelling of the cedar bucket and of living beech trees. And still they did not go home. It was a horse lot this time, a tall rail fence upon and along which men stood and sat and out of which one by one horses were led, to be walked and trotted and then cantered back and forth along the road while the slow swapping and buying went on and the sun began to slant westward, they—the three of them—watching and listening, the older brother with his muddy eyes and his steady, inevitable tobacco, the father commenting now and then on certain of the animals, to no one in particular.

It was after sundown when they reached home. They ate supper by lamplight, then, sitting on the doorstep, the boy watched the night fully accomplish, listening to the whippoorwills and the frogs, when he heard his mother's voice: "Abner! No! No! Oh, God. Oh, God. Abner!" and he rose, whirled, and saw the altered light through the door where a candle stub now burned in a bottle neck on the table and his father, still in the hat and coat, at once formal and burlesque as though dressed carefully for some shabby and ceremonial violence, emptying the reservoir of the lamp back into the five-gallon kerosene can from which it had been filled, while the mother tugged at his arm until he shifted the lamp to the other hand and flung her back, not savagely or viciously, just hard, into the wall, her hands flung out against the wall for balance, her mouth open and in her face the same quality of hopeless despair as had been in her voice. Then his father saw him standing in the door.

"Go to the barn and get that can of oil we were oiling the wagon with," he said. The boy did not move. Then he could speak.

"What..." he cried. "What are you..."

"Go get that oil," his father said. "Go."

Then he was moving, running, outside the house, toward the stable: this the old habit, the old blood which he had not been permitted to choose for himself, which had been bequeathed him willy nilly and which had run for so long (and who knew where, battening on what of outrage and savagery and lust) before it came to him. *I could keep on, he thought, I could run on and on and never look back, never need to see his face again. Only I can't. I can't*, the rusted can in his hand now, the liquid sploshing in it as he ran back to the house and into it, into the sound of his mother's weeping in the next room, and handed the can to his father.

"Ain't you going to even send a nigger?" he cried. "At least you sent a nigger before!"

This time his father didn't strike him. The hand came even faster than the blow had, the same hand which had set the can on the table with almost excruciating care flashing from the can toward him too quick for him to follow it, gripping him by the back of his shirt and on to tiptoe before he had seen it quit the can, the face stooping at him in breathless and frozen ferocity, the cold, dead voice speaking over him to the older brother who leaned against the table, chewing with that steady, curious, sidewise motion of cows:

"Empty the can into the big one and go on. I'll catch up with you."

"Better tie him up to the bedpost," the brother said.

"Do like I told you," the father said. Then the boy was moving, his bunched shirt and the hard, bony hand between his shoulder-blades, his toes just touching the floor, across the room and into the other one, past the sisters sitting with spread heavy thighs in the two chairs over the cold hearth, and to where his mother and aunt sat side by side on the bed, the aunt's arms about his mother's shoulders.

"Hold him," the father said. The aunt made a startled movement. "Not you," the father said. "Lennie. Take hold of him. I want to see you do it." His mother took him by the wrist. "You'll hold him better than that. If he gets loose don't you know what he is going to do? He will go up yonder." He jerked his head toward the road. "Maybe I'd better tie him."

"I'll hold him," his mother whispered.

"See you do then." Then his father was gone, the stiff foot heavy and measured upon the boards, ceasing at last.

Then he began to struggle. His mother caught him in both arms, he jerking and wrenching at them. He would be stronger in the end, he knew that. But he had no time to wait for it. "Lemme go!" he cried. "I don't want to have to hit you!"

"Let him go!" the aunt said. "If he don't go, before God, I am going there myself!"

"Don't you see I can't!" his mother cried. "Sarty! Sarty! No! No! Help me, Lizzie!"

Then he was free. His aunt grasped at him but it was too late. He whirled, running, his mother stumbled forward on to her knees behind him, crying to the nearer sister: "Catch him, Net! Catch him!" But that was too late too, the sister (the sisters were twins, born at the same time, yet either of them now gave the impression of being, encompassing as much living meat and volume and weight as any other two of the family) not yet having begun to rise from the chair, her head, face, alone merely turned, presenting to him in the flying instant an astonishing expanse of young female features untroubled by any surprise even, wearing only an expression of bovine interest. Then he was out of the room, out of the house, in the mild dust of the starlit road and the heavy rifeness of honeysuckle, the pale ribbon unspooling with terrific slowness under his running feet, reaching the gate at last and turning in, running, his heart and lungs drumming, on up the drive toward the lighted house, the lighted door. He did not knock, he burst in, sobbing for breath, incapable for the moment of speech; he saw the astonished face of the Negro in the linen jacket without knowing when the Negro had appeared.

"De Spain!" he cried, panted. "Where's..." then he saw the white man too emerging from a white door down the hall. "Barn!" he cried. "Barn!"

"What?" the white man said. "Barn?"

"Yes!" the boy cried. "Barn!"

"Catch him!" the white man shouted.

But it was too late this time too. The Negro grasped his shirt, but the entire sleeve, rotten with washing, carried away, and he was out that door too and in the drive again, and had actually never ceased to run even while he was screaming into the white man's face.

Behind him the white man was shouting, "My horse! Fetch my horse!" and he thought for an instant of cutting across the park and climbing the fence into the road, but he did not know the park nor how high the vine-massed fence might be and he dared not risk it. So he ran on down the drive, blood and breath roaring; presently he was in the road again though he could not see it. He could not hear either: the galloping mare was almost upon him before he heard her, and even then he held his course, as if the very urgency of his wild grief and need must in a moment more find him wings, waiting until the ultimate instant to hurl himself aside and into the weed-choked roadside ditch as the horse thundered past and on, for an instant in furious silhouette against the stars, the tranquil early summer night sky which, even before the shape of the horse and rider vanished, stained abruptly and violently upward: a long, swirling roar incredible and soundless, blotting the stars, and he springing up and into the road again, running again, knowing it was too late yet still running even after he heard the shot and, an instant later, two shots, pausing now without knowing he had ceased to run, crying "Pap! Pap!", running again before he knew he had begun to run, stumbling, tripping over something and scrabbling up again without ceasing to run, looking backward over his shoulder at the glare as he got up, running on among the invisible trees, panting, sobbing, "Father! Father!"

At midnight he was sitting on the crest of a hill. He did not know it was midnight and he did not know how far he had come. But there was no glare behind him now and he sat now, his back toward what he had called home for four days anyhow, his face toward the dark woods which he would enter when breath was strong again, small, shaking steadily in the chill darkness, hugging himself into the remainder of his thin, rotten shirt, the grief and despair now no longer terror and fear but just grief and despair. *Father. My father*, he thought. "He was brave!" he cried suddenly, aloud but not loud, no more than a whisper: "He was! He was in the war! He was in Colonel Sartoris' cav'ry[①]!" not knowing that his father had gone to that war a private in the fine old European sense, wearing no uniform, admitting the authority of and giving fidelity to no man or army or flag,

---

① cav'ry: cavalry.

going to war as Malbrouck① himself did: for booty—it meant nothing and less than nothing to him if it were enemy booty or his own.

The slow constellations wheeled on. It would be dawn and then sun-up after a while and he would be hungry. But that would be to-morrow and now he was only cold, and walking would cure that. His breathing was easier now and he decided to get up and go on, and then he found that he had been asleep because he knew it was almost dawn, the night almost over. He could tell that from the whippoorwills. They were everywhere now among the dark trees below him, constant and inflectioned and ceaseless, so that, as the instant for giving over to the day birds drew nearer and nearer, there was no interval at all between them. He got up. He was a little stiff, but walking would cure that too as it would the cold, and soon there would be the sun. He went on down the hill, toward the dark woods within which the liquid silver voices of the birds called unceasing—the rapid and urgent beating of the urgent and quiring heart of the late spring night. He did not look back.

《烧畜棚》(又译《烧马棚》)写于福克纳创作鼎盛期中的1938年,1939年作为该年度美国最佳短篇小说获得首届欧·亨利纪念奖,一直被视为福克纳最具代表性的短篇小说之一。

南方穷白人的生活是福克纳较为关注的题材。斯诺普斯(Snopes)这一穷白人家族的故事在福克纳后来写的《村子》(*The Hamlet*,1940)、《小镇》(*The Town*,1957)、《大宅》(*The Mansion*,1959)等长篇小说中得到了更为详细的表现。《烧畜棚》主要是通过描写他们与庄园主的激烈冲突来表现穷白人的。阿伯纳(Abner)擅入德斯潘(de Spain)的大宅、糟蹋他的地毯、烧他的畜棚等行为,都明确表现了阿伯纳对于庄园主的仇恨,以及誓死维护自尊的意志。但小说强调使他众叛亲离、自取灭亡的偏执与暴烈,也传达出作者对他的责备。

处于痛苦的成长期的男孩也是福克纳所感兴趣的。在《烧畜棚》里,萨蒂(Sarty)的痛苦不仅在于他必须承受过去的罪孽所产生的后果,比如在哈里斯的畜棚被烧之后,他被骂作"畜棚纵火犯",并被打得头破血流;还在于他必须做出艰难的选择,必须决定是按父亲的要求忠实于自己的血统,继续生活在"恐惧与绝望"之中,还是背叛血统,去追求德斯潘"漂亮、雪白"、"像法院一般"的大宅所象征的"和平与快乐"。萨蒂的最后选择无疑为他的追求创造了机会。但他天真,没有像阿伯纳那样认识到德斯潘的大宅建在黑人和白人的汗水之上,这又难免让人对他的未来感到担忧。萨蒂在福克纳的作品中没有再出现过。

---

① Malbrouck:马尔布鲁克,18世纪法国民谣《马尔布鲁克已赴战场》(Malbrouck Has Gone to the War)中的人物,常被看成约翰·丘吉尔(John Churchill),即第一代马尔伯勒(Marlborough)公爵。他靠非凡的军事才能从士兵升至中将,曾率英军战胜法王路易十四,是历史上的名将之一。但他也是一个有争议的人物,被指责为谋乱反上,唯利是图。

萨蒂当时没有认识到的还有阿伯纳为什么只生小火取暖,阿伯纳在内战中的真实表现等。而读者则可从叙述者的有关叙述中了解到他的这种幼稚以及他所不了解的其他情况。小说叙述者具有传统的第三人称叙述的全知视角,但他的叙述具有高度的选择性,主要选择叙述萨蒂所能看到、感到、想到的东西,使得叙述客观而又简洁。叙述者有时也站出来表达年幼的主人公尚不具备的洞见,从而加强了他可悲处境的感染力和他成熟过程的戏剧性。

思考题

1. What is the nature of the story's conflict? How does each of the story's six scenes serve to reveal, clarify, and intensify the conflict?

2. What seems to motivate Abner's violent, antisocial behaviour? Why does he try to make Sarty an accomplice to the burning of Major de Spain's barn? Why does Sarty finally defy him and try to warn Major de Spain?

3. What comments does the story offer about the social, moral, and economic values of the old and the new South?

推荐作品

"A Rose for Emily" (1931)
The Sound and the Fury (1929)
Absalom, Absalom! (1936)

参考资料

Blotner, Joseph. *Faulkner: A Biography.* 2 vols. New York: Random House, 1974.

Brooks, Cleanth. *William Faulkner: The Yoknapatawpha Country.* New Haven: Yale UP, 1963.

Polk, Noel, ed. *New Essays on The Sound and the Fury.* Beijing: Peking UP; Cambridge UP, 2006.

Wagner-Martin, Linda, ed. *New Essays on Go Down, Moses.* Beijing: Peking UP; Cambridge UP, 2006.

Weinstein, Philip M. *The Cambridge Companion to William Faulknr.* Cambridge: Cambridge UP, 1995.

第五单元

Ezra Pound
(1885—1972)
艾兹拉·庞德

作者简介

艾兹拉·庞德,诗人、批评家、翻译家。生于爱达荷州海雷市。16岁就读于宾夕法尼亚州大学,1906年获硕士学位。大学时代,庞德与后来同样叱咤诗坛的W.C.威廉斯为同窗好友,彼此影响至深,结为终生志同道合的朋友。在大学短暂执教两年后,庞德前往西班牙、意大利、英国和法国等欧洲国家考察,由此开始进行文学创作与出版活动,并对中国文学和日本文学产生了浓厚的兴趣。1914年结婚后,庞德更多地致力于诗歌创作和翻译等活动,1917年起担任颇有影响的刊物《诗歌》驻伦敦通信员,1924年移居意大利。二战中,庞德为意大利法西斯政权效力,通过意大利电台广播攻击美国。战争结束时,他在比萨被美军抓获,囚禁在露天的笼子里,但他坚持写作,完成了《比萨诗章》(Pisan Cantos)。庞德1945年返回美国因叛国罪被捕入狱,后因众多知名作家呼吁,以其精神不正常为理由未判罪而送进精神病医院。其间,他因《比萨诗章》于1948年获国会博林根图书馆奖。1958年,由于作家们的呼吁,庞德被释放,再度移居意大利,隐居威尼斯,直至辞世。他的主要诗歌作品还包括:《向塞克斯图斯·佩罗提乌斯致敬》(Homage to Sextus Propertius, 1918)以及《休·塞尔温·莫伯利》(Hugh Selwyn Mauberley, 1920);他最重要的作品当推长诗《诗章》(Cantos, 1915—1970)。庞德在20世纪美国诗歌史上具有重要的地位,主要基于他在两个方面的贡献:一是他个人不同凡响的诗歌探索与创作,二是他鼎力提携新秀,在理论与诗歌创作实践两个方面引领美国诗歌的发展,包括20世纪初他与美国诗人休姆一起发起意象派诗歌运动,并帮助乔伊斯、T.S.艾略特与弗罗斯特等人在创作初期发表作品。

作品

A Girl

The tree has entered my hands,
The sap① has ascended my arms,

---
① sap: 树液;汁液;精力;活力。

The tree has grown in my breast—
Downward,
The branches grow out of me, like arms.

Tree you are,
Moss① you are,
You are violets with wind above them.
A child—so high—you are,
And all this is folly② to the world.

　　《少女》一诗是庞德的短诗代表作之一，与《地铁站里》(In a Station of Metro)和《画》(The Picture)一样典型地体现了诗人所倡导的意象派诗歌的主要特征与风范。意象派诗歌崇尚再现具有鲜明特色的、处于静态的意象，并着力渲染诗人瞬间捕捉到这些意象时的感官体验，但诗中并不铺陈任何解说或评论性的内容。换言之，意象派诗歌是刻意突出意象作为诗歌艺术本源的作用，注重通过视觉来捕捉那些有内涵的事物，回避或者淡化概念性的内容，试图借此匡正诗歌中理性成分过于浓重的倾向。上述特征都在《少女》一诗中得以展现。该诗是庞德根据李白的名诗《玉阶怨》改写而成，比较李白的原作：

　　　　玉阶生白露，夜久侵罗袜。
　　　　却下水晶帘，玲珑望秋月。

　　不难发现，庞德之所以改写此诗是因为此诗契合意象派诗歌的要旨，或者说他在此诗中寻找到了共鸣抑或启迪。李白虽以"怨"字作为诗的标题，但诗中字面不见"怨"字，反倒是夜色中冰凉的露水浸湿罗袜，水晶帘掩映孤独，秋月照射寒意，凡此种种，无一不淋漓尽致地再现了深深的"怨"情。《少女》也是要复原《玉阶怨》的上述特征，以意象衬托出意境和情怀。

 思考题

1. What stylistic features can you find in this poem?
2. Some critics think that the theme of this poem departs from that of the original text by Li Bai. What do you think of it?

---

① moss：苔藓；指任何一种苔藓植物。
② folly：荒唐事；蠢事；邪恶；危险或犯法的愚蠢行为。

 **推荐作品**

"In a Station of the Metro"
"A Pact"
"The Picture"

参考资料

Ackroyd, Peter. *Ezra Pound and His World*. London: Thames and Hudson, 1980.

Brooker, Peter. *A Student's Guide to the Selected Poems of Ezra Pound*. London: Faber and Faber, 1979.

Hamilton, Scott. *Ezra Pound and the Symbolist Inheritance*. Princeton: princeton UP, 1992.

Wallace Stevens
(1879—1955)
华莱士·史蒂文斯

作者简介

　　华莱士·史蒂文斯，诗人、律师。生于宾夕法尼亚州雷丁市，父亲是一位成功而在当地颇有影响的律师。曾就读哈佛大学三年，后转学纽约法学院，1904年获得学士学位，并成为律师。1909年结婚。在哈佛大学学习期间，史蒂文斯萌生诗歌创作的欲望，曾在校刊发表少量习作。毕业后他虽然以律师为业，但始终没有放弃诗歌创作，直至36岁正式发表第一首诗作，1923年出版第一部诗集《簧风琴》(Harmonium)，可谓大器晚成。《簧风琴》首版只售出一百余册，但是却赢得了文学批评界极高的赞誉，由此奠定了史蒂文斯在美国诗歌界乃至诗歌史上的地位。史蒂文斯的诗歌创作长达四十余年，曾经获得许多殊荣，包括门罗诗歌奖、博林根诗歌奖、美国国家图书奖和普利策奖等，被誉为20世纪最重要的美国诗人之一，但他一生为人低调，素为世人称道。他的主要诗集还包括《秩序的概念》(Ideas of Order, 1935)、《猫头鹰的三叶草》(Owl's Clover, 1937)、《带蓝吉他的人》(The Man With the Blue Guitar, 1937)、《世界的各个部分》(Parts of a World, 1942)以及《关于最高虚构的札记》(Notes Toward a Supreme Fiction, 1942)。学术界一般认为，史蒂文斯的诗歌深邃难解，因为他主张诗歌的任务是阐发诗人对人、社会以及自然的广泛而独特的抽象思考。因此，他的主要诗作都具有两个显著的特色：一是较为抽象的思考贯穿诗歌的字里行间，二是主题丰富多变，体现出他宽广的视野与胸襟。

The Snow Man

One must have a mind of winter
To regard the frost and the boughs
Of the pine-trees crusted① with snow;

---

　　① crusted：有外皮的；用外皮(壳)覆盖的。

And have been cold a long time
To behold the junipers① shagged② with ice,
The spruces③ rough in the distant glitter

Of the January sun; and not to think
Of any misery in the sound of the wind,
In the sound of a few leaves,

Which is the sound of the land
Full of the same wind
That is blowing in the same bare place

For the listener, who listens in the snow,
And, nothing himself, beholds
Nothing that is not there and the nothing that is.

作为史蒂文斯脍炙人口的名篇之一,《雪人》可以从多重角度进行解读与赏析。由于受到庞德等意象派诗人的影响,史蒂文斯在描写冬天的景色时,将他宽广、敏锐而深邃的眼光所捕捉到的别有新意的意象以组合的方式呈现出来,例如诗歌开篇亭亭玉立的"雪人"、"白雪包裹的松树"、"在远方闪烁的粗糙的云杉"以及"残叶发出的声音"等等,犹如画龙点睛之笔,旋即将大自然的妩媚、纯洁,以及春夏秋冬周而复始的力量跃然纸上,而且冰雪覆盖的冬天所展示的妩媚多姿也反衬出"雪人"的渺小,能够给人带来富有哲理的想象。如果把这首诗看作诗人对人与自然之间关系的思考,或者说是对人类如何认识自己的思考,那么他笔下似乎处于休眠状态的自然就是一种自我投射,是心灵与自然景色美妙的契合。由此着眼,可以将该诗分为两个段落,前7行是第一段落,着重以视觉意象投射出"冬天的心灵",第二段落是从第7行后半部分到结尾,转而以听觉的力量展示"冬天的心灵"的孤独和深邃。诗歌的结尾叙写了一个物我交融的瞬间,宛如格言,隽永精辟,使诗中的张力达到了极至。

---

① junipers: 刺柏属丛木或树木;杜松。
② shagged: 精疲力尽的;树的枝叶不整齐、毛茸茸的样子。此处可能有双重含义。
③ spruces: 云杉,属于松柏科,四季常绿树,叶如针状,结球形果。

思考题

1. If the poem presents a picture of the harmony of nature and man, how does the poet attempt to inspire his readers in both visual and audio ways so that they may have access to perceiving that point?
2. What can you find if you look into the poem from the perspective of literary ecology?
3. What is your interpretation of the poem?

推荐作品

"Thirteen Ways of Looking at a Blackbird"
"Sunday Morning"
"The Emperor of Ice Cream"

参考资料

Baird, James. *The Dome and the Rock: Structure in the Poetry of Wallace Stevens.* Baltimore: Johns Hopkins Press, 1968.

Benamou, Michel. *Wallace Stevens and the Symbolist Imagination.* Princeton, New Jersey: Princeton UP, 1972.

Filreis, Alan. *Wallace Stevens and the Actual World.* Princeton, New Jersey: Princeton UP, 1991.

William Carlos Williams
(1883—1963)
威廉·卡洛斯·威廉斯

作者简介

　　威廉·卡洛斯·威廉斯，诗人、剧作家、散文家、儿科医生。生于新泽西州卢瑟福市，父亲经商，家境殷实。母亲喜爱绘画，并在威廉斯少年时代送其远赴日内瓦和巴黎学习。在宾夕法尼亚大学学习期间，威廉斯结识庞德，虽然专业有别，但因二人均钟情于诗歌创作，且志向与见解相投，成为终生莫逆之交。威廉斯虽然学医且终生以医生为业，但从中学时代开始写诗，并立志以行医谋生，以诗歌创作实现自己的理想。威廉斯是意象派诗人群体中的核心成员之一，诗歌创作与艺术观念的影响虽然不及T.S.艾略特等与其同时代的诗人，但对20世纪中叶的一些重要诗人，诸如艾伦·金斯堡与罗伯特·洛威尔等人产生了显见的影响。1913年在庞德的帮助下，他在伦敦出版了第一部诗集《性情》(The Tempers)，试图在欧洲拓展创作的空间。他的其他重要诗集包括《地狱中的柯拉》(Kora in Hell, 1920)、《春天及其他》(Spring and All, 1923)以及煌煌五卷本的史诗《帕特森》(Paterson, 1963)。其他体裁的作品还包括小说《白骡》(White Mule, 1937)。1963年，他谢世之后因诗集《来自布鲁盖尔的画像及其他》(Pictures from Brueghel and Other Poems, 1962)而获得普利策诗歌奖。威廉斯虽然与庞德、T.S.艾略特等声名显赫的人物属于同一时代的美国诗人，而且在其四十余年的诗歌创作生涯中也创作出了完全能够与前者相媲美的作品，但是就其创作思想与风格而言，他与他们差别迥异，反倒是与19世纪的爱默生、惠特曼、狄金森等诗人一脉相承，始终自觉地与欧洲文化传统拉开距离，孜孜追求具有美国民族特色的诗歌艺术。

The Uses of Poetry

I've fond anticipation of a day
O'erfilled① with pure diversion presently,

---

① o'erfilled: 充满的，装得太满的。

For I must read a lady poesy①
The while we glide by m0any a leafy bay,

Hid deep in rushes, where at random play
The glossy black winged May-flies, or whence flee
Hush-throated nestlings② in alarm,
Whom we have idly frighted with our boat's long sway.

For, lest o'ersaddened③ by such woes as spring
To rural peace from our meek onward trend,
What else more fit? We'll draw the latch-string

And close the door of sense; then satiate wend,
On poesy's transforming giant wing,
To worlds afar whose fruits all anguish mend.

就其创作思想而言,《诗歌的用途》一诗典型地反映出了威廉斯自觉摒弃欧洲诗歌传统,大胆探索,刻意追求具有美国民族特色的诗歌艺术风格。从形式特征来看,这首诗较为传统,诗句采用惠特曼之后的诗歌中常见的自由体,具有独白特征,如流水般自然而然地推心置腹,与威廉斯的名篇佳作《红色手推车》、《在墙之间》和《麻雀》等显然不同,利用诗文不规则排列所产生的几何造型,从而营造一种别开生面的视觉效果。在内容方面,该诗在第一节以女人为意象说明诗人所青睐的诗歌的特征。实际上,女性也始终是威廉斯在诗歌创作中关注的主要对象之一。诗的最后一节说明诗歌能够抚平人的心灵,消除人的痛楚,即使是在动荡不安的社会背景下也有其特定的价值和意义。

思考题

1. Can you summarize the main ideas the poet presents in the poem?
2. American literature is not devoid of poems that project principles or theories of poetry. Can you give other examples apart from this poem?

---

① poesy: 诗歌,作诗法,诗歌艺术。
② nestlings: 雏鸟,尤指因年幼不能离巢的雏鸟。
③ o'ersaddened: 过于忧愁,过于难过。

 "The Red Wheelbarrow"
"This Is Just to Say"
"Between Walls"

参考资料

Morris, Daniel. *The Writings of William Carlos Williams: Publicity for the Self.* Columbia: U of Missouri P, 1995.

Schmidt, Peter. *William Carlos Williams, the Arts, and Literary Tradition.* Baton Rouge: Louisiana State UP, 1988.

Whitaker, Thomas R. *William Carlos Williams.* Rev. ed. Twayne's United States Authors Ser. 139. Boston: Twayne, 1989.

Robert Frost
(1874—1963)
罗伯特·弗罗斯特

 作者简介

  罗伯特·弗罗斯特,诗人。生于加利福尼亚州旧金山市,父亲为记者,后从政,在儿子 11 岁时亡故。母亲为中学教师,收入微薄,加之外祖父多病,一家人勉强维持生计。弗罗斯特曾就读于达特茅斯学院和哈佛大学,但均中途辍学,在 30 岁之前的十余年间始终靠打零工谋生。1895 年结婚,有 6 个子女。弗罗斯特自幼喜好文学,自学写诗,20 岁时在《纽约独立报》发表第一首诗歌《我的蝴蝶》(My Butterfly)。20 世纪初叶,赴欧洲进行创作和发展是当时美国作家的时尚,弗罗斯特为之所动,1912 年举家迁居英国,开始了诗歌创作的一个辉煌时期。次年,他在庞德的帮助下出版了第一部诗集《少年的心愿》(A Boy's Will, 1913),1914 年出版第二部诗集《波士顿之北》(North of Boston),其中包括许多脍炙人口的诗作,例如《修墙》(Mending Wall)和《雇工之死》(The Death of the Hired Man)。他由此获得国际声誉,随后于 1915 年返回美国,在密歇根州立大学等多家大学任教。弗罗斯特曾四次荣获普利策诗歌奖,获奖次数之多,至今无人企及。1961 年 1 月 20 日,弗罗斯特应邀在美国总统约翰·F.肯尼迪总统的就职仪式上朗诵诗歌 The Gift Outright,因此举世瞩目。他的其他主要诗集还包括《山间洼地》(Mountain Interval, 1916)等。弗罗斯特的诗风不是以新奇取胜,而是在传统的诗歌形式上有所创新,他称之为"以旧形式表达新内容"。他擅长以象征性的手法描写树木花草等植物以及司空见惯的场景与意象,进而通过它们投射出诗人推崇的价值观念。弗罗斯特始终是美国最受欢迎的诗人之一,不能不说与他的诗风密切相关。

作品

Love and A Question

A Stranger came to the door at eve①,
  And he spoke the bridegroom fair.

---

① eve:常用于诗歌中,指黄昏;除夕;前夕;傍晚。

He bore a green-white stick in his hand,
  And, for all burden, care.
He asked with the eyes more than the lips
  For a shelter for the night,
And he turned and looked at the road afar
  Without a window light.

The bridegroom came forth into the porch
  With, 'Let us look at the sky,
And question what of the night to be,
  Stranger, you and I.'
The woodbine① leaves littered the yard,
  The woodbine berries were blue,
Autumn, yes, winter was in the wind;
  'Stranger, I wish I knew.'

Within, the bride in the dusk alone
  Bent over the open fire,
Her face rose-red with the glowing coal
  And the thought of the heart's desire.
The bridegroom looked at the weary road,
  Yet saw but her within,
And wished her heart in a case of gold
  And pinned with a silver pin.

The bridegroom thought it little to give
  A dole② of bread, a purse,
A heartfelt prayer for the poor of God,
  Or for the rich a curse;
But whether or not a man was asked
  To mar the love of two
By harboring③ woe in the bridal house,

---

① woodbine：忍冬，一种微黄色的花，也指任何一种攀生藤蔓植物。
② dole：施舍；施舍品；悲哀。
③ harboring：为……提供栖息地或者地点。

The bridegroom wished he knew.

弗罗斯特的诗歌创作特征之一是他能够在貌似平凡的事物中发现不平凡的深刻内涵，或者说他善于将似乎司空见惯的场景和意象与寓意深邃的思想和情感交织在一起，物我相依，其诗情画意耐人寻味。如同他在几乎家喻户晓的《未选择的路》(The Road Not Taken)一诗中刻画了一种难以抉择的困惑，《爱与问题》惟妙惟肖地展示了一种内心的张力，或者说是渲染了面对某些未知因素的时候人与人之间内心难以言表的困窘与互动。在弗罗斯特的笔下，一对生活拮据的新婚夫妇和一个富有的男性"陌生人"在一个黑夜的短暂时刻戏剧化地再现了爱、猜疑、陌生、贫富差异、恐惧以及无奈等复杂因素所构成的矛盾，由表及里，三个人彼此影响和牵制，能够使人更深刻地品味到"爱"的内涵。在诗歌的结尾，诗人并没有向读者提供明确的答案，而是选择了带有悬念的开放性结局，这一点与《修墙》等名篇不同。诗中的许多意象和表达方式都体现了弗罗斯特细腻而独到的眼光与文字表现能力，例如：陌生人"用眼睛而不是用嘴唇询问"这句诗优美而活灵活现地将这位过路客的谨慎而高雅的修养、对新郎的揣测以及与新郎的差异全然呈现在读者面前。

思考题

1. How does the poet dramatize the tension of love in this poem?
2. What devices does the poet use to depict the profundity of mind in the simplicity of verses?

"Mending Wall"
"The Road Not Taken"
"Stopping by Woods on a Snowy Evening"

参考资料

Oster, Judith. *Toward Robert Frost: The Reader and the Poet.* Athens: U of Georgia P, 1991.

Potter, James L. *Robert Frost Handbook.* U Park: Pennsylvania State UP, 1980.

Thompson, Lawrance R. *Fire and Ice: The Art and Thought of Robert Frost.* New York: Russell & Russell, 1961.

E. E. Cummings
(1894—1962)
E. E. 肯明斯

作者简介

　　E.E.肯明斯,诗人、小说家、画家。生于马萨诸塞州剑桥,父亲为哈佛大学教授,母亲出身世家,两人一道鼓励与指导肯明斯自幼开始学习写诗和绘画。1911年,肯明斯入哈佛大学,学习期间,他发现庞德的作品,倾心现代主义诗歌,参与创建了哈佛诗社,并与同学合作自费出版诗集《八位哈佛诗人》(*Eight Haward Poets*, 1917)。第一次世界大战期间,他曾自愿赴法国参加救护车队的工作,并把自己在法国战犯营的经历写成《巨人的房间》(*The Enormous Room*, 1922)。战后他在巴黎和纽约研习绘画,并继续进行诗歌创作,诗作多发表在《日晷》等先锋派的刊物上。肯明斯一生共有三次婚姻,前两次都以其被抛弃而告终,严重影响了他的诗歌创作。悲观与玩世不恭的特征见之于他在这一时期创作的部分诗歌。但他更主张诗歌的特色为幽默和表现喜怒哀乐的激情。就其创作而言,他长期致力于探索诗歌维新之路,例如别出心裁地将名词等非动词词性的词语用作动词,违反常规地使用标点符号和字母的大小写规则。他认为读者常常阅读而不光朗读诗歌,因此注意诗行及诗词在页面上的安排,甚至拆散词组或词,把它们按音节或字母排列成诗行,以产生视觉或视觉节奏的效果。他共出版了12部诗集,主要诗集包括《郁金香与烟囱》(*Tulips and Chimneys*, 1923)、《万岁》(*ViVa*, 1931)和《肯明斯诗选》(*Collected Poems*, 1938)。他去世后,他的全部诗作汇集为两卷本的《肯明斯诗歌全集》(*Complete Poems*, 1968)出版。

作品

Humanity i love you

Humanity i love you
because you would rather black the boots of
success than enquire whose soul dangles from his
watch-chain which would be embarrassing for both

parties and because you
unflinchingly① applaud all
songs containing the words country home and
mother when sung at the old howard②

Humanity i love you because
when you're hard up you pawn③ your
intelligence to buy a drink and when
you're flush④ pride keeps

you from the pawn shop and
because you are continually committing
nuisances⑤ but more
especially in your own house

Humanity i love you because you
are perpetually putting the secret of
life in your pants and forgetting
it's there and sitting down

on it
and because you are
forever making poems in the lap
of death Humanity

i hate you

作为"迷惘的一代"的代表人物之一,肯明斯最为人称道的是他在探索新的诗歌方面所做出的努力和贡献,包括他尝试将诗歌与绘画融为一炉,以及改变单词的字母拼写规律和格式,以便使诗歌的外在形式具有奇特的视觉效果,例如他的名诗《蚱蜢》

---

① unflinchingly:果敢地,不畏缩地,不妥协地。
② old Howard:指美国波士顿市区内一个表演歌舞杂耍的场所。
③ pawn:典当,抵押。
④ flush:丰富的,充足的,富足的。
⑤ nuisances:令人讨厌的东西,麻烦事,损害。

(r-p-o-p-h-e-s-s-a-g-r)和《我将》(I will be)等等。但是人们往往容易忽视他在一些采用较为传统的诗歌格式的诗歌中对人与社会中重大问题的观察和思考,而恰恰是在这些诗歌中,肯明斯表现出了他深刻而富有强烈责任感的一面。对于诗中的两个人物"i"与"Humanity",前者刻意打破规则,采用小写字母,与后者首字母的大写形成对比,以象征性的手法突出二者的差异,尤其是以前者之渺小反衬后者之狂妄自大。在当时反战的背景下,这首诗歌凸现了诗人对待战争的态度,以嘲讽的口吻针砭人性中的缺陷,从开篇的"人类,我爱你"转变为结尾的"人类……我恨你"。

思考题

1. Why does the poet begin with "Humanity i love you" and end with "i hate you"?
2. The poet does not use "i" in its conventional capital form. What meaning can you find in such a departure from the convention?

推荐作品

"when I have thought of you somewhat too"

"since feeling is first"

"come, gaze with me upon this dome"

参考资料

Dendinger, Lloyd N., ed. *E. E. Cummings: The Critical Reception.* New York: Burt Franklin, 1981.

Kidder, Rushworth M. *E. E. Cummings: An Introduction to the Poetry.* New York: Columbia UP, 1979.

Lane, Gary. *I am: A Study of E. E. Cummings' Poems.* Lawrence: UP of Kansas, 1976.

Langston Hughes
(1902—1967)
兰斯顿·休斯

作者简介

兰斯顿·休斯,生于密苏里州乔普林镇,童年随外祖母在堪萨斯州生活。13岁那年,外祖母去世,方与母亲共同生活。休斯上高中时就在校办杂志上发表诗作。1921年秋,他进入哥伦比亚大学学习,一年后辍学。其间,他对哈莱姆地区产生浓厚兴趣,迅速成为哈莱姆文学艺术圈的活跃分子,并最终成为哈莱姆文艺复兴的代言人和记录者。其自传《大海》(The Big Sea, 1940)至今仍是研究那场运动的第一手资料。1923年,他作为水手随货船访问了三十余个非洲港口。回国前,曾先后在巴黎、威尼斯等地居住。1925年,休斯创作的《疲惫的布鲁斯》(The Weary Blues)一诗获得《机会》杂志举办的文学竞赛诗歌类一等奖,他从此步入文坛。1926年,休斯的第一本诗集以《疲惫的布鲁斯》为名出版。同年,他得到七十多岁的白人富婆梅森(Charlotte Osgood Mason)的资助,进入宾夕法尼亚州的林肯大学学习。1927年,休斯发表第二部诗集《好衣服拿给犹太人》(Fine Clothes to the Jew),但未获成功。在梅森的说服下,休斯创作了长篇小说《并非无笑》(Not Without Laughter, 1930)。1930年两人发生争执,资助关系终止。这时,休斯在思想上转向左翼,开始在《新大众》(New Masses)杂志发表诗作,于1932年访问苏联,1933年访问上海。随后几年,休斯转向戏剧创作,他以美国南方黑白人通婚为题材的剧目《混血儿》(Mulatto)在百老汇上演并获得成功。1942年,休斯开始为美国黑人办的报纸《芝加哥卫士》(Chicago Defender)撰写专栏。1943年,幽默的贫民人物辛普尔(Jesse B. Semple或Simple)出现在这个专栏里,休斯借此讨论严肃的种族问题。因为辛普尔幽默可爱,专栏大获成功,故事连载了20年,被收入几部书出版发行。1947年,休斯用为百老汇音乐剧写歌词挣的钱实现了他在哈莱姆购房的梦想。1951年,他发表了著名的诗集《延迟的梦之蒙太奇》(Montage of a Dream Deferred)。其后,他又发表了20余部作品。休斯将美国黑人音乐明快的节奏运用到诗歌中,努力表现黑人的活力,被誉为"哈莱姆桂冠诗人"、"黑人民族桂冠诗人"。

The Weary Blues①

Droning a drowsy syncopated② tune,
Rocking back and forth to a mellow croon,
  I heard a Negro play.③
Down on Lenox Avenue④ the other night
By the pale dull pallor of an old gas light
  He did a lazy sway...
  He did a lazy sway...
To the tune o' those Weary Blues.
With his ebony hands on each ivory key⑤
He made that poor piano moan with melody.
  O Blues!
Swaying to and fro on his rickety stool
He played that sad raggy⑥ tune like a musical fool.
  Sweet Blues!
Coming from a black man's soul.
  O Blues!

---

  ① blues：布鲁斯音乐，原为美国南方黑人民间的一种即兴演唱形式，常表现悲伤的主题(美国人认为蓝色为忧郁、悲哀的颜色)，速度舒缓，节拍常为四二拍、四四拍，旋律多含切分节奏，常于大调音阶上降半音，而且带有滑音、颤音，使歌唱听起来哀声怨语，悲恸凄楚。布鲁斯演唱风格自由，生活气息浓厚，假声、呻吟、哭泣、嘟囔、呼喊都可以用来渲染表达情绪，烘托气氛。布鲁斯的发展经历了乡村布鲁斯、古典布鲁斯和城市布鲁斯三个阶段。乡村布鲁斯采用上升或下降的自然滑音，一般三句构成一段，没有固定的段数，可以即兴演唱很多段，有时采用班卓琴和吉他进行伴奏。古典布鲁斯，常有作曲者参与，不完全靠歌手即兴演唱，曲式更加规整，经常有爵士乐队伴奏。城市布鲁斯主要反映城市生活的感受，结构固定，四四拍，12 小节分成三句，每 4 小节为一句，第一、二句重复。伴奏可能是乐队，或者是钢琴，伴奏和声趋于规范。

  ② syncopated：被切分的；syncopation：切分音。

  ③ 诗的前三行为一个句子，从表面上看，出现了语法上的"无依着"现象，即前两行分词短语的逻辑主语和第三行句子主语不一致。这里，诗人通过这一结构表现布鲁斯音乐使歌手(分词短语的逻辑主语)和听众(句子主语)合二为一的效果，暗示布鲁斯音乐表达的不仅仅是个人情感，而是黑人的民族情感。

  ④ Lenox Avenue：纽约市哈莱姆区的一条主要街道。

  ⑤ With his ebony hands on each ivory key：注意该行中黑(ebony hands)白(ivory key)之间的关系，以及黑人乐手用白人乐器创造出自己的艺术形式的寓意。歌手低沉的歌声表现了"黑人的灵魂"(a black man's soul)，布鲁斯帮助黑人界定身份。乌黑的手敲击在乳白色的琴键上，使产生于西方文化的钢琴倾诉着黑人的悲伤，白人的音乐形式被黑人文化改变。

  ⑥ raggy：相当于 ragged，一般指衣衫褴褛的，这里指乐声狂躁刺耳。

In a deep song voice with a melancholy tone
I heard that Negro sing, that old piano moan—
  "Ain't got nobody in all this world,
  Ain't got nobody but ma self.
  I's gwine to quit ma frownin'
  And put ma troubles on the shelf."①

Thump, thump, thump, went his foot on the floor.
He played a few chords then he sang some more —
  "I got the Weary Blues
  And I can't be satisfied.
  Got the Weary Blues
  And can't be satisfied—
  I ain't happy no mo'
  And I wish that I had died."
And far into the night he crooned that tune.
The stars went out and so did the moon.
The singer stopped playing and went to bed
While the Weary Blues echoed through his head.
He slept like a rock or a man that's dead.

《疲倦的布鲁斯》一诗于1923年发表在纽约的《阿姆斯特丹新闻》(Amsterdam News)上。休斯在自传《大海》里说这首诗包含着他幼年在堪萨斯州最早听到的布鲁斯歌曲。诗歌用第一人称描述了一天夜晚在哈莱姆街道上听布鲁斯歌手演唱的情景,通过选词、重复句子、引用布鲁斯歌词表达悲哀之情和布鲁斯歌曲舒缓的节奏,从而使读者感受到布鲁斯歌手的情绪。无名歌手扭动着身躯,手弹钢琴,脚拍地板,用"懒洋洋的切分调"低沉哀婉地唱出自己的希望、孤独与失望。手脚上的活力同低沉的音调形成反差,揭示歌手内心的张力。诗歌引用了两段布鲁斯歌词,第一段为8小节,表现的是歌手决心忘却烦恼,面对生活的愿望。但是,相对第二段12小节,8小节显得短小,暗示实现这种愿望的渺茫,从而深化了歌手的孤独。第二段通过两句重复进一步强化歌手的疲惫、失落和绝望。忧伤的布鲁斯似乎成了歌手拥有的一切,既是他表达"黑

---

① 没有受过正规教育的美国黑人使用的英语,有不符合语法规范的地方,如用双重否定表示否定 Ain't got nobody, ain't 为助动词的否定式形式;ma: my; "I's gwine to": I'm going to; frownin': frowing。省音现象在美国黑人英语中常见。

人的灵魂"的途径,也是他得以展示自己生命活力的舞台。他用布鲁斯宣泄生活在白人主宰的社会里的孤独,让白人的钢琴发出黑人的呐喊。他通宵达旦地演唱,直到精疲力竭,内心的感受得到完全的释放,然后安然入睡。布鲁斯因此界定了他的身份,显然也打动了作为诗歌叙述人的听众,使他用另一种艺术形式表现出歌手孤独、疲惫的感情,以及歌手通过布鲁斯音乐拒绝接受现状,力图展示活力,维护尊严的复杂心理。

思考题

1. What figure of speech is used in the first line, and what effect does it have?
2. What effect does the monosyllabic rhyme of "tune" and "croon" have at the end of the first two lines?
3. How does the poet create a "rocking" or "swaying" effect?
4. How does the poem express pride in African-American forms of expression?
5. What do you think of the poet's use of "Sweet Blues" in line 14, against the title of "The Weary Blues"?

推荐作品

"The Negro Speaks of Rivers"
"Dreams"
"Dream Variations"
"I, Too"
"As I Grew Older"
"Madam and the Phone Bill"
"What happens to a dream deferred?"
"Let American be America Again"

参考资料

Emanuel, James A. *Langston Hughes*. New York: Twayne Publishers, 1997.
Tracy, Steven C. *Langston Hughes and the Blues*. Urbana: U of Illinois P, 1988.

第六单元
Eugene Gladstone O'Neill
(1888—1953)
尤金·格拉斯通·奥尼尔

作者简介

尤金·格拉斯通·奥尼尔,美国现代戏剧的奠基人。在他之前,已有一批美国剧作家不满当时充斥着美国剧坛的伤感喜剧和情节悲剧,致力于创作既有艺术价值,又受大众欢迎的剧作。奥尼尔更是对艺术孜孜以求,取得了前人无法企及的成就,使严肃戏剧成为美国现代戏剧的主流。美国许多重要的剧作家都受到他的影响;他也使美国戏剧走向世界,影响到其他许多国家的剧作家,其中包括中国的曹禺和洪深。奥尼尔于1936年获得诺贝尔文学奖;他也四度获得普利策戏剧奖,获奖剧作为:《天边外》(1920)、《安娜·克里斯蒂》(1921)、《奇异的插曲》(1928)、《进入黑夜的漫长旅程》(1956)。

奥尼尔的父亲是著名的戏剧演员,他年复一年地在各地巡演根据大仲马的小说改编的剧作《基督山伯爵》,而他们全家也随剧团四处漂泊。奥尼尔虽然有时也憎恨这种居无定所的生活,却也从小耳濡目染,血液中融进了对于戏剧的一手感觉。后来,奥尼尔在普林斯顿大学读过一年书,并在哈佛大学听过一年乔治·皮尔斯·贝克的著名的戏剧课;他十分喜欢尼采、叔本华、王尔德、波德莱尔、斯特林堡等作家。他也通过在世界各地的流浪和冒险经历,取得了丰富的生活体验。

奥尼尔从1913年开始创作,到1943年收笔,一共创作了50个剧本。他早期的剧作大多以大海为主题,真实地表现了海员的艰苦生活和他们对大海和陆地的复杂情感。他乐于尝试新的题材和表现手法:《琼斯皇帝》(1920)和《毛猿》(1922)运用了表现主义手法;《奇异的插曲》(1928)中有大量的意识流成分;《上帝的儿女都有翅膀》(1924)和《大神布朗》(1926)则利用面具揭示出人物的双重性格和内心的挣扎。奥尼尔对不同的文化成分十分敏感:《马可百万》(1928)对中国文化形象进行了美国式的塑造;《悲悼》(1931)将古希腊题材移植到新英格兰加以本土化改造。他后期的作品《送冰的人来了》(1939)和《进入黑夜的漫长旅程》(1956)是悲剧杰作。

奥尼尔剧作不断获得舞台重演,多部作品被改编成电影和电视作品。其中,被改编成电影的作品包括《安娜·克里斯蒂》(1923年的无声片;1930年由嘉宝主演的有声片)、《奇异的插曲》(1932)、《琼斯皇帝》(1933)、《啊,荒野!》(1935)、《漫长的返航》(1940)、《毛猿》(1944)、《悲悼》(1947)、《榆树下的欲望》(1958)、《送冰的人来了》(1973)、《进入黑夜的漫长旅程》(1962;1996)。

Long Day's Journey into Night

（第四幕选段）

TYRONE: (*Mechanically*) Drink hearty, lad. (*They drink. Tyrone again listens to sounds upstairs-with dread*) She's moving around a lot. I hope to God she doesn't come down.

EDMUND: (*Dully*)Yes. She'll be nothing but a ghost haunting the past by this time. (*He pauses—then miserably*) Back before I was born—

TYRONE: Doesn't she do the same with me? Back before she ever knew me.① You'd think the only happy days she's ever known were in her father's home, or at the Convent, praying and playing the piano. (*Jealous resentment in his bitterness*) As I've told you before, you must take her memories with a grain of salt②. Her wonderful home was ordinary enough. Her father wasn't the great, generous, noble Irish gentleman she makes out. He was a nice enough man, good company and a good talker. I liked him and he liked me. He was prosperous enough, too, in his wholesale grocery business, an able man. But he had his weakness. She condemns my drinking but she forgets his. It's true he never touched a drop till he was forty, but after that he made up for lost time. He became a steady champagne drinker, the worst kind. That was his grand pose, to drink only champagne. Well, it finished him quick—that and the consumption③—(*He stops with a guilty glance at his son.*)

EDMUND: (*Sardonically*) We don't seem able to avoid unpleasant topics, do we?

TYRONE: (*Sighs sadly*) No. (*Then with a pathetic attempt at heartiness*) What do you say to a game or two of casino, lad?

---

① 詹姆斯·蒂龙和小儿子埃德蒙正在谈论玛丽，父子两人似乎很有默契。埃德蒙刚说"在我出生之前"，詹姆斯马上就明白他的意思；如果不是因为生他而被庸医染上毒瘾，玛丽现在还会很幸福。所以，詹姆斯忙说，"她在认识我之前"才过着幸福的生活。

② with a grain / pinch of salt：with reservations, doubtfully, suspiciously, disbelievingly.

③ consumption：肺结核。埃德蒙也患有肺结核，詹姆斯无意中又提到这种当时的不治之症，所以感到内疚。

EDMUND: All right.

TYRONE: (*Shuffling the cards clumsily*) We can't lock up and go to bed till Jamie comes on the last trolley—which I hope he won't—and I don't want to go upstairs, anyway, till she's asleep.

EDMUND: Neither do I.

TYRONE: (*Keeps shuffling the cards fumblingly, forgetting to deal them*) As I was saying, you must take her tales of the past with a grain of salt. The piano playing and her dream of becoming a concert pianist. That was put in her head by the nuns flattering her. She was their pet. They loved her for being so devout. They're innocent women, anyway, when it comes to the world.① They don't know that not one in a million who shows promise ever rises to concert playing. Not that your mother didn't play well for a schoolgirl, but that's no reason to take it for granted she could have—

EDMUND: (*Sharply*) Why don't you deal, if we're going to play.

TYRONE: Eh? I am. (*Dealing with very uncertain judgment of distance*) And the idea she might have become a nun. That's the worst. Your mother was one of the most beautiful girls you could ever see. She knew it, too. She was a bit of a rogue and a coquette,② God bless her, behind all her shyness and blushes. She was never made to renounce the world. She was bursting with health and high spirits and the love of loving.

EDMUND: For God's sake, Papa! Why don't you pick up your hand?③

TYRONE: (*Picks it up—dully*) Yes, let's see what I have here. (*They both stare at their cards unseeingly. Then they both start. Tyrone whispers*) Listen!

EDMUND: She's coming downstairs.

TYRONE: (*Hurriedly*) We'll play our game. Pretend not to notice and she'll soon go up again.

EDMUND: (*Staring through the front parlor—with relief*) I don't see her. She must have started down and then turned back.

TYRONE: Thank God.

---

① come to: to be a question of. "如果涉及到人情世故，她们倒真是些不谙世事的女人"

② She was a bit of a rogue and a coquette.: 她有点调皮和调情。

③ Why don't you pick up your hand?: 你为什么不抓牌？

EDMUND: Yes. It's pretty horrible to see her the way she must be now. (*With bitter misery*) The hardest thing to take is the blank wall she builds around her.① Or it's more like a bank of fog in which she hides and loses herself. Deliberately, that's hell of it! You know something in her does it deliberately—to get beyond our reach, to be rid of us, to forget we're alive! It's as if, in spite of loving us, she hated us!

TYRONE: (*Remonstrates gently*) Now, now, lad. It's not her. It's the damned poison②.

EDMUND: (*Bitterly*) She takes it to get that effect. At least, I know she did this time! (*Abruptly*) My play, isn't it? Here. (*He plays a card.*)

TYRONE: (*Plays mechanically—gently reproachful*) She's been terribly frightened about your illness, for all her pretending. Don't be too hard on her, lad. Remember she's not responsible. Once that cursed poison gets a hold on anyone—

EDMUND: (*His face grows hard and he stares at his father with bitter accusation*) It never should have gotten a hold on her! I know damned well she's not to blame! And I know who is! You are! Your damned stinginess! If you'd spent money for a decent doctor when she was so sick after I was born, she'd never have known morphine existed! Instead you put her in the hands of a hotel quack who wouldn't admit his ignorance and took the easiest way out, not giving a damn what happened to her afterwards! All because his fee was cheap! Another one of your bargains!

TYRONE: (*Stung—angrily*) Be quiet! How dare you talk of something you know nothing about! (*Trying to control his temper*) You must try to see my side of it, too, lad. How was I to know he was that kind of a doctor? He had a good reputation—

EDMUND: Among the souses in the hotel bar, I suppose!

TYRONE: That's a lie! I asked the hotel proprietor to recommend the best—

EDMUND: Yes! At the same time crying poorhouse and making it plain you wanted a cheap one! I know your system!③ By God, I ought to after this afternoon!

---

① The hardest thing to take is the blank wall she builds around her.：最难接受她在自己四周建起的无形墙壁。
② poison：指毒品。
③ I know your system!：我知道你那一套！

TYRONE: (*Guiltily defensive*) What about this afternoon?
EDMUND: Never mind now. We're talking about Mama! I'm saying no matter how you excuse yourself you know damned well your stinginess is to blame—
TYRONE: And I say you're a liar! Shut your mouth right now, or—
EDMUND: (*Ignoring this*) After you found out she'd been made a morphine addict, why didn't you send her to a cure then, at the start, while she still had a chance? No, that would have meant spending some money! I'll bet you told her all she had to do was use a little will power! That's what you still believe in your heart, in spite of what doctors, who really know something about it, have told you!
TYRONE: You lie again! I know better than that now! But how was I to know then? What did I know of morphine? It was years before I discovered what was wrong. I thought she'd never got over her sickness, that's all. Why didn't I send her to a cure, you say? (*Bitterly*) Haven't I? I've spent thousands upon thousands in cures! A waste. What good have they done her? She always started again.
EDMUND: Because you've never given her anything that would help her want to stay off it! No home except this summer dump in a place she hates and you've refused even to spend money to make this look decent, while you keep buying more property, and playing sucker for every con man with a gold mine, or a silver mine, or any kind of get—rich—quick swindle! You've dragged her around on the road, season after season, on one—night stands, with no one she could talk to, waiting night after night in dirty hotel rooms for you to come back with a bun on① after the bars closed! Christ, is it any wonder she didn't want to be cured. Jesus, when I think of it I hate your guts②!
TYRONE: (*Strickenly*) Edmund! (*Then in a rage*) How dare you talk to your father like that, you insolent young cub! After all I've done for you.
EDMUND: We'll come to that, what you're doing for me!
TYRONE: (*Looking guilty again—ignores this*) Will you stop repeating your mother's crazy accusations, which she never makes unless it's the

---

① with a bun on：(俚)醉醺醺地。
② hate one's guts：极端仇恨某人。

poison talking? I never dragged her on the road against her will. Naturally, I wanted her with me. I loved her. And she came because she loved me and wanted to be with me. That's the truth, no matter what she says when she's not herself. And she needn't have been lonely. There was always the members of my company to talk to, if she'd wanted. She had her children, too, and I insisted, in spite of the expense, on having a nurse to travel with her.

EDMUND: (*Bitterly*) Yes, your one generosity, and that because you were jealous of her paying too much attention to us, and wanted us out of your way! It was another mistake, too! If she'd had to take care of me all by herself, and had that to occupy her mind, maybe she'd have been able—

TYRONE: (*Goaded into vindictiveness*) Or for that matter, if you insist on judging things by what she says when she's not in her right mind, if you hadn't been born she'd never—(*He stops ashamed.*)

EDMUND: (*Suddenly spent and miserable*) Sure. I know that's what she feels, Papa.

TYRONE: (*Protests penitently*) She doesn't! She loves you as dearly as ever mother loved a son! I only said that because you put me in such a God—damned rage, raking up the past, and saying you hate me—

EDMUND: (*Dully*) I didn't mean it, Papa. (*He suddenly smiles—kidding a bit drunkenly*) I'm like Mama, I can't help liking you, in spite of everything.

TYRONE: (*Grins a bit drunkenly in return*) I might say the same of you. You're no great shakes① as a son. It's a case of "A poor thing but mine own."② (*They both chuckle with real, if alcoholic, affection. Tyrone changes the subject*) What's happened to our game? Whose play is it?

EDMUND: Yours, I guess. (*Tyrone plays a card which Edmund takes and the game gets forgotten again.*)

TYRONE: You mustn't let yourself be too downhearted, lad, by the bad news you had today. Both the doctors promised me, if you obey orders at

---

① no great shakes：没本事；不算重要。
② 莎士比亚剧作《皆大欢喜》(V.iv.57—58)中的台词。

this place you're going, you'll be cured in six months, or a year at most.

EDMUND: (*His face hard again*) Don't kid me. You don't believe that.

TYRONE: (*Too vehemently*) Of course I believe it! Why shouldn't I believe it when both Hardy and the specialist—?

EDMUND: You think I'm going to die.

TYRONE: That's a lie! You're crazy!

EDMUND: —(*More bitterly*) So why waste money? That's why you're sending me to a state farm—

TYRONE: (*In guilty confusion*) What state farm? It's the Hilltown Sanatorium, that's all I know, and both doctors said it was the best place for you.

EDMUND: (*Scathingly*) For the money! That is, for nothing, or practically nothing. Don't lie, Papa! You know damned well Hilltown Sanatorium is a state institution! Jamie suspected you'd cry poorhouse to Hardy and he wormed the truth out of him.

TYRONE: (*Furiously*) That drunken loafer! I'll kick him out in the gutter! He's poisoned your mind against me ever since you were old enough to listen!

EDMUND: You can't deny it's the truth about the state farm, can you?

TYRONE: It's not true the way you look at it! What if it is run by the state? That's nothing against it. The state has the money to make a better place than any private sanatorium. And why shouldn't I take advantage of it? It's my right—and yours. We're residents. I'm a property owner. I help to support it. I'm taxed to death—

EDMUND: (*With bitter irony*) Yes, on property valued at a quarter of a million.

TYRONE: Lies! It's all mortgaged!

EDMUND: Hardy and the specialist know what you're worth. I wonder what they thought of you when they heard you moaning poorhouse and showing you wanted to wish me on charity!

TYRONE: It's a lie! All I told them was I couldn't afford any millionaire's sanatorium because I was land poor①. That's the truth!

EDMUND: And then you went to the Club to meet McGuire and let him stick you with another bum piece of property! (*As Tyrone starts to deny*)

---

① land poor (一般为 land-poor)：土地多而收入少的；因支付高额土地税而导致经济困难的。

Don't lie about it! We met McGuire in the hotel bar after he left you. Jamie kidded him about hooking you, and he winked and laughed!

TYRONE: (*Lying feebly*) He's a liar if he said—

EDMUND: Don't lie about it! (*With gathering intensity*) God, Papa, ever since I went to sea and was on my own, and found out what hard work for little pay was, and what it felt like to be broke, and starve, and camp on park benches because I had no place to sleep. I've tried to be fair to you because I knew what you'd been up against as a kid. I've tried to make allowances. Christ, you have to make allowances in this damned family or go nuts! I have tried to make allowances for myself when I remember all the rotten stuff I've pulled! I've tried to feel like Mama that you can't help being what you are where money is concerned. But God Almighty, this last stunt of yours is too much! It makes me want to puke! Not because of the rotten way you're treating me. To hell with that! I've treated you rottenly, in my way, more than once. But to think when it's a question of your son having consumption, you can show yourself up before the whole town as such a stinking old tightwad! Don't you know Hardy will talk and the whole damned town will know! Jesus, Papa, haven't you any pride or shame? (*Bursting with rage*) And don't think I'll let you get away with it! I won't go to any damned state farm just to save you a few lousy dollars to buy more bum property with! You stinking old miser—! (*He chokes huskily, his voice trembling with rage, and then is shaken by a fit of coughing.*)

TYRONE: (*Has shrunk back in his chair under this attack, his guilty contrition greater than his anger. He stammers*) Be quiet! Don't say that to me! You're drunk! I won't mind you. Stop coughing, lad. You've got yourself worked up over nothing. Who said you had to go to this Hilltown place? You can go anywhere you like. I don't give a damn what it costs. All I care about is to have you get well. Don't call me a stinking miser, just because I don't want doctors to think I'm a millionaire they can swindle. (*Edmund has stopped coughing. He looks sick and weak. His father stares at him frightenedly*) You look weak, lad. You'd better take a bracer.

EDMUND: (*Grabs the bottle and pours his glass brimful—weakly*) Thanks. (*He gulps down the whiskey.*)

TYRONE: (*Pours himself a big drink, which empties the bottle, and drinks it. His head bows and he stares dully at the cards on the table—vaguely*) Whose play is it? (*He goes on dully, without resentment*) A stinking old miser. Well, maybe you're right. Maybe I can't help being, although all my life since I had anything I've thrown money over the bar to buy drinks for everyone in the house, or loaned money to sponges I knew would never pay it back—(*With a loose-mouthed sneer of self-contempt*) But, of course, that was in barrooms, when I was full of whiskey. I can't feel that way about it when I'm sober in my home. It was at home I first learned the value of a dollar and the fear of the poorhouse. I've never been able to believe in my luck since. I've always feared it would change and everything I had would be taken away. But still, the more property you own, the safer you think you are. That may not be logical, but it's the way I have to feel. Banks fail, and your money's gone, but you think you can keep land beneath your feet. (*Abruptly his tone becomes scornfully superior*) You said you realized what I'd been up against as a boy. The hell you do! How could you? You've had everything—nurses, schools, college, though you didn't stay there. You've had food, clothing. Oh I know you had a fling of hard work with your back and hands, a bit of being homeless and penniless in a foreign land, and I respect you for it. But it was a game of romance and adventure to you. It was play.

EDMUND: (*Dully sarcastic*) Yes, particularly the time I tried to commit suicide at Jimmie the Priest's, and almost did.

TYRONE: You weren't in your right mind. No son of mine would ever—You were drunk.

EDMUND: I was stone cold sober. That was the trouble. I'd stopped to think too long.

TYRONE: (*With drunken peevishness*) Don't start your damned atheist morbidness again! I don't care to listen. I was trying to make plain to you—(*Scornfully*) What do you know of the value of a dollar?

When I was ten my father deserted my mother and went back to Ireland to die. Which he did soon enough, and deserved to, and I hope he's roasting in hell. He mistook rat poison for flour, or sugar, or something. There was gossip it wasn't by mistake but that's a lie. No one in my family ever—

EDMUND: My bet is, it wasn't by mistake.

TYRONE: More morbidness! Your brother put that in your head. The worst he can suspect is the only truth for him. But never mind. My mother was left, a stranger in a strange land, with four small children, me and a sister a little older and two younger than me. My two older brothers had moved to other parts. They couldn't help. They were hard put to it① to keep themselves alive. There was no damned romance in our poverty. Twice we were evicted from the miserable hovel we called home, with my mother's few sticks of furniture thrown out in the street, and my mother and sisters crying. I cried, too, though I tried hard not to, because I was the man of the family. At ten years old! There was no more school for me. I worked twelve hours a day in a machine shop, learning to make files. A dirty barn of a place where rain dripped through the roof, where you roasted in summer, and there was no stove in winter, and your hands got numb with cold, where the only light came through two small filthy windows, so on grey days I'd have to sit bent over with my eyes almost touching the files in order to see! You talk of work! And what do you think I got for it? Fifty cents a week! It's the truth! Fifty cents a week! And my poor mother washed and scrubbed for the Yanks by the day, and my older sister sewed, and my two younger stayed at home to keep the house. We never had clothes enough to wear, nor enough food to eat. Well I remember one Thanksgiving, or maybe it was Christmas, when some Yank in whose house mother had been scrubbing gave her a dollar extra for a present, and on the way home she spent it all on food. I can remember her hugging and kissing us and saying with tears of joy running down her tired face: "Glory be to God, for once in our lives we'll have enough for each

---

① hard put to it: 陷入困境；几乎无法。

of us!" (*He wipes tears from his eyes.*) A fine, brave, sweet woman. There never was a braver or finer.

EDMUND: (*Moved.*) Yes, she must have been.

TYRONE: Her one fear was she'd get old and sick and have to die in the poorhouse. (*He pauses—then adds with grim humor*) It was in those days l learned to be a miser. A dollar was worth so much then. And once you've learned a lesson, it's hard to unlearn it. You have to look for bargains. If I took this state farm sanatorium for a good bargain, you'll have to forgive me. The doctors did tell me it's a good place. You must believe that, Edmund. And I swear I never meant you to go there if you didn't want to. (*Vehemently*) You can choose any place you like! Never mind what it costs! Any place I can afford. Any place you like—within reason. (*At this qualification, a grin twitches Edmund's lips. His resentment has gone. His father goes on with an elaborately offhand, casual air.*) There was another sanatorium the specialist recommended. He said it had a record as good as any place in the country. It's endowed by a group of millionaire factory owners, for the benefit of their workers principally, but you're eligible to go there because you're a resident. There's such a pile of money behind it, they don't have to charge much. It's only seven dollars a week but you get ten times that value. (*Hastily*) I don't want to persuade you to anything, understand. I'm simply repeating what l was told.

EDMUND: (*Concealing his smile—casually*) Oh, I know that. It sounds like a good bargain to me. I'd like to go there. So that settles that. (*Abruptly he is miserably desperate again—dully*) It doesn't matter a damn now, anyway. Let's forget it! (*Changing the subject*) How about our game? Whose play is it?

TYRONE: (*Mechanically*) I don't know. Mine, I guess. No, it's yours. (*Edmund plays a card. His father takes it. Then about to play from his hand, he again forgets the game.*) Yes, maybe life overdid the lesson for me, and made a dollar worth too much and the time came when that mistake ruined my career as a fine actor. (*Sadly*) I've never admitted this to anyone before, lad, but tonight I'm so heartsick I

feel at the end of everything, and what's the use of fake pride and pretense. That God—damned play I bought for a song① and made such a great success in—a great money success—it ruined me with its promise of an easy fortune. I didn't want to do anything else, and by the time I woke up to the fact I'd become a slave to the damned thing and did try other plays, it was too late. They had identified me with that one part, and didn't want me in anything else. They were right, too. I'd lost the great talent I once had through years of easy repetition, never learning a new part, never really working hard. Thirty-five to forty thousand dollars net profit a season like snapping your fingers! It was too great a temptation. Yet before I bought the damned thing I was considered one of the three or four young actors with the greatest artistic promise in America. I'd worked like hell. I'd left a good job as a machinist to take supers'② parts because I loved the theater. I was wild with ambition. I read all the plays ever written. I studied Shakespeare as you'd study the Bible. I educated myself. I got rid of an Irish brogue you could cut with a knife③. I loved Shakespeare. I would have acted in any of his plays for nothing, for the joy of being alive in his great poetry. And I acted well in him. I felt inspired by him. I could have been a great Shakespearean actor, if I'd kept on. I know that! In 1874 when Edwin Booth④ came to the theater in Chicago where I was leading man, I played Cassius to his Brutus one night, Brutus to his Cassius the next, Othello to his Iago, and so on. The first night I played Othello, he said to our manager, "That young man is playing Othello better than I ever did!" (*Proudly*) That from Booth, the greatest actor of his day or any other! And it was true! And I was only twenty-seven years old! As I look back on it now, that night was the high spot in my career. I had life where I wanted it! And for a time after that I kept on upward with ambition high. Married your mother.

---

① for a song：花很少钱。1883 年，詹姆斯·奥尼尔买下了查尔斯·菲克纳改编的大仲马小说《基督山伯爵》的戏剧演出权，随后长期扮演该剧的男主人公，从而放弃了成为莎士比亚剧作演员的机会。

② super= supernumerary：跑龙套的配角。

③ an Irish brogue you could cut with a knife：浓重得都可以用刀割的爱尔兰口音。

④ Edwin Booth (1833—1893)：美国戏剧演员，被认为是当时最出色的哈姆莱特扮演者。

Ask her what I was like in those days. Her love was an added incentive to ambition. But a few years later my good bad luck made me find the big money-maker. It wasn't that in my eyes at first. It was a great romantic part I knew I could play better than anyone. But it was a great box office success from the start—and then life had me where it wanted me①—at from thirty-five to forty thousand net profit a season! A fortune in those days—or even in these. (*Bitterly*) What the hell was it I wanted to buy, I wonder, that was worth— Well, no matter. It's a late day for regrets. (*He glances vaguely at his cards.*) My play, isn't it?

EDMUND: (*Moved, stares at his father with understanding—slowly*) I'm glad you've told me this, Papa. I know you a lot better now.

TYRONE: (*With a loose, twisted smile*) Maybe I shouldn't have told you. Maybe you'll only feel more contempt for me. And it's a poor way to convince you of the value of a dollar. (*Then as if this phrase automatically aroused an habitual association in his mind, he glances up at the chandelier disapprovingly.*) The glare from those extra lights hurts my eyes. You don't mind if I turn them out, do you? We don't need them, and there's no use making the Electric Company rich.

EDMUND: (*Controlling a wild impulse to laugh—agreeably*) No, sure not. Turn them out.

TYRONE: (*Gets heavily and a bit waveringly to his feet and gropes uncertainly for the lights—his mind going back to its line of thought*) No, I don't know what the hell it was I wanted to buy. (*He clicks out one bulb.*) On my solemn oath, Edmund, I'd gladly face not having an acre of land to call my own, nor a penny in the bank— (*He clicks out another bulb.*) I'd be willing to have no home but the poorhouse in my old age if I could look back now on having been the fine artist I might have been. (*He turns out the third bulb, so only the reading lamp is on, and sits down again heavily. Edmund suddenly cannot hold back a burst of strained, ironical laughter. Tyrone is hurt.*) What the devil are you laughing at?

---

① I had life where I wanted it... life had me where it wanted me：我想让生活怎样，生活就会怎样……生活想要我怎样，我就得必须怎样。

EDMUND: Not at you, Papa. At life. It's so damned crazy.

TYRONE: (*growls*) More of your morbidness! There's nothing wrong with life. It's we who—(*He quotes*) "The fault, dear Brutus, is not in our stars, but in ourselves that we are underlings."① (*He pauses—then sadly*) The praise Edwin Booth gave my Othello. I made the manager put down his exact words in writing. I kept it in my wallet for years. I used to read it every once in a while until finally it made me feel so bad I didn't want to face it any more. Where is it now, I wonder? Somewhere in this house. I remember I put it away carefully—

EDMUND: (*With a wry ironical sadness*) It might be in an old trunk in the attic, along with Mama's wedding dress. (*Then as his father stares at him, he adds quickly*) For Pete's sake, if we're going to play cards, let's play. (*He takes the card his father had played and leads. For a moment, they play the game, like mechanical chess players. Then Tyrone stops, listening to a sound upstairs.*)

TYRONE: She's still moving around. God knows when she'll go to sleep.

EDMUND: (*pleads tensely*) For Christ's sake, Papa, forget it! (*He reaches out and pours a drink. Tyrone starts to protest, then gives it up. Edmund drinks. He puts down the glass. His expression changes. When he speaks it is as if he were deliberately giving way to drunkenness and seeking to hide behind a maudlin manner.*) Yes, she moves above and beyond us, a ghost haunting the past, and here we sit pretending to forget, but straining our ears listening for the slightest sound, hearing the fog drip from the eaves like the uneven tick of a rundown, crazy clock—or like the dreary tears of a trollop spattering in a puddle of stale beer on a honky-tonk table top②! (*He laughs with maudlin appreciation.*) Not so bad, that last, eh? Original, not Baudelaire③. Give me credit! (*Then with alcoholic talkativeness*) You've just told me some high spots in your memories. Want to hear mine? They're all connected with the sea. Here's one. When I was on the Squarehead④ square rigger,

---

① 见莎士比亚《裘力斯·凯撒》第一幕第二场。

② or like the dreary tears of a trollop spattering in a puddle of stale beer on a honky-tonk table top：或者像下等夜总会里妓女清然而下的泪水溅在桌上走了气的啤酒里（汪义群译文）。

③ Baudelaire：波德莱尔(1821—67)：法国诗人和批评家，以诗集《恶之花》(1857)而闻名于世。

④ Sqaurehead 号横帆船。

bound for Buenos Aires. Full moon in the Trades①. The old hooker driving fourteen knots. I lay on the bowsprit, facing astern, with the water foaming into spume under me, the masts with every sail white in the moonlight, towering high above me. I became drunk with the beauty and singing rhythm of it, and for a moment I lost myself—actually lost my life. I was set free! I dissolved in the sea, became white sails and flying spray, became beauty and rhythm, became moonlight and the ship and the high dim-starred sky! I belonged, without past or future, within peace and unity and a wild joy, within some thing greater than my own life, or the life of Man, to Life itself! To God, if you want to put it that way. Then another time, on the American Line②, when I was lookout on the crow's nest③ in the dawn watch. A calm sea, that time. Only a lazy ground swell④ and a slow drowsy roll of the ship. The passengers asleep and none of the crew in sight. No sound of man. Black smoke pouring from the funnels behind and beneath me. Dreaming, not keeping lookout, feeling alone, and above, and apart, watching the dawn creep like a painted dream over the sky and sea which slept together. Then the moment of ecstatic freedom came. The peace, the end of the quest, the last harbor, the joy of belonging to a fulfillment beyond men's lousy, pitiful, greedy fears and hopes and dreams! And several other times in my life, when I was swimming far out, or lying alone on a beach, I have had the same experience. Became the sun, the hot sand, green seaweed anchored to a rock, swaying in the tide. Like a saint's vision of beatitude. Like the veil of things as they seem drawn back by an unseen hand. For a second you see—and seeing the secret, are the secret. ⑤ For a second there is meaning! Then the hand lets the veil fall and you are alone, lost in the fog again, and you stumble on toward nowhere, for no good reason! (*He grins wryly.*) It was a great mistake, my being born a man, I would have

---

① 贸易风;信风

② the American Line：美国轮船公司。

③ crow's nest：桅上了望台。

④ ground swell：涌浪。

⑤ For a second you see—and seeing the secret, are the secret.：瞬息之间，你具有了观察力——你看到秘密，也就成为秘密本身。

been much more successful as a sea gull or a fish. As it is, I will always be a stranger who never feels at home, who does not really want and is not really wanted, who can never belong, who must always be a little in love with death!

TYRONE: (*Stares at him—impressed.*) Yes, there's the makings of a poet in you all right. (*Then protesting uneasily.*) But that's morbid craziness about not being wanted and loving death.

EDMUND: (*Sardonically.*) The makings of a poet. No, I'm afraid I'm like the guy who is always panhandling for a smoke. He hasn't even got the makings. He's got only the habit. I couldn't touch what I tried to tell you just now. I just stammered. That's the best I'll ever do, I mean, if I live. Well, it will be faithful realism, at least. Stammering is the native eloquence of us fog people. (*A pause. Then they both jump startledly as there is a noise from outside the house, as if someone had stumbled and fallen on the front steps. Edmund grins.*) Well, that sounds like the absent brother. He must have a peach[①] of a bun on.

TYRONE: (*Scowling.*) That loafer! He caught the last car, bad luck to it. (*He gets to his feet.*) Get him to bed, Edmund. I'll go out on the porch. He has a tongue like an adder when he's drunk. I'd only lose my temper. (*He goes out the door to the side porch as the front door in the hall bangs shut behind Jamie. Edmund watches with amusement Jamie's wavering progress through the front parlor. Jamie comes in. He is very drunk and woozy on his legs. His eyes are glassy, his face bloated, his speech blurred, his mouth slack like his father's, a leer on his lips.*)

JAMIE: (*Swaying and blinking in the doorway—in a loud voice.*) What ho! What ho!

EDMUND: (*Sharply.*) Nix on the loud noise![②]

JAMIE: (*Blinks at him.*) Oh, hello, Kid. (*With great seriousness.*) I'm as drunk as a fiddler's bitch[③].

EDMUND: (*Dryly.*) Thanks for telling me your great secret.

---

① peach：十分出色的事物。"他一定醉得够呛"。

② Nix on the loud noise!：别大声喧哗。

③ as drunk as a fiddler：酩酊大醉。Jamie 在这一惯用法后面加上了"bitch"这个不雅之词。

JAMIE: (*Grins foolishly.*) Yes. Unneshesary① information Number One, eh? (*He bends and slaps at the knees of his trousers.*) Had serious accident. The front steps tried to trample on me. Took advantage of fog to waylay me. Ought to be a lighthouse out there. Dark in here, too. (*Scowling.*) What the hell is this, the morgue? Lesh have some light on subjec.② (*He sways forward to the table, reciting Kipling③.*)

"Ford, ford, ford o' Kabul river,

Ford o' Kabul river in the dark!

Keep the crossing-stakes beside you, an' they will surely guide you

'Cross the ford o' Kabul river in the dark."

(*He fumbles at the chandelier and manages to turn on the three bulbs.*) Thash more like it. To hell with old Gaspard④. Where is the old tightwad?

EDMUND: Out on the porch.

JAMIE: Can't expect us to live in the Black Hole of Calcutta⑤. (*His eyes fix on the full bottle of whiskey.*) Say! Have I got the d.t.'s⑥? (*He reaches out fumblingly and grabs it.*) By God, it's real. What's matter with the Old Man tonight? Must be ossified to forget he left this out. Grab opportunity by the forelock.⑦ Key to my success. (*He slops a big drink into a glass.*)

EDMUND: You're stinking now. That will knock you stiff.

JAMIE: Wisdom from the mouth of babes. Can⑧ the wise stuff, Kid. You're still wet behind the ears.⑨ (*He lowers himself into a chair, holding*

---

① Jamie 因醉酒而口齿不清。Unneshesary＝Unnecessary；Lesh＝Let's；Thash＝That's； lash=last； aw right=all right; shatisfied=satisfied; Egzactly=Exactly。

② Lesh have some light on subjec.：让我们把话题挑明。

③ Rudyard Kipling (1865—1936)，英国小说家、诗人。他的诗作 Ford o' Kabul River 描写了第二次英国—阿富汗战争(1878—1880)中，英军在渡过喀布尔河时发生的多人溺水身亡的惨剧。

④ 法国作曲家简·罗伯特·普朗凯特 (1850—1903) 的歌剧《科尔内维尔的钟》(即下文中的 The Bells) 一剧中的吝啬鬼。

⑤ the Black Hole of Calcutta：英国东印度公司在加尔各答的监狱的名称。这座监狱面积约 20 平方米，只有两个小窗户。1756 年 6 月 20 日，孟加拉 (当时为印度莫卧儿帝国的一个部分) 的统治者从英国东印度公司手中夺取了加尔各答。据当时的英国守军将领说，146 名守城的欧洲俘虏被关进这座监狱，其中幸存者只有 23 名。后来，也有人怀疑这一数据，认为监狱里只关押了 64 人，其中 21 人生还。在一些西方人眼里，这一监狱是非人待遇的象征。

⑥ d. t.=delirium tremens，(医) 震战性谵妄

⑦ grab opportunity by the forelock：不让机会溜走。类似的说法还有：take time by the forelock；take occasion by the forelock。

⑧ can：(俚) 停止；放弃。"别玩聪明了"。

⑨ 你还乳臭未干。

the drink carefully aloft.)

EDMUND: All right. Pass out if you want to.

JAMIE: Can't, that's trouble. Had enough to sink a ship, but can't sink. Well, here's hoping. (*He drinks.*)

EDMUND: Shove over the bottle. I'll have one, too.

JAMIE: (*With sudden, big-brotherly solicitude, grabbing the bottle.*) No, you don't. Not while I'm around. Remember doctor's orders. Maybe no one else gives a damn if you die, but I do. My kid brother. I love your guts①, Kid. Everything else is gone. You're all I've got left. (*Pulling bottle closer to him.*) So no booze for you, if I can help it. (*Beneath his drunken sentimentality there is a genuine sincerity.*)

EDMUND: (*Irritably.*) Oh, lay off it.

JAMIE: (*Is hurt and his face hardens.*) You don't believe I care, eh? Just drunken bull. (*He shoves the bottle over.*) All right. Go ahead and kill yourself.

EDMUND: (*Seeing he is hurt—affectionately.*) Sure I know you care, Jamie, and I'm going on the wagon②. But tonight doesn't count. Too many damned things have happened today. (*He pours a drink.*) Here's how. (*He drinks.*)

JAMIE: (*Sobers up momentarily and with a pitying look.*) I know, Kid. It's been a lousy day for you. (*Then with sneering cynicism.*) I'll bet old Gaspard hasn't tried to keep you off booze. Probably give you a case to take with you to the state farm for pauper patients. The sooner you kick the bucket, the less expense. (*With contemptuous hatred.*) What a bastard to have for a father! Christ, if you put him in a book, no one would believe it!

EDMUND: (*Defensively.*) Oh, Papa's all right, if you try to understand him—and keep your sense of humor.

JAMIE: (*Cynically.*) He's been putting on the old sob act for you, eh? He can always kid you. But not me. Never again. (*Then slowly.*) Although, in a way, I do feel sorry for him about one thing. But he

---

① Jamie 将惯用法"hate one's guts"(恨死你了)改为"love one's guts"(爱死你了),以开玩笑的方式表达他对弟弟的感情。

② on the wagon: 发誓戒酒。

has even that coming to him[①]. He's to blame. (*Hurriedly.*) But to hell with that.   (*He grabs the bottle and pours another drink, appearing very drunk again.*) That lash drink's getting me. This one ought to put the lights out.   Did you tell Gaspard I got it out of Doc Hardy this sanatorium is a charity dump?

EDMUND: (*Reluctantly.*) Yes. I told him I wouldn't go there. It's all settled now. He said I can go anywhere I want. (*He adds, smiling without resentment.*) Within reason, of course.

JAMIE: (*Drunkenly imitating his father.*) Of course, lad. Anything within reason. (*Sneering.*) That means another cheap dump. Old Gaspard, the miser in "The Bells," that's a part he can play without make—up.

EDMUND: (*Irritably.*) Oh, shut up, will you. I've heard that Gaspard stuff a million times.

JAMIE: (*Shrugs his shoulders—thickly.*) Aw right, if you're shatisfied—let him get away with it. It's your funeral—I mean, I hope it won't be.

EDMUND: (*Changing the subject.*)   What did you do uptown tonight?   Go to Mamie Burns?

JAMIE: (*Very drunk, his head nodding.*) Sure thing. Where else could I find suitable feminine companionship?   And love.   Don't forget love. What is a man without a good woman's love?   A God—damned hollow shell.

EDMUND: (*Chuckles tipsily, letting himself go now and be drunk.*) You're a nut.

JAMIE: (*Quotes with gusto from Oscar Wilde's "The Harlot's House."*)[②]
"Then, turning to my love, I said,
'The dead are dancing with the dead,
The dust is whirring with the dust.'

But she—she heard the violin,
And left my side and entered in:
Love passed into the house of lust.

[①] 不过连这件事也要算在他头上。

[②] Oscar Wilde (1854—1900)：爱尔兰小说家、诗人、剧作家。他的诗作 The Harlot's House 有 12 诗节, 诗中"妓女之家"中幽灵般的居民随着斯特劳斯的华尔兹舞曲"真挚的爱心"翩翩起舞, 但爱情已经为性欲所淹没。

Then suddenly the tune went false,
The dancers wearied of the waltz..."
(*He breaks off, thickly.*) Not strictly accurate. If my love was with me, I didn't notice it. She must have been a ghost. (*He pauses.*) Guess which one of Mamie's charmers① I picked to bless me with her woman's love. It'll hand you a laugh, Kid. I picked Fat Violet.

EDMUND: (*Laughs drunkenly.*) No, honest? Some pick! God, she weighs a ton. What the hell for, a joke?

JAMIE: No joke. Very serious. By the time I hit Mamie's dump I felt very sad about myself and all the other poor bums in the world. Ready for a weep on any old womanly bosom. You know how you get when John Barleycorn② turns on the soft music inside you. Then, soon as I got in the door, Mamie began telling me all her troubles. Beefed③ how rotten business was, and she was going to give Fat Violet the gate. Customers didn't fall for Vi④. Only reason she'd kept her was she could play the piano. Lately Vi's gone on drunks and been too boiled⑤ to play, and was eating her out of house and home, and although Vi was a goodhearted dumbbell, and she felt sorry for her because she didn't know how the hell she'd make a living, still business was business, and she couldn't afford to run a home for fat tarts. Well, that made me feel sorry for Fat Violet, so I squandered two bucks of your dough to escort her upstairs. With no dishonorable intentions whatever. I like them fat, but not that fat. All I wanted was a little heart—to—heart talk concerning the infinite sorrow of life.

EDMUND: (*Chuckles drunkenly.*) Poor Vi! I'll bet you recited Kipling and Swinburne⑥ and Dowson⑦ and gave her "I have been faithful to thee, Cynara, in my fashion."

---

① 迷人的女人。指 Mamie Burns 妓院的妓女。
② John Barleycorn：大麦约翰(啤酒等含酒精饮料的拟人化名称)。
③ Beef (俚)：抱怨。
④ Vi: 即 Violet。
⑤ Boiled (俚)：醉酒。
⑥ Swinburne (1837—1909), 英国诗人和批评家。
⑦ Dowson (1867—1900), 英国颓废派抒情诗人。"I have been faithful to thee, Cynara, in my fashion"是他的一首诗作中的著名叠句。Cynara 在她父亲的饭店里做服务员；Dowson 爱上了她，但她却无法理解 Dowson 的爱，最后嫁给她父亲饭店里的一位男服务员。

JAMIE: (*Grins loosely.*) Sure—with the Old Master, John Barleycorn, playing soft music. She stood it for a while. Then she got good and① sore. Got the idea I took her upstairs for a joke. Gave me a grand bawling out. Said she was better than a drunken bum who recited poetry. Then she began to cry. So I had to say I loved her because she was fat, and she wanted to believe that, and I stayed with her to prove it, and that cheered her up, and she kissed me when I left, and said she'd fallen hard for me, and we both cried a little more in the hallway, and everything was fine, except Mamie Burns thought I'd gone bughouse.

EDMUND: (*Quotes derisively.*)
"Harlots and
Hunted have pleasures of their own to give,
The vulgar herd can never understand."②

JAMIE: (*Nods his head drunkenly.*) Egzactly! Hell of a good time, at that.③ You should have stuck around with me, Kid. Mamie Burns inquired after you. Sorry to hear you were sick. She meant it, too. (*He pauses—then with maudlin humor, in a ham-actor tone.*) This night has opened my eyes to a great career in store for me, my boy! I shall give the art of acting back to the performing seals, which are its most perfect expression. By applying my natural God-given talents in their proper sphere, I shall attain the pinnacle of success! I'll be the lover of the fat woman in Barnum and Bailey's circus④! (*Edmund laughs. Jamie's mood changes to arrogant disdain.*) Pah! Imagine me sunk to the fat girl in a hick town hooker shop! Me! Who have made some of the best-lookers on Broadway sit up and beg! (*He quotes from Kipling's "Sestina of the Tramp—Royal."*)
"Speakin' in general, I 'ave tried 'em all,
The 'appy roads that take you o'er the world."⑤

---

① Good and: very; entirely.
② 波德莱尔《巴黎的忧郁》中的诗句,引自 Symons 的英译。
③ Hell of a good time, at that.: 也算是大大地开心一场。At that: regardless of what has been said or implied。
④ 由 Phineas Taylor 和 James Bailey 于 1881 年共同创建的著名的马戏团。
⑤ Kipling 的诗作"流浪皇族的六节诗"用伦敦方言写成,诗中的叙事者鼓吹四处漂泊、追求各种冒险和体验的生活。I'ave=I have; 'appy=happy。

| | (*With sodden melancholy.*) Not so apt. Happy roads is bunk①. Weary roads is right. Get you nowhere fast. That's where I've got—nowhere. Where everyone lands in the end, even if most of the suckers won't admit it. |

EDMUND: (*Derisively.*) Can it! You'll be crying in a minute.

JAMIE: (*Starts and stares at his brother for a second with bitter hostility—thickly.*) Don't get—too damned fresh. (*Then abruptly.*) But you're right. To hell with repining! Fat Violet's a good kid. Glad I stayed with her. Christian act. Cured her blues. Hell of a good time. You should have stuck with me, Kid. Taken your mind off your troubles. What's the use coming home to get the blues over what can't be helped. All over—finished now—not a hope! (*He stops, his head nodding drunkenly, his eyes closing—then suddenly he looks up, his face hard, and quotes jeeringly.*)

"If I were hanged on the highest hill,
Mother o' mine, O mother o' mine!
I know whose love would follow me still …"②

EDMUND: (*Violently.*) Shut up!

JAMIE: (*In a cruel, sneering tone with hatred in it.*) Where's the hophead? Gone to sleep? (*Edmund jerks as if he'd been struck. There is a tense silence. Edmund's face looks stricken and sick. Then in a burst of rage he springs from his chair.*)

EDMUND: You dirty bastard! (*He punches his brother in the face, a blow that glances off the cheekbone. For a second Jamie reacts pugnaciously and half rises from his chair to do battle, but suddenly he seems to sober up to a shocked realization of what he has said and he sinks back limply.*)

JAMIE: (*Miserably.*) Thanks, Kid. I certainly had that coming③. Don't know what made me—booze talking—You know me, Kid.

EDMUND: (*His anger ebbing.*) I know you'd never say that unless—But God, Jamie, no matter how drunk you are, it's no excuse! (*He pauses—miserably.*) I'm sorry I hit you. You and I never scrap—

---

① bunk: 废话；空话。
② 这是 Kipling 为他自己的小说《湮灭之光》(*The Light that Failed*)所作的题诗的一部分。
③ have that / it coming: 得到应得的东西。

that bad. (*He sinks back on his chair.*)

JAMIE: (*Huskily.*) It's all right. Glad you did. My dirty tongue. Like to cut it out. (*He hides his face in his hands—dully.*) I suppose it's because I feel so damned sunk. Because this time Mama had me fooled. I really believed she had it licked. She thinks I always believe the worst, but this time I believed the best. (*His voice flutters.*) I suppose I can't forgive her—yet. It meant so much. I'd begun to hope, if she'd beaten the game, I could, too. (*He begins to sob, and the horrible part of his weeping is that it appears sober, not the maudlin tears of drunkenness.*)

EDMUND: (*Blinking back tears himself.*) God, don't I know how you feel! Stop it, Jamie!

JAMIE: (*Trying to control his sobs.*) I've known about Mama so much longer than you. Never forget the first time I got wise. Caught her in the act with a hypo.① Christ, I'd never dreamed before that any women but whores took dope! (*He pauses.*) And then this stuff of you getting consumption. It's got me licked. We've been more than brothers. You're the only pal I've ever had. I love your guts. I'd do anything for you.

EDMUND: (*Reaches out and pats his arm.*) I know that, Jamie.

JAMIE: (*His crying over—drops his hands from his face—with a strange bitterness.*) Yet I'll bet you've heard Mama and old Gaspard spill so much bunk about my hoping for the worst, you suspect right now I'm thinking to myself that Papa is old and can't last much longer, and if you were to die, Mama and I would get all he's got, and so I'm probably hoping—

EDMUND: (*Indignantly.*) Shut up, you damned fool! What the hell put that in your nut? (*He stares at his brother accusingly.*) Yes, that's what I'd like to know. What put that in your mind?

JAMIE: (*Confusedly—appearing drunk again.*) Don't be a dumbbell! What I said! Always suspected of hoping for the worst. I've got so I can't help—(*Then drunkenly resentful.*) What are you trying to do, accuse me? Don't play the wise guy with me! I've learned more of life than

---

① Caught her in the act with a hypo.: 当场发现她皮下注射毒品。

you'll ever know! Just because you've read a lot of highbrow junk, don't think you can fool me! You're only an overgrown kid! Mama's baby and Papa's pet! The family White Hope①! You've been getting a swelled head lately. About nothing! About a few poems in a hick town newspaper! Hell, I used to write better stuff for the Lit② magazine in college! You better wake up! You're setting no rivers on fire! You let hick town boobs flatter you with bunk about your future—(*Abruptly his tone changes to disgusted contrition. Edmund has looked away from him, trying to ignore this tirade.*) Hell, Kid, forget it. That goes for Sweeny③. You know I don't mean it. No one hopes more than I do you'll knock 'em all dead. No one is prouder you've started to make good. (*Drunkenly assertive.*) Why shouldn't I be proud? Hell, it's purely selfish. You reflect credit on me. I've had more to do with bringing you up than anyone. I wised you up about women, so you'd never be a fall guy④, or make any mistakes you didn't want to make! And who steered you on to reading poetry first? Swinburne, for example? I did! And because I once wanted to write, I planted it in your mind that someday you'd write! Hell, you're more than my brother. I made you! You're my Frankenstein⑤! (*He has risen to a note of drunken arrogance. Edmund is grinning with amusement now.*)

EDMUND: All right, I'm your Frankenstein. So let's have a drink. (*He laughs.*) You crazy nut!

JAMIE: (*Thickly.*) I'll have a drink. Not you. Got to take care of you. (*He reaches out with a foolish grin of doting affection and grabs his brother's hand.*) Don't be scared of this sanatorium business. Hell, you can beat that standing on your head. Six months and you'll be in the pink. Probably haven't got consumption at all. Doctors lot of fakers. Told me years ago to cut out booze or I'd soon be dead—and here I am. They're all con men. Anything to grab your dough. I'll

---

① white hope：人们寄予厚望的人或事。
② Lit：literature。
③ That goes for Sweeny.：这只是骗骗小孩。Sweeny：什么都相信的天真家伙。
④ fall guy：容易受骗的人。
⑤ Frankenstein：玛丽·雪莱著名小说中的人物,他创造了一个最终毁灭了他自己的怪物。有时也指 Frankenstein 所创造的怪物。

bet this state farm stuff is political graft game. Doctors get a cut for every patient they send.

EDMUND: (*Disgustedly amused.*) You're the limit!① At the Last Judgment, you'll be around telling everyone it's in the bag.②

JAMIE: And I'll be right. Slip a piece of change to the Judge and be saved, but if you're broke you can go to hell! (*He grins at this blasphemy and Edmund has to laugh. Jamie goes on.*) "Therefore put money in thy purse."③ That's the only dope④. (*Mockingly.*) The secret of my success! Look what it's got me! (*He lets Edmund's hand go to pour a big drink, and gulps it down. He stares at his brother with bleary affection—takes his hand again and begins to talk thickly but with a strange, convincing sincerity.*) Listen, Kid, you'll be going away. May not get another chance to talk. Or might not be drunk enough to tell you truth. So got to tell you now. Something I ought to have told you long ago—for your own good. (*He pauses—struggling with himself. Edmund stares, impressed and uneasy. Jamie blurts out.*) Not drunken bull⑤, but "in vino veritas"⑥ stuff. You better take it seriously. Want to warn you—against me. Mama and Papa are right. I've been rotten bad influence. And worst of it is, I did it on purpose.

EDMUND: (*Uneasily.*) Shut up! I don't want to hear—

JAMIE: Nix, Kid! You listen! Did it on purpose to make a bum of you. Or part of me did. A big part. That part that's been dead so long. That hates life. My putting you wise so you'd learn from my mistakes. Believed that myself at times, but it's a fake. Made my mistakes look good. Made getting drunk romantic. Made whores fascinating vampires instead of poor, stupid, diseased slobs they really are. Made fun of work as sucker's game. Never wanted you succeed and

---

① You're the limit!：没有人比你更过分。

② At the Last Judgment, you'll be around telling everyone it's in the bag.：在上帝的最后审判日，你也会在那儿告诉大家，一切都在掌握之中。

③ 这是莎士比亚的悲剧《奥赛罗》(I.iii.352)中的台词。剧中的反面人物伊阿古诱使迷恋苔丝德蒙娜的罗德利哥花钱来达到自己的目的。

④ dope：内部消息；内情。

⑤ bull：蠢话；空话；废话。

⑥ in vino veritas(拉)：酒醉吐真言。

make me look even worse by comparison. Wanted you to fail. Always jealous of you. Mama's baby, Papa's pet! (*He stares at Edmund with increasing enmity.*) And it was your being born that started Mama on dope. I know that's not your fault, but all the same, God damn you, I can't help hating your guts—!

EDMUND: (*Almost frightenedly.*) Jamie! Cut it out! You're crazy!

JAMIE: But don't get wrong idea, Kid. I love you more than I hate you. My saying what I'm telling you now proves it. I run the risk you'll hate me—and you're all I've got left. But I didn't mean to tell you that last stuff—go that far back①. Don't know what made me. What I wanted to say is, I'd like to see you become the greatest success in the world. But you'd better be on your guard. Because I'll do my damnedest to make you fail. Can't help it. I hate myself. Got to take revenge. On everyone else. Especially you. Oscar Wilde's "Reading Gaol" has the dope twisted. ② The man was dead and so he had to kill the thing he loved. That's what it ought to be. The dead part of me hopes you won't get well. Maybe he's even glad the game has got Mama again! He wants company, he doesn't want to be the only corpse around the house! (*He gives a hard, tortured laugh.*)

EDMUND: Jesus, Jamie! You really have gone crazy!

JAMIE: Think it over and you'll see I'm right. Think it over when you're away from me in the sanatorium. Make up your mind you've got to tie a can to③ me—get me out of your life—think of me as dead—tell people, "I had a brother, but he's dead." And when you come back, look out for me. I'll be waiting to welcome you with that "my old pal" stuff, and give you the glad hand, and at the first good chance I get stab you in the back.

EDMUND: Shut up! I'll be God-damned if I'll listen to you any more—

JAMIE: (*As if he hadn't heard.*) Only don't forget me. Remember I warned you—for your sake. Give me credit. Greater love hath no man than

---

① go that far back: 说这么久之前的事。

② Oscar Wilde's "Reading Gaol" has the dope twisted.: 奥斯卡·王尔德的《莱丁监狱》歪曲了真情。王尔德的诗作《莱丁监狱之歌》("The Ballad of Reading Goal")表达了对一位即将被绞死的犯人的同情。这位犯人杀害了自己的妻子，因此被判处死刑："The man had killed the thing he loved, / And so he had to die"。但诗中的叙事者却表达了对他的同情："Yet each man kills the thing he loves"。

③ tie a can to(俚): get rid of。

this, that he saveth his brother from himself.① (*Very drunkenly, his head bobbing.*) That's all. Feel better now. Gone to confession. Know you absolve me, don't you, Kid? You understand. You're a damned fine kid. Ought to be. I made you. So go and get well. Don't die on me.② You're all I've got left. God bless you, Kid. (*His eyes close. He mumbles.*) That last drink—the old K. O.③ (*He falls into a drunken doze, not completely asleep. Edmund buries his face in his hands miserably. Tyrone comes in quietly through the screen door from the porch, his dressing gown wet with fog, the collar turned up around his throat. His face is stern and disgusted but at the same time pitying. Edmund does not notice his entrance.*)

TYRONE: (*In a low voice.*) Thank God he's asleep. (*Edmund looks up with a start.*) I thought he'd never stop talking. (*He turns down the collar of his dressing gown.*) We'd better let him stay where he is and sleep it off. (*Edmund remains silent. Tyrone regards him—then goes on.*) I heard the last part of his talk. It's what I've warned you. I hope you'll heed the warning, now it comes from his own mouth. (*Edmund gives no sign of having heard. Tyrone adds pityingly.*) But don't take it too much to heart, lad. He loves to exaggerate the worst of himself when he's drunk. He's devoted to you. It's the one good thing left in him. (*He looks down on Jamie with a bitter sadness.*) A sweet spectacle for me! My first-born, who I hoped would bear my name in honor and dignity, who showed such brilliant promise!

EDMUND: (*Miserably.*) Keep quiet, can't you, Papa?

TYRONE: (*Pours a drink.*) A waste! A wreck, a drunken hulk, done with and finished! (*He drinks. Jamie has become restless, sensing his father's presence, struggling up from his stupor. Now he gets his eyes open to blink up at Tyrone. The latter moves back a step defensively, his face growing hard.*)

JAMIE: (*Suddenly points a finger at him and recites with dramatic*

---

① 这是对《圣经》的模仿。《圣经》的原文为："Greater love hath no man than this, that a man lay down his life for his friends" (John, XV: 13)。

② Don't die on me.: 不要死在我手上；不要死在我面前

③ K. O.: 拳击比赛中击倒对手的一击。

emphasis.)

"Clarence is come, false, fleeting, perjured Clarence,
That stabbed me in the field by Tewksbury.
Seize on him, Furies, take him into torment."①

(*Then resentfully*.) What the hell are you staring at? (*He recites sardonically from Rossetti②*.)

"Look in my face. My name is Might-Have-Been;
I am also called No More, Too Late, Farewell."

TYRONE: I'm well aware of that, and God knows I don't want to look at it.

EDMUND: Papa! Quit it!

JAMIE: (*Derisively*.) Got a great idea for you, Papa. Put on revival of "The Bells" this season. Great part in it you can play without make-up. Old Gaspard, the miser! (*Tyrone turns away, trying to control his temper.*)

EDMUND: Shut up, Jamie!

JAMIE: (*Jeeringly*.) I claim Edwin Booth never saw the day when he could give as good a performance as a trained seal. Seals are intelligent and honest. They don't put up any bluffs about the Art of Acting. They admit they're just hams earning their daily fish.

TYRONE: (*Stung, turns on him in a rage.*) You loafer!

EDMUND: Papa! Do you want to start a row that will bring Mama down? Jamie, go back to sleep! You've shot off your mouth too much already. (*Tyrone turns away.*)

JAMIE: (*Thickly*) All right, Kid. Not looking for argument. Too damned sleepy. (*He closes his eyes, his head nodding. Tyrone comes to the table and sits down, turning his chair so he won't look at Jamie. At once he becomes sleepy, too.*)

TYRONE: (*Heavily*.) I wish to God she'd go to bed so that I could, too. (*Drowsily*.) I'm dog tired. I can't stay up all night like I used to. Getting old—old and finished. (*With a bone-cracking yawn.*) Can't keep my eyes open. I think I'll catch a few winks. Why don't you

---

① 引自莎士比亚剧作《理查三世》(I.iv.55—57)。为了得到王位，理查派凶手去杀害自己的哥哥克莱伦斯。在凶手到达之前，克莱伦斯正在讲述他做的噩梦。这段引文是噩梦中"一个天使般的阴影"对克莱伦斯所讲的话。

② Gabriel Charles Dante Rossetti (1828—82)：英国画家、诗人。诗行引自"生活之屋：系列十四行诗"("The House of Life: a Sonnet-Sequence")。该诗表达了典型的失败感、负罪感、悔恨感。

do the same, Edmund? It'll pass the time until she—(*His voice trails off. His eyes close, his chin sags, and he begins to breathe heavily through his mouth. Edmund sits tensely. He hears something and jerks nervously forward in his chair, staring through the front parlor into the hall. He jumps up with a hunted, distracted expression. It seems for a second he is going to hide in the back parlor. Then he sits down again and waits, his eyes averted, his hands gripping the arms of his chair. Suddenly all five bulbs of the chandelier in the front parlor are turned on from a wall switch, and a moment later someone starts playing the piano in there—the opening of one of Chopin's simpler waltzes, done with a forgetful, stiff-fingered groping, as if an awkward schoolgirl were practicing it for the first time. Tyrone starts to wide-awakeness and sober dread, and Jamie's head jerks back and his eyes open. For a moment they listen frozenly. The playing stops as abruptly as it began, and Mary appears in the doorway. She wears a sky-blue dressing gown over her nightdress, dainty slippers with pompons on her bare feet. Her face is paler than ever. Her eyes look enormous. They glisten like polished black jewels. The uncanny thing is that her face now appears so youthful. Experience seems ironed out of it. It is a marble mask of girlish innocence, the mouth caught in a shy smile. Her white hair is braided in two pigtails which hang over her breast. Over one arm, carried neglectfully, trailing on the floor, as if she had forgotten she held it, is an old-fashioned white satin wedding gown, trimmed with duchesse lace*①. *She hesitates in the doorway, glancing round the room, her forehead puckered puzzledly, like someone who has come to a room to get something but has become absent-minded on the way and forgotten what it was. They stare at her. She seems aware of them merely as she is aware of other objects in the room, the furniture, the windows, familiar things she accepts automatically as naturally belonging there but which she is too preoccupied to notice.*)

---

① duchesse lace: 公爵夫人花边。从 1840 年前后到 19 世纪末,这种生产于布鲁塞尔的花边廉价而又畅销。其特点是用粗线编织成的凸起的花卉和叶子图案。

JAMIE: (*Breaks the cracking silence—bitterly, self-defensively sardonic.*) The Mad Scene. Enter Ophelia![1] (*His father and brother both turn on him fiercely. Edmund is quicker. He slaps Jamie across the mouth with the back of his hand.*)

TYRONE: (*His voice trembling with suppressed fury.*) Good boy, Edmund. The dirty blackguard! His own mother!

JAMIE: (*Mumbles guiltily, without resentment.*) All right, Kid. Had it coming. But I told you how much I'd hoped—(*He puts his hands over his face and begins to sob.*)

TYRONE: I'll kick you out in the gutter tomorrow, so help me God. (*But Jamie's sobbing breaks his anger, and he turns and shakes his shoulder, pleading.*) Jamie, for the love of God, stop it! (*Then Mary speaks, and they freeze into silence again, staring at her. She has paid no attention whatever to the incident. It is simply a part of the familiar atmosphere of the room, a background which does not touch her preoccupation; and she speaks aloud to herself, not to them.*)

MARY: I play so badly now. I'm all out of practice. Sister Theresa will give me a dreadful scolding. She'll tell me it isn't fair to my father when he spends so much money for extra lessons. She's quite right, it isn't fair, when he's so good and generous, and so proud of me. I'll practice every day from now on. But something horrible has happened to my hands. The fingers have gotten so stiff—(*She lifts her hands to examine them with a frightened puzzlement.*) The knuckles are all swollen. They're so ugly. I'll have to go to the Infirmary and show Sister Martha. (*With a sweet smile of affectionate trust.*) She's old and a little cranky, but I love her just the same, and she has things in her medicine chest that'll cure anything. She'll give me something to rub on my hands, and tell me to pray to the Blessed Virgin, and they'll be well again in no time. (*She forgets her hands and comes into the room, the wedding gown trailing on the floor. She glances around vaguely, her forehead puckered again.*) Let me see. What did I come here to

---

[1] 在莎士比亚的悲剧《哈姆莱特》中，Ophelia 因父亲被哈姆莱特杀害而变疯 (IV. v.)。而哈姆莱特本人也装疯。

find? It's terrible, how absent-minded I've become. I'm always dreaming and forgetting.

TYRONE: (*In a stifled voice.*) What's that she's carrying, Edmund?

EDMUND: (*Dully.*) Her wedding gown, I suppose.

TYRONE: Christ! (*He gets to his feet and stands directly in her path—in anguish.*) Mary! Isn't it bad enough—? (*Controlling himself—gently persuasive.*) Here, let me take it, dear. You'll only step on it and tear it and get it dirty dragging it on the floor. Then you'd be sorry afterwards. (*She lets him take it, regarding him from somewhere far away within herself, without recognition, without either affection or animosity.*)

MARY: (*With the shy politeness of a well-bred young girl toward an elderly gentleman who relieves her of a bundle.*) Thank you. You are very kind. (*She regards the wedding gown with a puzzled interest.*) It's a wedding gown. It's very lovely, isn't it? (*A shadow crosses her face and she looks vaguely uneasy.*) I remember now. I found it in the attic hidden in a trunk. But I don't know what I wanted it for. I'm going to be a nun—that is, if I can only find— (*She looks around the room, her forehead puckered again.*) What is it I'm looking for? I know it's something I lost. (*She moves back from Tyrone, aware of him now only as some obstacle in her path.*)

TYRONE: (*In hopeless appeal.*) Mary! (*But it cannot penetrate her preoccupation. She doesn't seem to hear him. He gives up helplessly, shrinking into himself, even his defensive drunkenness taken from him, leaving him sick and sober. He sinks back on his chair, holding the wedding gown in his arms with an unconscious clumsy, protective gentleness.*)

JAMIE: (*Drops his hand from his face, his eyes on the table top. He has suddenly sobered up, too—dully.*) It's no good, Papa. (*He recites from Swinburne's "A Leave-taking" and does it well, simply but with a bitter sadness.*)

"Let us rise up and part; she will not know.
Let us go seaward as the great winds go,

    Full of blown sand and foam; what help is here?
    There is no help, for all these things are so,
    And all the world is bitter as a tear.
    And how these things are, though ye strove to show,
    She would not know."

MARY: (*Looking around her.*) Something I miss terribly. It can't be altogether lost. (*She starts to move around in back of Jamie's chair.*)

JAMIE: (*Turns to look up into her face—and cannot help appealing pleadingly in his turn.*) Mama! (*She does not seem to hear. He looks away hopelessly.*) Hell! What's the use? It's no good. (*He recites from "A Leave-taking" again with increased bitterness.*)
    "Let us go hence, my songs; she will not hear.
    Let us go hence together without fear;
    Keep silence now, for singing-time is over,
    And over all old things and all things dear.
    She loves not you nor me as all we love her.
    Yea, though we sang as angels in her ear,
    She would not hear."

MARY: (*Looking around her.*) Something I need terribly. I remember when I had it I was never lonely nor afraid. I can't have lost it forever, I would die if I thought that. Because then there would be no hope. (*She moves like a sleepwalker, around the back of Jamie's chair, then forward toward left front, passing behind Edmund.*)

EDMUND: (*Turns impulsively and grabs her arm. As he pleads he has the quality of a bewilderedly hurt little boy.*) Mama! It isn't a summer cold! I've got consumption!

MARY: (*For a second he seems to have broken through to her. She trembles and her expression becomes terrified. She calls distractedly, as if giving a command to herself.*) No! (*And instantly she is far away again. She murmurs gently but impersonally.*) You must not try to touch me. You must not try to hold me. It isn't right, when I am hoping to be a nun. (*He lets his hand drop from her arm. She moves left to the front end of the sofa beneath the windows and sits down, facing front, her hands folded in her lap, in a demure school girlish pose.*)

JAMIE: (*Gives Edmund a strange look of mingled pity and jealous gloating.*) You damned fool. It's no good. (*He recites again from the Swinburne poem.*)

"Let us go hence, go hence; she will not see.

Sing all once more together; surely she,

She too, remembering days and words that were,

Will turn a little toward us, sighing; but we,

We are hence, we are gone, as though we had not been there.

Nay, and though all men seeing had pity on me,

She would not see."

TYRONE: (*Trying to shake off his hopeless stupor.*) Oh, we're fools to pay any attention. It's the damned poison. But I've never known her to drown herself in it as deep as this. (*Gruffly.*) Pass me that bottle, Jamie. And stop reciting that damned morbid poetry. I won't have it in my house! (*Jamie pushes the bottle toward him. He pours a drink without disarranging the wedding gown he holds carefully over his other arm and on his lap, and shoves the bottle back. Jamie pours his and passes the bottle to Edmund, who, in turn, pours one. Tyrone lifts his glass and his sons follow suit mechanically, but before they can drink Mary speaks and they slowly lower their drinks to the table, forgetting them.*)

MARY: (*Staring dreamily before her. Her face looks extraordinarily youthful and innocent. The shyly eager, trusting smile is on her lips as she talks aloud to herself.*) I had a talk with Mother Elizabeth. She is so sweet and good. A saint on earth. I love her dearly. It may be sinful of me but I love her better than my own mother. Because she always understands, even before you say a word. Her kind blue eyes look right into your heart. You can't keep any secrets from her. You couldn't deceive her, even if you were mean enough to want to. (*She gives a little rebellious toss of her head—with girlish pique.*) All the same, don't think she was so understanding this time. I told her I wanted to be a nun. I explained how sure I was of my vocation, that I had prayed to the Blessed Virgin to make me sure, and to find me worthy. I told Mother I had

had a true vision when I was praying in the shrine of Our Lady of Lourdes, on the little island in the lake. I said I knew, as surely as I knew I was kneeling there, that the Blessed Virgin had smiled and blessed me with her consent. But Mother Elizabeth told me I must be more sure than that, even, that I must prove it wasn't simply my imagination. She said, if I was so sure, then I wouldn't mind putting myself to a test by going home after I graduated, and living as other girls lived, going out to parties and dances and enjoying myself; and then if after a year or two I still felt sure, I could come back to see her and we would talk it over again. (*She tosses her head—indignantly.*) I never dreamed Holy Mother would give me such advice! I was really shocked. I said, of course, I would do anything she suggested, but I knew it was simply a waste of time. After I left her, I felt all mixed up, so I went to the shrine and prayed to the Blessed Virgin and found peace again because I knew she heard my prayer and would always love me and see no harm ever came to me so long as I never lost my faith in her. (*She pauses and a look of growing uneasiness comes over her face. She passes a hand over her forehead as if brushing cobwebs from her brain—vaguely.*) That was in the winter of senior year. Then in the spring something happened to me. Yes, I remember. I fell in love with James Tyrone and was so happy for a time. (*She stares before her in a sad dream. Tyrone stirs in his chair. Edmund and Jamie remain motionless.*)

CURTAIN

　　《进入黑夜的漫长旅程》是奥尼尔创作生涯晚期的呕心沥血之作,是奥尼尔一家悲剧生活的真实写照,是美国的悲剧杰作。奥尼尔在剧作的献辞中写道:这部剧作"以泪水和鲜血写成……对蒂龙一家受尽折磨的四个成员充满着深深的怜悯、谅解和宽恕之情"。根据奥尼尔的遗嘱,该剧不得上演,并只有在奥尼尔去世25年之后才可以出版。但奥尼尔的遗孀卡罗塔·蒙特利(Carlotta Monterey)并未遵从奥尼尔的遗愿,使该剧于1956年先后在斯

　　德哥尔摩和纽约两地上演,引起极大轰动。
　　剧作通过蒂龙一家一天的生活,浓缩了全家人痛苦的一生。小儿子埃德蒙身患

当时的不治之症肺结核,而母亲玛丽则染上毒瘾不能自拔。他们肉体上的痛苦逐渐引出了不堪回首的往事,辛酸的回忆带来了精神上的更大痛苦。原来,父亲詹姆斯·蒂龙本有可能成为著名的莎士比亚戏剧演员,但却为了丰厚的票房收入而四处巡演商业化的剧目《基督山伯爵》。他生性吝啬,在玛丽生产埃德蒙时请了庸医,使她染上毒瘾;为了省钱,即使埃德蒙身患绝症,他也只想把他送到廉价的公立疗养院。全家充满怨恨,男人们更是以酒浇愁,互相指责和谩骂。

剧中的大雾是重要的象征主义道具,与毒品和酒精一起,使现实消失在梦幻当中。剧终时,在酗酒后的三父子的注视下,玛丽在毒品的作用下,神情恍惚地拖着婚纱走了过来,仿佛实现了少女时的两个梦想:即成为修女和钢琴家。这是美国戏剧中最令人心碎的场面之一。

美丽的梦幻和丑陋的现实之间的冲突似乎也为这部悲剧带来了理解和和解:玛丽随丈夫四处巡演,居无定所,举目无亲,使自己的理想化为泡影,也造成了她以后的悲剧;蒂龙是一位爱尔兰移民,他早年的艰辛使他对贫困充满恐惧,也造成了他病态般的吝啬。这一切最终得到了理解。

1962年,《进入黑夜的漫长旅程》被搬上电影银幕,并获得广泛好评。这部由西德尼·鲁麦特导演、凯瑟琳·赫本主演的电影影响了批评界对于剧中人物的评价。此前,剧中谁是主要人物一直存有争议。在该片中,赫本扮演的女主人公的分量远远超过了男主人公,此后一般都认为玛丽·蒂龙,而不是詹姆斯·蒂龙,是剧中的主要人物。该剧还曾于1973年、1982年、1987年三次被改编为电视剧。1996年,加拿大又再次将该剧改编为电影。

思考题

1. What role does the past play in *Long Day's Journey into Night*?
2. What role do drugs and alcohol play within the play?
3. In what way is the "fog" important in the play?
4. What is the relationship between the two brothers?
5. What is the relationship between Tyrone and Mary?

推荐作品

Marco Millions (1924)
Strange Interlude (1928)
A Touch of the Poet (1939)
The Iceman Cometh (1939)
"Hughie" (1941)

参考资料

Manheim, Michael, ed. *The Cambridge Companion to Eugene O'Neill*. Shanghai: Shanghai Foreign Language Education Press, 2000.

Black, Stephen A. *Eugene O'Neill: Beyond Mourning and Tragedy*. Yale UP, 1999.

Houchin, John H. *The Critical Response to Eugene O'Neill*. Westport, Connecticut: Greenwood Press, 1993.

Berlin, Normand. *Eugene O'Neill*. Macmillan, 1982.

II

1945—2000

第七单元
Ralph(Waldo)Ellison
(1914—1994)
拉尔夫·埃里森

作者简介

拉尔夫·埃里森,黑人小说家、杂文家,生于俄克拉荷马市,自幼酷爱音乐,上高中期间开始演奏小号。1933年高中毕业时获得音乐奖学金,进入阿拉巴马州塔斯克基黑人学院(Tuskegee Institute)学习音乐。阿拉巴马州的种族隔离政策和学院视爵士乐为野蛮音乐的保守思想使他大为不快,1936年,他离开学院到纽约学习雕塑。在纽约,他结识了兰斯顿·休斯和理查德·赖特,受二人的影响,加上他在塔斯克基学院期间曾经被海明威、肖伯纳、艾略特等人的著作吸引的因素,他加入了美国联邦作家项目(Federal Writers' Project),开始写杂文、书评和短篇小说。1942年,埃里森退出联邦作家工程,担任《黑奴季刊》(Negro Quaterly)执行编辑。第二次世界大战结束后,他开始创作《看不见的人》(又译《无形人》,Invisible Man, 1952),该书出版前,埃里森共发表9个短篇小说和10多篇评论文章。《看不见的人》一鸣惊人,被誉为"划时代的小说"、"现代美国人生活的史诗",1953年获得美国国家图书奖,评审委员会赞扬作家的"文学冒险勇气"。此后,该书再版数十次,1982年和2002年分别发行了作品发表30周年和50周年纪念版。1965年,《看不见的人》被《图书周报》的民意测验列为"第二次世界大战后美国最卓越的小说";甚至到1982年,还连续16周高居最畅销作品排行榜;2000年,在美国现代书库(The Modern Library)所评选的20世纪100种最佳英语小说中列第19位。在这部以主人公寻求"自我"为主题的小说里,埃里森运用众多艺术手段,力图赋予无名主人公超越种族的感受,着力把黑人经受的种族压迫升华为人类经受的社会压迫。1960年,埃里森发表短篇小说《乡下佬来了》(And Hickman Arrives),这本是他计划中另一部反映美国黑人生活的长篇力作的一部分。不幸的是,1967年,已经写了368页的手稿被毁之一炬。但他继续辛勤耕耘,1994年去世时留下一部约2000页手稿的未完成长篇小说,后经学者卡拉瀚(John F. Callahan)整理节选,于1999年以《六一九》(又译《六月庆典》,Juneteenth)为名出版。埃里森生前曾在哥伦比亚、耶鲁、芝加哥、纽约等大学讲学或任教,获得过"自由勋章"(1969)、"文学艺术骑士勋章"(1970)、"国家艺术勋章"(1985)等众多奖励和学术头衔,还发表了两部论文集:《影子与行动》(Shadow and Act, 1964)和《走向领地》(Going to the Territory, 1986)。

King of the Bingo Game①

The woman in front of him was eating roasted peanuts that smelled so good that he could barely contain his hunger. He could not even sleep and wished they'd hurry and begin the bingo game. There, on his right, two fellows were drinking wine out of a bottle wrapped in a paper bag, and he could hear soft gurgling in the dark. His stomach gave a low, gnawing growl. "If this was down South," he thought, "all I'd have to do is lean over and say, 'Lady, gimme a few of those peanuts, please ma'am,' and she'd pass me the bag and never think nothing of it." Or he could ask the fellows for a drink in the same way. Folks down South stuck together that way; they didn't even have to know you. But up here it was different. Ask somebody for something, and they'd think you were crazy. Well, I ain't crazy. I'm just broke, 'cause I got no birth certificate to get a job, and Laura 'bout to die 'cause we got no money for a doctor. But I ain't crazy②. And yet a pinpoint of doubt was focused in his mind as he glanced toward the screen and saw the hero stealthily entering a dark room and sending the beam of a flashlight③

---

① Bingo: 一种赌博游戏,一般翻译为宾果(或宾戈),16世纪起源于意大利,18世纪流行欧洲,后经狂欢节商贩传到美国。1929年12月,在佐治亚州的亚特兰大狂欢节上,推销员爱德文·洛(Edwin S. Lowe)发现一个帐篷里人们正在兴奋地玩一种游戏,大家都热切地等待着叫号,当叫到的号同某人卡片上的相同时,那人便在数字上放一粒豆子(bean),当某人的豆子排成一排时,他就大喊一声"Beago!"爱德文·洛还发现玩游戏的人兴致甚浓,赶都赶不走,他意识到这种游戏有巨大的市场潜力。回到纽约后,爱德文·洛照葫芦画瓢,也邀请朋友玩起了这种游戏。情景正如他预料的那样,其中一女士眼看自己的一排豆子即将成行,激动不已,等到她赢得游戏时,舌头发紧,结巴了好一阵子也没能喊出"Beago",而是说成了"B-b-bingo!"爱德文·洛也备感兴奋,决定推广这一游戏,并称之为"Bingo"。现在,美国的宾果游戏通常在游戏厅进行,游戏使用的卡片多分为5行5列,对应"Bingo"的5个字母,卡上有24个数字加上一个空格。在75以内随机抽取数字,在1—15中选择B对应的数字,16—30中选择I对应的数字,31—45中选择N对应的数字,46—60中选择G对应的数字,61—75中选择O对应的数字。由专业人士叫号,游戏者根据叫号,迅速在自选的卡上找到这些数字,并做出标记。一人所做标记垂直、水平或对角线成行者获胜。

② 故事开头部分描写一个来自南方的黑人痛苦孤独的心理。他客居他乡,身无分文,而且因为没有身份证而无法找工作,饥肠辘辘在北方一家电影院里等待着电影结束,为的是从将在电影院举行的宾果游戏中得奖以为其重病在床的妻子罗拉(Laura)治病。如同理查德·赖特在《土生子》里表现的一样,电影院成为黑人产生美国梦、幻想实现美国梦的场所。故事里的主人公已经多次到过电影院,所以他从曾经奴役过黑人的南方来到象征自由的北方,而且相信自己可以通过工作或博彩获得成功。然而,事实上,饥饿、南北方文化差异以及妻子的疾病使他身心交瘁、无助无奈,甚至担心别人会把他当作疯子(这一点也为故事的发展埋下了伏笔)。自由与束缚、黑人与白人、南方与北方、疯狂与清醒、理想与现实等众多冲突开始显现。故事中的主人公显然没有受过什么教育,使用的是黑人英语: ain't 为 be 动词的否定式形式;有很多吞音现象, 'bout=about, 'cause=because。

③ the beam of a flashlight: 手电光。黑暗中的白光具有象征意义。

along a wall of bookcases. This is where he finds the trapdoor①, he remembered. The man would pass abruptly through the wall and find the girl tied to a bed, her legs and arms spread wide, and her clothing torn to rags. He laughed softly to himself. He had seen the picture three times, and this was one of the best scenes.

On his right the fellow whispered wide-eyed to his companion, "Man, look a-yonder!"

"Damn!"

"Wouldn't I like to have her tied up like that..."

"Hey! That fool's letting her loose!"

"Aw, man, he loves her."②

"Love or no love!"

The man moved impatiently beside him, and he tried to involve himself in the scene. But Laura was on his mind. Tiring quickly of watching the picture he looked back to where the white beam③ filtered from the projection room above the balcony. It started small and grew large, specks of dust dancing in its whiteness as it reached the screen. It was strange how the beam always landed right on the screen and didn't mess up and fall somewhere else. But they had it all fixed. Everything was fixed. Now suppose when they showed that girl with her dress torn the girl started taking off the rest of her clothes, and when the guy came in he didn't untie her but kept her there and went to taking off his own clothes? That would be something to see. If a picture got out of hand like that those guys up there would go nuts④. Yeah, and there'd be so many folks in here you couldn't find a seat for nine months! A strange sensation played over his skin. He shuddered. Yesterday he'd seen a bedbug on a woman's neck as they walked out into the bright street. But exploring his thigh through a hole in his pocket he found only goose pimples and old scars.

The bottle gurgled again. He closed his eyes. Now a dreamy music was accompanying the film and train whistles were sounding in the distance, and he was a boy again walking along a railroad trestle⑤ down South, and seeing the train

---

① trapdoor：暗门，因为 trap 具有"陷阱"之意，可以将该词理解为双关，或象征。
② 两个黑人男子（因为 man 是黑人之间打招呼的方式，相当于"老兄""哥儿们"。）对电影里被捆在床上，衣服被撕烂的女孩不怀好意的调侃一方面说明他们精神空虚，另一方面也说明他们没有认识到女孩也代表他们自己所处的境地，黑人和妇女都是白人男子霸权主义的受害者。
③ white beam：（电影放映机发出的）白光，象征白人控制的技术和权力（下文有"They had it all fixed."）。
④ nuts：疯子。这里指这些观众会因此而疯狂。
⑤ railroad trestle：铁路桥。下文中的也是此意。

coming, and running back as fast as he could go, and hearing the whistle blowing, and getting off the trestle to solid ground just in time, with the earth trembling beneath his feet, and feeling relieved as he ran down the cinder-strewn embankment① onto the highway, and looking back and seeing with terror that the train had left the track and was following him right down the middle of the street, and all the white people laughing as he ran screaming...②

"Wake up there, buddy! What the hell do you mean hollering like that? Can't you see we trying to enjoy this here picture?"

He stared at the man with gratitude.

"I'm sorry, old man," he said. "I musta been dreaming."

"Well, here, have a drink. And don't be making no noise like that, damm!"

His hands trembled as he tilted his head. It was not wine, but whiskey. Cold rye whiskey. He took a deep swoller, decided it was better not to take another, and handed the bottle back to its owner.

"Thanks, old man," he said.

Now he felt the cold whskey breaking a warm path straight through the middle of him, growing hotter and sharper as it moved. He had not eaten all day, and it made him light-headed. The smell of the peanuts stabbed him like a knife, and he got up and found a seat in the middle aisle. But no sooner did he sit than he saw a row of intense-faced young girls, and got up again, thinking, "You chicks musta been Lindy-hopping somewhere."③ He found a seat several rows ahead as the lights came on, and he saw the screen disappear behind a heavy red and gold curtain; then the curtain rising, and the man with the microphone and a uniformed attendant coming on the stage.

He felt for his bingo cards, smiling. The guy at the door wouldn't like it if he knew about his having *five* cards. Well, not everyone played the bingo game; and even with five cards he didn't have much of a chance. For Laura, though, he had to have faith. He studied the cards, each with its different numerals, punching the

---

① the cinder-strewn embankment：铺满炉渣的路堤。

② 主人公睡着后做了一个噩梦。现实与梦幻的交织使故事具有超现实主义特征，梦中脱轨追赶他的火车是白人技术和权力的另一个象征物。

③ You chicks musta been Lindy-hopping somewhere.：chick：(俚) 少妇；musta=must have。"你们这帮小娘儿们肯定是跑到哪里去跳爵士舞了。" Lindy Hop, 又称 Jitterbug, 一种随爵士乐节拍跳的快速舞，名称来自 1927 年林德伯格首次飞越大西洋后的新闻报道标题："LINDY HOPS THE ATLANTIC"。主人公连续换座位是在寻找光亮之处，为游戏做准备。

free center hole① in each and spreading them neatly across his lap; and when the lights faded he sat slouched in his seat so that he could look from his cards to the bingo wheel with but a quick shifting of his eyes.

  Ahead, at the end of the darkness, the man with the microphone was pressing a button attached to a long cord and spinning the bingo wheel and calling out the number each time the wheel came to rest. And each time the voice rang out his finger raced over the cards for the number. With five cards he had to move fast. He became nervous; there were too many cards, and the man went too fast with his grating voice. Perhaps he should just select one and throw the others away. But he was afraid. He became warm. Wonder how much Laura's doctor would cost? Damn that, watch the cards! And with despair he heard the man call three in a row which he missed on all five cards. This way he'd never win...

  When he saw the row of holes punched across the third card, he sat paralyzed and heard the man call three more numbers before he stumbled forward, screaming.

  "Bingo! Bingo!"

  "Let that fool up there," someone called.

  "Get up there, man!"

  He stumbled down the aisle and up the steps to the stage into a light so sharp and bright that for a moment it blinded him, and he felt that he had moved into the spell of some strange, mysterious power②. Yet it was as familiar as the sun, and he knew it was the perfectly familiar bingo.

  The man with the microphone was saying something to the audience as he held out his card. A cold light flashed from the man's finger as the card left his hand. His knees trembled. The man stepped closer, checking the card against the numbers chalked on the board. Suppose he had made a mistake? The pomade on the man's hair made him feel faint, and he backed away. But the man was checking the card over the microphone now, and he had to stay. He stood tense, listening.

  "Under the O, forty-four," the man chanted. "Under the I, seven. Under the G, three. Under the B, ninety-six. Under the N, thirteen!"

  His breath came easier as the man smiled at the audience.

---

 ① the free center hole：游戏卡片中间没有数字号码的空格。主人公为了增加赢钱的机会，拿了5张卡片，属游戏中的欺诈行为。

 ② 明亮刺眼的光让他感到像是被某种神秘的力量迷住了。象征意义极强，注意主持人称呼主人公的词。

"Yes sir, ladies and gentlemen, he's one of the chosen people①!"

The audience rippled with laughter and applause.

"Step right up to the front of the stage."

He moved slowly forward, wishing that the light was not so bright.

"To win tonight's jackpot of $36.90 the wheel must stop between the double zero, understand?"②

He nodded, knowing the ritual from the many days and nights he had watched the winners march across the stage to press the button that controlled the spinning wheel and receive the prizes. And now he followed the instructions as though he'd crossed the slippery stage a million prize-winning times.

The man was making some kind of a joke, and he nodded vacantly. So tense had he become that he felt a sudden desire to cry and shook it away. He felt vaguely that his whole life was determined by the bingo wheel③; not only that which would happen now that he was at last before it, but all that had gone before, since his birth, and his mother's birth and the birth of his father. It had always been there, even though he had not been aware of it, handing out the unlucky cards and numbers of his days. The feeling persisted, and he started quickly away. I better get down from here before I make a fool of myself, he thought.

"Here, boy," the man called. "You haven't started yet."

Someone laughed as he went hesitantly back.

"Are you all reet?"④

He grinned at the man's jive talk, but no words would come, and he knew it was not a convincing grin. For suddenly he knew that he stood on the slippery brink of some terrible embarrassment.

"Where are you from, boy?" the man asked.

"Down South."

"He's from down South, ladies and gentlemen," the man said. "Where from? Speak right into the mike."

"Rocky Mont," he said, "Rock'Mont, North Car'lina."

"So you decided to come down off that mountain to the U.S.," the man

---

① the chosen people：上帝的选民，清教徒认为上帝要拯救其灵魂的那一少部分人。主持人这里的意思是"他是个幸运儿！"但是，把这个清教徒自以为是的词用在一个黑人身上颇具讽刺意味。

② jackpot：头奖，累计奖金。有人认为把奖金总数写成 36.90 美元是有意通过 3 的倍数消解三位一体的神学观念。两个零，即"00"，代表多层意义的缺失，甚至包括主人公和他妻子的死。

③ the bingo wheel：游戏盘，可理解为"幸运之盘"、"命运之盘"的含义。

④ Are you all reet?：Are you all right? 注意主持人居高临下的话语。

laughed. He felt that the man was making a fool of him, but then something cold was placed in his hand, and the lights were no longer behind him.

Standing before the wheel he felt alone, but that was somehow right, and he remembered his plan. He would give the wheel a short quick twirl. Just a touch of the button. He had watched it many times, and always it came close to double zero when it was short and quick. He steeled himself; the fear had left, and he felt a profound sense of promise, as though he were about to be repaid for all the things he'd suffered all his life. Trembling, he pressed the button. There was a whirl of lights, and in a second he realized with finality that though he wanted to, he could not stop. It was as though he held a high-powered line in his naked hand. His nerves tightened. As the wheel increased its speed it seemed to draw him more and more into his power, as though it held his fate; and with it came a deep need to submit, to whirl, to lose himself in its swirl of color. He could not stop it now, he knew. So let it be.

The button rested snugly in his palm where the man had placed it. And now he became aware of the man beside him, advising him through the microphone, while behind the shadowy audience hummed with noisy voices. He shifted his feet. There was still that feeling of helplessness within him, making part of him desire to turn back, even now that the jackpot was right in his hand. He squeezed the button until his fist ached. Then, like the sudden shriek of a subway whistle, a doubt tore through his head. Suppose he did not spin the wheel long enough? What could he do, and how could he tell? And then he knew, even as he wondered, that as long as he pressed the button, he could control the jackpot. He and only he could determine whether or not it was to be his. Not even the man with the microphone could do anything about it now. He felt drunk. Then, as though he had come down from a high hill into a valley of people, he heard the audience yelling.

"Come down from there, you jerk①!"

"Let somebody else have a chance...."

"Ole Jack thinks he done found the end of the rainbow..."②

The last voice was not unfriendly, and he turned and smiled dreamily into

---

① jerk：(俚)笨蛋。

② Ole Jack thinks he done found the end of the rainbow...：那家伙以为他梦想成真了…… Ole：old；Jack 不是故事主人公的名字，相当于"那家伙"、"那个老兄"。the end of the rainbow 来自典故 the pot of gold at the end of the rainbow，意为不可能实现的愿望。

the yelling mouths. Then he turned his back squarely on them.

"Don't take too long, boy," a voice said.

He nodded. They were yelling behind him. Those folks did not understand what had happened to him. They had been playing the bingo game day in and night out for years, trying to win rent money or hamburger change. But not one of those wise guys had discovered this wonderful thing. He watched the wheel whirling past the numbers and experienced a burst of exaltation: This is God! This is the really truly God! He said it aloud, "This is God!"

He said it with such absolute conviction① that he feared he would fall fainting into the footlights. But the crowd yelled so loud that they could not hear. Those fools, he thought. I'm here trying to tell them the most wonderful secret in the world, and they're yelling like they gone crazy. A hand fell upon his shoulder.

"You'll have to make a choice now, boy. You've taken too long."

He brushed the hand violently away.

"Leave me alone, man. I know what I'm doing!"

The man looked surprised and held on to the microphone for support. And because he did not wish to hurt the man's feelings he smiled, realizing with a sudden pang that there was no way of explaining to the man just why he had to stand there pressing the button forever.

"Come here," he called tiredly.

The man approached, rolling the heavy microphone across the stage.

"Anybody can play this bingo game, right?" he said.

"Sure, but..."

He smiled, feeling inclined to be patient with this slick looking white man with his blue sport shirt and his sharp gabardine② suit.

"That's what I thought," he said. "Anybody can win the jackpot as long as they get the lucky number, right?"

"That's the rule, but after all..."

"That's what I thought," he said. "And the big prize goes to the man who knows how to win it?"

The man nodded speechlessly.

"Well then, go on over there and watch me win like I want to. I ain't going to hurt nobody," he said, "and I'll show you how to win. I mean to show the

---

① absolute conviction: 深信无疑。

② sharp: (俚) 时髦的, 漂亮的; gabardine: 华达呢。

whole world how it's got to be done."

And because he understood, he smiled again to let the man know that he held nothing against him for being white and impatient. Then he refused to see the man any longer and stood pressing the button, the voices of the crowd reaching him like sounds in distant streets. Let them yell. All the Negroes down there were just ashamed because he was black like them. He smiled inwardly, knowing how it was. Most of the time he was ashamed of what Negroes did himself. Well, let them be ashamed for something this time. Like him. He was like a long thin black wire that was being stretched and wound upon the bingo wheel; wound until he wanted to scream; wound, but this time himself controlling the winding and the sadness and the shame, and because he did, Laura would be all right. Suddenly the lights flickered. He staggered backwards. Had something gone wrong? All this noise. Didn't they know that although he controlled the wheel, it also controlled him, and unless he pressed the button forever and forever and ever it would stop, leaving him high and dry, dry and high on this hard high slippery hill and Laura dead? There was only one chance; he had to do whatever the wheel demanded. And gripping the button in despair, he discovered with surprise that it imparted a nervous energy. His spine tingled. He felt a certain power.

Now he faced the raging crowd with defiance, its screams penetrating his eardrums like trumpets shrieking from a juke-box①. The vague faces glowing in the bingo lights gave him a sense of himself that he had never known before. He was running the show, by God! They had to react to him, for he was their luck. This is *me*, he thought. Let the bastards yell. Then someone was laughing inside him, and he realized that somehow he had forgotten his own name. It was a sad, lost feeling to lose your name, and a crazy thing to do. That name had been given him by the white man who had owned his grandfather a long lost time ago down South. But maybe those wise guys knew his name.

"Who am I?" he screamed.

"Hurry up and bingo, you jerk!"

They didn't know either, he thought sadly. They didn't even know their own names, they were all poor nameless bastards. Well, he didn't need that old name; he was reborn. For as long as he pressed the button he was The-man-who-pressed-the-button-who-held-the-prize-who-was-the-King-of-Bingo. That was the

---

① juke-box：(美口)投币唱片播放机。

way it was, and he'd have to press the button even if nobody understood, even though Laura did not understand.

"Live!" he shouted.

The audience quieted like the dying of a huge fan.

"Live, Laura, baby. I got holt of it now①, sugar. Live!"

He screamed it, tears streaming down his face. "I got nobody but YOU!"

The screams tore from his very guts. He felt as though the rush of blood to his head would burst out in baseball seams of small red droplets, like a head beaten by police clubs. Bending over he saw a trickle of blood splashing the toe of his shoe. With his free hand he searched his head. It was his nose. God, suppose something has gone wrong? He felt that the whole audience had somehow entered him and was stamping its feet in his stomach and he was unable to throw them out. They wanted the prize, that was it. They wanted the secret for themselves. But they'd never get it; he would keep the bingo wheel whirling forever, and Laura would be safe in the wheel. But would she? It had to be, because if she were not safe the wheel would cease to turn; it could not go on. He had to get away, vomit all, and his mind formed an image of himself running with Laura in his arms down the tracks of the subway just ahead of an A train, running desperately *vomit* with people screaming for him to come out but knowing no way of leaving the tracks because to stop would bring the train crushing down upon him and to attempt to leave across the other tracks would mean to run into a hot third rail as high as his waist which threw blue sparks that blinded his eyes until he could hardly see.

He heard singing and the audience was clapping its hands.

Shoot the liquor to him, Jim, boy!

Clap-clap-clap

Well a-calla the cop②

He's blowing his top!

Shoot the liquor to him, Jim, boy!

Bitter anger grew within him at the singing. They think I'm crazy. Well let'em laugh. I'll do what I got to do.

He was standing in an attitude of intense listening when he saw that they were watching something on the stage behind him. He felt weak. But when he

---

① I got holt of it now.: I got hold of it now. 主人公以为自己控制住了一切,反复用 control, power 等词。

② a-calla the cop: Call the police.

turned he saw no one. If only his thumb did not ache so. Now they were applauding. And for a moment he thought that the wheel had stopped. But that was impossible, his thumb still pressed the button. Then he saw them. Two men in uniform beckoned from the end of the stage. They were coming toward him, walking in step, slowly, like a tap-dance team returning for a third encore[①]. But their shoulders shot forward, and he backed away, looking wildly about. There was nothing to fight them with. He had only the long black cord which led to a plug somewhere back stage, and he couldn't use that because it operated the bingo wheel. He backed slowly, fixing the men with his eyes as his lips stretched over his teeth in a tight, fixed grin; moved toward the end of the stage and realizing that he couldn't go much further, for suddenly the cord became taut and he couldn't afford to break the cord. But he had to do something. The audience was howling. Suddenly he stopped dead, seeing the men halt, their legs lifted as in an interrupted step of a slow-motion dance. There was nothing to do but run in the other direction and he dashed forward, slipping and sliding. The men fell back, surprised. He struck out violently going past.

"Grab him!"

He ran, but all too quickly the cord tightened, resistingly, and he turned and ran back again. This time he slipped them, and discovered by running in a circle before the wheel he could keep the cord from tightening. But this way he had to flail his arms to keep the men away. Why couldn't they leave a man alone? He ran, circling.

"Ring down the curtain," someone yelled. But they couldn't do that. If they did the wheel flashing from the projection room would be cut off. But they had him before he could tell them so, trying to pry open his fist, and he was wrestling and trying to bring his knees into the fight and holding on to the button, for it was his life. And now he was down, seeing a foot coming down, crushing his wrist cruelly, down, as he saw the wheel whirling serenely above.

"I can't give it up." he screamed. Then quietly, in a confidential tone, "Boys, I really can't give it up."

It landed hard against his head. And in the blank moment they had it away from him, completely now. He fought them trying to pull him up from the stage as he watched the wheel spin slowly to a stop. Without surprise he saw it rest at

---

[①] like a tap-dance team returning for a third encore: tap-dance: 踢踏舞; encore: 应观众要求加演。像是应观众要求第三次还场演出的踢踏舞队。

double-zero.

"You see," he pointed bitterly.

"Sure, boy, sure, it's O.K.," one of the men said smiling.

And seeing the man bow his head to someone he could not see, he felt very, very happy; he would receive what all the winners received.

But as he warmed in the justice of the man's tight smile he did not see the man's slow wink, nor see the bow-legged man behind him step clear of the swiftly descending curtain and set himself for a blow①. He only felt the dull pain exploding in his skull, and he knew even as it slipped out of him that his luck had run out on the stage.

《宾果游戏之王》最初于1944年发表,融现实主义情节和超现实主义手法于一体。无名黑人主人公试图通过宾果游戏筹取为妻子治病款项的叙事线索将黑人在美国被奴役的历史与孤立无援的现状之间的反差交织在一起,解构了通过个人努力取得成功、北方是黑人获得自由平等的天堂等美国神话。故事还通过隐喻、象征、梦境、幻觉等手法创造了一个虚实共存的情景,显现了黑人在美国无助无望的残酷社会现实。一个身无分文的黑人,无名无姓、无依无靠,抱着改变命运的希望,从南方山区走进北方都市;然而,身份(证)的缺失制约着他(工作)的权利,妻子的重病既加重他的责任又增添了他的孤立。万般无奈之时,他走进电影院,饥肠辘辘地从电影人物的行为和自己的想象中获得虚幻的自由和权力。博彩中,他侥幸地握住了控制游戏转盘的按钮,于是自以为控制了命运的车轮,要与历史和命运抗争,试图改变游戏规则不让转盘停下,结果被砸死在制造幻想的电影院的舞台上。电影和游戏一样,都是主流社会通过幻觉奴役他者的文化霸权工具,"他们把一切都安排好了"。象征命运或社会力量的白色亮光和火车让他睁不开眼、喘不出气,北方工业文明同南方种植园经济一样压榨着黑人;象征机会的游戏转盘给予他力量,让他忘却过去的屈辱,成为西方文化(电影)中的英雄人物,然而他最终还是在一个警察向另一个警察挤眼的瞬间成为牺牲品,在赢得游戏的同时失去自身的存在。无名黑人的故事就像一则寓言揭示了生活在现代美国社会的人的困境:生活在自由的国度却受各种枷锁束缚,人与人(黑人与黑人、黑人与白人)之间隔阂重重,工作不像清教宣传的那样会得到报偿(有人没有工作权利,有人因工作失去理智),取胜却一无所获。

① set himself for a blow: 跑开。

思考题

1. Where does the action of the story take place? What is the significance of this setting?
2. Why does the protagonist, an African American, miss the American South? What does that suggest about the alternatives open to such a person?
3. Is the protagonist's sense of power hallucination or insight?
4. What is the significance of the nameless protagonist's forgetting his own name?
5. What are the symbolic meanings of the bingo wheel?

推荐作品

Invisible Man (1952)

参考资料

Busby, Mark. *Ralph Ellison*. Boston: Twayne Publishers, 1991.

Graham, Maryemma and Amritjit Singh, eds. *Conversations with Ralph Ellison.* UP of Mississippi, 1995.

Jackson, Lawrence. *Ralph Ellision: Emergence of Genius.* New York: John Wiley & Sons, 2002

O'Meally, Robert G. *The Craft of Ralph Ellison*. Cambridge, Mass.: Harvard UP, 1980.

---, ed. *New Essays on Invisible Man*. Beijing: Peking UP; Cambridge UP, 2006.

第八单元

John Updike
(1932—)

约翰·厄普代克

作者简介

约翰·厄普代克,美国当代重要作家,出生于宾夕法尼亚州一个教师家庭。他在哈佛大学读书时就显露才华,经常为学生幽默杂志撰稿、作画。毕业后,他到英国学习美术一年,回国后曾在《纽约客》(New Yorker)杂志任记者。厄普代克的作品体裁包括了小说、诗歌、散文、戏剧、文学评论。他的主要长篇小说包括《兔子,跑吧!》(Rabbit, Run, 1960)、《马人》(又译《半人半马》,The Centaur, 1963)、《夫妇们》(又译《成双成对》,Couples, 1968)、《兔子归来》(Rabbit Redux, 1971)、《都是星期天的一个月》,(A Month of Sundays, 1975)、《嫁给我:一段浪漫史》(Marry Me: A Romance, 1976)、《兔子富了》(Rabbit is Rich, 1981)、《罗杰教授的版本》(Roger's Version, 1986)、《S》(S., 1988)、《兔子安息》(Rabbit at Rest, 1990)、《巴西》(Brazil, 1994)、《圣洁百合》(In the Beauty of the Lilies, 1996)、《末日来临》(Toward the End of the Time, 1997)、《葛特露和克劳迪斯》(Gertrude and Claudius, 2000)、《寻找我的面容》(Seek My Face, 2002)等。短篇小说集包括《同一道门》(The Same Door, 1959)、《鸽羽和其他故事》(Pigeon Feathers and Other Stories, 1962)、《音乐学校》(The Music School, 1966)、《爱的插曲:短篇及续集》(Licks of Love: Short Stories and a Sequel, 2000)(其中收有"兔子"系列的续集,中篇小说《兔子受到了怀念》(Rabbit Remembered)、《短篇小说集》(The Collected Stories: 1953—1975, 2003)等。厄普代克的作品多次获奖。其中,"兔子"系列小说中的《兔子富了》获得了美国国家图书奖、美国书评界奖和普利策奖。其后,该系列的另一部小说《兔子安息》又获得了美国书评界奖和普利策奖。厄普代克的创作手法主要是现实主义的,同时他也关注欧洲、拉丁美洲作家的不同的创作风格和实验,并在自己的创作中尝试不同方法,如《巴西》中的魔幻现实主义,《末日来临》中的科幻技巧等。厄普代克的主要作品以20世纪50年代以来社会现实为背景,细致入微地刻画了当代美国中产阶级的生存状态以及个人面对家庭、性爱、信仰危机等诸多问题时的心路历程和行为选择。

尽管按厄普代克的说法,写评论与小说和诗歌创作的差别如同"海上行船"与"紧靠海岸"之间的差别,但他自己却不仅是著作等身的作家,同时也是多产的评论家。除了为《纽约客》、《纽约时报书评》(The New York Times Book Review)、《纽约书评》(The New York Review of Books)等刊物撰写大量评论文章外,他已结集出版了多本散文评论,如《紧靠海岸》(Hugging the Shore, 1983)、《看看而已》(Just Looking, 1989)、《看了又看:关于美国艺术的论述》(Still Looking: Essays on American Art, 2005) 等。其中 1983 年出版的《紧靠海岸》更是获得了 1983 年美国书评界奖。

厄普代克是少数受到公众和学界高度关注的在世作家之一。他两度成为《时代周刊》的封面人物,而受到同样待遇的只有乔伊斯、海明威、福克纳和辛克莱·刘易斯其他四位小说家。《现代小说研究》(Modern Fiction Studies)两次出版厄普代克专刊,而享此殊荣的只有乔伊斯、詹姆斯、康拉德、沃尔夫、福克纳和海明威其他六位作家。然而,厄普代克的文学成就在学界尚有完全不同的看法。

Separating

The day was fair. Brilliant. All that June the weather had mocked the Maples' internal misery with solid sunlight—golden shafts and cascades of green in which their conversations had wormed unseeing, their sad murmuring selves the only stain in Nature. Usually by this time of the year they had acquired tans; but when they met their elder daughter's plane on her return from a year in England they were almost as pale as she, though Judith was too dazzled by the sunny opulent jumble of her native land to notice. They did not spoil her homecoming by telling her immediately. Wait a few days, let her recover from jet lag, had been one of their formulations, in that string of gray dialogues—over coffee, over cocktails, over Cointreau①—that had shaped the strategy of their dissolution, while the earth performed its annual stunt of renewal unnoticed beyond their closed windows. Richard had thought to leave at Easter; Joan had insisted they wait until the four children were at last assembled, with all exams passed and ceremonies attended, and the bauble of summer to console them. So he had drudged away, in love, in dread, repairing screens, getting the mowers sharpened, rolling and patching their new tennis court.

The court, clay, had come through its first winter pitted and windswept bare of redcoat. Years ago the Maples had observed how often, among their friends, divorce followed a dramatic home improvement, as if the marriage were making one last twitchy effort to live; their own worst crisis had come amid the plaster

---

① Cointreau:一种甜酒。

dust and exposed plumbing of a kitchen renovation. Yet, a summer ago, as canary-yellow bulldozers gaily churned a grassy, daisy-dotted knoll into a muddy plateau, and a crew of pigtailed young men raked and tamped clay into a plane, this transformation did not strike them as ominous, but festive in its impudence; their marriage could rend the earth for fun①. The next spring, waking each day at dawn to a sliding sensation as if the bed were being tipped, Richard found the barren tennis court, its net and tapes still rolled in the barn, an environment congruous with his mood of purposeful desolation, and the crumbling of handfuls of clay into cracks and holes (dogs had frolicked on the court in a thaw; rivulets had evolved trenches) an activity suitably elemental and interminable. In his sealed heart he hoped the day would never come.

Now it was here. A Friday. Judith was reacclimated; all four children were assembled, before jobs and camps and visits again scattered them. Joan thought they should be told one by one. Richard was for making an announcement at the table. She said, "I think just making an announcement is a cop-out. They'll start quarrelling and playing to each other instead of focussing. They're each individuals, you know, not just some corporate obstacle to your freedom."

"O.K., O.K. I agree." Joan's plan was exact. That evening, they were giving Judith a belated welcome-home dinner, of lobster and champagne. Then, the party over, they, the two of them, who nineteen years before would push her in a baby carriage along Tenth Street to Washington Square②, were to walk her out of the house, to the bridge across the salt creek, and tell her, swearing her to secrecy. Then Richard Jr., who was going directly from work to a rock concert in Boston, would be told, either late when he returned on the train or early Saturday morning before he went off to his jobs; he was seventeen and employed as one of a golf-course maintenance crew. Then the two younger children, John and Margaret, could, as the morning wore on, be informed.

"Mopped up, as it were," Richard said.

"Do you have any better plan? That leaves you the rest of Saturday to answer any questions, pack, and make your wonderful departure."

"No," he said, meaning he had no better plan, and agreed to hers, though it had an edge of false order, a plea for control in the semblance of its achievement,

---

① but festive in its impudence; their marriage could rend the earth for fun.: its impudence 在这里指把原来遍布花草的小丘推成平地的冒失行为; rend the earth for fun 这里指前面所说的行为是为了取乐而破坏了大地的原貌。

② along Tenth Street to Washington Square: 该地点位于纽约市。

like Joan's long chore lists and financial accountings and, in the days when he first knew her, her too copious lecture notes. Her plan turned one hurdle for him into four—four knife-sharp walls, each with a sheer blind drop① on the other side.

  All spring he had been morbidly conscious of insides and outsides, of barriers and partitions. He and Joan stood as a thin barrier between the children and the truth. Each moment was a partition, with the past on one side and the future on the other, a future containing this unthinkable *now*. Beyond four knifelike walls a new life for him waited vaguely. His skull cupped a secret, a white face, a face both frightened and soothing, both strange and known, that he wanted to shield from tears, which he felt all about him, solid as the sunlight. So haunted, he had become obsessed with battening down the house against his absence, replacing screens and sash cords, hinges and latches—a Houdini② making things snug before his escape.

  The lock. He had still to replace a lock on one of the doors of the screened porch. The task, like most such, proved more difficult than he had imagined. The old lock, aluminum frozen by corrosion, had been deliberately rendered obsolete by manufacturers. Three hardware stores had nothing that even approximately matched the mortised hole its removal (surprisingly easy) left. Another hole had to be gouged, with bits too small and saws too big, and the old hole fitted with a block of wood—the chisels dull, the saw rusty, his fingers thick with lack of sleep. The sun poured down, beyond the porch, on a world of neglect. The bushes already needed pruning, the windward side of the house was shedding flakes of paint, rain would get in when he was gone, insects, rot, death. His family, all those he would lose, filtered through the edges of his awareness as he struggled with screw holes, splinters, opaque instructions, minutiae of metal.

  Judith sat on the porch, a princess returned from exile. She regaled them with stories of fuel shortages, of bomb scares in the Underground, of Pakistani workmen loudly lusting after her as she walked past on her way to dance school. Joan came and went, in and out of the house, calmer than she should have been, praising his struggles with the lock as if this were one more and not the last of their chain of shared chores. The younger of his sons, John, now at fifteen suddenly, unwittingly handsome, for a few minutes held the rickety screen door

---

 ① blind drop：指陡然下落的地形。

 ② Houdini：胡迪尼(Harry Houdini, 1874—1926)美国魔术师和脱逃表演大师,常将自己锁在看似无法脱逃的牢笼中,在限定的时间内挣脱出来。

while his father clumsily hammered and chiselled, each blow a kind of sob in Richard's ears. His younger daughter, having been at a slumber party, slept on the porch hammock through all the noise—heavy and pink, trusting and forsaken. Time, like the sunlight, continued relentlessly; the sunlight slowly slanted. Today was one of the longest days. The lock clicked, worked. He was through. He had a drink; he drank it on the porch, listening to his daughter. "It was so sweet," she was saying, "during the worst of it, how all the butcher's and bakery shops kept open by candlelight. They're all so plucky and cute. From the papers, things sounded so much worse here—people shooting people in gas lines①, and everybody freezing."

Richard asked her, "Do you still want to live in England forever?" Forever: the concept, now a reality upon him, pressed and scratched at the back of his throat.

"No," Judith confessed, turning her oval face to him, its eyes still childishly far apart, but the lips set as over something succulent and satisfactory. "I was anxious to come home. I'm an American." She was a woman. They had raised her; he and Joan had endured together to raise her, alone of the four. The others had still some raising left in them. Yet it was the thought of telling Judith—the image of her, their first baby, walking between them arm in arm, to the bridge—that broke him. The partition between himself and the tears broke. Richard sat down to the celebratory meal with the back of his throat aching; the champagne, the lobster seemed phases of sunshine; he saw them and tasted them through tears. He blinked, swallowed, croakily joked about hay fever. The tears would not stop leaking through; they came not through a hole that could be plugged but through a permeable spot in a membrane, steadily, purely, endlessly, fruitfully. They became, his tears, a shield for himself against these others—their faces, the fact of their assembly, a last time as innocents, at a table where he sat the last time as head. Tears dropped from his nose as he broke the lobster's back; salt flavored his champagne as he sipped it; the raw clench at the back of his throat was delicious. He could not help himself.

His children tried to ignore his tears. Judith on his right, lit a cigarette, gazed upward in the direction of her too energetic, too sophisticated exhalation; on her other side, John earnestly bent his face to the extraction of the last morsels—legs,

---

① in gas lines：为给汽车加油排起的队伍。

tail segments—from the scarlet corpse. Joan, at the opposite end of the table, glanced at him surprised, her reproach displaced by a quick grimace, of forgiveness, or of salute to his superior gift of strategy. Between them, Margaret, no longer called Bean, thirteen and large for her age, gazed from the other side of his pane of tears as if into a shop-window at something she coveted—at her father, a crystalline heap of splinters and memories. It was not she, however, but John who, in the kitchen, as they cleared the plates and carapaces away, asked Joan the question: *Why is Daddy crying?*

Richard heard the question but not the murmured answer. Then he heard Bean cry, "Oh, no-oh!"—the faintly dramatized exclamation of one who had long expected it.

John returned to the table carrying a bowl of salad. He nodded tersely at his father and his lips shaped the conspiratorial words "She told."

"Told what?" Richard asked aloud, insanely.

The boy sat down as if to rebuke his father's distraction with the example of his own good manners and said quietly, "The separation."

Joan and Margaret returned; the child, in Richard's twisted vision, seemed diminished in size, and relieved, relieved to have had the boogeyman[①] at last proved real. He called out to her—the distances at the table had grown immense—"You knew, you always knew," but the clenching at the back of his throat prevented him from making sense of it. From afar he heard Joan talking, levelly, sensibly, reciting what they had prepared: it was a separation for the summer, and experiment. She and Daddy both agreed it would be good for them; they needed space and time to think; they liked each other but did not make each other happy enough, somehow.

Judith, imitating her mother's factual tone, but in her youth off-key, too cool, said, "I think it's silly. You should either live together or get divorced."

Richard's crying, like a wave that has crested and crashed, had become tumultuous, but it was overtopped by another tumult, for John, who had been so reserved, now grew larger and larger at the table. Perhaps his younger sister's being credited with knowing set him off. "Why didn't you *tell* us?" he asked, in a large round voice quite unlike his own. "You should have *told* us you weren't getting along."

---

① boogeyman: bogeyman.

Richard was startled into attempting to force words through his tears. "We *do* get along, that's the trouble, so it doesn't show even to us—" "That we do not love each other" was the rest of the sentence; he couldn't finish it.

Joan finished for him, in her style. "And we've always, *especially*, loved our children."

John was not mollified. "What do you care about *us*?" he boomed. "We're just little things you *had*." His sister's laughing forced a laugh from him, which he turned hard and parodistic: "Ha ha *ha*." Richard and Joan realized simultaneously that the child was drunk, on Judith's homecoming champagne. Feeling bound to keep the center of the stage, John took a cigarette from Judith's pack, poked it into his mouth, let it hang from his lower lip, and squinted like a gangster.

"You're not little things we had," Richard called to him. "You're the whole point. But you're grown. Or almost."

The boy was lighting matches. Instead of holding them to his cigarette (for they had never seen him smoke; being "good" had been his way of setting himself apart), he held them to his mother's face, closer and closer, for her to blow out. Then he lit the whole folder—a hiss and then a torch, held against his mother's face. Prismed by tears, the flame filled Richard's vision; he didn't know how it was extinguished. He heard Margaret say, "Oh stop showing off," and saw John, in response, break the cigarette in two and put the halves entirely into his mouth and chew, sticking out his tongue to display the shreds to his sister.

Joan talked to him, reasoning—a fountain of reason, unintelligible. "Talked about it for year... our children must help us... Daddy and I both want..." As the boy listened, he carefully wadded a paper napkin into the leaves of his salad, fashioned a ball of paper and lettuce, and popped it into his mouth, looking around the table for the expected laughter. None came. Judith said, "Be mature," and dismissed a plume of smoke.

Richard got up from this stifling table and led the boy outside. Though the house was in twilight, the outdoors still brimmed with light, the long waste light of high summer. Both laughing, he supervised John's spitting out the lettuce and paper and tobacco into the pachysandra①. He took him by the hand—a square gritty hand, but for its softness a man's②. Yet, it held on. They ran together up

---

① pachysandra：草本植物，常用于草坪。
② but for its softness a man's：要不是还显得柔软，就会被当作成人的手了。

into the field, past the tennis court. The raw banking left by the bulldozers was dotted with daisies. Past the court and a flat stretch where they used to play family baseball stood a soft green rise glorious in the sun, each weed and species of grass distinct as illumination on parchment. "I'm sorry, so sorry," Richard cried. "You were the only one who ever tried to help me with all the goddam jobs around this place."

Sobbing, safe within his tears and the champagne, John explained, "It's not just the separation, it's the whole crummy year, I *hate* that school, you can't make any friends, the history teacher's a scud①."

They sat on the crest of the rise, shaking and warm from their tears but easier in their voices, and Richard tried to focus on the child's sad year—the weekdays long with homework, the weekends spent in his room with model airplanes, while his parents murmured down below, nursing their separation. How selfish, how blind, Richard thought; his eyes felt scoured. He told his son, "We'll think about getting you transferred. Life's too short to be miserable."

They had said what they could, but did not want the moment to heal, and talked on, about the school, about the tennis court, whether it would ever again be as good as it had been that first summer. They walked to inspect it and pressed a few more tapes more firmly down. A little stiltedly, perhaps trying to make too much of the moment, to prolong it, Richard led the boy to the spot in the field where the view was best, of the metallic blue river, the emerald marsh, the scattered islands velvet with shadow in th low light, the white bits of beach far away. "See," he said. "It goes on being beautiful. It'll be here tomorrow."

"I know," John answered, impatiently. The moment had closed.

Back in the house, the others had opened some white wine, the champagne being drunk, and still sat at the table, the three females, gossiping. Where Joan sat had become the head. She turned, showing him a tearless face, and asked, "All right?"

"We're fine," he said, resenting it, though relieved, that the party went on without him.

In bed she explained, "I couldn't cry I guess because I cried so much all spring. It really wasn't fair. It's your idea, and you made it look as though I was kicking you out."

---

① scud: 令人反感的人。

"I'm sorry," he said. "I couldn't stop. I wanted to but couldn't."

"You *didn't* want to. You loved it. You were having your way, making a general announcement."

"I love having it over," he admitted. "God, those kids were great. So brave and funny." John, returned to the house, had settled to a model airplane in his room, and kept shouting down to them, "I'm O.K. No sweat." "And the way," Richard went on, cozy in his relief, "they never questioned the reasons we gave. Not thought of a third person. Not even Judith."

"That *was* touching," Joan said.

He gave her a hug. "You were great too. Thank you." Guiltily, he realized he did not feel separated.

"You still have Dickie to do," she told him. These words set before him a black mountain in the darkness; its cold breath, its near weight affected his chest. Of the four children Dickie was most nearly his conscience. Joan did not need to add, "That's one piece of your dirty work I won't do for you."

"I know. I'll do it. You go to sleep."

Within minutes, her breathing slowed, became oblivious and deep. It was quarter to midnight. Dickie's train from the concert would come in at one-fourteen. Richard set the alarm for one. He had slept atrociously for weeks. But whenever he closed his lids some glimpse of the last hours scorched them— Judith exhaling toward the ceiling in a kind of aversion, Bean's mute staring, the sunstruck growth of the field where he and John had rested. The mountain before him moved closer, moved within him; he was huge, momentous. The ache at the back of his throat felt stale. His wife slept as if slain beside him. When, exasperated by his hot lids, his crowded heart, he rose from bed and dressed, she awoke enough to turn over. He told her then, "If I could undo it all, I would."

"Where would you begin?" she asked. There was no place. Giving him courage, she was always giving him courage. He put on shoes without socks in the dark. The children were breathing in their rooms, the downstairs was hollow. In their confusion they had left lights burning. He turned off all but one, the kitchen overhead. The car started. He had hoped it wouldn't. He met only moonlight on the road; it seemed a diaphanous companion, flickering in the leaves along the roadside, haunting his rearview mirror like a pursuer, melting under his headlights. The center of town, not quite deserted, was eerie at this hour. A young cop in uniform kept company with a gang of T-shirted kids on the steps of the bank. Across from the railroad station, several bars kept open. Customers, mostly young, passed in and out of the warm night, savoring summer's novelty. Voices shouted from cars as they passed; an immense conversation seemed in progress. Richard parked and in his weariness put his head on the passenger seat, out of the commotion and wheeling lights. It was as when, in the movies, an assassin grimly carries his mission through the jostle of a carnival—except the movies cannot show the precipitous, palpable slope you cling to within. You cannot climb back down; you can only fall. The synthetic fabric of the car seat, warmed by his cheek, confided to him an ancient, distant scent of vanilla.

A train whistle caused him to lift his head. It was on time; he had hoped it would be late. The slender drawgates descended. The bell of approach tingled happily. The great metal body, horizontally fluted, rocked to a stop, and sleepy teen-agers disembarked, his son among them. Dickie did not show surprise that his father was meeting him at this terrible hour. He sauntered to the car with two friends, both taller than he. He said "Hi" to his father and took the passenger's seat with an exhausted promptness that expressed gratitude. The friends got into the back, and Richard was grateful; a few more minutes' postponement would be won by driving them home.

He asked, "How was the concert?"

"Groovy," one boy said from the back seat.

"It bit," the other said.

"It was O.K.," Dickie said, moderate by nature, so reasonable that in his childhood the unreason of the world had given him headaches, stomach aches, nausea. When the second friend had been dropped off at his dark house, the boy blurted, "Dad, my eyes are killing me with hay fever! I'm out there cutting that mothering grass all day!"

"Do we still have those drops?"

"They didn't do any good last summer."

"They might this." Richard swung a U-turn on the empty street. The drive home took a few minutes. The mountain was here, in his throat. "Richard," he said, and felt the boy, slumped and rubbing his eyes, go tense at his tone, "I didn't come to meet you just to make your life easier. I came because your mother and I have some news for you, and you're a hard man to get ahold of these days. It's sad news."

"That's O.K." The reassurance came out soft, but quick, as if released from the tip of a spring.

Richard had feared that his tears would return and choke him, but the boy's manliness set an example, and his voice issued forth steady and dry. "It's sad news, but it needn't be tragic news, at least for you. It should have no practical effect on your life, though it's bound to have an emotional effect. You'll work at your job, and go back to school in September. Your mother and I are really proud of what you're making of your life; we don't want that to change at all."

"Yeah," the boy said lightly, on the intake of his breath, holding himself up. They turned the corner; the church they went to loomed like a gutted fort. The home of the woman Richard hoped to marry stood across the green. Her bedroom light burned.

"Your mother and I," he said, "have decided to separate. For the summer. Nothing legal, no divorce yet. We want to see how it feels. For some years now, we haven't been doing enough for each other, making each other as happy as we should be. Have you sensed that?"

"No," the boy said. It was an honest, unemotional answer: true or false in a quiz.

Glad for the factual basis, Richard pursued, even garrulously, the details. His apartment across town, his utter accessibility, the split vacation arrangements, the advantages to the children, the added mobility and variety of the summer. Dickie listened, absorbing. "Do the others know?"

Richard described how they had been told.

"How did they take it?"

"The girls pretty calmly. John flipped out; he shouted and ate a cigarette and made a salad out of his napkin and told us how much he hated school."
His brother chuckled. "He did?"

"Yeah. The school issue was more upsetting for him than Mom and me. He seemed to feel better for having exploded."

"He did?" The repetition was the first sign that he was stunned.

"Yes. Dickie, I want to tell you something. This last hour, waiting for your train to get in, has been about the worst of my life. I hate this. *Hate* it. My father would have died before doing it to me." He felt immensely lighter, saying this. He had dumped the mountain on the boy. They were home. Moving swiftly as a shadow, Dickie was out of the car, through the bright kitchen. Richard called after him, "Want a glass of milk or anything?"

"No thanks."

"Want us to call the course tomorrow and say you're too sick to work?"

"No, that's all right." The answer was faint, delivered at the door to his room; Richard listened for the lam of a tantrum. The door closed normally. The sound was sickening.

Joan had sunk into the first deep trough of sleep and was slow to awake. Richard had to repeat, "I told him."

"What did he say?"

"Nothing much. Could you go say good night to him? Please."

She left their room, without putting on a bathrobe. He sluggishly changed back into his pajamas and walked down the hall. Dickie was already in bed, Joan was sitting beside him, and the boy's bedside clock radio was murmuring music. When she stood, an inexplicable light—the moon? —outlined her body through the nightie. Richard sat on the warm place she had indented on the child's narrow mattress. He asked him, "Do you want the radio on like that?"

"It always is."

"Doesn't it keep you awake? It would me."

"No."

"Are you sleepy?"

"Yeah."

"Good. Sure you want to get up and go to work? You've had a big night."

"I want to."

Away at school this winter he had learned for the first time that you can go short of sleep and live. As an infant he had slept with an immobile, sweating intensity that had alarmed his babysitters. As the children aged, he became the first to go to bed, earlier for a time than his younger brother and sister. Even now, he would go slack in the middle of a television show, his sprawled legs hairy and brown. "O.K. Good boy, Dickie, listen. I love you so much, I never knew how much until now. No matter how this works out, I'll always be with you. Really."

Richard bent to kiss an averted face but his son, sinewy, turned and with wet cheeks embraced him and gave him a kiss, on the lips, passionate as a woman's. In his father's ear he moaned one word, the crucial, intelligent word: *"Why?"*

Why. It was a whistle of wind in a crack, a knife thrust, a window thrown open on emptiness. The white face was gone, the darkness was featureless. Richard had forgotten why.

《分居》(1975)是梅普尔斯夫妇系列故事中的一篇。作者自己的婚姻历程与故事主人公的婚姻架构有相当的对应。故事中,梅普尔斯夫妇像其他中产阶级家庭的生活一样,物质上富足,行事也显得井井有条:他们承担培育子女成长的职责,扮演各自的家庭社会角色,努力完成对其他家庭成员的应尽义务,他们遵循主流中产阶级的自由、平等、个人主义价值,甚至梅普尔斯夫妇宣布分居消息的计划都象征性地具有"秩序"的意味。然而,这只是一种"虚假"的秩序感。从主人公心理活动和外在言行中看出,无论如何抉择,他都无法逃脱错综复杂的情感矛盾和迷茫。即便他愿意时光倒退,也根本"无处着落"。故事几处描写他心灵体验的无助"滑落"、"坠落"感。分居究竟是"为什么?"他竟然"忘记了"其理性依据,这样的抉择只是"打开窗户后面对的虚空"。的确,在现代美国,以宗教为基础的道德秩序早已失去往昔的权威,让位于理性。虽然以个人权利和功利主义为基础建立的社会、经济秩序能够给个人提供追求物欲满足的自由,但是对厄普代克和他作品中的主人公所代表的、具有深厚宗教传统的美国个人来说,普遍的"理性化"本身并不能给个人人生意义的追求提供依据和心灵秩序,而观念开放时代的家庭解体和情欲旋涡更是凸显出缺失的个人信念支点。作者将事物细节与心理描述有机地交织在一起:理查德对加固房屋的执着和内心关于屏障和禁锢的联想,子女对父母分居的反应和父爱与责任交织的歉疚感,对家庭的留恋以及寻求新爱的情感纠葛,而这些交错的细节是当代个人生存现状的现实主义写照。故事叙述采用第三人称视角中的有限全知视角:即,读者只能看到男主人公的内心活动。

思考题

1. What secret does Richard keep in his mind?
2. How does John react to the news?
3. Is John more upset about school than about his parents' separation? Why or why not?
4. How does Dickie take the news?
5. How does Richard feel about his new life?

推荐作品

Rabbit, Run (1960)
"A&P" (1961)
Couples (1968)

参考资料

Boswell, Marshall. *John Updike's Rabbit Tetralogy: Mastered Irony in Motion.* Columbia: U of Missouri P, 2001.

Greiner, Donald J. *John Updike's Novels.* Athens: Ohio UP, 1984.

Trachtenberg, Stanley, ed. *New Essays on Rabbit Run.* Beijing: Peking UP; Cambridge UP, 2006

Updike, John. *Conversations with John Updike.* Ed. James Plath. Jackson: UP of Mississippi, 1994.

第九单元
Saul Bellow
(1915—2005)
索尔·贝娄

作者简介

索尔·贝娄,犹太裔小说家,生于加拿大的魁北克,后移居芝加哥。贝娄先后就读于芝加哥大学和西北大学,1937 年获社会学和人类学学士学位。同年在威斯康星大学做研究工作,二战期间曾在商船运输部门服役。曾在普林斯顿大学、明尼苏达大学、芝加哥大学和波士顿大学任教,2005 年 4 月去世。

早期作品包括《晃来晃去的人》(*Dangling Man*, 1944),《受害者》(*The Victim*, 1947),《只争朝夕》(*Seize the Day*, 1956)。有评论家认为,这些作品虽然出色,但在许多方面不如《奥吉·玛琪历险记》(*The Adventures of Augie March*, 1953,获美国国家图书奖)、《雨王汉德逊》(*Henderson The Rain King*, 1959)、《赫尔索格》(*Herzog*, 1964,获美国国家图书奖)、《赛姆勒先生的行星》(*Mr. Sammler's Planet*, 1964,获美国国家图书奖)、《洪堡的礼物》(*Humboldt's Gift*, 1975,获普利策奖)。1976 年因其作品反映出"对人类的理解以及对当代文化的细致分析"而荣获诺贝尔文学奖。《院长的十二月》(*The Dean's December*, 1982)不同于之前作者的自嘲作品,是"真实而严肃的自画像"。评论家马尔科姆·布拉德伯里认为,该作品"代表贝娄对当代社会最有力的反抗"。《愁思伤情》(*More Die of Heartbreak*, 1987)深入细致地刻画出当代美国社会中欲望对个人的折磨。小说《拉维尔斯坦》(*Ravelstein*, 2000)以作者在芝加哥大学的好友艾伦·布卢姆(Alan Bloom)为原型。第一部非虚构作品《往返耶路撒冷:个人报道》(*To Jerusalem and Back: A Personal Account*)于 1976 问世,记录了他逗留以色列期间的个人生活和文学创作。贝娄还发表过《最后的分析》(*The Last Analysis*, 1965) 以及三个短剧。出版的短篇故事集有《莫斯比的回忆及其他故事》(*Mosby's Memoirs and Other Stories*, 1968)和《出言不逊者及其他故事》(*Him with His Foot in His Mouth and Other Stories*, 1984)。贝娄的作品主要以他最为熟悉的芝加哥为背景,探索现代犹太人如何悲喜交加地在物欲横流的世界中寻找生活"更崇高的意义"。贝娄叙事技巧精湛,语言丰富多彩,善于捕捉生活场景,并赋以深刻寓意。他曾说:"最普通的犹太人对话中都会充满历史、神话、宗教典故。"

A Silver Dish

WHAT DO YOU DO ABOUT DEATH—IN THIS CASE, the death of an old father? If you're a modern person, sixty years of age, and a man who's been around, like Woody Selbst, what do you do? Take this matter of mourning, and take it against a contemporary background. How, against a contemporary background, do you mourn an octogenarian① father, nearly blind, his heart enlarged, his lungs filling with fluid, who creeps, stumbles, gives off the odors, the moldiness or gassiness, of old men. I mean! As Woody put it, be realistic. Think what times these are. The papers daily give it to you—the Lufthansa pilot in Aden is described by the hostages on his knees, begging the Palestinian terrorists not to execute him, but they shoot him through the head. Later they themselves are killed. And still others shoot others, or shoot themselves. That's what you read in the press, see on the tube, mention at dinner. We know now what goes daily through the whole of the human community, like a global death-peristalsis②.

Woody, a businessman in South Chicago, was not an ignorant person. He knew more such phrases than you would expect a tile contractor (offices, lobbies, lavatories) to know. The kind of knowledge he had was not the kind for which you get academic degrees. Although Woody had studied for two years in a seminary, preparing to be a minister. Two years of college during the Depression was more than most high-school graduates could afford. After that, in his own vital, picturesque, original way (Morris, his old man, was also, in his days of nature, vital and picturesque), Woody had read up on many subjects, subscribed to Science and other magazines that gave real information, and had taken night courses at De Paul and Northwestern in ecology, criminology, existentialism. Also he had traveled extensively in Japan, Mexico, and Africa, and there was an African experience that was especially relevant to mourning. It was this: on a launch near the Murchison Falls in Uganda, he had seen a buffalo calf seized by a crocodile from the bank of the White Nile. There were giraffes along the tropical river, and hip-

---

① octogenarian: 80岁到90岁(的人)的。
② peristalsis: (生理)蠕动。

popotamuses, and baboons, and flamingos and other brilliant birds crossing the bright air in the heat of the morning, when the calf, stepping into the river to drink, was grabbed by the hoof and dragged down. The parent buffaloes couldn't figure it out. Under the water the calf still threshed, fought, churned the mud. Woody, the robust traveler, took this in as he sailed by, and to him it looked as if the parent cattle were asking each other dumbly what had happened. He chose to assume that there was pain in this, he read brute grief into it①. On the White Nile, Woody had the impression that he had gone back to the pre-Adamite② past, and he brought reflections on this impression home to South Chicago. He brought also a bundle of hashish③ from Kampala. In this he took a chance with the customs inspectors, banking perhaps on his broad build, frank face, high color. He didn't look like a wrongdoer, a bad guy; he looked like a good guy. But he liked taking chances. Risk was a wonderful stimulus. He threw down his trenchcoat on the customs counter. If the inspectors searched the pockets, he was prepared to say that the coat wasn't his. But he got away with it, and the Thanksgiving turkey was stuffed with hashish. This was much enjoyed. That was practically the last feast at which Pop, who also relished risk or defiance, was present, The hashish Woody had tried to raise in his backyard from the Africa seeds didn't take. But behind his warehouse, where the Lincoln Continental was parked, he kept a patch of marijuana. There was no harm at all in Woody, but he didn't like being entirely within the law. It was simply a question of self-respect.

After that Thanksgiving, Pop gradually sank as if he had a slow leak. This went on for some years. In and out of the hospital, he dwindled, his mind wandered, he couldn't even concentrate enough to complain, except in exceptional moments on the Sundays Woody regularly devoted to him. Morris, an amateur who once was taken seriously by Willie Hoppe, the great pro④ himself, couldn't execute the simplest billiard shots anymore. He could only conceive shots; he began to theorize about impossible three-cushion⑤ combinations. Halina, the Polish woman with whom Morris had lived for over forty years as man and wife, was too old herself now to run to the hospital. So Woody had to do it. There was Woody's

---

① he read brute grief into it：他看出野兽也有悲伤。
② pre-Adamite：人类出现前的。
③ hashish：大麻。
④ pro：专业人员。
⑤ three-cushion：(台)三边的(指每一击使球三次撞边的)。

mother, too—a Christian convert—needing care; she was over eighty and frequently hospitalized. Everybody had diabetes and pleurisy and arthritis and cataracts and cardiac pacemakers①. And everybody had lived by the body, but the body was giving out.

There were Woody's two sisters as well, unmarried, in their fifties, very Christian, very straight, still living with Mama in an entirely Christian bungalow. Woody, who took full responsibility for them all, occasionally had to put one of the girls (they had become sick girls) in a mental institution. Nothing severe. The sisters were wonderful women, both of them gorgeous once, but neither of the poor things was playing with a full deck②. And all the factions had to be kept separate—Mama, the Christian convert; the fundamentalist③ sisters; Pop, who read the Yiddish paper as long as he could still see print; Halina, a good Catholic. Woody, the seminary forty years behind him, described himself as an agnostic④. Pop had no more religion than you could find in the Yiddish paper, but he made Woody promise to bury him among Jews, and that was where he lay now, in the Hawaiian shirt Woody had bought for him at the tilers' convention in Honolulu. Woody would allow no undertaker's assistant to dress him, but came to the parlor and buttoned the stiff into the shirt himself, and the old man went down looking like Ben-Gurion⑤ in a simple wooden coffin, sure to rot fast. That was how Woody wanted it all. At the graveside, he had taken off and folded his jacket, rolled up his sleeves on thick freckled biceps, waved back the little tractor standing by, and shoveled the dirt himself. His big face, broad at the bottom, narrowed upward like a Dutch house. And, his small good lower teeth taking hold of the upper lip in his exertion, he performed the final duty of a son. He was very fit, so it must have been emotion, not the shoveling, that made him redden so. After the funeral, he went home with Halina and her son, a decent Polack like his mother, and talented, too—Mitosh played the organ at hockey and basketball games in the Stadium, which took a smart man because it was a rabble-rousing kind of occupation—and they had some drinks and comforted the old girl. Halina was true blue, always one hundred percent for Morris.

---

① pleurisy：肋膜炎。arthritis：关节炎。cataract：白内障。cardiac pacemaker：心脏电子起搏器。
② neither of the poor things was playing with a full deck：她俩脑子没一个够用的。
③ fundamentalist：原教旨主义的。
④ agnostic：不可知论者。
⑤ Ben-Gurion：本·古里安(1886—1973)，犹太复国主义运动领导人，1930年组成以色列工人党，自任领袖，是以色列国主要创建者和首任总理兼国防部长。

Then for the rest of the week Woody was busy, had jobs to run, office responsibilities, family responsibilities. He lived alone; as did his wife; as did his mistress: everybody in a separate establishment. Since his wife, after fifteen years of separation, had not learned to take care of herself, Woody did her shopping on Fridays, filled her freezer. He had to take her this week to buy shoes. Also, Friday night he always spent with Helen—Helen was his wife de facto[①]. Saturday he did his big weekly shopping. Saturday night he devoted to Mom and his sisters. So he was too busy to attend to his own feelings except, intermittently, to note to himself, "First Thursday in the grave." "First Friday, and fine weather." "First Saturday; he's got to be getting used to it." Under his breath he occasionally said, "Oh, Pop."

But it was Sunday that hit him, when the bells rang all over South Chicago—the Ukrainian, Roman Catholic, Greek, Russian, African Methodist churches[②], sounding off one after another. Woody had his offices in his warehouse, and there had built an apartment for himself, very spacious and convenient, in the top story. Because he left every Sunday morning at seven to spend the day with Pop, he had forgotten by how many churches Selbst Tile Company was surrounded. He was still in bed when he heard the bells, and all at once he knew how heartbroken he was. This sudden big heartache in a man of sixty, a practical, physical, healthy-minded, and experienced man, was deeply unpleasant. When he had an unpleasant condition, he believed in taking something for it. So he thought: What shall I take? There were plenty of remedies available. His cellar was stocked with cases of Scotch whisky, Polish vodka, Armagnac, Moselle, Burgundy[③]. There were also freezers with steaks and with game and with Alaskan king crab. He bought with a broad hand—by the crate and by the dozen. But in the end, when he got out of bed, he took nothing but a cup of coffee. While the kettle was heating, he put on his Japanese judo-style suit and sat down to reflect.

Woody was moved when things were honest. Bearing beams[④] were honest, undisguised concrete pillars inside highrise apartments were honest. It was bad to cover up anything. He hated faking. Stone was honest. Metal was honest. These Sunday bells were very straight. They broke loose, they wagged and rocked, and

---

① de facto：(拉)实际上的，事实上的。
② African Methodist churches：非洲循道宗教堂。
③ Armagnac：阿马尼亚克酒。Moselle：(德国)摩泽尔白葡萄酒。Burgundy：勃艮第葡萄酒。
④ bearing beams：过梁。

the vibrations and the banging did something for him—cleansed his insides, purified his blood. A bell was a one-way throat, had only one thing to tell you and simply told it. He listened.

He had had some connections with bells and churches. He was after all something of a Christian. Born a Jew, he was a Jew facially, with a hint of Iroquois or Cherokee①, but his mother had been converted more than fifty years ago by her brother-in-law, the Reverend Doctor Kovner. Kovner, a rabbinical② student who had left the Hebrew Union College in Cincinnati to become a minister and establish a mission, had given Woody a partly Christian upbringing. Now, Pop was on the outs with these fundamentalists. He said that the Jews came to the mission to get coffee, bacon, canned pineapple, day-old bread, and dairy products. And if they had to listen to sermons, that was okay—this was the Depression and you couldn't be too particular—but he knew they sold the bacon.

The Gospels said it plainly: "Salvation is from the Jews."③

Backing the Reverend Doctor were wealthy fundamentalists, mainly Swedes, eager to speed up the Second Coming④ by converting all Jews. The foremost of Kovner's backers was Mrs. Skoglund, who had inherited a large dairy business from her late husband. Woody was under her special protection.

Woody was fourteen years of age when Pop took off with Halina, who worked in his shop, leaving his difficult Christian wife and his converted son and his small daughters. He came to Woody in the backyard one spring day and said, "From now on you're the man of the house." Woody was practicing with a golf club, knocking off the heads of dandelions. Pop came into the yard in his good suit, which was too hot for the weather, and when he took off his fedora⑤ the skin of his head was marked with a deep ring and the sweat was sprinkled over his scalp—more drops than hairs. He said, "I'm going to move out." Pop was anxious, but he was set to go—determined. "It's no use. I can't live a life like this." Envisioning the life Pop simply had to live, his free life, Woody was able to picture him in the billiard parlor, under the El tracks in a crap game, or playing poker at Brown and Koppel's upstairs. "You're going to be the man of

---

① Iroquois: 易洛魁人(北美印第安人)。Cherokee: 彻罗基人(北美印第安人)。
② rabbinical: 拉比的;(尤指中世纪的)拉比著作(或学识、教诲、语言等)的。
③ Salvation is from the Jews.: 拯救来自犹太人。
④ Second Coming: (宗)(世界末日前的)基督复临。
⑤ fedora: 浅顶软呢男帽。

the house," said Pop. "It's okay. I put you all on welfare.① I just got back from Wabansia Avenue, from the relief station." Hence the suit and the hat. "They're sending out a caseworker." Then he said, "You got to lend me money to buy gasoline—the caddie money② you saved."

Understanding that, couldn't get away without his help, Woody turned over to him all he had earned at the Sunset Ridge Country Club in Winnetka. Pop felt that the valuable life lesson he was transmitting was worth far more than these dollars, and whenever he was conning his boy a sort of high-priest expression came down over his bent nose, his ruddy face. The children, who got their finest ideas at the movies, called him Richard Dix. Later, when the comic strip came out, they said he was Dick Tracy③.

As Woody now saw it, under the tumbling bells, he had bankrolled④ his own desertion. Ha ha! He found this delightful; and especially Pop's attitude of "That'll teach you to trust your father." For this was a demonstration on behalf of real life and free instincts, against religion and hypocrisy. But mainly it was aimed against being a fool, the disgrace of foolishness. Pop had it in for the Reverend Doctor Kovner,⑤ not because he was an apostate⑥ (Pop couldn't have cared less); not because the mission was a racket (he admitted that the Reverend Doctor was personally honest), but because Doctor Kovner behaved foolishly, spoke like a fool, and acted like a fiddler. He tossed his hair like a Paganini (this was Woody's addition; Pop had never even heard of Paganini). Proof that he was not a spiritual leader was that he converted Jewish women by stealing their hearts. "He works up all those broads," said Pop. "He doesn't even know it himself, I swear he doesn't know how he gets them."

From the other side, Kovner often warned Woody, "Your father is a dangerous person. Of course, you love him; you should love him and forgive him, Voodrow, but you are old enough to understand he is leading a life of wice."

It was all petty stuff: Pop's sinning was on a boy level and therefore made a big impression on a boy. And on Mother. Are wives children, or what? Mother

---

① I put you all on welfare.: 我给你们都办了接受政府福利救济。
② caddie money: 当高尔夫球场服务员赚得的钱。
③ Dick Tracy: 1931 年起在美国报刊上登载的连环画中的大侦探, 后又在电台、电视、电影中出现。
④ bankroll: 为……提供资金。
⑤ Pop had it in for the Reverend Doctor Kovner.: (口) 爸爸对 Reverend Doctor Kovner 有恶感; 总是与 Reverend Doctor Kovner 过不去。
⑥ apostate: 叛教者。

often said, "I hope you put that brute in your prayers. Look what he has done to us. But only pray for him, don't see him." But he saw him all the time. Woodrow was leading a double life, sacred and profane. He accepted Jesus Christ as his personal redeemer. Aunt Rebecca took advantage of this. She made him work. He had to work under Aunt Rebecca. He filled in for① the janitor at the mission and settlement house②. In winter, he had to feed the coal furnace, and on some nights he slept near the furnace room, on the pool table. He also picked the lock of the storeroom. He took canned pineapple and cut bacon from the flitch③ with his pocketknife. He crammed himself with uncooked bacon. He had a big frame to fill out.④

  Only now, sipping Melitta coffee, he asked himself: Had he been so hungry? No, he loved being reckless. He was fighting Aunt Rebecca Kovner when he took out his knife and got on a box to reach the bacon. She didn't know, she couldn't prove that Woody, such a frank, strong, positive boy, who looked you in the eye, so direct, was a thief also. But he was also a thief. Whenever she looked at him, he knew that she was seeing his father. In the curve of his nose, the movements of his eyes, the thickness of his body, in his healthy face, she saw that wicked savage Morris.

  Morris, you see, had been a street boy in Liverpool—Woody's mother and her sister were British by birth. Morris's Polish family, on their way to America, abandoned him in Liverpool because he had an eye infection and they would all have been sent back from Ellis Island. They stopped awhile in England, but his eyes kept running and they ditched him. They slipped away, and he had to make out alone in Liverpool at the age of twelve. Mother came of better people. Pop, who slept in the cellar of her house; fell in love with her. At sixteen, scabbing⑤ during a seamen's strike, he shoveled his way across the Atlantic and jumped ship in Brooklyn. He became an American, and America never knew it. He voted without papers, he drove without a license, he paid no taxes, he cut every corner⑥. Horses, cards, billiards, and women were his lifelong interests, in ascending order. Did he love anyone (he was so busy)? Yes, he loved Halina. He loved his

---

 ① fill in for: 临时补缺、替代。
 ② settlement house: 街坊文教馆(指为城市等贫民区民供教育、娱乐等社会服务的场所)。
 ③ flitch: 烟熏猪肋条肉。
 ④ He had a big frame to fill out.: 他的大骨架需要食物填充起来。
 ⑤ scab: (美口)顶替罢工工人去上工。
 ⑥ cut every corner: (不按常规而)用简便方法办事。

son. To this day, Mother believed that he had loved her most and always wanted to come back. This gave her a chance to act the queen, with her plump wrists and faded Queen Victoria face. "The girls are instructed never to admit him," she said. The Empress of India speaking.

Bell-battered Woodrow's soul was whirling this Sunday morning, indoors and out, to the past, back to his upper corner of the warehouse, laid out with such originality—the bells coming and going, metal on naked metal, until the bell circle expanded over the whole of steel-making, oil-refining, power-producing mid-autumn South Chicago, and all its Croatians, Ukrainians, Greeks, Poles, and respectable blacks heading for their churches to hear Mass or to sing hymns.

Woody himself had been a good hymn singer. He still knew the hymns. He had testified, too. He was often sent by Aunt Rebecca to get up and tell a churchful of Scandihoovians that he, a Jewish lad, accepted Jesus Christ. For this she paid him fifty cents. She made the disbursement. She was the book-keeper, fiscal chief, general manager of the mission. The Reverend Doctor didn't know a thing about the operation. What the Doctor supplied was the fervor. He was genuine, a wonderful preacher. And what about Woody himself? He also had fervor. He was drawn to the Reverend Doctor. The Reverend Doctor taught him to lift up his eyes, gave him his higher life. Apart from this higher life, the rest was Chicago—the ways of Chicago, which came so natural that nobody thought to question them. So, for instance, in 1933 (what ancient, ancient times!), at the Century of Progress World's Fair, when Woody was a coolie and pulled a rickshaw, wearing a peaked straw hat and trotting with powerful, thick legs, while the brawny red farmers—his boozing① passengers —were laughing their heads off and pestered him for whores, he, although a freshman at the seminary, saw nothing wrong, when girls asked him to steer a little business their way, in making dates and accepting tips from both sides. He necked in② Grant Park with a powerful girl who had to go home quickly to nurse her baby. Smelling of milk, she rode beside him on the streetcar to the West Side, squeezing his rickshaw puller's thigh and wetting her blouse. This was the Roosevelt Road car. Then, in the apartment where she lived with her mother, he couldn't remember that there were any husbands around. What he did remember was the strong milk odor. Without inconsistency, next morning he did New Testament Greek: The light shineth in darkness—to fos

---

① boozing：狂饮的。
② neck in：(美口)亲吻，拥抱。

en te skotia fainei—and the darkness comprehended it not.

And all the while he trotted between the shafts on the fairgrounds he had one idea, nothing to do with these horny giants having a big time in the city: that the goal, the project, the purpose was (and he couldn't explain why he thought so; all evidence was against it)—God's idea was that this world should be a love world, that it should eventually recover and be entirely a world of love. He wouldn't have said this to a soul, for he could see himself how stupid it was—personal and stupid. Nevertheless, there it was at the center of his feelings. And at the same time, Aunt Rebecca was right when she said to him, strictly private, close to his ear even, "You're a little crook, like your father."

The Reverend Doctor preached, Rebecca preached, rich Mrs. Skoglund preached from Evanston, Mother preached. Pop also was on a soapbox. Everyone was doing it. Up and down Division Street, under every lamp, almost, speakers were giving out: anarchists, Socialists, Stalinists, single-taxers, Zionists, Tolstoyans①, vegetarians, and fundamentalist Christian preachers—you name it. A beef, a hope, a way of life or salvation, a protest. How was it that the accumulated gripes of all the ages took off so when transplanted to America?②

And that fine Swedish immigrant Aase (Osie, they pronounced it), who had been the Skoglunds' cook and married the eldest son, to become his rich, religious widow—she supported the Reverend Doctor. In her time she must have been built like a chorus girl. And women seem to have lost the secret of putting up their hair in the high basketry fence of braid she wore. Aase took Woody under her special protection and paid his tuition at the seminary. And Pop said... But on this Sunday, at peace as soon as the bells stopped banging, this velvet autumn day when the grass was finest and thickest, silky green: before the first frost, and the blood in your lungs is redder than summer air can make it and smarts with oxygen, as if the iron in your system was hungry for it, and the chill was sticking it to you in every breath... Pop, six feet under, would never feel this blissful sting gain. The last of the bells still had the bright air streaming with vibrations.

On weekends, the institutional vacancy of decades came back to the warehouse and crept under the door of Woody's apartment. It felt as empty on Sundays as churches were during the week. Before each business day, before the

---

① single-taxer: 主张单一税制者。Zionist: 犹太复国主义者。Tolstoyans: 信奉托尔斯泰哲学学者。

② How was it that the accumulated gripes of all the ages took off so when transplanted to America?: 各个时代累积的痛苦怎么一到美国就全部开始发作了呢？

trucks and the crews got started, Woody jogged five miles in his Adidas suit. Not on this day still reserved for Pop, however. Although it was tempting to go out and run off the grief. Being alone hit Woody hard this morning. He thought: Me and the world; the world and me. Meaning that there always was some activity to interpose, an errand or a visit, a picture to paint (he was a creative amateur), a massage, a meal—a shield between himself and that troublesome solitude which used the world as its reservoir. But Pop! Last Tuesday, Woody had gotten into the hospital bed with Pop because he kept pulling out the intravenous needles[①]. Nurses stuck them back, and then Woody astonished them all by climbing into bed to hold the struggling old guy in his arms. "Easy, Morris, Morris, go easy." But Pop still groped feebly for the pipes.

When the tolling stopped, Woody didn't notice that a great lake of quiet had come over his kingdom, the Selbst Tile warehouse. What he heard and saw was an old red Chicago streetcar, one of those trams the color of a stockyard steer. Cars of this type went out before Pearl Harbor—clumsy, big-bellied, with tough rattan seats and brass grips for the standing passengers. Those cars used to make four stops to the mile, and ran with a wallowing motion. They stank of carbolic or ozone and throbbed when the air compressors were being charged. The conductor had his knotted signal cord to pull, and the motorman beat the foot gong with his mad heel.

Woody recognized himself on the Western Avenue line and riding through a blizzard with his father, both in sheepskins and with hands and faces raw, the snow blowing in from the rear platform when the doors opened and getting into the longitudinal cleats of the floor. There wasn't warmth enough inside to melt it. And Western Avenue was the longest car line in the world, the boosters said, as if it was a thing to brag about. Twenty-three miles long, made by a draftsman with a T square, lined with factories, storage buildings, machine shops, used-car lots, trolley barns, gas stations, funeral parlors, six-flats, utility buildings, and junkyards, on and on from the prairies on the south to Evanston on the north. Woodrow and his father were going north to Evanston, to Howard Street, and then some, to see Mrs. Skoglund. At the end of the line they would still have about five blocks to hike. The purpose of the trip? To raise money for Pop. Pop had talked him into this. When they found out, Mother and Aunt Rebecca would

---

① intravenous needles：静脉注射针。

be furious, and Woody was afraid, but he couldn't help it.

Morris had come and said, "Son, I'm in trouble. It's bad."

"What's bad, Pop?"

"Halina took money from her husband for me and has to put it back before old Bujak misses it. He could kill her."

"What did she do it for?"

"Son, you know how the bookies① collect? They send a goon②. They'll break my head open."

"Pop! You know I can't take you to Mrs. Skoglund."

"Why not? You're my kid, aren't you? " The old broad wants to adopt you, doesn't she? Shouldn't I get something out of it for my trouble? What am I— outside? And what about Halina? She puts her life on the line, but my own kid says no.

"Oh, Bujak wouldn't hurt her."

"Woody, he'd beat her to death."

Bujak? Uniform in color with his dark-gray work clothes, short in the legs, his whole strength in his tool-and-die-maker's③ forearms and black fingers; and beat-looking—there was Bujak for you. But, according to Pop, there was big, big violence in Bujak, a regular boiling Bessemer④ inside his narrow chest. Woody could never see the violence in him. Bujak wanted no trouble. If anything, maybe he was afraid that Morris and Halina would gang up on him and kill him, screaming. But Pop was no desperado murderer. And Halina was a calm, serious woman. Bujak kept his savings in the cellar (banks were going out of business). The worst they did was to take some of his money, intending to put it back. As Woody saw him, Bujak was trying to be sensible. He accepted his sorrow. He set minimum requirements for Halina: cook the meals, clean the house, show respect. But at stealing Bujak might have drawn the line, for money was different, money was vital substance. If they stole his savings he might have had to take action, out of respect for the substance, for himself—self-respect. But you couldn't be sure that Pop hadn't invented the bookie, the goon, the theft—the whole thing. He was capable of it, and you'd be a fool not to suspect him. Morris knew that Mother and

---

① bookie：(口)赛马等赌注登记经纪人。
② goon：(俚)打手,受雇的流氓。
③ tool-and-die-maker：工具和模具制作者。
④ Bessemer：以发明家贝塞麦命名的转炉。

Aunt Rebecca had told Mrs. Skoglund how wicked he was. They had painted him for her in poster colors--purple for vice, black for his soul, red for Hell flames: a gambler, smoker, drinker, deserter, and atheist. So Pop was determined to reach her. It was risky for everybody. The Reverend Doctor's operating costs were met by Skoglund Dairies. The widow paid Woody's seminary tuition; she bought dresses for the little sisters.

Woody, now sixty, fleshy and big, like a figure for the victory of American materialism, sunk in his lounge chair, the leather of its armrests softer to his fingertips than a woman's skin, was puzzled and, in his depths, disturbed by certain blots within him, blots of light in his brain, a blot combining pain and amusement in his breast (how did that get there?). Intense thought puckered the skin between his eyes with a strain bordering on headache. Why had he let Pop have his way? Why did he agree to meet him that day, in the dim rear of the poolroom?

"But what will you tell Mrs. Skoglund?"

"The old broad? Don't worry, there's plenty to tell her, and it's all true. Ain't I trying to save my little laundry-and-cleaning shop? Isn't the bailiff coming for the fixtures next week?" And Pop rehearsed his pitch① on the Western Avenue car. He counted on Woody's health and his freshness. Such a straightforward-looking body was perfect for a con.

Did they still have such winter storms in Chicago as they used to have? Now they somehow seemed less fierce. Blizzards used to come straight down from Ontario, from the Arctic, and drop five feet of snow in an afternoon. Then the rusty green platform cars, with revolving brushes at both ends, came out of the barns to sweep the tracks. Ten or twelve streetcars followed in slow processions, or waited, block after block.

There was a long delay at the gates of Riverview Park, all the amusements covered for the winter, boarded up—the dragon's-back high-rides, the Bobs, the Chute, the Tilt-a-Whirl②, all the fun machinery put together by mechanics and electricians, men like Bujak the tool-and-die-maker, good with engines. The blizzard was having it all its own way behind the gates, and you couldn't see far inside; only a few bulbs burned behind the palings. When Woody wiped the vapor from the glass, the wire mesh of the window guards was stuffed solid at eye level with snow. Looking higher, you saw mostly the streaked wind horizontally driv-

---

① pitch：(美口)商品推销员的行话。
② the Bobs, the Chute, the Tilt-a-Whirl：都指儿童娱乐项目。

ing from the north. In the seat ahead, two black coal heavers, both in leather Lindbergh flying helmets, sat with shovels between their legs, returning from a job. They smelled of sweat, burlap sucking, and coal. Mostly dull with black dust, they also sparkled here and there.

There weren't many riders. People weren't leaving the house. This was a day to sit legs stuck out beside the stove, mummified by both the outdoor and the indoor forces. Only a fellow with an angle, like Pop, would go and buck① such weather. A storm like this was out of the compass, and you kept the human scale by having a scheme to raise fifty bucks. Fifty soldiers! Real money in 1933.

"That woman is crazy for you," said Pop.

"She's just a good woman, sweet to all of us."

"Who knows what she's got in mind. You're a husky kid. Not such a kid, either."

"She's a religious woman. She really has religion."

"Well, your mother isn't your only parent. She and Rebecca and Kovner aren't going to fill you up with their ideas. I know your mother wants to wipe me out of your life. Unless I take a hand, you won't even understand what life is. Because they don't know those silly Christers."

"Yes, Pop."

"The girls I can't help. They're too young. I'm sorry about them, but I can't do anything. With you it's different."

He wanted me like himself, an American.

They were stalled in the storm, while the cattle-colored car waited to have the trolley reset in the crazy wind, which boomed, tingled, blasted. At Howard Street they would have to walk straight into it, due north.

"You'll do the talking at first," said Pop.

Woody had the makings of a salesman, a pitchman. He was aware of this when he got to his feet in church to testify before fifty or sixty people. Even though Rebecca made it worth his while, he moved his own heart when he spoke up about his faith. But occasionally, without notice, his heart went away as he spoke religion and he couldn't find it anywhere. In its absence, sincere behavior got him through. He had to rely for delivery on his face, his voice—on behavior. Then his eyes came closer and closer together.

---

① buck：顶着……前进。You kept the human scale by having a scheme to raise fifty bucks.：你想方设法筹五十块钱好维持人的生活标准。Fifty soldiers：五十块钱。

And in this approach of eye to eye he felt the strain of hypocrisy. The twisting of his face threatened to betray him. It took everything he had to keep looking honest. So, since he couldn't bear the cynicism of it, he fell back on mischievousness. Mischief was where Pop came in. Pop passed straight through all those divided fields, gap after gap, and arrived at his side, bent-nosed and broad-faced. In regard to Pop, you thought of neither sincerity nor insincerity. Pop was like the man in the song: he wanted what he wanted when he wanted it. Pop was physical; Pop was digestive, circulatory, sexual. If Pop got serious, he talked to you about washing under the arms or in the crotch or of drying between your toes or of cooking supper, of baked beans and fried onions, of draw poker① or of a certain horse in the fifth race at Arlington. Pop was elemental. That was why he gave such relief from religion and paradoxes, and things like that. Now, Mother *thought* she was spiritual, but Woody knew that she was kidding herself. Oh, yes, in the British accent she never gave up she was always talking to God or about Him—please God, God willing, praise God. But she was a big substantial bread-and-butter down-to-earth woman, with down-to-earth duties like feeding the girls, protecting, refining, keeping pure the girls. And those two protected doves grew up so overweight, heavy in the hips and thighs, that their poor heads looked long and slim. And mad. Sweet but cuckoo—Paula cheerfully cuckoo, Joanna depressed and having episodes.

"I'll do my best by you, but you have to promise, Pop, not to get me in Dutch with② Mrs. Skoglund."

"You worried because I speak bad English? Embarrassed? I have a mockie accent③?"

"It's not that. Kovner has a heavy accent, and she doesn't mind."

"Who the hell are those freaks to look down on me? You're practically a man and your dad has a right to expect help from you. He's in a fix. And you bring him to her house because she's bighearted, and you haven't got anybody else to go to."

"I got you, Pop."

The two coal trimmers stood up at Devon Avenue, One of them wore a woman's coat. Men wore women's clothing in those years, and women men's,

---

① draw poker：抽彩（得奖）。
② get in Dutch with：(俚)处于困境(或苦恼中)；失宠；受嫌疑的。
③ mockie accent：(美俚)犹太口音。

when there was no choice. The fur collar was spiky with the wet, and sprinkled with soot. Heavy, they dragged their shovels and got off at the front. The slow car ground on, very slow. It was after four when they reached the end of the line, and somewhere between gray and black, with snow spouting and whirling under the street lamps. In Howard Street, autos were stalled at all angles and abandoned. The sidewalks were blocked. Woody led the way into Evanston, and Pop followed him up the middle of the street in the furrows made earlier by trucks. For four blocks they bucked the wind and then Woody broke through the drifts to the snowbound mansion, where they both had to push the wrought-iron gate because of the drift behind it. Twenty rooms or more in this dignified house and nobody in them but Mrs. Skoglund and her servant Hjordis, also religious.

As Woody and Pop waited, brushing the slush from their sheepskin collars and Pop wiping his big eyebrows with the ends of his scarf, sweating and freezing, the chains began to rattle and Hjordis uncovered the air holes of the glass storm door by turning a wooden bar. Woody called her "monk-faced." You no longer see women like that, who put no female touch on the face. She came plain, as God made her. She said, "Who is it and what do you want?"

"It's Woodrow Selbst. Hjordis? It's Woody."

"You're not expected."

"No, but we're here."

"What do you want?"

"We came to see Mrs. Skoglund."

"What for do you want to see her?"

"Just tell her we're here."

"I have to tell her what you came for, without calling up first."

"Why don't you say it's Woody with his father, and we wouldn't come in a snowstorm like this if it wasn't important."

The understandable caution of women who live alone. Respectable old-time women, too. There was no such respectability now in those Evanston houses, with their big verandas and deep yards and with a servant like Hjordis, who carried at her belt keys to the pantry and to every closet and every dresser drawer and every padlocked bin in the cellar. And in High Episcopal Christian Science Women's Temperance Evanston[①], no tradespeople rang at the front door. Only invited

---

① High Episcopal Christian Science Women's Temperance Evanston：埃文斯顿高级圣工会基督教科学派妇女戒酒协会。

guests. And here, after a ten-mile grind through the blizzard, came two tramps from the West Side. To this mansion where a Swedish immigrant lady, herself once a cook and now a philanthropic widow, dreamed, snowbound, while frozen lilac twigs clapped at her storm windows, of a new Jerusalem and a Second coming and a Resurrection and a Last Judgment. To hasten the Second Coming, and all the rest, you had to reach the hearts of these scheming bums arriving in a snowstorm.

Sure, they let us in.

Then in the heat that swam suddenly up to their mufflered chins Pop and Woody felt the blizzard for what it was; their cheeks were frozen slabs. They stood beat, itching, trickling in the front hall that was a hall, with a carved newel post staircase and a big stained-glass window at the top. Picturing Jesus with the Samaritan① woman. There was a kind of Gentile closeness to the air. Perhaps when he was with Pop, Woody made more Jewish observations than he would otherwise. Although Pop's most Jewish characteristic was that Yiddish was the only language he could read a paper in. Pop was with Polish Halina, and Mother was with Jesus Christ, and Woody ate uncooked bacon from the flitch. Still, now and then he had a Jewish impression.

Mrs. Skoglund was the cleanest of women—her fingernails, her white neck, her ears—and Pop's sexual hints to Woody all went wrong because she was so intensely clean, and made Woody think of a waterfall, large as she was, and grandly built. Her bust was big. Woody's imagination had investigated this. He thought she kept things tied down tight, very tight. But she lifted both arms once to raise a window and there it was, her bust, beside him, the whole unbindable thing. Her hair was like the raffia② you had to soak before you could weave with it in a basket class—pale, pale. Pop, as he took his sheepskin off, was in sweaters, no jacket. His darting looks made him seem crooked. Hardest of all for these Selbsts with their bent noses and big, apparently straightforward faces was to look honest. All the signs of dishonesty played over them. Woody had often puzzled about it. Did it go back to the muscles, was it fundamentally a jaw problem—the projecting angles of the jaws? Or was it the angling that went on in the heart? The girls called Pop Dick Tracy, but Dick Tracy was a good guy. Whom could Pop convince? Here Woody caught a possibility as it flitted by. Precisely because of

---

① Samaritan：原指巴勒斯坦北部撒马利亚王国人，现泛指乐善好施者。Gentile：非犹太人的。
② raffia：酒椰叶纤维。

the way Pop looked, a sensitive person might feel remorse for condemning unfairly or judging unkindly. Just because of a face? Some must have bent over backward. Then he had them. Not Hjordis. She would have put Pop into the street then and there, storm or no storm. Hjordis was religious, but she was wised up, too. She hadn't come over in steerage and worked forty years in Chicago for nothing.

Mrs. Skoglund, Awse (Osie), led the visitors into the front room. This, the biggest room in the house, needed supplementary heating. Because of fifteen-foot ceilings and high windows, Hjordis had kept the parlor stove burning. It was one of those elegant parlor stoves that wore a nickel crown, or miter, and this miter, when you moved it aside, automatically raised the hinge of an iron stove lid. That stove lid underneath the crown was all soot and rust, the same as any other stove lid. Into this hole you tipped the scuttle and the anthracite[①] chestnut rattled down. It made a cake or dome of fire visible through the small isinglass[②] frames. It was a pretty room, three-quarters paneled in wood. The stove was plugged into the flue of the marble fireplace, and there were parquet floors and Axminster carpets[③] and cranberry-colored tufted Victorian upholstery, and a kind of Chinese étagère,[④] inside a cabinet, lined with mirrors and containing silver pitchers, trophies won by Skoglund cows, fancy sugar tongs and cut-glass pitchers and goblets. There were Bibles and pictures of Jesus and the Holy Land and that faint Gentile odor, as if things had been rinsed in a weak vinegar solution.

"Mrs. Skoglund, I brought my dad to you. I don't think you ever met him," said Woody.

"Yes, Missus, that's me, Selbst."

Pop stood short but masterful in the sweaters, and his belly sticking out, not soft but hard. He was a man of the hard-bellied type. Nobody intimidated Pop. He never presented himself as a beggar. There wasn't a cringe in him anywhere. He let her see at once by the way he said "Missus" that he was independent and that he knew his way around. He communicated that he was able to handle himself with women. Handsome Mrs. Skoglund, carrying a basket woven out of her own hair, was in her fifties—eight, maybe ten years his senior.

"I asked my son to bring me because I know you do the kid a lot of good. It's

---

① anthracite：无烟煤。
② isinglass：鱼胶。
③ parquet floor：镶木地板。Axminster carpet：阿克斯明斯特绒头地毯（取名来自原产地英国德文郡的阿克斯明斯特）。
④ étagère：(法)放置古玩及小摆设的陈列架。

natural you should know both of his parents."

"Mrs. Skoglund, my dad is in a tight corner and I don't know anybody else to ask for help."

This was all the preliminary Pop wanted. He took over and told the widow his story about the laundry-and-cleaning business and payments overdue, and explained about the fixtures and the attachment notice, and the bailiff's office and what they were going to do to him; and he said, "I'm a small man trying to make a living."

"You don't support your children," said Mrs. Skoglund.

"That's right," said Hjordis.

"I haven't got it. If I had it, wouldn't I give it? There's bread lines and soup lines all over town. Is it just me? What I have I divvy① with. I give the kids. A bad father? You think my son would bring me if I was a bad father into your house? He loves his dad, he trusts his dad, he knows his dad is a good dad. Every time I start a little business going I get wiped out. This one is a good little business, if I could hold on to that little business. Three people work for me, I meet a payroll, and three people will be on the street, too, if I close down. Missus, I can sign a note and pay you in two months. I'm a common man, but I'm a hard worker and a fellow you can trust."

Woody was startled when Pop used the word "trust." It was as if from all four corners a Sousa band② blew a blast to warn the entire world: "Crook! This is a crook!" But Mrs. Skoglund, on account of her religious preoccupations, was remote. She heard nothing. Although everybody in this part of the world, unless he was crazy, led a practical life, and you'd have nothing to say to anyone, your neighbors would have nothing to say to you, if communications were not of a practical sort, Mrs. Skoglund, with all her money, was unworldly—two-thirds out of this world.

"Give me a chance to show what's in me," said Pop, "and you'll see what I do for my kids."

So Mrs. Skoglund hesitated, and then she said she'd have to go upstairs, she'd have to go to her room and pray on it and ask for guidance—would they sit down and wait. There were two rocking chairs by the stove. Hjordis gave Pop a grim look (a dangerous person) and Woody a blaming one (he brought a danger-

---

① divvy: (俚)分享,分配。
② Sousa: 美国乐队指挥兼作曲家。Sousa band: 管乐队。

ous stranger and disrupter to injure two kind Christian ladies). Then she went out with Mrs. Skoglund.

As soon as they left, Pop jumped up from the rocker and said in anger, "What's this with the praying? She has to ask God to lend me fifty bucks?"

Woody said, "It's not you, Pop, it's the way these religious people do."

"No," said Pop. "She'll come back and say that God wouldn't let her."

Woody didn't like that; he thought Pop was being gross and he said, "No, she's sincere. Pop, try to understand: she's emotional, nervous, and sincere, and tries to do right by everybody."

And Pop said, "That servant will talk her out of it. She's a toughie. It's all over her face that we're a couple of chiselers."

"What's the use of us arguing," said Woody. He drew the rocker closer to the stove. His shoes were wet through and would never dry. The blue flames fluttered like a school of fishes in the coal fire. But Pop went over to the Chinese-style cabinet or étagère and tried the handle, and then opened the blade of his penknife and in a second had forced the lock of the curved glass door. He took out a silver dish.

"Pop, what is this?" said Woody.

Pop, cool and level, knew exactly what this was. He relocked the étagère, crossed the carpet, listened. He stuffed the dish under his belt and pushed it down into his trousers. He put the side of his short thick finger to his mouth.

So Woody kept his voice down, but he was all shook up. He went to Pop and took him by the edge of his hand. As he looked into Pop's face, he felt his eyes growing smaller and smaller, as if something were contracting all the skin on his head. They call it hyperventilation when everything feels tight and light and close and dizzy. Hardly breathing, he said, "Put it back, Pop."

Pop said, "It's solid silver; it's worth dough."

"Pop, you said you wouldn't get me in Dutch."

"It's only insurance in case she comes back from praying and tells me no. If she says yes, I'll put it back."

"How?"

"It'll get back. If I don't put it back, you will."

"You picked the lock. I couldn't. I don't know how."

"There's nothing to it."

"We're going to put it back now. Give it here."

"Woody, it's under my fly, inside my underpants. Don't make such a noise about nothing."

"Pop, I can't believe this."

"For cry-ninety-nine,① shut your mouth. If I didn't trust you I wouldn't have let you watch me do it. You don't understand a thing. What's with you?"

"Before they come down, Pop, will you dig that dish out of your long johns."

Pop turned stiff on him. He became absolutely military. He said, "Look, I order you!"

Before he knew it, Woody had jumped his father and begun to wrestle with him. It was outrageous to clutch your own father, to put a heel behind him, to force him to the wall. Pop was taken by surprise and said loudly, "You want Halina killed? Kill her! Go on, you be responsible." He began to resist, angry, and they turned about several times, when Woody, with a trick he had learned in a Western movie and used once on the playground, tripped him and they fell to the ground. Woody, who already outweighed the old man by twenty pounds, was on top. They landed on the floor beside the stove, which stood on a tray of decorated tin to protect the carpet. In this position, pressing Pop's hard belly, Woody recognized that to have wrestled him to the floor counted for nothing. It was impossible to thrust his hand under Pop's belt to recover the dish. And now Pop had turned furious, as a father has every right to be when his son is violent with him, and he freed his hand and hit Woody in the face. He hit him three or four times in midface. Then Woody dug his head into Pop's shoulder and held tight only to keep from being struck and began to say in his ear, "Jesus, Pop, for Christ sake remember where you are. Those women will be back!" But Pop brought up his short knee and fought and butted him with his chin and rattled Woody's teeth. Woody thought the old man was about to bite him. And because he was a seminarian, he thought: Like an unclean spirit. And held tight. Gradually Pop stopped threshing and struggling. His eyes stuck out and his mouth was open, sullen. Like a stout fish. Woody released him and gave him a hand up. He was then overcome with many many bad feelings of a sort he knew the old man never suffered. Never, never. Pop never had these groveling emotions. There was his whole superiority. Pop had no such feelings. He was like a horseman from Central Asia. It was

---

① for cry-ninety-nine.: 够了,别说了。

Mother, from Liverpool, who had the refinement, the English manners. It was the preaching Reverend Doctor in his black suit. You have refinements, and all they do is oppress you? The hell with that.

The long door opened and Mrs. Skoglund stepped in, saying, "Did I imagine, or did something shake the house?"

"I was lifting the scuttle to put coal on the fire and it fell out of my hand. I'm sorry I was so clumsy," said Woody.

Pop was too huffy to speak. With his eyes big and sore and the thin hair down over his forehead, you could see by the tightness of his belly how angrily he was fetching his breath, though his mouth was shut.

"I prayed," said Mrs. Skoglund.

"I hope it came out well," said Woody.

"Well, I don't do anything without guidance, but the answer was yes, and I feel right about it now. So if you'll wait, I'll go to my office and write a check. I asked Hjordis to bring you a cup of coffee. Coming in such a storm."

And Pop, consistently a terrible little man, as soon as she shut the door, said, "A check? Hell with a check. Get me the greenbacks."

"They don't keep money in the house. You can cash it in her bank tomorrow. But if they miss that dish, Pop, they'll stop the check, and then where are you?"

As Pop was reaching below the belt, Hjordis brought in the tray. She was very sharp with him. She said, "Is this a place to adjust clothing, Mister? A men's washroom?"

"Well, which way is the toilet, then?" said Pop.

She had served the coffee in the seamiest mugs in the pantry, and she bumped down the tray and led Pop down the corridor, standing guard at the bathroom door so that he shouldn't wander about the house.

Mrs. Skoglund called Woody to her office and after she had given him the folded check said that they should pray together for Morris. So once more he was on his knees, under rows and rows of musty marbled-cardboard files, by the glass lamp by the edge of the desk, the shade with flounced edges, like the candy dish. Mrs. Skoglund, in her Scandinavian accent—an emotional contralto—raising her voice to Jesus-uh Christ-uh, as the wind lashed the trees, kicked the side of the house, and drove the snow seething on the windowpanes, to send light-uh, give guidance-uh, put a new heart-uh in Pop's bosom. Woody asked God only to make Pop put the dish back. He kept Mrs. Skoglund on her knees as long as possible. Then he thanked her, shining with candor (as much as he knew how), for her Christian generosity and he said, "I know that Hjordis has a cousin who works at the Evanston YMCA. Could she please phone him and try to get us a room tonight so that we don't have to fight the blizzard all the way back? We're almost as close to the Y as to the car line. Maybe the cars have even stopped running."

Suspicious Hjordis, coming when Mrs. Skoglund called to her, was burning now. First they barged in, made themselves at home, asked for money, had to have coffee, probably left gonorrhea① on the toilet seat. Hjordis, Woody remembered, was a woman who wiped the doorknobs with rubbing alcohol after guests had left. Nevertheless, she telephoned the Y and got them a room with two cots for six bits.

Pop had plenty of time, therefore, to reopen the étagère, lined with reflecting glass or German silver (something exquisitely delicate and tricky), and as soon as the two Selbsts had said thank you and goodbye and were in midstreet again up to the knees in snow, Woody said, "Well, I covered for you. Is that thing back?"

"Of course it is," said Pop.

They fought their way to the small Y building, shut up in wire grille and resembling a police station—about the same dimensions. It was locked, but they made a racket on the grille, and a small black man let them in and shuffled them upstairs to a cement corridor with low doors. It was like the small-mammal house in Lincoln Park. He said there was nothing to eat, so they took off their wet pants, wrapped themselves tightly in the khaki army blankets, and passed out on their cots.

First thing in the morning, they went to the Evanston National Bank and got the fifty dollars. Not without difficulties. The teller went to call Mrs. Skoglund and was absent a long time from the wicket.

"Where the hell has he gone?" said Pop.

But when the fellow came back, he said, "How do you want it?"

Pop said, "Singles." He told Woody, "Bujak stashes① it in one-dollar bills."

But by now Woody no longer believed Halina had stolen the old man's money.

---

① gonorrhea: 淋病。

Then they went into the street, where the snow-removal crews were at work. The sun shone broad, broad, out of the morning blue, and all Chicago would be releasing itself from the temporary beauty of those vast drifts.

"You shouldn't have jumped me last night, Sonny."

"I know, Pop, but you promised you wouldn't get me in Dutch."

"Well, it's okay. We can forget it, seeing you stood by me."

Only, Pop had taken the silver dish. Of course he had, and in a few days Mrs. Skoglund and Hjordis knew it, and later in the week they were all waiting for Woody in Kovner's office at the settlement house. The group included the Reverend Doctor Crabbie, head of the seminary, and Woody, who had been flying along, level and smooth, was shot down in flames.② He told them he was innocent. Even as he was falling, he warned that they were wronging him. He denied that he or Pop had touched Mrs. Skoglund's property. The missing object—he didn't even know what it was—had probably been misplaced, and they would be very sorry on the day it turned up. After the others were done with him, Dr. Crabbie said that until he was able to tell the truth he would be suspended from the seminary, where his work had been unsatisfactory anyway. Aunt Rebecca took him aside and said to him, "You are a little crook, like your father. The door is closed to you here."

To this Pop's comment was "So what, kid?"

"Pop, you shouldn't have done it."

"No? Well, I don't give a care, if you want to know. You can have the dish if you want to go back and square yourself with all those hypocrites③."

"I didn't like doing Mrs. Skoglund in the eye, she was so kind to us."

"Kind?"

"Kind."

"Kind has a price tag."

Well, there was no winning such arguments with Pop. But they debated it in various moods and from various elevations and perspectives for forty years and more, as their intimacy changed, developed, matured.

"Why did you do it, Pop? For the money? What did you do with the fifty

---

① stash：藏起来。

② who had been flying along, level and smooth, was shot down in flames.：一直平稳顺利地飞翔, 却被击中坠入枪火中。

③ square yourself with all those hypocrites：要求所有那些伪善者宽恕你。

bucks?" Woody, decades later, asked him that.

"I settled with the bookie, and the rest I put in the business."

"You tried a few more horses."

"I maybe did. But it was a double, Woody. I didn't hurt myself, and at the same time did you a favor."

"It was for me?"

"It was too strange of a life. That life wasn't *you*, Woody. All those women... Kovner was no man, he was an in-between. Suppose they made you a minister? Some Christian minister! First of all, you wouldn't have been able to stand it, and second, they would throw you out sooner or later."

"Maybe so."

"And you wouldn't have converted the Jews, which was the main thing they wanted."

"And what a time to bother the Jews," Woody said. "At least *I* didn't bug① them."

Pop had carded him back to his side of the line, blood of his blood, the same thick body walls, the same coarse grain. Not cut out for a spiritual life. Simply not up to it.

Pop was no worse than Woody, and Woody was no better than Pop. Pop wanted no relation to theory, and yet he was always pointing Woody toward a position—a jolly, hearty, natural, likable, unprincipled position. If Woody had a weakness, it was to be unselfish. This worked to Pop's advantage, but he criticized Woody for it, nevertheless. "You take too much on yourself," Pop was always saying. And it's true that Woody gave Pop his heart because Pop was so selfish. It's usually the selfish people who are loved the most. They do what you deny yourself, and you love them for it. You give them your heart.

Remembering the pawn ticket for the silver dish, Woody startled himself with a laugh so sudden that it made him cough. Pop said to him after his expulsion from the seminary and banishment from the settlement house, "You want in again? Here's the ticket. I hocked that thing. It wasn't so valuable as I thought."

"What did they give?"

"Twelve-fifty was all I could get. But if you want it you'll have to raise the dough yourself, because 1 haven't got it anymore."

---

① bug:（俚）烦扰。

176

"You must have been sweating in the bank when the teller went to call Mrs. Skoglund about the check."

"I was a little nervous," said Pop. "But I didn't think they could miss the thing so soon."①

That theft was part of Pop's war with Mother. With Mother, and Aunt Rebecca, and the Reverend Doctor. Pop took his stand on realism. Mother represented the forces of religion and hypochondria. In four decades, the fighting never stopped. In the course of time, Mother and the girls turned into welfare personalities and lost their individual outlines. Ah, the poor things, they became dependents and cranks. In the meantime, Woody, the sinful man, was their dutiful and loving son and brother. He maintained the bungalow—this took in roofing, pointing②, wiring, insulation, air-conditioning—and he paid for heat and light and food, and dressed them all out of Sears, Roebuck and Wieboldt's, and bought them a TV, which they watched as devoutly as they prayed. Paula took courses to learn skills like macramé③-making and needlepoint, and sometimes got a little job as recreational worker in a nursing home. But she wasn't steady enough to keep it. Wicked Pop spent most of his life removing stains from people's clothing. He and Halina in the last years ran a Cleanomat in West Rogers Park—a so-so business resembling a laundromat—which gave him leisure for billiards, the horses, rummy and pinochle. Every morning he went behind the partition to check out the filters of the cleaning equipment. He found amusing things that had been thrown into the vats with the clothing—sometimes, when he got lucky, a locket chain or a brooch. And when he had fortified the cleaning fluid, pouring all that blue and pink stuff in from plastic jugs, he read the *Forward* over a second cup of coffee, and went out, leaving Halina in charge. When they needed help with the rent, Woody gave it.

After the new Disney World was opened in Florida, Woody treated all his dependents to a holiday. He sent them down in separate batches, of course. Halina enjoyed this more than anybody else. She couldn't stop talking about the address given by an Abraham Lincoln automaton. "Wonderful, how he stood up and moved his hands, and his mouth. So real! And how beautiful he talked." Of them

---

① But I didn't think they could miss the thing so soon.：可我没想到她们那么快就发现丢了那样东西。
② pointing：(建)用水泥等勾嵌砖石墙等的砌缝。
③ macramé：(家具装饰用)流苏，花边。

all, Halina was the soundest, the most human, the most honest. Now that Pop was gone, Woody and Halina's son, Mitosh, the organist at the Stadium, took care of her needs over and above Social Security, splitting expenses. In Pop's opinion, insurance was a racket. He left Halina nothing but some out-of-date equipment.

Woody treated himself, too. Once a year, and sometimes oftener, he left his business to run itself, arranged with the trust department at the bank to take care of his gang, and went off. He did that in style, imaginatively, expensively. In Japan, he wasted little time on Tokyo. He spent three weeks in Kyoto and stayed at the Tawaraya Inn, dating from the seventeenth century or so. There he slept on the floor, the Japanese way, and bathed in scalding water. He saw the dirtiest strip show on earth, as well as the holy places and the temple gardens. He visited also Istanbul, Jerusalem, Delphi, and went to Burma and Uganda and Kenya on safari①, on democratic terms with drivers, Bedouins②, bazaar merchants. Open, lavish, familiar, fleshier and fleshier but (he jogged, he lifted weights) still muscular—in his naked person beginning to resemble a Renaissance courtier in full costume—becoming ruddier every year, an outdoor type with freckles on his back and spots across the flaming forehead and the honest nose. On the Nile, below Murchison Falls, those fever trees③ rose huge from the mud, and hippos on the sandbars belched at the passing launch, hostile. One of them danced on his spit of sand, springing from the ground and coming down heavy, on all fours. There, Woody saw the buffalo calf disappear, snatched by the crocodile.

Mother, soon to follow Pop, was being lightheaded these days. In company, she spoke of Woody as her boy—"What do you think of my Sonny?"—as though he was ten years old. She was silly with him, her behavior was frivolous, almost flirtatious. She just didn't seem to know the facts. And behind her all the others, like kids at the playground, were waiting their turn to go down the slide: one on each step, and moving toward the top.

Over Woody's residence and place of business there had gathered a pool of silence of the same perimeter as the church bells while they were ringing, and he mourned under it, this melancholy morning of sun and autumn. Doing a life survey, taking a deliberate look at the gross side of his case—of the other side as well, what there was of it. But if this heartache continued, he'd go out and run it

---

① safari: 徒步旅游队。

② Bedouins: 贝都因人; 游牧人。

③ fever tree: 蓝桉树。

off. A three-mile jog—five, if necessary. And you'd think that this jogging was an entirely physical activity, wouldn't you? But there was something else in it. Because, when he was a seminarian, between the shafts of his World's Fair rickshaw, he used to receive, pulling along (capable and stable), his religious experiences while he trotted. Maybe it was all a single experience repeated. He felt truth coming to him from the sun. He received a communication that was also light and warmth. It made him very remote from his horny Wisconsin passengers, those farmers whose whoops and whore cries he could hardly hear when he was in one of his states. And again out of the flaming of the sun would come to him a secret certainty that the goal set for this earth was that it should be filled with good, saturated with it. After everything preposterous, after dog had eaten dog, after the crocodile death had pulled everyone into his mud. It wouldn't conclude as Mrs. Skoglund, bribing him to round up the Jews and hasten the Second Coming, imagined it, but in another way. This was his clumsy intuition. It went no further. Subsequently, he proceeded through life as life seemed to want him to do it.

There remained one thing more this morning, which was explicitly physical, occurring first as a sensation in his arms and against his breast and, from the pressure, passing into him and going into his breast.

It was like this: When he came into the hospital room and saw Pop with the sides of his bed raised, like a crib, and Pop, so very feeble, and writhing, and toothless, like a baby, and the dirt already cast into his face, into the wrinkles—Pop wanted to pluck out the intravenous needles and he was piping his weak death noise. The gauze patches taped over the needles were soiled with dark blood. Then Woody took off his shoes, lowered the side of the bed, and climbed in and held him in his arms to soothe and still him. As if he were Pop's father, he said to him, "Now, Pop. Pop." Then it was like the wrestle in Mrs. Skoglund's parlor, when Pop turned angry like an unclean spirit and Woody tried to appease him, and warn him, saying, "Those women will be back!" Beside the coal stove, when Pop hit Woody in the teeth with his head and then became sullen, like a stout fish. But this struggle in the hospital was weak—so weak! In his great pity, Woody held Pop, who was fluttering and shivering. From those people, Pop had told him, you'll never find out what life is, because they don't know what it is. Yes, Pop—well, what is it, Pop? Hard to comprehend that Pop, who was dug in for eighty-three years and had done all he could to stay, should now want nothing but to free himself. How could Woody allow the old man to pull the intravenous

needles out? Willful Pop, he wanted what he wanted when he wanted it. But what he wanted at the very last Woody failed to follow, it was such a switch①.

After a time, Pop's resistance ended. He subsided and subsided. He rested against his son, his small body curled there. Nurses came and looked. They disapproved, but Woody, who couldn't spare a hand to wave them out, motioned with his head toward the door. Pop, whom Woody thought he had stilled, only had found a better way to get around him. Loss of heat was the way he did it. His heat was leaving him. As can happen with small animals while you hold them in your hand, Woody presently felt him cooling. Then, as Woody did his best to restrain him, and thought he was succeeding, Pop divided himself. And when he was separated from his warmth, he slipped into death. And there was his elderly, large, muscular son, still holding and pressing him when there was nothing anymore to press. You could never pin down that self-willed man. When he was ready to make his move, he made it—always on his own terms. And always, always, something up his sleeve②. That was how he was.

作品赏析

《银盘子》选自1984年出版的《出言不逊者及其他故事》。通过讲述有犹太血统的主人公伍迪(Woody)在美国经济大萧条时期的成长故事，用讽刺辛辣的笔触揭示出犹太人的宗教信仰以及个人道德危机。大萧条时期美国的移民生活对犹太人产生隔离影响，造成犹太人信仰危机，使犹太人在迫切需要接受功利性基督教会提供的生活援助的同时，又对基督教是否真正具备拯救灵魂这一神圣功效产生质疑。青年时代的伍迪徘徊在艰辛的物质生活与岌岌可危的宗教信仰之间；而当中年时代的伍迪享受着实现美国梦所带来的物质成功之时，也咀嚼着美国的犹太移民特有的酸涩；耳顺之年的伍迪在百感交集的回忆中，似乎要通过回忆父亲笃信犹太教来解除自己的信仰困惑，而父亲的话语背后时刻交织着不同宗教教堂鸣响的钟声。伍迪的这种两难境地恐怕正是贝娄向犹太人以及其他读者提出的问题。

《银盘子》展示了贝娄独特的叙事技巧，故事开端采用第二人称直截了当的问句，让读者设身处地体验主人公伍迪的丧父之痛以及他魂牵梦绕的精神困惑。故事展开后，采用由意象引发的意识流手法，例如，伍迪对他从非洲带回大麻并塞入感恩节火鸡腹内的这段回忆，通过火鸡这一意象，自然过渡到对父亲最后一次在家吃火鸡这一令人心酸场景的描写，之后笔锋一转，又回到伍迪对父亲的回忆，突出了伍迪对父亲的理解不断深化的过程。故事的叙述往返于以伍迪为内聚焦与全知视角之

---

① switch：(口) 调换, 交换；(欺骗性的)掉包。
② something up his sleeve：总有锦囊妙计；留有……一招。

间,通过不断切换主观与客观的认知视角,读者的认识不断丰富,叙述的可信性也不断增强。贯穿全文的教堂钟声这一象征高度深化了故事的主旨,既烘托出笃信犹太教的父亲的孤独,又折射出伍迪对包括自己在内的新一代美国犹太人的迷茫和反思。此外,圣经中的银杯典故(Genesis 44:4 "A Silver Cup in a Sack")是深入理解本文宗教内涵的重要线索。

思考题

1. What kind of person is Morris?
2. How do you characterize Mrs. Skoglund?
3. What does Woody think of his father?
4. Why do you think Morris says "Kind has a price tag"?
5. How is Woody's wrestle with his father at the hospital similar to and different from that in Mrs. Skoglund's parlor?
6. What narrative techniques are used to enhance the theme?

推荐作品

Herzog (1964)
Humboldt's Gift (1975)
The Dean's December (1982)

参考资料

Atalas, James. *Bellow: A Biography.* Rpt. ed. New York: Modern Library, 2002.

Bach, Gerhard, et al., eds. *Small Planets: Saul Bellow and the Art of Short Fiction.* East Lansing: Michigan State UP, 2000.

Cronin, Gloria L. and B. Siegel, eds. *Conversations with Saul Bellow.* Jackson: UP of Mississippi, 1994.

Kramer, Mincheal P., ed. *New Essays on Size the Day.* Beijing: Peking UP; Cambridge UP, 2006.

第十单元
Flannery O'Connor
(1925—1964)
弗兰纳里·奥康纳

作者简介

弗兰纳里·奥康纳，美国现代南方女作家，1925年3月出生于佐治亚州萨凡纳，1950年患上红斑狼疮，1964年8月英年早逝。她早年曾就读于天主教学校，随后分别在佐治亚州女子学院与爱荷华大学学习。奥康纳从年轻时起就开始遭受疾病和残疾困扰，大半生都是在位于米尔基维尔的母亲的农场上度过的，闲时喂养孔雀。但是，她不顾病魔的折磨，始终笔耕不辍。其代表作品主要包括两部长篇小说《智血》(*Wise Blood*，又译《慧血》，1952)，《暴力夺魁》(*The Violent Bear It Away*, 1960)；另外还有几部短篇小说和散文集，其中《好人难寻》(*A Good Man Is Hard to Find*, 1955)与《殊途同归》(*Everything that Rises must Converge*, 1965)中的一些作品被誉为本世纪美国最优秀的短篇小说作品。在她去世以后，一些文学随笔与评论被收入《神秘与习俗：散文拾零》(*Mystery and Manners*, 1969)，生前的书信被结集成册《生存习惯》(*The Habit of Being*, 1979)。1971年出版的《短篇小说全集》(*The Complete Short Stories*)收有她生前未曾发表过的作品12篇。

奥康纳以短篇小说见长。如施咸荣先生所讲，"作为南方作家，她的创作带有南方文学的显著特征：浓厚的历史意识、细腻的心理描写和怪诞的人物形象。"在多数作品中，奥康纳主要描写的是20世纪四五十年代美国南方的农村生活，常以怪诞手法揭示人类在现代社会中的道德畸形，因此与同时期的卡森·麦卡勒斯(Carson McCullers, 1917—1967)、杜鲁门·卡波特(Truman Capote, 1924—1984)等作家一起被视为"南方哥特流派"(Southern Gothic School of Writing)的代表人物。关于这一流派名称，奥康纳曾经宣称，"凡是出自南方的事物都会被北方读者称作怪诞，而怪诞的事物却又被他们当作现实主义了。"另外，南方地区多以基督教新教为主流，奥康纳虽然身为南方作家，她的创作思想却带有天主教家庭背景的深刻烙印。在她看来，"上帝(对罪人)施加的恩典(the action of grace)往往会改变一个人物"，而她笔下的"所有故事都关系到恩典是如何在一个毫无悔罪之意的人物身上产生影响的"。

A Good Man Is Hard to Find (1953)

THE GRANDMOTHER didn't want to go to Florida. She wanted to visit some of her connections in east Tennessee and she was seizing at every chance to change Bailey's mind. Bailey was the son she lived with, her only boy. He was sitting on the edge of his chair at the table, bent over the orange sports section of the *Journal*. "Now look here, Bailey," she said, "see here, read this," and she stood with one hand on her thin hip and the other rattling the newspaper at his bald head. "Here this fellow that calls himself The Misfit[①] is aloose from the Federal Pen[②] and headed toward Florida and you read here what it says he did to these people. Just you read it. I wouldn't take my children in any direction with a criminal like that aloose in it. I couldn't answer to my conscience if I did."

Bailey didn't look up from his reading so she wheeled around then and faced the children's mother, a young woman in slacks, whose face was as broad and innocent as a cabbage and was tied around with a green head-kerchief that had two points on the top like rabbit's ears. She was sitting on the sofa, feeding the baby his apricots out of a jar. "The children have been to Florida before," the old lady said. "You all ought to take them somewhere else for a change so they would see different parts of the world and be broad. They never have been to east Tennessee."

The children's mother didn't seem to hear her but the eight-year-old boy, John Wesley, a stocky child with glasses, said, "If you don't want to go to Florida, why dontcha[③] stay at home?" He and the little girl, June Star, were reading the funny papers on the floor.

"She wouldn't stay at home to be queen for a day," June Star said without raising her yellow head.

"Yes and what would you do if this fellow, The Misfit, caught you?" the grandmother asked.

"I'd smack his face," John Wesley said.

---

① The Misfit:不合时宜的人,不适应环境的人。
② Federal Pen:联邦监狱,Pen 是 Penitentiary 的口语简称。
③ dontcha:口语体,实为 don't you。

"She wouldn't stay at home for a million bucks①," June Star said. "Afraid she'd miss something. She has to go everywhere we go."

"All right, Miss," the grandmother said. "Just remember that the next time you want me to curl your hair."

June Star said her hair was naturally curly.

The next morning the grandmother was the first one in the car, ready to go. She had her big black valise that looked like the head of a hippopotamus in one corner, and underneath it she was hiding a basket with Pitty Sing, the cat, in it. She didn't intend for the cat to be left alone in the house for three days because he would miss her too much and she was afraid he might brush against one of the gas burners and accidentally asphyxiate② himself. Her son, Bailey, didn't like to arrive at a motel with a cat.

She sat in the middle of the back seat with John Wesley and June Star on either side of her. Bailey and the children's mother and the baby sat in front and they left Atlanta at eight forty-five with the mileage on the car at 55890. The grandmother wrote this down because she thought it would be interesting to say how many miles they had been when they got back. It took them twenty minutes to reach the outskirts of the city.

The old lady settled herself comfortably, removing her white cotton gloves and putting them up with her purse on the shelf in front of the back window. The children's mother still had on slacks and still had her head tied up in a green kerchief, but the grandmother had on a navy blue straw sailor hat with a bunch of white violets on the brim and a navy blue dress with a small white dot in the print. Her collars and cuffs were white organdy③ trimmed with lace and at her neckline she had pinned a purple spray of cloth violets containing a sachet. In case of an accident, anyone seeing her dead on the highway would know at once that she was a lady.

She said she thought it was going to be a good day for driving, neither too hot nor too cold, and she cautioned Bailey that the speed limit was fifty-five miles an hour and that the patrolmen hid themselves behind billboards and small clumps of trees and sped out after you before you had a chance to slow down. She

---

① buck：(口)美元。

② asphyxiate：使窒息。

③ organdy：一种细薄的棉织品,蝉翼纱；sachet：(熏衣等用的)香袋,香料袋。从这段描述可见,老祖母服饰讲究,显然经过一番刻意装扮。

pointed out interesting details of the scenery: Stone Mountain①; the blue granite that in some places came up to both sides of the highway; the brilliant red clay banks slightly streaked with purple; and the various crops that made rows of green lace-work on the ground. The trees were full of silver-white sunlight and the meanest of them sparkled. The children were reading comic magazines and their mother had gone back to sleep.

"Let's go through Georgia fast so we won't have to look at it much," John Wesley said.

"If I were a little boy," said the grandmother, "I wouldn't talk about my native state that way. Tennessee has the mountains and Georgia has the hills."

"Tennessee is just a hillbilly② dumping ground," John Wesley said, "and Georgia is a lousy state too."

"You said it③," June Star said.

"In my time," said the grandmother, folding her thin veined fingers, "children were more respectful of their native states and their parents and everything else. People did right then. Oh look at the cute little pickaninny④!" she said and pointed to a Negro child standing in the door of a shack. "Wouldn't that make a picture, now?" she asked and they all turned and looked at the little Negro out of the back window. He waved.

"He didn't have any britches on," June Star said.

"He probably didn't have any," the grandmother explained. "Little niggers in the country don't have things like we do. If I could paint, I'd paint that picture," she said.

The children exchanged comic books.

The grandmother offered to hold the baby and the children's mother passed him over the front seat to her. She set him on her knee and bounced him and told him about the things they were passing. She rolled her eyes and screwed up her mouth and stuck her leathery thin face into his smooth bland one. Occasionally he gave her a faraway⑤ smile. They passed a large cotton field with five or six graves fenced in the middle of it, like a small island. "Look at the graveyard!" the

---

① Stone Mountain：美国佐治亚州的石山公园。
② hillbilly：山地内部的贫农，山地人。
③ You said it.：对了，让你说着了。
④ pickaninny：(贬)黑人小孩。
⑤ faraway：恍惚的，心不在焉的。

grandmother said, pointing it out. "That was the old family burying ground. That belonged to the plantation."

"Where's the plantation?" John Wesley asked.

"Gone With the Wind①," said the grandmother. "Ha. Ha."

When the children finished all the comic books they had brought, they opened the lunch and ate it. The grandmother ate a peanut butter sandwich and an olive and would not let the children throw the box and the paper napkins out the window. When there was nothing else to do they played a game by choosing a cloud and making the other two guess what shape it suggested. John Wesley took one the shape of a cow and June Star guessed a cow and John Wesley said, no, an automobile, and June Star said he didn't play fair, and they began to slap each other over the grandmother.

The grandmother said she would tell them a story if they would keep quiet. When she told a story, she rolled her eyes and waved her head and was very dramatic. She said once when she was a maiden lady she had been courted by a Mr. Edgar Atkins Teagarden from Jasper, Georgia. She said he was a very good-looking man and a gentleman and that he brought her a watermelon every Saturday afternoon with his initials cut in it, E. A. T. Well, one Saturday, she said, Mr. Teagarden brought the watermelon and there was nobody at home and he left it on the front porch and returned in his buggy to Jasper, but she never got the watermelon, she said, because a nigger boy ate it when he saw the initials, E. A. T.! This story tickled John Wesley's funny bone② and he giggled and giggled but June Star didn't think it was any good. She said she wouldn't marry a man that just brought her a watermelon on Saturday. The grandmother said she would have done well to marry Mr. Teagarden because he was a gentleman and had bought Coca-Cola stock when it first came out and that he had died only a few years ago, a very wealthy man.

They stopped at The Tower for barbecued sandwiches. The Tower was a part stucco and part wood filling③ station and dance hall set in a clearing outside of Timothy. A fat man named Red Sammy Butts ran it and there were signs stuck here and there on the building and for miles up and down the highway saying,

---

① Gone With the Wind.：随风而逝。这里是双关语，暗指以南北战争为背景、反映南方种植园兴衰的流行小说《飘》。

② funny bone：肘部尺骨端，幽默感。

③ part stucco and part wood filling：一半粉饰灰泥，一半油灰。

TRY RED SAMMY'S FAMOUS BARBECUE. NONE LIKE FAMOUS RED SAMMY'S! RED SAM! THE FAT BOY WITH THE HAPPY LAUGH. A VETERAN! RED SAMMY'S YOUR MAN!

Red Sammy was lying on the bare ground outside The Tower with his head under a truck while a gray monkey about a foot high, chained to a small chinaberry tree, chattered nearby. The monkey sprang back into the tree and got on the highest limb as soon as he saw the children jump out of the car and run toward him.

Inside, The Tower was a long dark room with a counter at one end and tables at the other and dancing space in the middle. They all sat down at a board table next to the nickelodeon① and Red Sam's wife, a tall burnt-brown woman with hair and eyes lighter than her skin, came and took their order. The children's mother put a dime in the machine and played "The Tennessee Waltz②," and the grandmother said that tune always made her want to dance. She asked Bailey if he would like to dance but he only glared at her. He didn't have a naturally sunny disposition like she did and trips made him nervous. The grandmother's brown eyes were very bright. She swayed her head from side to side and pretended she was dancing in her chair. June Star said play something she could tap to so the children's mother put in another dime and played a fast number and June Star stepped out onto the dance floor and did her tap routine③.

"Ain't she cute?" Red Sam's wife said, leaning over the counter. "Would you like to come be my little girl?"

"No I certainly wouldn't," June Star said. "I wouldn't live in a broken-down place like this for a million bucks!" and she ran back to the table.

"Ain't she cute?" the woman repeated, stretching her mouth politely.

"Arn't you ashamed?" hissed the grandmother.

Red Sam came in and told his wife to quit lounging on the counter and hurry up with these people's order. His khaki trousers reached just to his hip bones and his stomach hung over them like a sack of meal swaying under his shirt. He came over and sat down at a table nearby and let out a combination sigh and yodel④.

---

① nickelodeon：五分钱娱乐场，一种旧式自动点唱机。
② The Tennessee Waltz：《田纳西华尔兹》(又译《田纳西圆舞曲》)，美国著名乡村歌手帕蒂·佩奇(Patti Page)的招牌曲，1951年全美十大畅销歌曲之首，20世纪50年代舞会必播经典，被田纳西州选为州歌。歌曲曲调婉转，表现出女主人公在发生爱情变故后的忧伤之余对感情得失进行的思考，带有一种幽怨伤感的怀旧情愫。
③ tap routine：踢踏舞舞步。
④ yodel：岳得尔歌（一种流行于瑞士和奥地利山民间的民歌）。

"You can't win," he said. "You can't win," and he wiped his sweating red face off with a gray handkerchief. "These days you don't know who to trust," he said. "Ain't that the truth?"

"People are certainly not nice like they used to be," said the grandmother.

"Two fellers① come in here last week," Red Sammy said, "driving a Chrysler. It was a② old beat-up car but it was a good one and these boys looked all right to me. Said they worked at the mill and you know I let them fellers charge the gas they bought? Now why did I do that?"

"Because you're a good man!" the grandmother said at once.

"Yes'm③, I suppose so," Red Sam said as if he were struck with this answer.

His wife brought the orders, carrying the five plates all at once without a tray, two in each hand and one balanced on her arm. "It isn't a soul in this green world of God's that you can trust," she said. "And I don't count nobody out of that, not nobody," she repeated, looking at Red Sammy.

"Did you read about that criminal, The Misfit, that's escaped?" asked the grandmother.

"I wouldn't be a bit surprised if he didn't attact this place right here," said the woman. "If he hears about it being here, I wouldn't be none surprised to see him. If he hears it's two cent in the cash register, I wouldn't be a tall surprised if he..."

"That'll do," Red Sam said. "Go bring these people their Co'-Colas," and the woman went off to get the rest of the order.

"A good man is hard to find," Red Sammy said. "Everything is getting terrible. I remember the day you could go off and leave your screen door unlatched. Not no more."

He and the grandmother discussed better times. The old lady said that in her opinion Europe was entirely to blame for the way things were now. She said the way Europe acted you would think we were made of money and Red Sam said it was no use talking about it, she was exactly right. The children ran outside into the white sunlight and looked at the monkey in the lacy chinaberry tree. He was busy catching fleas on himself and biting each one carefully between his teeth as

---

① feller：(口)家伙,伙计,相当于 fellow。
② 这里的 a 应为 an。讲话人受教育程度不高,语法和发音都不甚规范,下文还有类似错误出现。
③ Yes'm："Yes, Madam"的口语形式。

188

if it were a delicacy①.

They drove off again into the hot afternoon. The grandmother took cat naps② and woke up every few minutes with her own snoring. Outside of Toombsboro she woke up and recalled an old plantation that she had visited in this neighborhood once when she was a young lady. She said the house had six white columns across the front and that there was an avenue of oaks leading up to it and two little wooden trellis arbors on either side in front where you sat down with your suitor after a stroll in the garden. She recalled exactly which road to turn off to get to it. She knew that Bailey would not be willing to lose any time looking at an old house, but the more she talked about it, the more she wanted to see it once again and find out if the little twin arbors were still standing. "There was a secret panel in this house," she said craftily, not telling the truth but wishing that she were, "and the story went that all the family silver was hidden in it when Sherman came through but it was never found…"

"Hey!" John Wesley said. "Let's go see it! We'll find it! We'll poke all the woodwork and find it! Who lives there? Where do you turn off at? Hey Pop, can't we turn off there?"

"We never have seen a house with a secret panel!" June Star shrieked. "Let's go to the house with the secret panel! Hey Pop, can't we go see the house with the secret panel!"

"It's not far from here, I know," the grandmother said. "It wouldn't take over twenty minutes."

Bailey was looking straight ahead. His jaw was as rigid as a horseshoe. "No," he said.

The children began to yell and scream that they wanted to see the house with the secret panel. John Wesley kicked the back of the front seat and June Star hung over her mother's shoulder and whined desperately into her ear that they never had any fun even on their vacation, that they could never do what THEY wanted to do. The baby began to scream and John Wesley kicked the back of the seat so hard that his father could feel the blows in his kidney.

"All right!" he shouted and drew the car to a stop at the side of the road. "Will you all shut up? Will you all just shut up for one second? If you don't shut up, we won't go anywhere."

---

① delicacy：美味佳肴。
② cat nap：打瞌睡。

"It would be very educational for them," the grandmother murmured.

"All right," Bailey said, "but get this: this is the only time we're going to stop for anything like this. This is the one and only time."

"The dirt road that you have to turn down is about a mile back," the grandmother directed. "I marked it when we passed."

"A dirt road," Bailey groaned.

After they had turned around and were headed toward the dirt road, the grandmother recalled other points about the house, the beautiful glass over the front doorway and the candle-lamp in the hall. John Wesley said that the secret panel was probably in the fireplace.

"You can't go inside this house," Bailey said. "You don't know who lives there."

"While you all talk to the people in front, I'll run around behind and get in a window," John Wesley suggested.

"We'll all stay in the car," his mother said. They turned onto the dirt road and the car raced roughly along in a swirl of pink dust. The grandmother recalled the times when there were no paved roads and thirty miles was a day's journey. The dirt road was hilly and there were sudden washes in it and sharp curves on dangerous embankments. All at once they would be on a hill, looking down over the blue tops of trees for miles around, then the next minute, they would be in a red depression① with the dust-coated trees looking down on them.

"This place had better turn up in a minute," Bailey said, "or I'm going to turn around."

The road looked as if no one had traveled on it in months.

"It's not much farther," the grandmother said and just as she said it, a horrible thought came to her. The thought was so embarrassing that she turned red in the face and her eyes dilated and her feet jumped up, upsetting her valise in the corner. The instant the valise moved, the newspaper top she had over the basket under it rose with a snarl and Pitty Sing, the cat, sprang onto Bailey's shoulder.

The children were thrown to the floor and their mother, clutching the baby, was thrown out the door onto the ground; the old lady was thrown into the front seat. The car turned over once and landed right-side-up in a gulch off the side of

---

① depression：低洼地。

the road. Bailey remained in the driver's seat with the cat—gray-striped with a broad white face and an orange nose—clinging to his neck like a caterpillar.

As soon as the children saw they could move their arms and legs, they scrambled out of the car, shouting, "We've had an ACCIDENT!" The grandmother was curled up under the dashboard, hoping she was injured so that Bailey's wrath would not come down on her all at once. The horrible thought she had had before the accident was that the house she had remembered so vividly was not in Georgia but in Tennessee.

Bailey removed the cat from his neck with both hands and flung it out the window against the side of a pine tree. Then he got out of the car and started looking for the children's mother. She was sitting against the side of a red gutted ditch, holding the screaming baby, but she only had a cut down her face and a broken shoulder. "We've had an ACCIDENT!" the children screamed in a frenzy of delight.

"But nobody's killed," June Star said with disappointment as the grandmother limped out of the car, her hat still pinned to her head but the broken front brim standing up at a jaunty angle and the violet spray hanging off the side. They all sat down in the ditch, except the children, to recover from the shock. They were all shaking.

"Maybe a car will come along," said the children's mother hoarsely.

"I believe I have injured an organ," said the grandmother, pressing her side, but no one answered her. Bailey's teeth were clattering. He had on a yellow sport shirt with bright blue parrots designed in it and his face was as yellow as the shirt. The grandmother decided that she would not mention that the house was in Tennessee.

The road was about ten feet above and they could see only the tops of the trees on the other side of it. Behind the ditch they were sitting in there were more woods, tall and dark and deep. In a few minutes they saw a car some distance away on top of a hill, coming slowly as if the occupants were watching them. The grandmother stood up and waved both arms dramatically to attract their attention. The car continued to come on slowly, disappeared around a bend and appeared again, moving even slower, on top of the hill they had gone over. It was a big black battered hearse-like automobile. There were three men in it.

It came to a stop just over them and for some minutes, the driver looked

down with a steady expressionless gaze to where they were sitting, and didn't speak. Then he turned his head and muttered something to the other two and they got out. One was a fat boy in black trousers and a red sweat shirt with a silver stallion embossed on the front of it. He moved around on the right side of them and stood staring, his mouth partly open in a kind of loose grin. The other had on khaki pants and a blue striped coat and a gray hat pulled down very low, hiding most of his face. He came around slowly on the left side. Neither spoke.

The driver got out of the car and stood by the side of it, looking down at them. He was an older man than the other two. His hair was just beginning to gray and he wore silver-rimmed spectacles that gave him a scholarly look. He had a long creased face and didn't have on any shirt or undershirt. He had on blue jeans that were too tight for him and he was holding a black hat and a gun. The two boys also had guns.

"We've had an ACCIDENT!" the children screamed.

The grandmother had the peculiar feeling that the bespectacled man was someone she knew. His face was as familiar to her as if she had known him all her life but she could not recall who he was. He moved away from the car and began to come down the embankment, placing his feet carefully so that he wouldn't slip. He had on tan and white shoes and no socks, and his ankles were red and thin. "Good afternoon," he said. "I see you all had you a little spill."

"We turned over twice!" said the grandmother.

"Oncet," he corrected. "We seen it happen. Try their car and see will it run, Hiram," he said quietly to the boy with the gray hat.

"What you got that gun for?" John Wesley asked. "Whatcha gonna① do with that gun?"

"Lady," the man said to the children's mother, "would you mind calling them children to sit down by you? Children make me nervous. I want all you all to sit down right together there where you're at."

"What are you telling US what to do for?" June Star asked.

Behind them the line of woods gaped like a dark open mouth. "Come here," said the mother.

"Look here now," Bailey began suddenly, "we're in a predicament②! We're in..."

───────────────

① Whatcha gonna: What're you going to...?
② predicament: 困境。此处不仅指一家人此前发生的车祸,而且贝利忽然意识到了对方的身份。

192

The grandmother shrieked. She scrambled to her feet and stood staring. "You're The Misfit!" she said. "I recognized you at once!"

"Yes'm," the man said, smiling slightly as if he were pleased in spite of himself to be known, "but it would have been better for all of you, lady, if you hadn't of reckernized me."

Bailey turned his head sharply and said something to his mother that shocked even the children. The old lady began to cry and The Misfit reddened.

"Lady," he said, "don't you get upset. Sometimes a man says things he don't mean. I don't reckon he meant to talk to you thataway."

"You wouldn't shoot a lady, would you?" the grandmother said and removed a clean handkerchief from her cuff and began to slap at her eyes with it.

The Misfit pointed the toe of his shoe into the ground and made a little hole and then covered it up again. "I would hate to have to," he said.

"Listen," the grandmother almost screamed, "I know you're a good man. You don't look a bit like you have common blood. I know you must come from nice people!"

"Yes mam," he said, "finest people in the world." When he smiled he showed a row of strong white teeth. "God never made a finer woman than my mother and my daddy's heart was pure gold," he said. The boy with the red sweat shirt had come around behind them and was standing with his gun at his hip. The Misfit squatted down on the ground. "Watch them children, Bobby Lee," he said. "You know they make me nervous." He looked at the six of them huddled together in front of him and he seemed to be embarrassed as if he couldn't think of anything to say. "Ain't a cloud in the sky," he remarked, looking up at it. "Don't see no sun but don't see no cloud neither."

"Yes, it's a beautiful day," said the grandmother. "Listen," she said, "you shouldn't call yourself The Misfit because I know you're a good man at heart. I can just look at you and tell."

"Hush!" Bailey yelled. "Hush! Everybody shut up and let me handle this!" He was squatting in the position of a runner about to sprint forward but he didn't move.

"I pre-chate① that, lady," The Misfit said and drew a little circle in the ground with the butt of his gun.

---

① pre-chate：应为 appreciate。这里的不规范拼写体现讲话人的不规范发音,类似处理上下文出现多处。

"It'll take a half a hour to fix this here car," Hiram called, looking over the raised hood of it.

"Well, first you and Bobby Lee get him and that little boy to step over yonder with you," The Misfit said, pointing to Bailey and John Wesley. "The boys want to ast you something," he said to Bailey. "Would you mind stepping back in them woods there with them?"

"Listen," Bailey began, "we're in a terrible predicament! Nobody realizes what this is," and his voice cracked. His eyes were as blue and intense as the parrots in his shirt and he remained perfectly still.

The grandmother reached up to adjust her hat brim as if she were going to the woods with him but it came off in her hand. She stood staring at it and after a second she let it fall on the ground. Hiram pulled Bailey up by the arm as if he were assisting an old man. John Wesley caught hold of his father's hand and Bobby Lee followed. They went off toward the woods and just as they reached the dark edge, Bailey turned and supporting himself against a gray naked pine trunk, he shouted, "I'll be back in a minute, Mamma, wait on me!"

"Come back this instant!" his mother shrilled but they all disappeared into the woods.

"Bailey Boy!" the grandmother called in a tragic voice but she found she was looking at The Misfit squatting on the ground in front of her. "I just know you're a good man," she said desperately. "You're not a bit common!"

"Nome, I ain't a good man," The Misfit said after a second as if he had considered her statement carefully, "but I ain't the worst in the world neither. My daddy said I was a different breed of dog from my brothers and sisters. 'You know,' Daddy said, 'it's some that can live their whole life out without asking about it and it's others has to know why it is, and this boy is one of the latters. He's going to be into everything!" He put on his black hat and looked up suddenly and then away deep into the woods as if he were embarrassed again. "I'm sorry I don't have on a shirt before you ladies," he said, hunching his shoulders slightly. "We buried our clothes that we had on when we escaped and we're just making do until we can get better. We borrowed these from some folks we met," he explained.

"That's perfectly all right," the grandmother said. "Maybe Bailey has an extra shirt in his suitcase."

"I'll look and see terrectly," The Misfit said.

"Where are they taking him?" the children's mother screamed.

"Daddy was a card himself," The Misfit said. "You couldn't put anything over on him. He never got in trouble with the Authorities though. Just had the knack of handling them."

"You could be honest too if you'd only try," said the grandmother. "Think how wonderful it would be to settle down and live a comfortable life and not have to think about somebody chasing you all the time."

The Misfit kept scratching in the ground with the butt of his gun as if he were thinking about it. "Yes'm, somebody is always after you," he murmured.

The grandmother noticed how thin his shoulder blades were just behind his hat because she was standing up looking down on him. "Do you ever pray?" she asked.

He shook his head. All she saw was the black hat wiggle between his shoulder blades. "Nome," he said.

There was a pistol shot from the woods, followed closely by another. Then silence. The old lady's head jerked around. She could hear the wind move through the tree tops like a long satisfied insuck of breath. "Bailey Boy!" she called.

"I was a gospel singer for a while," The Misfit said. "I been most everything. Been in the arm service, both land and sea, at home and abroad, been twict married, been an undertaker, been with the railroads, plowed Mother Earth, been in a tornado, seen a man burnt alive oncet," and he looked up at the children's mother and the little girl who were sitting close together, their faces white and their eyes glassy. "I even seen a woman flogged[①]," he said.

"Pray, pray," the grandmother began, "pray, pray..."

"I never was a bad boy that I remember of," The Misfit said in an almost dreamy voice, " but somewheres along the line I done something wrong and got sent to the penitentiary. I was buried alive," and he looked up and held her attention to him by a steady stare.

"That's when you should have started to pray," she said "What did you do to get sent to the penitentiary that first time?"

---

① flog: 鞭笞, 鞭打。逃犯声称曾经看到一名妇女遭到鞭笞, 同时他简述了自身经历的人生不幸、看到的暴行, 这对他的人生观形成都有深刻影响。

"Turn to the right, it was a wall," The Misfit said, looking up again at the cloudless sky. "Turn to the left, it was a wall. Look up it was a ceiling, look down it was a floor. I forget what I done, lady. I set there and set there, trying to remember what it was I done and I ain't recalled it to this day. Oncet in a while, I would think it was coming to me, but it never come."

"Maybe they put you in by mistake," the old lady said vaguely.

"Nome," he said. "It wasn't no mistake. They had the papers on me."

"You must have stolen something," she said.

The Misfit sneered slightly. "Nobody had nothing I wanted," he said. "It was a head-doctor at the penitentiary said what I had done was kill my daddy but I known that for a lie. My daddy died in nineteen ought nineteen of the epidemic flu and I never had a thing to do with it. He was buried in the Mount Hopewell Baptist churchyard and you can go there and see for yourself."

"If you would pray," the old lady said, "Jesus would help you."

"That's right," The Misfit said.

"Well then, why don't you pray?" she asked trembling with delight suddenly.

"I don't want no hep," he said. "I'm doing all right by myself."

Bobby Lee and Hiram came ambling back from the woods. Bobby Lee was dragging a yellow shirt with bright blue parrots in it.

"Thow me that shirt, Bobby Lee," The Misfit said. The shirt came flying at him and landed on his shoulder and he put it on. The grandmother couldn't name what the shirt reminded her of. "No, lady," The Misfit said while he was buttoning it up, "I found out the crime don't matter. You can do one thing or you can do another, kill a man or take a tire off his car, because sooner or later you're going to forget what it was you done and just be punished for it."

The children's mother had begun to make heaving noises as if she couldn't get her breath. "Lady," he asked, "would you and that little girl like to step off yonder with Bobby Lee and Hiram and join your husband?"

"Yes, thank you," the mother said faintly. Her left arm dangled helplessly and she was holding the baby, who had gone to sleep, in the other. "Hep that lady up, Hiram," The Misfit said as she struggled to climb out of the ditch, "and Bobby Lee, you hold onto that little girl's hand."

"I don't want to hold hands with him," June Star said. "He reminds me of a pig."

The fat boy blushed and laughed and caught her by the arm and pulled her off into the woods after Hiram and her mother.

Alone with The Misfit, the grandmother found that she had lost her voice. There was not a cloud in the sky nor any sun. There was nothing around her but woods. She wanted to tell him that he must pray. She opened and closed her mouth several times before anything came out. Finally she found herself saying, "Jesus. Jesus," meaning, Jesus will help you, but the way she was saying it, it sounded as if she might be cursing.

"Yes'm," The Misfit said as if he agreed. "Jesus thown everything off balance. It was the same case with Him as with me except He hadn't committed any crime and they could prove I had committed one because they had the papers on me. Of course," he said, "they never shown me my papers. That's why I sign myself now. I said long ago, you get you a signature and sign everything you do and keep a copy of it. Then you'll know what you done and you can hold up the crime to the punishment and see do they match and in the end you'll have something to prove you ain't been treated right. I call myself The Misfit," he said, "because I can't make what all I done wrong fit what all I gone through in punishment."

There was a piercing scream from the woods, followed closely by a pistol report[①]. "Does it seem right to you, lady, that one is punished a heap and another ain't punished at all?"

"Jesus!" the old lady cried. "You've got good blood! I know you wouldn't shoot a lady! I know you come from nice people! Pray! Jesus, you ought not to shoot a lady. I'll give you all the money I've got!"

"Lady," The Misfit said, looking beyond her far into the woods, "there never was a body that give the undertaker a tip."

There were two more pistol reports and the grandmother raised her head like a parched old turkey hen crying for water and called, "Bailey Boy, Bailey Boy!" as if her heart would break.

"Jesus was the only One that ever raised the dead," The Misfit continued, "and He thouldn't have done it. He thown everything off balance. If He did what He said, then it's nothing for you to do but thow away everything and follow Him, and if He didn't, then it's nothing for you to do but enjoy the few minutes you got left the best way you can—by killing somebody or burning down his

---

① a pistol report: 一声枪响。

house or doing some other meanness to him. No pleasure but meanness," he said and his voice had become almost a snarl.

"Maybe He didn't raise the dead," the old lady mumbled, not knowing what she was saying and feeling so dizzy that she sank down in the ditch with her legs twisted under her.

"I wasn't there so I can't say He didn't," The Misfit said. "I wisht I had of been there," he said, hitting the ground with his fist. "It ain't right I wasn't there because if I had of been there I would of known. Listen lady," he said in a high voice, "if I had of been there I would of known and I wouldn't be like I am now." His voice seemed about to crack and the grandmother's head cleared for an instant. She saw the man's face twisted close to her own as if he were going to cry and she murmured, "Why you're one of my babies. You're one of my own children!" She reached out and touched him on the shoulder. The Misfit sprang back as if a snake had bitten him and shot her three times through the chest. Then he put his gun down on the ground and took off his glasses and began to clean them.

Hiram and Bobby Lee returned from the woods and stood over the ditch, looking down at the grandmother who half sat and half lay in a puddle of blood with her legs crossed under her like a child's and her face smiling up at the cloudless sky.

Without his glasses, The Misfit's eyes were red-rimmed and pale and defenseless-looking. "Take her off and thow her where you thown the others," he said, picking up the cat that was rubbing itself against his leg.

"She was a talker, wasn't she?" Bobby Lee said, sliding down the ditch with a yodel.

"She would of been a good woman," The Misfit said, "if it had been somebody there to shoot her every minute of her life."

"Some fun!"① Bobby Lee said.

"Shut up, Bobby Lee" The Misfit said. "It's no real pleasure in life."

---

① Some fun!: 真有乐子!

第十单元

作品赏析

　　《好人难寻》是奥康纳最有名的两个短篇小说之一（另一个是《善良的乡下人》）。小说以黑色幽默与暴力结合的文字讲述了一个虚构的宗教寓言故事。主人公是一个自以为是的饶舌老太太。一个假日里，她与儿子、儿媳、孙子和孙女一家人带上婴儿一起出去玩，一路上唠唠叨叨讨人嫌。由于她的记忆失误，众人走错了路，汽车翻了，而此时却恰好碰上了出发前一天在报纸上看到的通缉逃犯"不合时宜的人"。老太太认出了他，一家六口因此招来了杀身之祸，被分成三批杀掉，老太太是最后一个，即使临死前的幡然悔悟也没能使她免遭杀戮。

　　南方生活题材、天主教思想背景和怪诞风格是奥康纳小说创作的三个突出特点，这三个特点在《好人难寻》这个短篇里得到了集中体现。首先，与欧茨的《何去何从》（见本书第二十章）如出一辙，《好人难寻》取材于新闻报道中的真实案件。小说以作者所熟悉的南方地理环境和历史时代为背景展开叙事，上个世纪50年代的帕蒂·佩奇风靡全国的流行歌曲《田纳西华尔兹》构成了回响在整个故事中的一个主旋律，与老太太的"田纳西情结"相呼应，营造了一种南方所特有的排他性怀旧情绪。在一定程度上，怀旧之旅中的车祸和谋杀事件正是由这种情绪间接导致的破坏性后果。同时，人物的语言也保留了鲜活的口语体特征，具有浓郁的美国南方特色。

　　谈到宗教对文学创作的影响，奥康纳曾经指出，"具有基督教精神关怀的作家会发现现实生活中的扭曲与自身的不一致性，作家的困难是如何让这种扭曲在读者面前呈现出来，而他们对这种生活早已心安理得……你只能对着半聋的家伙嚷嚷，让半瞎的人看大而明亮的图画。"在小说创作中，奥康纳自觉地扮演着一个先知先觉的角色，她认为唤醒人们的宗教意识需要通过暴力去触及人的灵魂，使之在暴力的非常状态下获得灵魂救赎。具体到《好人难寻》，在暴力构成的压力下，死神的迫近让老太太将目光从自我转向了他者，瞬间苏醒的慈悲心促使她在死前那一刻终于放弃了自我封闭带来的优越感，发自内心地对逃犯说出"你就是我的一个孩子呀！"这样的话来。可以说，尽管难逃肉体灭亡的悲惨结局，但是对他者在上帝面前的平等地位的认可却使她获得了灵魂的救赎。

　　另外，对于奥康纳来说，不仅仅是暴力，荒诞也是现实生活中的一部分。值得注意的是，在《好人难寻》里，人物形象不仅经过了夸张变形的艺术加工，而且被贴上各种动物的标签：兔子耳朵一样的头巾、河马头形状的旅行袋等等。特别是，面对死亡时的黑色幽默反衬出现实生活的内在荒诞性和残酷性。

思考题

1. What do you think of the family relationships?
2. Who is mainly responsible for the family's tragedy? Why?
3. What prompted the grandmother to say to the Misfit, "Why you're one of my babies. You're one of my own children!"? What kind of revelation occurred to the old lady at the last moment?
4. "She would of been a good woman," The Misfit said, "if it had been somebody there to shoot her every minute of her life." How do you understand this comment in relation to the author's view of violence?
5. Where might the author's sympathy lie?

推荐作品

Wise Blood (1952)

"Good Country People" (1955)

"Everything that Rises must Converge" (1965)

参考资料

Cash, W. J. *Flannery O'Connor: A life*. Knoxville: U of Tennessee P, 2002.

Grimshaw, James A. *The Flannery O'Connor Companion*. Westport CT: Greenwood Press, 1981.

Kreyling, Michael, ed. *New Essays on Wise Blood*. Beijing: Peking UP; Cambridge UP, 2006

Paulson, SM. *Flannery O'Connor: A Study of the Short Fiction*. Boston: Twa-yne Publishers, 1988.

第十一单元
Allen Ginsberg
(1926—1997)
艾伦·金斯堡

作者简介

艾伦·金斯堡(又译金斯伯格),诗人。生于新泽西州纽瓦克市,父亲为中学英语教师,为人厚道谨慎;母亲为犹太移民,因为是共产党员在俄国遭受迫害而患有精神疾病。金斯堡曾就读哥伦比亚大学,主修经济,但热衷于诗歌创作,并发表诗歌。其间,他结识了威廉·巴勒斯(William S. Burroughs)与杰克·凯鲁亚克(Jack Kerouac)等后来投身文学创作的同学,志同道合,形成一个颇有特色的文学创作群体,史称"垮掉的一代"(the Beat Generation)。后因生活放荡不羁,吸食毒品,破坏学校的秩序等原因,金斯堡被开除学籍。1956年,他发表了诗集《嚎叫及其他》(Howl and Other Poems),以其反传统的主题内容和效仿惠特曼的诗歌风格震撼了美国诗坛,其诗集中还包括他最负盛名的一些诗篇,诸如《加利福尼亚的超级市场》(A Supermarket in California)。金斯堡的一生可谓跌宕起伏,一度缺乏稳定的生活,长期周游各州,靠打零工谋生,并曾因窝赃而被捕入狱。他也曾成为纽约布鲁克林学院的杰出教授,还曾当选美国的人文艺术学院院士,得过古根海姆(Guggenheim)基金会的资助。在50年代和60年代特殊的环境下,他参与反战游行、民权运动和吸毒、同性恋等反文化活动。这些经历实际上也成为他诗歌的主要内容。金斯堡共出版了11部诗集,主要包括《卡迪西及其他》(Kaddish and Other Poems, 1961)、《现实三明治》(Reality Sandwiches, 1963)、《星球消息》(Planet News, 1961—1967)以及荣获美国国家图书奖的《美国的堕落》(The Fall of America: Poems of These States, 1965—1971)等。1984年金斯堡访问中国,写了一些回忆中国之行的诗歌,收集在《白色的尸衣》(White Shroud Poems, 1980—1985, 1986)和《向世界祝福》(Cosmopolitan Greetings: Poems, 1986—1992, 1994)。最后一部诗集《死亡的荣誉》(Death and Fame Poems, 1995—1997)在他去世后于1999年出版。金斯堡是20世纪美国诗歌历史上不可或缺的重要代表人物。

On the Conduct of the World Seeking Beauty Against Government

Is that the only way we can become like Indians, like Rhinoceri①,
like Quartz Crystals②, like organic farmers, like what we imagine
Adam & Eve to've been, caressing each other with trembling limbs
before the Snake of Revolutionary Sex wrapped itself round
The Tree of Knowledge③? What would Roque Dalton④ joke about lately
teeth chattering like a machine gun as he dabated mass tactics
with his Companeros⑤? Necessary to kill the Yanquis⑥ with big bomb
Yes but don't do it by yourself, better consult your mother
to get the Correct Line of Thought,   if not consult Rimbaud⑦ once he got his leg cut off
or Lenin after his second stroke sending a message thru Mrs Krupskaya
to the rude Georgian, & just before his deathly fit when the Cheka⑧ aides outside
his door looked in coldly assuring him his affairs were in good hands no need to move—What sickness at the
pit of his stomach moved up to
his brain?
What thought Khlebnikov⑨ on the hungry train exposing his stomach to the sun?

---

① Rhinoceri：犀牛。
② Quartz Crystals：水晶，石英，雕玻璃，晶体。
③ Tree of Knowledge：指《圣经》中的智慧之树，位于伊甸园的中心，亚当和夏娃违反上帝的旨意，偷吃树上的禁果，构成"原罪"。
④ Roque Dalton：萨尔瓦多诗人、革命家。1935 年出生，1975 年被处以极刑。
⑤ Companeros：志同道合的人，伙伴。
⑥ Yanquis：专指美国人，有别于其他拉丁美洲人。
⑦ Rimbaud：兰波（Arthur Rimbaud，1854—1891），法国诗人。
⑧ Cheka：(苏联)契卡，肃反委员会的简称。
⑨ Khlebnikov：赫列勃尼科夫（Velimir Vladimirovich Khlebnikov，1855—1922），俄国诗人、未来主义流派创始人。

Or Mayakovsky① before the bullet hit his brain, what sharp propaganda for action
on the Bureaucratic Battlefield in the Ministry of Collective Agriculture in Ukraine?
What Slogan for Futurist architects or epic hymn for masses of Communist Party Card holders in Futurity②
on the conduct of the world seeking beauty against Government?

金斯堡作为美国社会批评者的形象贯穿其主要诗作,这首诗也不例外。该诗沿袭了《嚎叫》一诗的主题,从一个处于社会边缘地带的"另类"人物的视角对当时美国社会中普遍存在的严重问题发出了愤怒的抗议,诗的标题中的"反政府"就凸现了诗的主题。就诗的风格而言,金斯堡推崇19世纪美国诗人惠特曼,并尽力仿效,诗句摒弃传统的音步和韵律,自由地使用口语风格的长句,犹如瀑布一泻千里,以此展现边缘人物向政府和权力叫板时所表现的磅礴气势,犹如庞大的示威人群发出的怒吼。大量使用意象组合也是该诗的一个特点,从"亚当与夏娃"到"乌克兰集体农业部",从"革命性的蛇"到"马雅可夫斯基",典型地体现了金斯堡以表现愤懑情绪见长的诗人思维奔逸、藐视权力、挪揄传统、自命不凡的特征。金斯堡的诗歌有别于注重音韵格律的传统诗歌。著名诗歌评论家海伦·文德莱曾说,"金斯堡借以唤醒／提高意识最有效方式是他的极富节奏感的冲动力通过长长的浪花般滚动起伏的诗句表达出来。"对于有人批评诗人意象杂乱的观点,文德莱则说,他的诗是"对美国的透视",他用"类似电影的手法对现实发生细节进行处理,令人身临其境"。这对于不了解诗中涉及的社会、文化、政治事件和人物,甚至地理知识以及他的家世友人的读者制造了一定的困难。

思考题

1. If you take this poem as an example for a comparative study, in what way do you think that Allen Ginsberg was influenced by Walt Whitman?
2. When you look into the narrative traits of the poem, whom do you think Allen Ginsberg intends to denote in his use of "we"?

---

① Mayakovsky:马雅可夫斯基(Vladimir Vladimirovich Mayakovsky, 1893—1930),苏联诗人。
② Futurity:未来,来世。

 **推荐作品**

"Howl"

"A Supermarket in California"

参考资料

Graham, Caveney. *Screaming with Joy: The Life of Allen Ginsberg*. New York: Broadway Books, 1999.

Lewis Hyde, ed. *On the Poetry of Allen Ginsberg*. Ann Arbor: U of Michigan P, 1984.

Paul Cornel Portuges. *The Visionary Poetics of Allen Ginsberg*. Santa Barbara, California: Ross-Erickson, 1978.

Robert Lowell
(1917—1977)
罗伯特·洛威尔

作者简介

罗伯特·洛威尔,诗人,"自白派"诗歌的代表人物之一。生于马萨诸塞州波士顿市,父亲为海军军官。他的父母及前辈中不乏颇有建树的文学家,如19世纪赫赫有名的诗人詹姆斯·拉塞尔·洛威尔(James Russell Lowell)以及20世纪的知名意象派诗人艾米·洛威尔(Amy Lowell)。在哈佛大学期间,洛威尔开始对诗歌创作感兴趣,两年后追随"逃亡派"诗人艾伦·塔特(Allen Tate)到田纳西并入肯庸学院受塔特和约翰·兰塞姆(John Crowe Ransom)等诗人的栽培。大学毕业后,他前往路易斯安那州立大学进一步深造,师从当时走红的新批评派核心人物罗伯特·潘·沃伦(Robert Penn Warren)与克林斯·布鲁克斯(Cleanth Brooks)。1940年,他首次结婚,配偶是小说家简恩·斯塔福德(Jean Stafford),但很快离异;此后又两度结婚,但均不美满,后因与第三位夫人发生口角而猝死在出租汽车上。二战期间,他参军在德国服役,目睹战争的血腥与残酷,萌生反战思想,拒绝执行军务,因此被捕入狱。战后,洛威尔专注于诗歌创作,成就非凡。他的第一部诗集《威利爵爷的城堡》(*Lord Weary's Castle*, 1947),取材于苏格兰民谣,荣获普利策诗歌奖。1959年出版的诗集《人生研究》(*Life Studies*)获得美国国家图书奖。其他作品还包括获得普利策奖的诗集《海豚》(*The Dolphin*, 1973)。

作　品

Man and Wife

Tamed by *Miltown*①, we lie on Mother's bed;
the rising sun in war paint dyes us red;
in broad daylight her gilded bed-posts② shine,

---
① Miltown:眠尔通,药名:即一种安眠药;安宁。
② bed-posts:床柱,床角的垂直柱子。

abandoned, almost Dionysian①.
At last the trees are green on Marlborough② Street,
blossoms on our magnolia ignite
the morning with their murderous five day's white.
All night I've held your hand,
as if you had
a fourth time faced the kingdom of the mad—
its hackneyed③ speech, its homicidal④ eye—
and dragged me home alive... Oh my *Petite*,
clearest of all God's creatures, still all air and nerve:
you were in your twenties, and I,
once hand on glass
and heart in mouth,
outdrank the Rahvs⑤ in the heat
of Greenwich Village⑥, fainting at your feet—
too boiled and shy
and poker-faced⑦ to make a pass,
while the shrill verve
of your invective⑧ scorched the traditional South.

Now twelve years later, you turn your back.
Sleepless, you hold
your pillow to your hollows like a child,
your old-fashioned tirade⑨—
loving, rapid, merciless—
breaks like the Atlantic Ocean on my head.

---

① Dionysian：酒神节的；放荡的；源于古希腊神话中的酒神狄俄尼索斯(Dionysus)，指与狄俄尼索斯有关的。

② Marlborough：也称 Marlboro，指美国马萨诸塞州中东部一城市，位于伍斯特市东北偏东方向，1657 年开始有人定居。

③ hackneyed：陈词滥调的，老生常谈的，不新奇的。

④ homicidal：杀人的，可导致杀人的。

⑤ the Rahvs：一种酒精饮料。

⑥ Greenwich Village：格林威治村，位于美国纽约市曼哈顿的一个居民区，1910 年后成为艺术家和作家的聚居地。

⑦ poker-faced：没有表情的，神情木然的，一本正经的。

⑧ invective：非难的，漫骂的，恶言的。

⑨ tirade：抨击；激烈演说；愤怒的或激烈的长篇言辞，通常为挑剔或谴责性质。

 洛威尔的诗歌题材和主题都非常广泛,从思考现实问题到改写古代的民谣,展示了他宽阔的视野和胸怀。他与同时代的许多诗人一样,诸如金斯堡和西尔维娅·普拉斯,在很大程度上动用"自白"手法,即毫无顾忌地叙说自身非同一般、刻骨铭心的经历和感受,强烈关注个人的生活境遇以及内心世界的感受,而并非像古希腊的诗人荷马那样凭借想象与传说就能够写就事关人类命运和国家社稷的史诗。在《夫与妻》一诗中,作为主人公的叙事者讲述了他与妻子在服用"眠尔通"之后进入似睡非睡的幻觉状态,由此无拘无束地倾诉了心灵中痛苦不安的感受。位于诗歌之首的"被眠尔通制服以后",提示读者主人公与妻子在服用安眠药之前的苦楚与疯狂。在诗的结尾,"妻子"的愤懑再一次像"大西洋一样"倾泻而出,"丈夫"也再一次领略到了"司空见惯的长篇唠叨"。虽然这一幕仅仅是主人公在幻觉中的感受,但在"自白派"诗人看来,只有在解除意识束缚的状况下的"自白"才能展示最真实的内心世界。

 思考题

1. What do you think the poet means when he refers to Dionysus in the poem?
2. How does the poet represent the habitual but gnawing tension between the husband and his wife?

 "Skunk Hour"
"To Skeak of Woe that Is in Marriage"
"Walking in the Blue"

参考资料

Perloff, Marjorie. *The Poetic Art of Robert Lowell*. Ithaca: Cornell UP, 1973.
Rudman, Mark. *Robert Lowell: An Introduction to the Poetry*. New York: Columbia UP, 1983.
Tillinghast, Richard. *Robert Lowell' Life and Work: Damaged Grandeur*. Ann Arbor: U of Michigan P, 1995.

Elizabeth Bishop
(1911—1979)
伊丽莎白·毕晓普

 作者简介

　　伊丽莎白·毕晓普,女诗人、翻译家。生于马萨诸塞州伍斯特市,襁褓时母亲多病,6岁时父亲早亡,由亲戚抚养成人。她在13岁时发现惠特曼、狄金森等诗人、小说家,1930年就读瓦莎学院,先主修作曲和钢琴,后因身体不佳转学英语,由此对诗歌创作发生兴趣,并在校园中创办了一种文学刊物。大学期间,她经人介绍结识诗人玛丽安·摩尔(Marianne Moore)。摩尔比她大24岁,已经成名,对她有很大的影响。毕晓普性格独特,终身未婚,大学毕业后周游北美和欧洲的许多国家,并客居巴西长达17年之久。这段生活对她的文学创作与翻译产生了重要影响。回国后,毕晓普受聘哈佛大学,哈佛的文化氛围也对她的创作产生了显见的影响。就学术界和读者大众对其诗歌创作的认同而言,她取得了同时代美国诗人中无人可以比拟的成就,曾经荣获所有的诗歌奖项。1955年,她诗集《北与南》(*North & South*, 1946)与《寒春》(*A Cold Spring*, 1955)获得普利策诗歌奖。1976年,她成为荣获诺斯达特国际文学奖(*Neustat International for Literature Prize*)的第一位美国作家。她翻译的文学作品包括《20世纪巴西诗歌选集》(*An Anthology of the Twentieth-Century Brazilian Poetry*, 1972)。

作 品

Sestina①

September rain falls on the house.
In the failing light, the old grandmother
sits in the kitchen with the child
beside the Little Marvel Stove②,

---

① sestina: 六节诗,一种诗体,由法国普罗旺斯抒情诗人率先使用,结构是由六个六行诗节和一个三行收尾诗节组成;通常第一诗节末尾出现的词需要在其他诗节中以不同顺序重复,并用作收尾诗节的最后一个词。

② the Little Marvel Stove: 一种火炉。

reading the jokes from the almanac①,
laughing and talking to hide her tears.

She thinks that her equinoctial tears
and the rain that beats on the roof of the house
were both foretold by the almanac,
but only known to a grandmother.
The iron kettle sings on the stove.
She cuts some bread and says to the child,

It's time for tea now; but the child
is watching the teakettle's small hard tears
dance like mad on the hot black stove,
the way the rain must dance on the house.
Tidying up, the old grandmother
hangs up the clever almanac
on its string. Birdlike, the almanac
hovers② half open above the child,
hovers above the old grandmother
and her teacup full of dark brown tears.
She shivers and says she thinks the house
feels chilly, and puts more wood in the stove.

It was to be, says the Marvel Stove.
I know what I know, says the almanac.
With crayons the child draws a rigid house
and a winding pathway. Then the child
puts in a man with buttons like tears
and shows it proudly to the grandmother.

But secretly, while the grandmother
busies herself about the stove,
the little moons fall down like tears

---

① almanac：年历，历书，年鉴。
② hover：盘旋，徘徊，踌躇。

from between the pages of the almanac
into the flower bed① the child
has carefully placed in the front of the house.

Time to plant tears, says the almanac.
The grandmother sings to the marvellous stove
and the child draws another inscrutable② house.

该诗的体裁别有特色,采用了美国诗人很少使用的六节诗,这一特征与庞德等人在20世纪初叶改写中国古典诗词、模仿日本的俳句和借鉴欧洲文学传统所产生的影响有关。惠特曼和狄金森之后,美国诗人始终崇尚推陈出新,借鉴其他民族和文化中的诗体也属于这一范畴的努力。六节诗原本流行于法国普罗旺斯,主题大多是吟颂爱情和浪漫的故事,节奏舒缓,韵律规范,适合于讲述情感细腻的经历。在这首诗中,毕晓普娴熟地驾驭了这种别具风格的诗体,讲述了一个貌似童话但令人心酸的故事,使诗歌的内容与形式完美地交融为一个整体。诗歌规范的格式也提示诗中讲述的故事只是主人公循环往复的现实生活中的一幕。诗中的叙事者采用了旁观的第三人称视角,毕晓普往往借此回避自我的直接流露,而更青睐暗示或者间接提示的手法。诗中没有提及"孩童"的父母,但是孩子的孤独、沉默、眼泪以及与年历和火炉的对话都会使读者感受到父母的缺失对一个幼小的生命和心灵的巨大影响。作为女诗人,毕晓普没有使用金斯堡等当时在美国诗坛呼风唤雨的人物所惯常使用的宏大背景和大气磅礴的语言文字,但她的诗歌的魅力在于从平凡的生活细节中发掘出震撼人心的价值和意义。当"孩童"用幼小的手"画了一个男人,他的纽扣宛如一滴滴泪水",又如当孩子将茶壶中滴落在火炉上的水滴视为"泪珠",观看它们"疯狂地在黑色的火炉上跳舞",毕晓普期待读者感受到的不仅仅是孩子的命运以及对于这种命运的同情,还应当有对现实的责问。

思考题

1. Can you summarize the main metrical and rhythmical features of the poem?
2. Apart from the third-person narrator, what other devices does the poet use in the poem so as to mirror the life of "the grandmother" and "the child" in an objective way?

---

① flower bed:花床,花圃,花坛。
② inscrutable:高深莫测的,不可思议的,神秘的。

第十一单元

推荐作品

"The Moose"
"The Fish"
"A Cold Spring"

参考资料

Doreski, C. K. *Elizabeth Bishop: The Restraints of Language*. New York: Oxford UP, 1993.

Schwartz, Lloyd and Sybil P. Estess, eds. *Elizabeth Bishop and Her Art*. Ann Arbor: U of Michigan P, 1983.

Stevenson, Anne. *Elizabeth Bishop*. New York: Twayne, 1966.

Robert Creeley
(1926—2005)
罗伯特·克里莱

 作者简介

  罗伯特·克里莱,诗人、小说家、编辑。生于马萨诸塞州阿林顿市,父亲为医生,在克里莱幼年时亡故。在哈佛大学学习期间,他开始写诗并在校刊上发表;后转学至黑山学院,获得学士学位,并担任《黑山评论》的编辑。黑山学院是"黑山派"诗歌的发祥地,克里莱在此与查尔斯·奥森(Charles Olsen)以及罗伯特·邓肯(Robert Duncan)等诗人结识,并以其创作和理论使该学院成为20世纪50年代和60年代美国诗歌的一个中心。他们主张,诗歌创作应当采用与当时主流的格律诗体和广征博引的学院派诗风不同风格的"放射体",强调口语性和自然的音乐性,将诗人的"能"传递给自己的读者。克里莱曾周游北美、欧洲和亚洲的许多国家,并几度作为富布莱特专家在芬兰和尼泊尔等国家任教。1978年以后担任纽约州立大学诗歌教授。他的诗歌以风格清新、情真意切、文字简洁明快见长,在国内外出版60部诗集,可谓当代最高产的美国诗人。他的主要作品包括《诗选》(*Selected Poems*, 1976)、《记忆花园》(*Memory Gardens*, 1986)、《生与死》(*Life & Death*, 1998),以及《准时》(*Just in Time*, 2001)。其他作品还包括小说《岛》(*The Island*, 1963)。他曾荣获许多奖项,包括美国诗歌协会奖以及波林根奖。

作品

Water Music

The words are a beautiful music
The words bounce like in water.

Water music,
loud in the clearing

off the boats,

birds, leaves.

They look for a place
To sit and eat—

no meaning,
no point.

　　克里莱的诗歌素来以高度聚焦的题材、短小精悍的诗篇、简洁清新的风格与崇尚诗歌的音乐性而见长,在美国诗坛独树一帜。他几乎从不使用恢宏的背景和完整的叙事结构,完全不同于惠特曼、T. S.艾略特、金斯堡,甚至弗罗斯特等各种流派的经典诗人的风格,尽管他也受到了金斯堡和威廉斯的影响。可以说,《水音乐》实际上是以浓缩而优美的方式体现了克里莱的诗歌创作原则。如该诗所示,克里莱可谓惜字如金,许多诗篇只有十几个字构成,但是着意追求意象的清新与诗句的音乐美感。他将他理想中的诗称为"水音乐",自然而然地使人感受到这一形象的比喻所昭示的诗的特性:在形式上,应当具有自然的音乐性,清澈如泉,舒展如云,追求内心与外在现实的和谐,不事雕琢,但沁人心脾;在内涵方面,诗文字面上"没有意义",也不追求表层的意义,而是期盼读者在诗人创造的美妙语境中感悟到诗的主旨。

思考题

1. What lyrical and musical qualities can you find in this poem?
2. Some people hold the idea that imagery plays a more important role in the poems whose narrative structure is loose. Do you agree or not? Why?

"The World"
"Time"
"The Whip"

参考资料

Foster, Edward Halsey. "Robert Creeley, Poetics of Solitude." *Understanding the Black Mountain Poets*. Columbia: U of South Carolina P, 1994.

Mandel, Ann. *Measures: Robert Creeley's Poetry*. Toronto: The Coach House Press, 1974.

Wilson, John, ed. *Robert Creeley's Life and Work: A Sense of Increment*. Ann Arbor: U of Michigan P, 1988.

Robert Hayden
(1913—1980)
罗伯特·海登

作者简介

  罗伯特·海登,美国国会图书馆第一个黑人"诗歌顾问"(后改称为"美国桂冠诗人"),生于底特律的贫民区,亲生父母在他出生后不久即离异,被邻居海登家收养。养父母不休的争吵和打骂,以及自身的近视和矮小,使少年罗伯特郁郁寡欢,只好从书籍中寻找慰藉。海登就读于芝加哥城市学院(后改名为韦恩州立大学),主修西班牙语,1936 年以一学分之差辍学,加入美国联邦作家项目,开始研究美国黑人历史和民间文化,为后来的诗歌创作积累了素材。1940 年,海登发表第一部诗集《尘土中的心形》(*Heart-Shape in the Dust*)。1941 年,他进入密歇根大学攻读英语硕士学位,1942 年师从奥登(W. H. Auden),在诗歌创作上取得很大进步。从 1946 年起,他到南方的菲斯克大学(Fisk University)任教 23 年,陆续发表《狮子与弓箭手》(*The Lion and the Archer*, 1948)、《时间的数字:诗集》(*Figures of Time: Poems*, 1955)、《记忆的歌谣》(*A Ballad of Remembrance*, 1962)和《诗选》(*Selected Poems*, 1966)。1969 年重返密歇根大学,舌笔同耕,发表了《哀悼时的言语》(*Words in the Mourning Time*, 1970)、《夜间绽开的尾须》(*The Night-Blooming Cereus*, 1972)和《上飘的天使》(*Angle of Ascent*, 1975),成为重要的美国诗人。1975 年,因为"对诗歌杰出的贡献"被美国诗院奖励每年一万美元的创作奖金。次年,被任命为国会图书馆的诗歌顾问。1980 年 1 月,应卡特总统之邀到白宫参加诗人庆祝活动,同年 2 月去世,遗著《美国日志》于 1982 年出版。海登是巴哈伊教徒,信奉世界大同、民族友爱,认为诗人不应该是民族的代言人,政治和种族标准不应该用在对"好诗"与"坏诗"的判断上。然而,他的很多诗歌反映的仍是黑人的情感和体验。海登善于运用诗歌细节性技巧,通过压缩、委婉陈述、并列组合、蒙太奇等手法提升诗歌的象征浓度,诗作洗炼优美,受到越来越多的读者的喜爱。

Those Winter Sundays[①]

Sundays too my father got up early
and put his clothes on in the blueblack[②] cold,
then with cracked hands that ached
from labor in the weekday weather made
banked fires[③] blaze. No one ever thanked him.

I'd wake and hear the cold splintering[④], breaking.
When the rooms were warm, he'd call,
and slowly I would rise and dress,
fearing the chronic angers[⑤] of that house,
Speaking indifferently to him,
who had driven out the cold
and polished my good shoes[⑥] as well.
What did I know, what did I know
of love's austere and lonely offices[⑦]?

---

①《冬天的早晨》用清晰、准确的语言描绘了一位父亲在冬天的早晨任劳任怨地为孩子生火驱寒的往事,最后又通过成熟的"我"对童年的反思,抒发父子间复杂的感情和"我"对爱的深刻理解。全诗十四行,有人因此称之为"十四行诗"。虽然本诗在最后两行点明主题,但是全诗的分阙方法、音步和韵式都不同于彼得拉克诗体、莎士比亚体和斯宾塞体三种传统的十四行诗。

② in the blueblack cold:在冻得人发青的黑暗的寒冷中。blue 可以指人的肤色发青、发紫、发灰;black 指天还未亮,一片漆黑。

③ banked fires:封炉的火,用火灰掩盖的火。

④ splinter:撕裂,刺穿。这里 splintering 和 breaking 两个词一起生动地展示"我"听到寒冷被火驱散的情景。

⑤ the chronic angers:慢性愤怒。一说指父子间的敌对情绪;另一说指诗人的养母(Sue Ellen Hayden),因其婚姻不幸福,常发脾气;亦可理解为贫困家庭因生活所迫而滋生的不满情绪。

⑥ good shoes:星期天是上教堂的日子,人们一般都穿最好的衣服,所以父亲为养子擦亮了那双好鞋。

⑦ office:一词多义,既可以因父亲艰辛劳作的实质和单词的复数形式,把它理解为"照料、帮助",又可以根据上文中孩子对父亲淡漠的态度,理解为"职责",甚至还可以理解为"礼仪"。前者表示成年的"我"感受到父亲对自己的爱怜之情,后者则表示儿时的"我"认为父亲所作的一切都是他应尽的职责。

第十一单元

 作品赏析

《冬天的早晨》于1962年发表在《记忆的歌谣》(*A Ballad of Remembrance*)里。诗歌展示了诗人卓越的文字能力和对复杂情感的细腻表现能力,通过"我"对父爱的缓慢认识过程揭示了"我"对儿时不知感恩(比如:"No one ever thanked him","Speaking indifferently to him")的复杂心理。诗歌开头两句通过"too"一词说明父亲终年累月含辛茹苦,没有休息日,又通过父亲在黑暗中起床穿衣暗示了他默默无闻的奉献。3—5行,通过对父亲用粗糙疼痛的手为家人生火的具体描写表现了父亲的自我牺牲精神,然而这一切却没有人领情,第5行后半句"没谁感谢他",突兀地衬托了父亲的孤独。第一阕中[k]音的反复出现不仅让全阕诗有一气呵成、浑然一体之势,而且也让人联想到火烧劈柴的声音。第二阕写"我"的感受和行为,将无形的寒冷描绘成可以撕裂、可以破碎的有形之物,通过黑暗和寒冷的破碎引出光明和温暖的到来,"我"在温暖的房间慢腾腾地穿着衣服。然而一幅温馨的图画突然又被家庭内部的"慢性愤怒"所破坏,[k]音(在 chronic 中)的出现似乎将这一愤怒同父亲变形的手(cracked hands)和炉火(banked fire)联系到一起,愤怒主体和原因的含混更加准确地揭示了家庭关系的复杂性。第三阕从父子心存隔阂、疏于交流、缺乏热情的过去,到长大成人后的儿子认识到父亲生火驱寒、擦亮皮鞋的关爱之后的现在,表现了觉醒后的"我"黯然神伤的心理。父爱朴实无华,甚至带有几分酸苦,显得严厉,不被理解,然而,它真真切切地存在,给家庭以温暖,等到"我"意识到这些时,已经没有机会再向父亲道谢或者回报父亲了,可谓"子欲养,而亲不待也",只得借助诗歌这种情感的载体聊表思念了。

思考题

1. Who is the speaker (narrator or persona)? What's the story of this poem?
2. What do you know about the father?
3. What are the emotions of the speaker to his father?
4. What do you think the word "offices" mean in the last line?
5. What's the significance of the word "Sundays" in the title? Will it make any difference if it is changed to "mornings"?

推荐作品

"The Whipping"
"Night, Death, Mississippi"
"Middle Passage"
"Runagate, Runagate"

参考资料

Fetrow, Fred M. *Robert Hayden*. Boston: Twayne, 1984.

Hatcher, John. *From the Auroral Darkness: The Life and Poetry of Robert Hayden*. Oxford: George Ronald, 1984.

Williams, Pontheolla T. *Robert Hayden: A Critical Analysis of His Poetry*. Urbana: U of Illinois P, 1987.

Sylvia Plath
(1932—1963)
西尔维娅·普拉斯

作者简介

西尔维娅·普拉斯,诗人、小说家。生于马萨诸塞州波士顿市,父亲是大学教师,因病在普拉斯8岁时亡故。父亲之死对年幼的普拉斯影响巨大,使她对人生与死亡产生了复杂的想法,如同她后来在一首题为《爸爸》(Daddy, 1966)的诗中所描述的那样,爱、怀念、恐惧、失望、孤独、猜疑等形形色色的感受与概念交织在一起,充斥了她幼稚的心灵。这种复杂的心理特征始终与她形影不离,并导致其悲剧性的早逝。她在1950年获史密斯学院的奖学金前往该校学习,学业优异,但因没能入选参加哈佛大学的写作班而自杀未遂。后来在剑桥大学学习期间,她与英国诗人泰德·休斯(Ted Hughes)相爱并结婚,7年后先患产后忧郁症,随后发现丈夫婚后有私情,与之分居,由于贫困无法生活而产生绝望,自杀身亡。

她生前出版的两部诗集是:《冬天的船》(A Winter Ship, 1960)、《巨人的石像及其他》(The Colossus and Other Poems, 1960)。她生命中的最后6个月是她的创作高峰期,平均每天写2—3首诗篇,由此将"自白派"诗歌推向其成就的巅峰。她去世以后出版的诗集包括《爱丽尔》(Ariel, 1965)和《渡湖》(Crossing The Water, 1971)。1982年,她的诗歌汇集出版,获得了普利策奖。普拉斯创作的唯一一部小说是《钟罩》(The Bell Jar, 1963),其中许多内容与她曾经自杀的生活经历相吻合,自传色彩充斥字里行间。在当今文学批评界,由于女权主义批评理论的发展,加上普拉斯独特的个性与命运,她正在获得越来越多的关注。

作品

Last Words

I do not want a plain box, I want a sarcophagus①
With tigery② stripes, and a face on it

---
① sarcophagus: 石棺;源于希腊语,常指古埃及、古希腊、古罗马雕刻精美的石制棺椁。
② tigery: 斑驳的;有花斑的。

Round as the moon, to stare up.
I want to be looking at them when they come
Picking among the dumb minerals, the roots.
I see them already—the pale, star-distance faces.
Now they are nothing, they are not even babies.
I imagine them without fathers or mothers, like the first gods.
They will wonder if I was important.
I should sugar① and preserve my days like fruit!
My mirror is clouding over—
A few more breaths, and it will reflect nothing at all.
The flowers and the faces whiten to a sheet.

I do not trust the spirit. It escapes like steam
In dreams, through mouth-hole or eye-hole. I can't stop it.
One day it won't come back. Things aren't like that.
They stay, their little particular lusters
Warmed by much handling. They almost purr②
When the soles of my feet grow cold,
The blue eye of my tortoise③ will comfort me.
Let me have my copper cooking pots, let my rouge pots
Bloom about me like night flowers, with a good smell.
They will roll me up in bandages, they will store my heart
Under my feet in a neat parcel.
I shall hardly know myself. It will be dark,
And the shine of these small things sweeter than the face of Ishtar④.

由于其特殊的生活经历，普拉斯创作的许多诗歌都以讨论死亡或者描述死亡的感受为主题，《遗言》可以说是一个范例。惠特曼、狄金森以及梭罗等19世纪美国诗人也热衷于在诗歌中思考死亡，但他们描写死亡的诗歌一般都不会给读者带来恐惧，因为他们的思考与描述主要是侧重于理性的探索，是一种空灵的想象。对他们来说，探索死亡

① sugar：粉饰；美化；用甜言蜜语描述。
② purr：发出一种轻柔且颤动的声音。
③ tortoise：龟；常指在陆地生存的乌龟。
④ Ishtar：伊师塔，古巴比伦和亚述神话中专司爱情、生育及战争的女神。

就如同探索社会现实中其他需要探索的事物一样。相比之下,就主题而言,普拉斯则是侧重描述死亡对她作为一个活生生的人的意义,描绘她在"死亡"之后的感受。她对死亡的认识,甚至向往,在一定程度上是将其视为一种生命的力量,明显带有病态的特征,例如在《拉萨露丝夫人》(Lady Lazarus, 1966)中将死亡称为"美妙的""艺术",并描述自己死亡的过程。20世纪50年代和60年代的美国诗人乃至其它文学体裁的作家都或多或少具有这一特有的共性,如金斯堡、罗伯特·克里莱等作家以吸毒或者同性恋来表达对社会的不满和抗争。从技巧的角度来看,诗的张力主要是借助于诗中叙事者"我"跨越生死界限的对话,以及诗人巧妙地使用"石棺"、"沉默的物质"、"最原始的神明"、"夜色中的花朵"以及古巴比伦女神"伊师塔"等意象。这些代表死亡的意象也使得读者能够窥视普拉斯复杂而充满矛盾的内心世界以及她对生活和艺术所做的痛苦的探索。

 思考题

1. How and why does the poet attempt to universalize a depressing and even hopeless mood in the poem?
2. If you do not have to relate the subject-matter of the poem to the tragic life of Sylvia Plath, what thematic significance can you find in this poem?

 推荐作品

"Daddy"
"Mirror"
"The Bee Meeting"

参考资料

Bloom, Harold, ed. *Sylvia Plath: Comprehensive Research and Study Guide.* Chelsea House Publishers, 2001.
Hughes, Ted. "On Sylvia Plath." *A Quarterly Review* 14.2 (1994): 1–10.
Newman, Charles. *The Art of Sylvia Plath.* Bloomington: Indiana UP, 1970.

第十二单元
Edward Franklin Albee
(1928—)

爱德华·富兰克林·阿尔比

作者简介

爱德华·阿尔比,20世纪美国最重要的剧作家之一。他幼年被富裕的养父母收养,但与他们(尤其是养母)的关系紧张。由于他的经历,他最成功的剧作也大多描写家庭关系。他在纽约及附近的西切斯特县(Westchester County)长大,中学时曾多次转学,后上过一年大学。他早年写过诗歌和一部未发表的长篇小说,而在50年代后期开始进行戏剧创作。阿尔比早期的独幕剧,包括《动物园故事》(1959)、《贝茜·斯密斯之死》(1960)、《沙盒》(1960)、《美国梦》(1961)等,精辟地批评了所谓美国的价值观,奠定了他作为一位重要剧作家的地位。而他的第一部多幕剧《谁害怕弗吉尼亚·沃尔夫?》(1962;电影1966)是他最主要的作品之一。他以后的剧作包括《伤心咖啡馆之歌》(1963;电影1991;改编自卡森·麦卡勒斯的长篇小说)、《小爱丽斯》(1964)、《微妙的平衡》(1966;电影1973年)、《盒子》与《毛泽东主席语录》("两部互相关联的剧作";1968)、《海景》(1975)、《三臂男人》(1983)、《一部关于婴儿的剧》(1998)、《三位高个女人》(1999)、《山羊,或谁是西尔维亚》(2002)等。他的剧作大多具有荒诞戏剧的典型特征,剧中人物无法或不愿意与他人交流;他们内心孤独,得不到同情也并不同情他人。

阿尔比是一位严肃、博学的主流剧作家;与尤金·奥尼尔、田纳西·威廉斯、阿瑟·米勒一起,他能够跻身于美国一流的主流剧作家之列。但是,他也是一位具有高度反叛精神的剧作家,不断颠覆现行的社会价值观念。在他2002年的剧作《山羊,或谁是西尔维亚》中,他描写了建筑师马丁生活中的两天。马丁的事业如日中天;他与妻子斯蒂薇情投意合;他们夫妻得体地接受了儿子是同性恋的消息。后来,事情却急转直下:原来马丁一直在与一只他称为西尔维亚的山羊恋爱和做爱。剧终时,斯蒂薇拖着被她杀戮的山羊血淋淋地走上了舞台。像他以往的多部剧作一样,该剧也描写了家庭生活;但该剧对人兽恋的宽容,似乎预示着同性恋之类的关系已成为常态。对山羊的杀戮似乎也是祭祀的典礼:在古希腊,悲剧的原意是"山羊歌";这种类似似乎点明了该剧的当代悲剧意义。

阿尔比在当代的影响持久不衰。他的重要剧目不断重演,而他的最新剧作《家庭生活》(2004)也受到评论界的重视。这部剧作是45年前的《动物园故事》的前传,描写彼得在到动物园的前一天,与妻子安妮之间的故事。这部剧作也许是对阿尔比所有"家庭生活"戏剧的回归和总结。

Who's Afraid of Virginia Woolf?

GEORGE:　...Now, take our son①...

HONEY:　Who?

GEORGE:　Our son... Martha's and my little joy!

NICK (*Moving toward the bar*):　Do you mind if I...?

GEORGE:　No, no; you go right ahead.

MARTHA:　George...

GEORGE (*Too kindly*):　Yes, Martha?

MARTHA:　Just what are you doing?

GEORGE:　Why, Love, I was talking about our son.

MARTHA:　Don't.

GEORGE:　Isn't Martha something? Here we are, on the eve of our boy's homecoming, the eve of his twenty-first birthday, the eve of his majority ...and Martha says don't talk about him.

MARTHA:　Just... don't.

GEORGE:　But I want to, Martha! It's very important we talk about him. Now bunny② and the... houseboy or stud here, whichever he is③... don't know much about junior, and I think they should.

MARTHA:　Just... don't.

GEORGE (*Snapping his fingers at* NICK):　You. Hey, you! You want to play bringing up baby, don't you!

NICK (*Hardly civil*):　Were you snapping at me?

GEORGE:　That's right. (*Instructing him*) *You* want to hear about our bouncy boy.

---

① take our son: 以我们的儿子为例。

② bunny: 小兔子，可爱的女郎；指 Honey。她 26 岁，长相平平，继承了父亲的一大笔遗产。Nick 因她怀孕才与他结婚，但她却对怀孕极为恐惧。在剧中，她因醉酒而一直在呕吐，对身边发生的事情不闻不问，是剧中最无心计的人物。最后，她克服了自己的恐惧，决心生育孩子，以承担起生活的责任。

③ houseboy: 家童；stud: 种马。乔治怀疑 Dick 与玛莎发生了性关系，但又不敢肯定，所以一直在试探。"家童"不应该对女主人有非分之想，而"种马"的意思则显而易见。

NICK (*Pause; then, shortly*): Yeah; sure.

GEORGE (*To* HONEY): And you, my dear? You want to hear about him, too, don't you.

HONEY: Whom?

GEORGE: Martha's and my son.

HONEY: Oh, you have a child? (MARTHA *and* NICK *laugh uncomfortably*)

GEORGE: Oh, indeed; do we ever! Do you want to talk about him, Martha, or shall I? Hunh?

MARTHA (*A smile that is a sneer*): Don't, George.

GEORGE: All rightie. Well, now; let's see. He's a nice kid, really, in spite of his home life; I mean, most kids'd grow up neurotic, what with① Martha here carrying on the way she does: sleeping 'til four in the P.M., climbing all over the poor bastard, trying to break the bathroom door down to wash him in the tub when he's sixteen, dragging strangers into the house at all hours...

MARTHA (*Rising*): O. K. YOU!

GEORGE (*Mock concern*): Martha!

MARTHA: That's enough!

GEORGE: Well, do you want to take over?

HONEY (*To* NICK): Why would anybody want to wash somebody who's sixteen years old?

NICK (*Slamming his drink down*): Oh, for Christ's sake, Honey!

HONEY (*Stage whisper*②): Well, why?!

GEORGE: Because it's her baby-poo③.

MARTHA: ALL RIGHT!! (*By rote; a kind of almost-tearful recitation*) Our son. You want our son? You'll have it.

GEORGE: You want a drink, Martha?

MARTHA (*Pathetically*): Yes.

NICK (*To* MARTHA *kindly*): We don't have to hear about it... if you don't want to.

GEORGE: Who says so? You in a position to set the rules around here?

NICK (*Pause; tight-lipped*): No.

---

① what with: 由于，因为。

② golf club: 高尔夫球俱乐部往往是财富的象征，俱乐部会员一般都是社会名流和富人。

③ -poo: 表示轻蔑或者弱小的单词后缀。

GEORGE: Good boy; you'll go far. All right, Martha; your recitation, please.

MARTHA (*From far away*①): What, George?

GEORGE (*Prompting*): "Our son..."

MARTHA: All right. Our son. Our son was born in a September night, a night not unlike tonight, though tomorrow, and twenty... one... years ago.

GEORGE (*Beginning of quiet asides*): You see? I told you.

MARTHA: It was an easy birth...

GEORGE: Oh, Martha; no. You labored... how you labored.

MARTHA: It was an easy birth... once it had been... accepted, relaxed into.

GEORGE: Ah... yes. Better.

MARTHA: It was an easy birth, once it had been accepted, and I was young.

GEORGE: And I was younger... (*Laughs quietly to himself*)

MARTHA: And I was young, and he was a healthy child, a red, bawling child, with slippery firm limbs...

GEORGE: ...Martha thinks she saw him at delivery...

MARTHA: ...with slippery, firm limbs, and a full head of black, fine, fine hair which, oh, later, later, became blond as the sun, our son②.

GEORGE: He was a healthy child.

MARTHA: And I had wanted a child... oh, I had wanted a child.

GEORGE (*Prodding her*): A son? A daughter?

MARTHA: A child! (*Quieter*) A child. And I had my child.

GEORGE: Our child.

MARTHA (*With great sadness*): Our child. And we raised him...(*Laughs, briefly, bitterly*) yes, we did; we raised him...

GEORGE: With teddy bears and an antique bassinet from Austria... and *no nurse*.

MARTHA: ...with teddy bears and transparent floating goldfish, and a pale blue bed with cane at the headboard when he was older, cane which he wore through... finally... with his little hands... in his... sleep...

GEORGE: ...nightmares...

MARTHA: ...sleep... He was a restless child...

GEORGE: ...(*Soft chuckle, head-shaking of disbelief*)... Oh Lord...

---

① from far away：心不在焉。

② sun 和 son 发音一样，构成双关语。在莎士比亚的剧作《哈姆莱特》中，也有类似的双关。

MARTHA: ...sleep... and a croup tent... a pale green croup tent, and the shining kettle hissing in the one light of the room that time he was sick①... those four days... and animal crackers, and the bow and arrow he kept under his bed...

GEORGE: ...the arrows with rubber cups at their tip...

MARTHA: ...at their tip, which he kept beneath his bed...

GEORGE: Why? Why, Martha?

MARTHA: ...for fear... for fear of...

GEORGE: For fear. Just that: for fear.

MARTHA: (*Vaguely waving him off; going on*) ...and...and sandwiches on Sunday night, and Saturdays... (*Pleased recollection*) ...and Saturdays the banana boat, the whole peeled banana, scooped out on top, with green grapes for the crew, a double line of green grapes, and along the sides, stuck to the boat with toothpicks, orange slices... SHIELDS.

GEORGE: And for the oar?

MARTHA (*Uncertainly*) A... carrot?

GEORGE: Or a swizzle stick②, whatever was easier.

MARTHA: No. A carrot. And his eyes were green... green with... if you peered so deep into them... so deep... bronze... bronze parentheses around the irises... such green eyes!

GEORGE: ...blue, green, brown...

MARTHA: ...and he loved the sun!...He was tan before and after everyone... and in the sun his hair... became... fleece.

GEORGE (*Echoing her*): ...fleece...

MARTHA: ...beautiful, beautiful boy.

GEORGE: Absolve, Domine, animas omnium fidelium defunctorum ab omni vinculo delictorum.③

MARTHA: ...and school... and summer camp ... and sledding... and swimming...

GEORGE: Et gratia tua illis succurrente, mereantur evadere judicium ultionis.④

---

① croup：儿童哮喘；croup tent：治疗哮喘的氧气帐。烧一壶开水也是为了增加湿度，缓解哮喘症状。

② swizzle stick：调酒棒。

③ Absolve, Domine, animas omnium fidelium defunctorum ab omni vinculo delictorum.：(拉)天主，求你赦免所有虔诚者的一切罪行(杨敦惠译，下同)。出自"安魂曲"中的"联唱曲"(Tractus)。拉丁语的"安魂曲"在西方极为流行，很多著名作曲家都为之谱曲，其中包括莫扎特、柏辽兹、凯鲁比尼、德沃夏克、威尔第、布鲁克纳、佛瑞、迪律弗莱等。

④ 本句出处同上：(拉)借着你的慈悲之助，希望他们能够逃脱惩罚式的判决。

MARTHA (*Laughing, to herself*): ...and how he broke his arm... how funny it was... oh, no, it hurt him! ...but, oh, it was funny... in a field, his very first cow, the first he'd ever seen... and he went into the field, to the cow, where the cow was grazing, head down, busy... and he moo'd at it! (*Laughs ibid*①) He moo'd at it and the beast, oh, surprised, swung its head up and moo'd at him, all three years of him, and he ran, startled, and he stumbled... fell... and broke his poor arm. (*Laughs, ibid*) Poor lamb.

GEORGE: Et lucis aeternae beatitudine perfrui.②

MARTHA: George cried! Helpless ...George... cried. I carried the poor lamb. George snuffling beside me, I carried the child, having fashioned a sling... and across the great fields.

GEORGE: In Paradisum deducant te Angeli.③

MARTHA: And as he grew... and as he grew... oh! so wise! ...he walked evenly between us... (*She spreads her hands*) ... a hand out to each of us for what we could offer by way of support, affection, teaching, even love... and these hands, still, to hold us off a bit, for mutual protection, to protect us all from George's ...weakness... and my necessary greater strength... to protect himself... and *us*.

GEORGE: In memoria aeterna erit justus: ab auditione mala non timebit.④

MARTHA: So wise; so wise.

NICK (*To* GEORGE): What is this? What are you doing?

GEORGE: Shhhhh.

HONEY: Shhhhh.

NICK (*Shrugging*): O.K.

MARTHA: So beautiful; so wise.

GEORGE (*Laughs quietly*): All truth being relative.

MARTHA: It was true! Beautiful; wise; perfect.

GEORGE: There's a real mother talking.

HONEY: (*Suddenly; almost tearfully*) I want a child.

---

① ibid：同前。指同前一条舞台说明一样，"自己发笑"。

② Et lucis aeternae beatitudine perfrui.：（拉）并享有永生的快乐。

③ In Paradisum deducant te Angeli.：（拉）愿天使引导你进入天堂（中文译者不详）。出自"安魂曲"中的"在天堂"（In Paradisum）。

④ In memoria aeterna erit justus: ab auditione mala non timebit.：（拉）正直的人将留存于不朽的回忆中；他将不畏邪恶的审听（杨敦惠译）。出自"安魂曲"中的"阶台经"（Graduale）。

NICK: Honey...

HONEY (*More forcefully*): I want a child!

GEORGE: On principle?

HONEY (*in tears*): I want a child. I want a baby.

MARTHA: (*Waiting out the interruption, not really paying it any mind*) Of course, this state, this perfection... couldn't last. Not with George... not with George around.

GEORGE (*To the others*): There; you see? I knew she'd shift.

HONEY: Be still!

GEORGE (*Mock awe*): Sorry... mother.

NICK: Can't you be still?

GEORGE (*Making a sign at* NICK): Dominus vobiscum.①

MARTHA: Not with George around. A drowning man takes down those nearest. George tried, but, oh, God, how I fought him. God, how I fought him.

GEORGE (*A satisfied laugh*): Ahhhhhhhh.

MARTHA: Lesser states can't stand those above them. Weakness, imperfection cries out against strength, goodness and innocence. And George tried.

GEORGE: How did I try, Martha? How did I try?

MARTHA: How did you... what?... No! No... he grew... our son grew... up; he is grown up; he is away at school, college. He is fine, everything is fine.

GEORGE (*Mocking*): Oh, come on, Martha!

MARTHA: No. That's all.

GEORGE: Just a minute! You can't cut a story off like that, sweetheart. You started to say something... now you say it!

MARTHA: No!

GEORGE: Well, I will.

MARTHA: No!

GEORGE: You see, Martha, here, stops just when the going gets good... just when things start getting a little rough. Now, Martha, here, is a misunderstood little girl; she really is. Not only does she have a

---

① Dominus vobiscum.：(拉)愿主与你们同在。

husband who is a bog... a younger-than-she-is bog albeit... not only does she have a husband who is a bog, she has as well a tiny problem with spiritous liquors—like she can't get enough...

MARTHA (*Without energy*): No more, George.

GEORGE: ...and on top of all that, poor weighed-down girl, PLUS a father who really doesn't give a damn whether she lives or dies, who couldn't care less *what* happens to his only daughter ...on top of all that she has a *son*. She has a son who fought her every inch of the way, who didn't want to be turned into a weapon against his father, who didn't want to be used as a goddamn club whenever Martha didn't get things like she wanted them!

MARTHA (*Rising to it*): Lies! Lies!!

GEORGE: Lies? All right. A son who would *not* disown his father, who came to him for advice, for information, for love that wasn't mixed with sickness—and you know what I mean, Martha!—who could not tolerate the slashing, braying residue that called itself his MOTHER. MOTHER? HAH!!

MARTHA (*Cold*): All right, you. A son who was so ashamed of his father he asked me once if it—possibly—wasn't true, as he had heard, from some cruel boys, maybe, that he was not our child; who could not tolerate the shabby failure his father had become....

GEORGE: Lies!

MARTHA: Lies? Who would not bring his girl friends to the house...

GEORGE: ...in shame of his mother...

MARTHA: ...of his father! Who writes letters only to me!

GEORGE: Oh, so you think! To me! At my office!

MARTHA: Liar!

GEORGE: I have a stack of them!

MARTHA: YOU HAVE NO LETTERS!

GEORGE: And you have?

MARTHA: He has no letters. A son... a son who spends his summers away... away from his family... ON ANY PRETEXT... because he can't stand the shadow of a man flickering around the edges of a house...

GEORGE: ...who spends his summers away... and he does! Who spends his summers away because there isn't room for him in a house full of

empty bottles, lies, strange men, and a harridan who...

MARTHA: Liar!!

GEORGE: Liar?

MARTHA: ...A son who I have raised as best I can against... vicious odds, against the corruption of weakness and petty revenges...

GEORGE: ...A son who is, deep in his gut, sorry, to have been born...

(BOTH TOGETHER)

MARTHA	GEORGE
I have tried, oh God I have tried; the one thing... the one thing I've tried to carry pure and unscathed through the sewer of this marriage; through the sick nights, and the pathetic, stupid days, through the derision and the laughter... *God*, the laughter, through one failure after another, one failure compounding another failure, each attempt more sickening, more numbing than the one before; the one thing, the one *person* I have tried to protect, to raise above the mire of this vile, crushing marriage; the one light in all this hopeless... *darkness*... our SON.	Libera me, Domine, de morte aeterna, in die illa trelnenda: Quando caeli movendi sunt et terra: Dum veneris judicare saeculum per ignem. Tremens factus sum ego, et timeo, dum discussio venerit, atque ventura ira. Quando caeli movendi sunt et terra. Dies illa, dies irae, calamitatis et miseriae; dies magna et amara valde. Dum veneris judicare saeculum per ignem. Requiem aeternam dona eis, Domine: et lux perpetua luceat eis. Libera me Domine de morte aeterna in die illa tremenda quando caeli mo vendi sunt et terra: Dum veneris judicare saeculum per ignem.[1]

(*End together*)

HONEY (*Her hands to her ears*): STOP IT!! STOP IT!!

GEORGE (*With a hand sign*):　　Kyrie, eleison. Christe, eleison. Kyrie, eleison.[2]

---

[1] 本段的拉丁语出自"安魂曲"中的"答唱曲"(Responsorium)，其中有叠句。译文为："天主，在那可怕的一天里，请从永恒的死亡中将我拯救出来；届时天地都将震撼，而你将以地狱之火来审判人世。惊惧与颤抖遍布我身，我极度害怕即将来临的审判与神怒。届时天地都将震撼。那一天，神怒之日，充满深刻的绝望与无限的悲惨，那将会是伟大而极其痛苦的一天。届时你将以地狱之火来审判人世。天主，赐予他们永恒的安息吧，也让永续的光芒照耀他们"(杨敦惠译)。

[2] Kyrie, eleison. Christe, eleison. Kyrie, eleison.：(拉)主，怜悯我们吧。基督，怜悯我们吧。主，怜悯我们吧(译者不详)。出自"安魂曲"中的"慈悲经"(Kyrie，又译"垂怜经")。

HONEY: JUST STOP IT!!

GEORGE: Why, baby? Don't you like it?

HONEY (*Quite hysterical*): You... can't... do... this!

GEORGE (*Triumphant*): Who says!

HONEY: I! Say!

NICK: Is this game over?

HONEY: Yes! Yes, it is.

GEORGE: Ho-ho! Not by a long shot. (*To* MARTHA) I've got a little surprise for you, baby. It's about sunny-Jim.

MARTHA: No more, George.

GEORGE: YES!

NICK: Leave her be!

GEORGE: I'M RUNNING THIS SHOW! (*To* MARTHA) Sweetheart, I'm afraid I've got some bad news for you... for us, of course. Some rather sad news.

(HONEY *begins weeping, head in hands*)

MARTHA (*Afraid, suspicious*): What is this?

GEORGE (*Oh, so patiently*): Well, Martha, while you were out of the room, while the... two of you were out of the room... I mean, I don't know where, hell, you both must have been somewhere (*Little laugh*)... While you were out of the room, for a while... well, the doorbell chimed... and... well, it's hard to tell you, Martha...

MARTHA (*A strange throaty voice*): Tell me.

GEORGE: ...and...what it was... it was good old Western Union[①], some little boy about seventy.

MARTHA (*Involved*): Crazy Billy?

GEORGE: Yes, Martha, that's right... crazy Billy... and he had a telegram, and it was for us, and I have to tell you about it.

MARTHA (*As if from a distance*): Why didn't they phone it? Why did they bring it; why didn't they telephone it?

GEORGE: Some telegrams you have to deliver, Martha; some telegrams you can't phone.

MARTHA (*Rising*): What do you mean?

---

① Western Union：西联汇款。美国的特快汇款机构, 现已遍布全球。

GEORGE: Martha... I can hardly bring myself to say it. (*Sighing heavily*) Well, Martha... I'm afraid our boy isn't coming home for his birthday.

MARTHA: Of course he is.

GEORGE: No, Martha.

MARTHA: Of course he is. I say he is!

GEORGE: He... can't.

MARTHA: He is! I say so!

GEORGE: Martha... (*Long pause*) ...our son is... dead. (*Silence*) He was... killed... late in the afternoon... (*Silence*) (*A tiny chuckle*) on a country road, with his learner's permit in his pocket, he swerved, to avoid a porcupine, and drove straight into a...

MARTHA (*Rigid fury*): YOU... CAN'T... DO ... THAT!

GEORGE: ...large tree.

MARTHA: YOU CANNOT DO THAT!

NICK (*Softly*): Oh my God. (HONEY *is weeping louder*)

GEORGE (*Quietly, dispassionately*): I thought you should know.

NICK: Oh my God; no.

MARTHA (*Quivering with rage and loss*): NO! NO! YOU CANNOT DO THAT! YOU CAN'T DECIDE THAT FOR YOURSELF! I WILL NOT LET YOU DO THAT!

GEORGE: We'll have to leave around noon, I suppose...

MARTHA: I WILL NOT LET YOU DECIDE THESE THINGS!

GEORGE: ...because there are matters of identification, naturally, and arrangements to be made...

MARTHA (*Leaping at* GEORGE, *but ineffectual*): YOU CAN'T DO THIS! (NICK *rises, grabs hold of* MARTHA, *pins her arms behind her back*) I WON'T LET YOU DO THIS, GET YOUR HANDS OFF ME!

GEORGE: (*As* NICK *holds on; right in* MARTHA'S *face*) You don't seem to understand, Martha; I haven't done anything. Now, pull yourself together. Our son is DEAD! Can you get that into your head?

MARTHA: YOU CAN'T DECIDE THESE THINGS.

NICK: Lady, please.

MARTHA: LET ME GO!

GEORGE: Now listen, Martha; listen carefully. We got a telegram; there was a car accident, and he's dead. POUF! Just like that! Now, how do you like it?

MARTHA (*A howl which weakens into a moan*): NOOOOOOOooooo.

GEORGE (*To* NICK): Let her go. (MARTHA *slumps to the floor in a sitting position*) She'll be all right now.

MARTHA (*Pathetic*): No; no, he is not dead; he is not dead.

GEORGE: He is dead. Kyrie, eleison. Christe, eleison. Kyrie, eleison.

MARTHA: You can*not*. You may not decide these things.

NICK (*Leaning over her; tenderly*): He hasn't decided anything, lady. It's not his doing. He doesn't have the power...

GEORGE: That's right, Martha; I'm not a god. I don't have the power over life and death, do I?

MARTHA: YOU CAN'T KILL HIM! YOU CAN'T HAVE HIM DIE!

NICK: Lady... please...

MARTHA: YOU CAN'T!

GEORGE: There was a telegram, Martha.

MARTHA (*Up; facing him*): Show it to me! Show me the telegram!

GEORGE (*Long pause; then, with a straight face*): I ate it.

MARTHA (*A pause; then with the greatest disbelief possible, tinged with hysteria*): What did you just say to me?

GEORGE (*Barely able to stop exploding with laughter*): I... ate... it. (MARTHA *stares at him for a long moment, then spits in his face*)

GEORGE (*With a smile*): Good for you, Martha.

NICK (*To* GEORGE): Do you think that's the way to treat her at a time like this? Making an ugly goddamn joke like that? Hunh?

MARTHA (*To* GEORGE, *coldly*): You're not going to get away with this.

GEORGE (*With disgust*): YOU KNOW THE RULES, MARTHA! FOR CHRIST'S SAKE, YOU KNOW THE RULES!!

MARTHA: NO!

NICK (*With the beginnings of a knowledge he cannot face*): What are you two talking about?

GEORGE: I can kill him, Martha, if I want to.

MARTHA: HE IS OUR CHILD!

GEORGE: Oh yes, and you bore him, and it was a good delivery...

MARTHA: HE IS OUR CHILD!

GEORGE: AND I HAVE KILLED HIM!

MARTHA: NO!

GEORGE: YES! (*Long silence*)

NICK (*Very quietly*): I think I understand this.

GEORGE (*Ibid*): Do you?

NICK (*Ibid*): Jesus Christ, I think I understand this.

GEORGE (*Ibid*): Good for you, buster.

NICK (*Violently*): JESUS CHRIST I THINK I UNDERSTAND THIS!

MARTHA (*Great sadness and loss*): You have no right... you have no right at all...

GEORGE (*Tenderly*): I have the right, Martha. We never spoke of it; that's all. I could kill him any time I wanted to.

MARTHA: But why? Why?

GEORGE: You broke our rule, baby. You mentioned him ...you mentioned him to someone else.

MARTHA (*Tearfully*): I did not. I never did.

GEORGE: Yes, you did.

MARTHA: Who? WHO?!

HONEY (*Crying*): To me, You mentioned him to me.

MARTHA (*Crying*): I FORGET! Sometimes... sometimes when it's night, when it's late, and... and everybody else is... talking... I forget and I... want to mention him... but I... HOLD ON... I hold on... but I've wanted to... so often... oh, George, you've *pushed* it... there was no need... there Was no need for *this*. I *mentioned* him... all right... but you didn't have to push it over the EDGE. You didn't have to... kill him.

GEORGE: Requiescat in pace.①

HONEY: Amen.

MARTHA: You didn't have to have him die, George.

GEORGE: Requiem aeternam dona eis, Domine.

HONEY: Et lux perpetua luceat eis.②

MARTHA: That wasn't ...needed. (*A long silence*)

GEORGE (*Softly*): It will be dawn soon. I think the party's over.

---

① Requiescat in pace.：(拉)愿他灵魂安眠。

② Requiem aeternam dona eis, Domine. Et lux perpetua luceat eis.：(拉)天主，赐予他们永恒的安息吧，也让永续之光芒照耀他们"(杨敦惠译)。出自"安魂曲"中的"领主曲"(Communio)。

NICK (*To* GEORGE; *quietly*): You couldn't have... any?

GEORGE: We couldn't.

MARTHA (*A hint of communion in this*): We couldn't.

GEORGE (*To* NICK *and* HONEY): Home to bed, children; it's way past your bedtime.

NICK (*His hand out to* HONEY): Honey?

HONEY (*Rising, moving to him*): Yes.

GEORGE (MARTHA *is sitting on the floor by a chair now*): You two go now.

NICK: Yes.

HONEY: Yes.

NICK: I'd like to...

GEORGE: Good night.

NICK (*Pause*): Good night.

(NICK *and* HONEY *exit;* GEORGE *closes the door after them; looks around the room; sighs, picks up a glass or two, takes it to the bar*) (*This whole last section very softly, very slowly*)

GEORGE: Do you want anything, Martha?

MARTHA (*Still looking away*): No... nothing.

GEORGE: All fight. (*Pause*) Time for bed.

MARTHA: Yes.

GEORGE: Are you tired?

MARTHA: Yes.

GEORGE: I am.

MARTHA: Yes.

GEORGE: Sunday tomorrow; all day.

MARTHA: Yes. (*A long silence between them*) Did you... did you... have to?

GEORGE (*Pause*): Yes.

MARTHA: It was...? You had to?

GEORGE (*Pause*): Yes.

MARTHA: I don't know.

GEORGE: It was... time.

MARTHA: Was it?

GEORGE: Yes.

MARTHA (*Pause*): I'm cold.

GEORGE:　It's late.

MARTHA:　Yes.

GEORGE (*Long silence*): It will be better.

MARTHA (*Long silence*): I don't... know.

GEORGE:　It will be... maybe.

MARTHA:　I'm... not ...sure.

GEORGE:　No.

MARTHA:　Just... us?

GEORGE:　Yes.

MARTHA:　I don't suppose, maybe, we could...

GEORGE:　No, Martha.

MARTHA:　Yes. No.

GEORGE:　Are you all right?

MARTHA:　Yes. No.

GEORGE (*Puts his hand gently on her shoulder; she puts her head back, and sings to her, very softly*):　Who's afraid of Virginia Woolf
　　　　　　　　　　　　　　　　　　Virginia Woolf
　　　　　　　　　　　　　　　　　　Virginia Woolf,

MARTHA:　I... am... George...

GEORGE:　Who's afraid of Virginia Woolf...

MARTHA:　I... am... George... I... am...

(GEORGE *nods, slowly*)

(*Silence; tableau*)

CURTAIN

作品赏析　　《谁害怕弗吉尼亚·沃尔夫?》描写了一对知识夫妻的婚姻关系。46岁的乔治是某大学历史系的副教授,而他52岁的妻子玛莎则是该校校长的女儿。他们的婚姻生活虽有默契,但也时有摩擦。在某一周末晚上,他们之间的摩擦终于爆发。当天晚上,他们参加在玛莎父亲家举办的晚会归来,两人都有几分醉意。这时,玛莎告诉乔治,她已邀请尼克夫妇于凌晨二时来家中小酌。尼克年仅30岁,刚到该校生物系任教。他们到乔治家后,即成为主人夫妇吵架的听众,后来又参与了他们的争斗。玛莎一直认为乔治没有进取心,没有利用校长女婿的有利条件谋求升职。在酒精的作用下,她公开羞辱乔治。而乔治则利用自己能言善辩,与她反唇相讥。为了激怒乔治,玛莎故意与年轻且有魅力的尼克调情;0 而乔治的报复则是宣称他们的儿子死了:原来,他们一直想象自己有一个儿子,以作为自己失败的生活的安慰。剧作结束时,尼克夫妇离去,乔治和玛莎又只能单独面对对方。我们不知道在这场风波之后,他们会更好地珍惜对方,还是再也无法医治留下的创伤。

　　本剧的剧名来自当天晚会上被加工过的一首童谣。童谣原名为"谁害怕大坏狼?"(Who's afraid of the Big Bad Wolf?)"Wolf"与"Woolf"同音,所以就被这些知识界人士唱成了他们圈子内的人物:英国著名女作家弗吉尼亚·沃尔夫(1882—1941)。沃尔夫的作品描写人类的异化和生活的空虚,而她自己也有诸多心理问题,最后溺水自杀。原本的童谣其实也表现了生活中的恐惧和灾难:在童谣的三只小猪中,有两只因为未加防备而落入狼口。这首加工过的童谣似乎也是剧作的"主旋律",被剧中人物用来表达自己的情感。

　　阿尔比认为戏剧不仅是文学作品,而且也是音乐和雕塑作品。所以,他的剧作虽然以对话来推动情节的发展,但却具有很好的音乐感和节奏感。由于讲究雕塑的造型,阿尔比对于舞台道具也运用到了极致。在本剧中,主人公家中的家具就像他们的生活一样杂乱无章、拥挤不堪。

　　1966年,本剧被改编为一部十分成功的影片。著名影星理查得·伯顿和伊莉莎白·泰勒分别扮演男女主人公——35岁的泰勒扮演52岁的玛莎。影片未采用当时已经流行的"染印法彩色"(Technicolor),而摄制成纪录片风格的黑白片;在大多封闭的空间,以写实、不加修饰的风格,表现出主人公迷惘的内心世界。该片保留了原剧中大部分亵渎不敬和谈论性爱的语言,对当时的电影审查制度提出挑战。在发行时,华纳兄弟电影公司规定18岁以下人士只能在家长指导下观看,开了所谓"家长指导级影片"的先河,也促成了电影分级制度的实施。

思考题

1. Nick says: "I think I understand this." What does he understand?
2. What game is being played? Why do the characters play a game?
3. How are reality and illusion mixed up in the play?
4. Why do Martha and George keep fighting each other in front of Honey and Nick?
5. What human relationships does the play reflect?

 推荐作品

The Zoo Story (1959)
The Ballad of a Sad Café (1963)
A Delicate Balance (1966)

参考资料

Bottoms, Stephen, ed. *The Cambridge Companion to Edward Albee*. Cambridge, UK; New York: Cambridge UP, 2005.

---, ed. *Who's Afraid of Virginia Woolf?* Cambridge; New York: Cambridge UP, 2000.

第十三单元
Toni Morrison
(1931—)
托妮·莫里森

作者简介

　　托妮·莫里森,当代黑人女作家,生于俄亥俄州洛里恩的一个工人家庭。1953年,从霍华德大学获得英语文学学士学位,1955年从康奈尔大学获得文学硕士学位,之后到南德克萨斯大学任教,1957年返回霍华德大学。1958年和哈罗德·莫里森(Harold Morrison)结婚,两人1964年离婚,托妮·莫里森同时进行文学创作,养育两个儿子,在兰登书屋担任编辑。1967年她被提升为高级编辑并调往纽约工作,1970年发表处女作《最蓝的眼睛》(The Bluest Eye),受到评论界的赞扬。此后一直到1983年,莫里森在从事编辑工作的同时,继续从事文学创作,并先后在纽约州立大学、耶鲁大学和巴尔德学院教授英语。作为编辑,她力推青年黑人作家的作品,所主编的《黑人之书》(The Black Book, 1974)被称为美国黑人史的百科全书;作为作家,她先后发表了《秀拉》(Sula, 1974)、《所罗门之歌》(Song of Solomon, 1977)和《柏油娃》(Tar Baby, 1981),从不同的角度揭示了美国黑人的生活体验,《所罗门之歌》荣获美国图书评论家协会大奖。1987年,莫里森发表了被许多人认为是他代表作的《娇女》(Beloved,又译《宠儿》、《爱娃》等),用魔幻现实主义和意识流的手法,通过母亲宁肯亲手杀死女儿也不愿让她回到奴隶制,以及被杀的女儿阴魂不散,18年后重返人间的故事,深刻揭露了奴隶制的残暴及其对美国黑人的影响。该书获得极大的成功,1988年获得普利策文学奖。《娇女》、《爵士乐》(Jazz, 1992)和《天堂》(Paradise, 1998)被莫里森称为"爱的三部曲",同时也勾勒出美国黑人历史的脉络。莫里森的作品构思独特,具有史诗般的震撼力;语言诗化,具有丰富的表现力;叙事诡秘,具有浓厚的感染力;心理揭示深刻,具有锐利的穿透力,深受评论界和普通读者的青睐。1993年莫里森因"以其富于洞察力和诗情画意的小说把美国现实的一个重要方面写活了"荣获诺贝尔文学奖,成为获此殊荣的第一个黑人女性。1987年,莫里森出任普林斯顿大学罗伯特·戈新教席教授(the Robert F. Goheen Professor),讲授文学创作至今。她曾在多所大学演讲,其中在哈佛大学所做的关于白人作家作品对黑人形象"他者"化的演讲结集出版,即《黑暗里的游戏》(Playing in the Dark: Whiteness and the Literary Imagination, 1993)。2003年,她发表新作《爱》(Love)。莫里森还著有剧本《做梦的艾美特》(Dreaming Emmett, 1986)和童话诗《大盒子》(The Big Box, 1999)。

作 品

Beloved①

A FULLY DRESSED woman② walked out of the water. She barely gained the dry bank of the stream before she sat down and leaned against a mulberry tree. All day and all night she sat there, her head resting on the trunk in a position abandoned③ enough to crack the brim in her straw hat. Everything hurt but her lungs most of all. Sopping wet and breathing shallow she spent those hours trying to negotiate the weight of her eyelids④. The day breeze blew her dress dry; the night wind wrinkled it. Nobody saw her emerge or came accidentally by. If they had, chances are⑤ they would have hesitated before approaching her. Not because she was wet, or dozing or had what sounded like asthma, but because amid all that she was smiling. It took her the whole of the next morning to lift herself from the ground and make her way through the woods past a giant temple of boxwood to the field and then the yard of the slate-gray house. Exhausted again, she sat down on the first handy place—a stump not far from the steps of 124⑥. By then keeping her eyes open was less of an effort. She could manage it for a full two minutes or more. Her neck, its circumference no wider than a parlor-service saucer, kept bending and her chin brushed the bit of lace edging her dress.

Women who drink champagne when there is nothing to celebrate can look like that: their straw hats with broken brims are often askew; they nod in public places; their shoes are undone. But their skin is not like that of the woman

---

①《娇女》第五章，原书共分三部分十八章，作家为三个部分编了 1、2、3 的序号，对各章却既不写标题，也不加序号。因为作家把本书献给了"六千万甚至更多"死于贩奴途中的黑人同胞，这种做法似乎暗指屈死的黑人无名无姓的状况。

② A fully dressed woman：《娇女》的主人公瑟丝不堪忍受奴隶主的污辱，克服重重困难，九死一生逃到了俄亥俄河北岸，同婆婆和先期到达的三个孩子相聚。28 天后，奴隶主追来抓人。情急之下，瑟丝锯断刚刚会爬的女儿的喉咙，以免亲骨肉再受奴役之苦。瑟丝从监狱出来后，以自己的身体作为代价，换取石匠为冤死的女儿刻 "Beloved" 一词墓碑。本章出现的这个女孩，一般认为就是瑟丝女儿的阴魂还阳，因为她名叫 "Beloved"，正好 19—20 岁，肤色光滑细嫩，语言能力低下，喜爱甜食，从（羊）水中来。然而，也有人认为她是那个被白人关在一间小屋当作泄欲工具的非洲女奴。

③ abandoned：放任的，无拘无束的。

④ trying to negotiate the weight of her eyelids：试图解决眼皮的重量问题（想努力睁开眼）。

⑤ chances are：后面跟一个完整的从句，指从句的情况很有可能出现。

⑥ 124：瑟丝住房的门牌号，小说现在层面和部分往事的背景，小说的三个部分都从这座房子写起。有评论说，房子象征着贩运黑人的船，成倍数递增的门牌号码映射贩奴途中堆积如山的死尸。

240

breathing near the steps of 124. She had new skin, lineless and smooth, including the knuckles of her hands①.

By late afternoon when the carnival was over, and the Negroes were hitching rides② home if they were lucky—walking if they were not—the woman had fallen asleep again. The rays of the sun struck her full in the face, so that when Sethe, Denver and Paul D③ rounded the curve in the road all they saw was a black dress, two unlaced shoes below it, and Here Boy④ nowhere in sight.

"Look," said Denver. "What is that?"

And, for some reason she could not immediately account for, the moment she got close enough to see the face, Sethe's bladder filled to capacity⑤. She said, "Oh, excuse me," and ran around to the back of 124. Not since she was a baby girl, being cared for by the eight-year-old girl who pointed out her mother to her, had she had an emergency that unmanageable. She never made the outhouse. Right in front of its door she had to lift her skirts, and the water she voided was endless. Like a horse, she thought, but as it went on and on she thought, No, more like flooding the boat when Denver was born. So much water Am⑥ said, "Hold on, Lu. You going to sink us you keep that up." But there was no stopping water breaking form a breaking womb and there was no stopping now. She hoped Paul D wouldn't take it upon himself to come looking for her and be obliged to see her squatting in front of her own privy making a mudhole too deep to be witnessed without shame. Just about the time she started wondering if the carnival would accept another freak, it stopped. She tidied herself and ran around to the porch. No one was there. All three were inside—Paul D and Denver standing before the stranger, watching her drink cup after cup of water.

"She said she was thirsty," said Paul D. He took off his cap. "Mighty thirsty look like."

---

① 女孩耷拉脑袋(Her neck... kept bending...)，皮肤光滑细嫩，都表明她还是个婴儿。

② hitch rides：hitchhike，搭免费便车。

③ Sethe, Denver and Paul D：小说中的三个主要人物。Sethe 18 年前为了避免亲生骨肉受奴役之苦亲手杀死了女儿；Denver 是 Sethe 在逃往北方的路上生的另一个女儿；Paul D 原和 Sethe 及其丈夫在同一个种植园当奴隶，现在 124 号院和 Sethe 同居。这里，Paul D 带 Sethe 母女参加狂欢节归来。

④ Here Boy：瑟丝家养的狗。一说狗的失踪源于鬼魂的出现。

⑤ Sethe's bladder filled to capacity：瑟丝膀胱充盈。瑟丝见到这个女孩时突然感到内急，还没跑到厕所(She never made the outhouse.)就狂泻不止，让她不禁想起生孩子的情景。整个情景就是在暗示外来的女孩是瑟丝破羊水后生下的孩子。

⑥ Amy：瑟丝向北方逃跑途中遇到的离家出走的善良穷白人女孩，帮助瑟丝治伤并为丹芙接生。她想当然地把瑟丝称为 Lu。

The woman gulped water from a speckled tin cup and held it out for more. Four times Denver filled it, and four times the woman drank as though she had crossed a desert. When she was finished a little water was on her chin, but she did not wipe it away. Instead she gazed at Sethe with sleepy eyes. Poorly fed, thought Sethe, and younger than her clothes suggested—good lace at the throat, and a rich woman's hat. Her skin was flawless except for three vertical scratches① on her forehead so fine and thin they seemed at first like hair, baby hair before it bloomed and roped into the masses of black yarn under her hat.

"You from around here?" Sethe asked her.

She shook her head no and reached down to take off her shoes. She pulled her dress up to the knees and rolled down her stockings. When the hosiery was tucked into the shoes, Sethe saw that her feet were like her hands, soft and new. She must have hitched a wagon ride, thought Sethe. Probably one of those West Virginia girls looking for something to beat a life of tobacco and sorghum. Sethe bent to pick up the shoes.

"What might your name be?" asked Paul D.

"Beloved," she said, and her voice was so low and rough each one looked at the other two. They heard the voice first—later the name.

"Beloved. You use a last name, Beloved?" Paul D asked her.

"Last?" She seemed puzzled. Then "No," and she spelled it for them, slowly as though the letters were being formed as she spoke them.

Sethe dropped the shoes; Denver sat down and Paul D smiled. He recognized the careful enunciation of letters by those, like himself, who could not read but had memorized the letters of their name. He was about to ask who her people were but thought better of it. A young coloredwoman drifting was drifting from ruin.② He had been in Rochester four years ago and seen five women arriving with fourteen female children. All their men—brothers, uncles, fathers husbands, sons—had been picked off one by one by one. They had a single piece of paper directing them to a preacher on DeVore Street. The War had been over four or five years then, but nobody white or black seemed to know it. Odd clusters and strays of Negroes wandered the back roads and cowpaths from Schenectady to Jackson. Dazed but insistent, they searched each other out for word of a cousin, an aunt, a friend who once said, "Call on me. Anytime you get near Chicago, just

---

① three vertical scratches：暗示瑟丝锯杀女儿时留下的伤口。
② A young coloredwoman... ruin.：一个年轻的黑人女孩外出流浪肯定是在逃避灾难。

call on me." Some of them were running form family that could not support them, some to family; some were running from dead crops, dead kin, life threats, and took-over land.   Boys younger than Buglar and Howard①,   configurations and blends of families of women and children②, while elsewhere, solitary, hunted and hunting for, were men, men, men. Forbidden public transportation, chased by debt and filthy "talking sheets,"③ they followed secondary routes, scanned the horizon for signs and counted heavily on each other.   Silent,   except for social courtesies, when they met one another they neither described nor asked about the sorrow that drove them from one place to another.   The whites didn't bear speaking on. Everybody knew.

So he did not press the young woman with the broken hat about where from or how come. If she wanted them to know and was strong enough to get through the telling, she would. What occupied them at the moment was what it might be that she needed. Underneath the major question, each harbored another. Paul D wondered at the newness of her shoes. Sethe was deeply touched by her sweet name;   the remembrance of glittering headstone④ made her feel especially kindly toward her. Denver, however, was shaking. She looked at this sleepy beauty and wanted more.

Sethe hung her hat on a peg and turned graciously toward the girl. "That's a pretty name, Beloved. Take off your hat, why don't you, and I'll made us something. We just got back from the carnival over near Cincinnati. Everything in there is something to see."

Bolt upright in the chair, in the middle of Sethe's welcome, Beloved had fallen asleep again.

"Miss. Miss." Paul D shook her gently. "You want to lay down a spell?"⑤

She opened her eyes to slits and stood up on her soft new feet which, barely capable of their job, slowly bore her to the keeping room. Once there, she collapsed on Baby Suggs'⑥ bed. Deven removed her hat and put the quilt with two squares of color over her feet. She was breathing like a steam engine.

---

① Buglar and Howard：瑟丝的两个儿子，因为不堪忍受家里闹鬼，13岁时双双离家出走。
② configurations and blends of families of women and children：由妇女和儿童构建组合的家庭。
③ talking sheets：指三K党成员，他们用白布裹身掩盖身份。
④ glittering headstone：指瑟丝以身体作交换，为冤死的女儿买了一块墓石并让石匠在上刻下Beloved 7个字母，并漆成红色。
⑤ You want to lay down a spell?：你想躺一会儿吗？spell：一段时间。
⑥ Baby Suggs：瑟丝已故的婆婆。

"Sounds like croup,"① said Paul D, closing the door.

"Is she feverish? Denver, could you tell?"

"No. She's cold."

"Then she is. Fever goes form hot to cold."

"Could have the cholera," said Paul D.

"Reckon?"

"All that water. Sure sign."

"Poor thing. And nothing in this house to give her for it. She'll just have to ride it out. That's a hateful sickness if ever there was one."

"She's not sick!" said Denver, and the passion in her voice made them smile.

Four days she slept, waking and sitting up only for water. Denver tended her, watched her sound sleep, listened to her labored breathing and, out of love and a breakneck possessiveness that charged her, hid like a personal blemish Beloved's incontinence②. She rinsed the sheets secretly, after Sethe③ went to the restaurant and Paul D went scrounging for barges to help unload. She boiled the underwear and soaked it in bluing, praying the fever would pass without damage. So intent was her nursing, she forgot to eat or visit the emerald closet.

"Beloved?" Denver would whisper. "Beloved?" and when the black eyes opened a slice all she could say was "I'm here. I'm still here."

Sometimes, when Beloved lay dreamy-eyed for a very long time, saying nothing, licking her lips and heaving deep sighs, Denver panicked. "What is it?" she would ask.

"Heavy," murmured Beloved. "This place is heavy."

"Would you like to sit up?"

"No," said the raspy voice.

It took three days for Beloved to notice the orange patches in the darkness of the quilt. Denver was pleased because it kept her patient awake longer. She seemed totally taken with those faded scraps of orange, even made the effort to lean on her elbow and stroke them. An effort that quickly exhausted her, so Denver rearranged the quilt so its cheeriest part was in the sick girl's sight line.

---

① croup：喉头炎。

② (Denver) hid like a personal blemish Beloved's incontinence.：丹芙掩盖 Beloved 小便失禁之事，好像那是她自己的什么瑕疵似的。Beloved's incontinence 作动词 hid 的宾语。

③ Sethe 在一家餐馆工作，Paul D 靠打短工挣钱。

Patience, something Denver had never known, overtook her. As long as her mother did not interfere, she was a model of compassion, turning waspish, though, when Sethe tried to help.

"Did she take a spoonful of anything today?" Sethe inquired.

"She shouldn't eat with cholera."

"You sure that's it? Was just a hunch① of Paul D's."

"I don't know, but she shouldn't eat anyway just yet."

"I think cholera people puke all the time."

"That's even more reason, ain't it?"

"Well she shouldn't starve to death either, Denver."

"Leave us alone, Ma'am. I'm taking care of her."

"She say anything?"

"I'd let you know if she did."

Sethe looked at her daughter and thought, Yes, she has been lonesome. Very lonesome.

"Wonder where Here Boy got off to?" Sethe thought a change of subject was needed.

"He won't be back," said Denver.

"How you know?"

"I just know." Denver took a square of sweet bread off the plate.

Back in the keeping room, Denver was about to sit down when Beloved's eyes flew wide open. Denver felt her heart race. It wasn't that she was looking at that face for the first time with no trace of sleep in it, or that the eyes were big and black. Nor was it that the whites of them were much too white—blue-white. It was that deep down in those big black eyes there was no expression at all.

"Can I get you something?"

Beloved looked at the sweet bread in Denver's hands and Denver held it out to her. She smiled then and Denver's heart stopped bouncing and sat down—relieved and easeful like a traveler who had made it home.

From that moment and through everything that followed, sugar could always be counted on to please her. It was as though sweet things were what she was born for. Honey as well as the wax it came in, sugar sandwiches, the sludgy molasses gone hard and brutal in the can, lemonade, taffy and any type of dessert Sethe

---

① hunch: (口)预感。

brought home from the restaurant. She gnawed a cane stick to flax and kept the strings in her mouth long after the syrup had been sucked away. Denver laughed, Sethe smiled and Paul D said it made him sick to his stomach.

Sethe believed it was a recovering body's need—after an illness—for quick strength. But it was a need that went on and on into glowing health because Beloved didn't go anywhere. There didn't seem anyplace for her to go. She didn't mention one, or have much of an idea of what she was doing in that part of the country or where she had been. They believed the fever had caused her memory to fail just as it kept her slow-moving. A young woman, about nineteen or twenty, and slender, she moved like a heavier one or an older one, holding on to furniture, resting her head in the palm of her hand as though it was too heavy for a neck alone.

"You just gonna feed her? From now on?" Paul D, feeling ungenerous, and surprised by it, heard the irritability in his voice.

"Denver likes her. She's no real trouble. I thought we'd wait till her breath was better. She still sounds a little lumbar to me."

"Something funny 'bout that gal,"① Paul D said, mostly to himself.

"Funny how?"

"Acts sick, sounds sick, but she don't look sick. Good skin, bright eyes and strong as a bull."

"She's not strong. She can hardly walk without holding on to something."

"That's what I mean. Can't walk, but I seen her pick up the rocker② with one hand."

"You didn't."

"Don't tell *me*. Ask Denver. She was right there with her."

"Denver! Come in here a minute."

Denver stopped rinsing the porch and stuck her head in the window.

"Paul D says you and him saw Beloved pick up the rocking chair single-headed. That so?"

Long, heavy lashes made Denver's eyes seem busier than they were; deceptive, even when she held a steady gaze as she did now on Paul D. "No," she said. "I didn't see no such thing."

---

① Something funny 'bout that gal.: There is something funny about that girl. 保罗 D 原为奴隶，文盲，所以说话不合乎语法规范。

② rocker: 摇椅。Beloved 表面弱不禁风，实际上却力大如牛，说明她是鬼魂。

Paul D frowned but said nothing. If there had been an open latch between them, it would have closed.

《娇女》根据真实的历史故事,用断断续续的叙述碎片,零散地将 1873 年辛辛那提城郊蓝石路 124 号的现实和 1855 年肯塔基州"甜蜜之家"种植园的过去交织在一起。在过去层面,黑人在奴隶制下遭受着非人的待遇:白人奴隶主教育白人少年列出黑人的"人的属性"和"动物属性",拿尺子测量黑人的身子。白人少年不仅把瑟丝(Sethe)毒打得皮开肉绽,甚至还残暴地践踏了她的母性权利,把她按倒在地,吸取她育婴的奶水。瑟丝历经千难万险,九死一生成功逃到北方。为了不让亲身骨肉再受奴役之苦,她亲手锯断自己刚刚会爬、还没有名字的女儿的喉咙。从监狱出来后,瑟丝用自己的身体换取石匠为冤死的女儿刻"娇女"(Beloved)墓碑。在现实层面,往事挥之不去,"娇女"冤魂不散,闹得奶奶因精神崩溃而死亡,两个哥哥离家出走,妈妈和妹妹备受孤立,郁郁寡欢。保罗·D(Paul D)到来,驱散鬼魂,和瑟丝同居,准备开始新生活。但是,"娇女"又以 19—20 岁少女的肉身还阳,回来索取母爱,使瑟丝几乎崩溃。最后,黑人集体赶走"娇女",帮助瑟丝迎接新生活。小说旨在揭示奴隶制无穷的贻害,所以着力表现过去对现实的影响。第五章讲述的是"娇女"的冤魂在瑟丝的住所徘徊 18 年后以肉身还阳的情景。这个女孩的出现打破了瑟丝、保罗·D 和丹芙(Denver)三人间刚刚建立起的和谐,使得瑟丝不得不面对她一直努力忘却的过去,给予丹芙摆脱孤独的希望,疏远了保罗·D 同瑟丝母女的关系。丹芙对女孩的同情、依恋和保护既是她孤独的表现,又是她对过去好奇的流露。但这个 19 岁左右的女孩既有血有肉,又缥缈恍惚,既天真无邪,又魔力无边,虽然有 18 年前那个冤死的女孩的一些特征,其身份并不确定。她也可能是死在贩奴船上被扔到大西洋的某个黑人少女的亡灵,抑或是现实中某个刚刚逃离白人虎口的姑娘,这个形象因此模糊了历史和现时,具有更为普遍的象征意义。

思考题

1. What notable features of style have you noticed from this chapter?
2. What symbolic circumstances attend Beloved's return to Bluestone 124?
3. What characteristics or behaviors indicate that Beloved is like an infant?
4. Who does each of the other characters think Beloved is?
5. Why does Denver deny seeing Beloved pick up the rocker with one hand?

推荐作品

The Bluest Eye (1970)
Song of Solomon (1977)
Sula (1974)

参考资料

David, Ron. *Toni Morrison Explained: A Reader's Map to the Novels*. New York: Random House, 2000.

Grewal, Gurleen. *Circles of Sorrow, Lines of Struggle: The Novels of Toni Morrison*. Baton Rouge: Louisiana State UP, 1999.

Peach, Linden. *Toni Morrison*. 2nd ed. New York: Macmillan, 2000.

Smith, Valerie, ed. *New Essays on Song of Solomon*. Beijing: Peking UP; Cambridge UP, 2006.

第十四单元
Thomas Pynchon
(1937—)
托马斯·品钦

作者简介

　　托马斯·品钦，小说家，以形式新颖、内容复杂而著称。获得美国国家图书奖的《万有引力之虹》(Gravity's Rainbow, 1973)奠定了他在美国后现代主义文学中的核心地位。此书广泛运用戏仿、混合和多重叙述声音等技巧，深刻嘲讽了情节、人物和主题等传统文学要素。

　　第一部小说《V.》(1963)出版以后，他本人也变成了一个谜。他不爱抛头露面，谢绝采访、拍照，除了偶尔发表书评和文章，与外界没有什么交往。对他知之甚少的人们就捕风捉影地编出许多故事。传说他第一部小说出版时，出版社为编写《作者简介》派了一位摄影师去给他拍照。摄影师找到他下榻的旅馆房间，开门的人告诉他品钦过一小时就回来。一小时后摄影师再来时，发现房间已被客人退了。有人甚至认为品钦根本就不存在，那些作品并不是他写的。1976年的《梭霍新闻》(Soho News)上就有一篇文章说品钦其实就是塞林格(J. D. Salinger)。不久，品钦给文章作者去信，说自己确实存在，那些书也确实是他写的。

　　关于这个"确实存在"的品钦，人们所确知的只是他1937年5月8日生于纽约的格兰科夫(Glen Cove)，1953年毕业于牡蛎湾高级中学(Oyster Bay High School)。他的一张常见的照片就是出自他高中毕业时的集体照。照片上，他短发、长脸、凹眼，身穿白衬衫、黑外套，个子显然不小。高中毕业后，他进入康奈尔大学学习工程物理，其间停学在美国海军里服役两年，又返回母校改修英语，于1959年获得文学学士学位。之后，他在纽约的格林威治村住过一段时间，又于1960年去西雅图的波音公司编写技术资料，直到他第一部小说出版。他的其他小说有《拍卖第四十九批》(The Crying of Lot 49, 1966)、《葡萄园》(Vineland, 1990)和《梅森与狄克森》(Mason & Dixon, 1997)。

　　品钦的小说关注第二次世界大战中发展起来的由工业、军事、大众传媒和娱乐行业等构成的巨大社会网络，描写这张网络从欧洲源头延伸到当代美国的发展过程。他的作品背景广阔，大量借用了科学理论、历史事实和大众文化。他的人物多而常变，情节繁而无序。他运用讽刺、幽默、悬念等多种技巧表现了一个阴暗但又并非无望的当代社会。

Entropy①

Boris has just given me a summary of his views. He is a weather prophet. The weather will continue bad, he says. There will be more calamities, more death, more despair. Not the slightest indication of a change anywhere... We must get into step, a lockstep toward the prison of death. There is no escape. The weather will not change.

——*Tropic of Camcer*②

Downstairs, Meatball Mulligan's lease-breaking party was moving into its 40th hour. On the kitchen floor, amid a litter of empty champagne fifths, were Sandor Rojas and three friends, playing spit in the ocean and staying on Heidseck③ and benzedrine pills. In the living room Duke, Vincent, Krinkles and Paco sat crouched over a 15-inch speaker which had been bolted into the top of a wastepaper basket, listening to 27 watts' worth of *The Heroes' Gate at Kiev*④. They all wore hornrimmed sunglasses and rapt expressions, and smoked funny-looking cigarettes which contained not, as you might expect, tobacco, but an adulterated form of *cannabis sativa*⑤. This group was the Duke di Angelis quartet. They recorded for a local label called Tambú and had to their credit one ten 10" LP entitled *Songs of Outer Space*⑥. From time to time one of them would flick the ashes from his cigarette into the speaker cone to watch them dance around. Meatball himself was sleeping over by the window, holding an empty magnum to his chest as if it were a teddy bear. Several government girls, who worked for people like the State Department and NSA, had passed out on couches, chairs and in one case the bathroom sink.

---

① Entropy：熵，多个科学领域里的术语，指一切物体都将进入的混沌状态。在理论物理学里，熵指所有物质的温度都降到相同的水平，丧失了能做机械功的热能，也就是说，这时的宇宙达到了"热死亡"的状态。在通信理论中，熵指因为信息量过大，超过了人们所能理解的能力，而导致的通信停止。在社会学理论中，熵指任何社会都将必然堕入的混沌状态。

② Tropic of Camcer：美国作家米勒(Henry Miller, 1891—1980)1934 年发表的小说。

③ Heidseck：法国香槟酒。

④ The Heroes' Gate at Kiev：俄国作曲家穆索尔斯基(Modest Petrovich Mussorgsky, 1831—1881)的作品。

⑤ cannabis sativa：大麻。

⑥ Songs of Outer Space：具有反讽意味的标题，因为外层空间没有传递声波的空气，所以也就没有声音和歌声。

This was in early February of '57 and back then there were a lot of American expatriates around Washington, D.C., who would talk, every time they met you, about how someday they were going to go over to Europe for real but right now it seemed they were working for the government. Everyone saw a fine irony in this. They would stage, for instance, polyglot parties where the newcomer was sort of ignored if he couldn't carry on simultaneous conversations in three or four languages. They would haunt American delicatessens for weeks at a stretch and invite you over for bulghour and lamb① in tiny kitchens whose walls were covered with bullfight posters. They would have affairs with sultry girls from Andalucía or the Midi② who studied economics at Georgetown. Their Dôme③ was a collegiate Rathskeller out on Wisconsin Avenue called the Old Heidelberg and they had to settle for cherry blossoms instead of lime trees when spring came, but in its lethargic way their life provided, as they said, kicks.

At the moment, Meatball's party seemed to be gathering its second wind. Outside there was rain. Rain splatted against the tar paper on the roof and was fractured into a fine spray off the noses, eyebrows and lips of wooden gargoyles under the eaves, and ran like drool down the windowpanes. The day before, it had snowed and the day before that there had been winds of gale force and before that the sun had made the city glitter bright as April, though the calendar read early February. It is a curious season in Washington, this false spring. Somewhere in it are Lincoln's Birthday and the Chinese New Year, and a forlornness in the streets because cherry blossoms are weeks away still and, as Sarah Vaughan④ has put it, spring will be a little late this year. Generally crowds like the one which would gather in the Old Heidelberg on weekday afternoons to drink Würtzburger⑤ and to sing Lili Marlene⑥(not to mention The Sweetheart of Sigma Chi) are inevitably and incorrigibly Romantic. And as every good Romantic knows, the soul (*spiritus, ruach, pneuma*)⑦ is nothing, substantially, but air; it is only natural that warpings in the atmosphere should be recapitulated in those who breathe it. So that over and above the public components—holidays, tourist attractions—there are pri-

---

① bulghour and lamb：碎小麦（bulgur）烧羊肉，中东的一道菜。
② Andalucía：西班牙南部的一个地区。Midi：法国南部。
③ Le Dôme：一法国咖啡馆，作家、艺术家和 20 世纪 20 年代移居法国的美国人的聚集地。
④ Sarah Vaughan：沃恩（1924—1990），美国爵士乐歌手。
⑤ Würtzburger：德国 Würtzburg 酿制的啤酒。
⑥ Lili Marlene：德国抒情歌曲，第二次世界大战中流行于德国和同盟国军队中。
⑦ spiritus, ruach, pneuma：拉丁语、希伯来语和希腊语里的"soul"。

vate meanderings, linked to the climate as if this spell were a *stretto*① passage in the year's fugue: haphazard weather, aimless loves, unpredicted commitments: months one can easily spend *in* fugue, because oddly enough, later on, winds, rains, passions of February and March are never remembered in that city, it is as if they had never been.

The last bass notes of the *The Heroes' Gate* boomed up through the floor and woke Callisto from an uneasy sleep. The first thing he became aware of was a small bird he has been holding gently between his hands, against his body. He turned his head sidewise on the pillow to smile down at it, at its blue hunched-down head and sick, lidded eyes, wondering how many more nights he would have to give it warmth before it was well again. He had been holding the bird like that for three days: it was the only way he knew to restore its health. Next to him the girl stirred and whimpered, her arm thrown across her face. Mingled with the sounds of the rain came the first tentative, querulous morning voices of the other birds, hidden in philodendrons and small fan palms: patches of scarlet, yellow and blue laced through this Rousseau-like② fantasy, this hothouse jungle it had taken him seven years to weave together. Hermetically sealed, it was a tiny enclave of regularity in the city's chaos, alien to the vagaries of the weather, of national politics, of any civil disorder. Through trial-and-error Callisto had perfected its ecological balance, with the help of the girl its artistic harmony, so that the swayings of its plant life, the stirrings of its birds and human inhabitants were all as integral as the rhythms of a perfectly-executed mobile. He and the girl could no longer, of course, be omitted from that sanctuary; they had become necessary to its unity. What they needed from outside was delivered. They did not go out.

"Is he all right," she whispered. She lay like a tawny question mark facing him, her eyes suddenly huge and dark and blinking slowly. Callisto ran a finger beneath the feathers at the base of the bird's neck; caressed it gently. "He's going to be well, I think. See: he hears his friends beginning to wake up." The girl had heard the rain and the birds even before she was fully awake. Her name was Aubade: she was part French and part Annamese, and she lived on her own curious and lonely planet, where the clouds and the odor of poincianas, the bitterness of wine and the accidental fingers at the small of her back or feathery against her breasts came to her reduced inevitably to the terms of sound: of music which e-

---

① stretto：(意大利语)狭窄。作为音乐术语，指赋格曲中紧密的和应或声音的重叠。
② Henri Rousseau：卢梭(1844—1910)，法国原始派画家。

merged at intervals from a howling darkness of discordancy. "Aubade," he said, "go see." Obedient, she arose; padded to the window, pulled aside the drapes and after a moment said: "It is 37. Still 37." Callisto frowned. "Since Tuesday, then," he said. "No change." Henry Adams[①], three generations before his own, had stared aghast at Power; Callisto found himself now in much the same state over Thermodynamics[②], the inner life of that power, realizing like his predecessor that the Virgin and the dynamo stand as much for love as for power; that the two are indeed identical; and that love therefore not only makes the world go round but also makes the boccie ball spin, the nebula precess[③]. It was this latter or sidereal element which disturbed him. The cosmologists had predicted an eventual heat-death for the universe (something like Limbo: form and motion abolished, heat-energy identical at every point in it); the meteorologists, day-to-day, staved it off by contradicting with a reassuring array of varied temperatures.

Bur for three days now, despite the changeful weather, the mercury had stayed at 37 degrees Fahrenheit. Leery at omens of apocalypse, Callisto shifted beneath the covers. His fingers pressed the bird more firmly, as if needing some pulsing or suffering assurance of an early break in the temperature.

It was that last cymbal crash that did it. Meatball was hurled wincing into consciousness as the synchronized wagging of heads over the wastebasket stopped. The final hiss remained for an instant in the room, then melted into the whisper of rain outside. "Aarrgghh," announced Meatball in the silence, looking at the empty magnum. Krinkles, in slow motion, turned, smiled and held out a cigarette. "Tea time[④], man," he said. "No, no," said Meatball. "How many times I got to tell you guys. Not at my place. You ought to know, Washington is lousy with Feds." Krinkles looked wistful. "Jeez, Meatball," he said, "you don't want to do nothing no more." "Hair of dog," said Meatball. "Only hope. Any juice left?" He began to crawl toward the kitchen. "No champagne, I don't think," Duke said. "Case of tequila behind the icebox." They put on an Earl Bostic[⑤] side. Meatball paused at the kitchen door, glowering at Sandor Rojas. "Lemons," he said after some thought. He crawled to the refrigerator and got out three

---

① Henry Adams：亚当斯(1838—1918)，美国历史学家。
② 根据热力学三定律，宇宙间的能量守恒，既不能被创造，又不能被消除；热量必然从高温物体传向低温物体，最后达到温度平衡(熵)；有一个绝对零度。
③ the nebula precess：星际的一团围绕一呈锥状自转的中轴旋转的气体或尘埃。
④ tea time：抽大麻的时间。
⑤ Earl Bostic：博斯蒂克(1913—1965)，美国爵士乐萨克斯管吹奏者。

lemons and some cubes, found the tequila and set about restoring order to his nervous system. He drew blood once cutting the lemons and had to use two hands squeezing them and his foot to crack the ice tray but after about ten minutes he found himself, through some miracle, beaming down into a monster tequila sour. "That looks yummy," Sandor Rojas said. "How about you make me one." Meatball blinked at him. "*Kitchi lofass a shegibe*,"① he replied automatically, and wandered away into the bathroom. "I say," he called out a moment later to no one in particular. "I say, there seems to be a girl or something sleeping in the sink." He took her by the shoulder and shook. "Wha," she said. "You don't look too comfortable," Meatball said. "Well," she agreed. She stumbled to the shower, turned on the cold water and sat down crosslegged in the spray. "That's better," she smiled.

"Meatball," Sandor Rojas yelled from the kitchen. "Somebody is trying to come in the window. A burglar, I think. A second-story man." "What are you worrying about," Meatball said. "We're on the third floor." He loped back into the kitchen. A shaggy woebegone figure stood out on the fire escape, raking his fingernails down the windowpane. Meatball opened the window. "Saul," he said.

"Sort of wet out," Saul said. He climbed in, dripping. "You heard, I guess."

"Miriam left you," Meatball said, "or something, is all I heard."

There was a sudden flurry of knocking at the front door. "Do come in," Sandor Rojas called. The door opened and there were three coeds from George Washington, all of whom were majoring in philosophy. They were each holding a gallon of Chianti. Sandor leaped up and dashed into the living room. "We heard there was a party," one blonde said. "Young blood," Sandor shouted. He was an ex-Hungarian freedom fighter who had easily the worst chronic case of what certain critics of the middle class have called Don Giovannism② in the District of Columbia. *Purche porti la gonnella, voi sapete quel che fa.*③ Like Pavlov's dog:④ a contralto voice or a whiff of Arpège and Sandor would begin to salivate. Meat-

---

① kitchi lofass a shegibe.：（匈牙利忌语）相当于英语的"Up yours."

② Don Giovannism：强行追求女人的做法，以西班牙传说中放荡不羁的唐璜（Don Juan，意大利语称作 Don Giovanni）的名字命名。

③ Purche porti la gonnella, voi sapete quel che fa.：（意大利语）如果她穿裙子，你就知道他会干什么。出自莫扎特（Wolfgang Amadeus Mozart, 1756—1791）的歌剧《唐璜》（1787）第一幕里仆人（Leporello）列举唐璜征服女性的事例时的所言。

④ Ivan Petrovich Pavlov：巴甫洛夫（1849—1936），俄国生理学家，曾在狗身上造成条件反射，使它一听到铃声就流口水。1904 年，他因在研究消化作用的特征方面的贡献而获诺贝尔奖。

ball regarded the trio blearily as they filed into the kitchen; he shrugged. "Put the wine in the icebox," he said "and good morning."

Aubade's neck made a golden bow as she bent over the sheets of foolscap, scribbling away in the green murk of the room. "As a young man at Princeton," Callisto was dictating, nestling the bird against the gray hairs of his chest, "Callisto had learned a mnemonic device for remembering the Laws of Thermodynamics: you can't win, things are going to get worse before they get better, who says they're going to get better. At the age of 54, confronted with Gibbs'[①] notion of the universe, he suddenly realized that undergraduate cant had been oracle, after all. That spindly maze of equations became, for him, a vision of ultimate, cosmic heat-death. He had known all along, of course, that nothing but a theoretical engine or system ever runs at 100% efficiency; and about the theorem of Clausius[②], which states that the entropy of an isolated system always continually increases. It was not, however, until Gibbs and Boltzmann[③] brought to this principle the methods of statistical mechanics that the horrible significance of it all dawned on him: only then did he realize that the isolated system—galaxy, engine, human being, culture, whatever—must evolve spontaneously toward the Condition of the More Probable. He was forced, therefore, in the sad dying fall of middle age, to a radical reevaluation of everything he had learned up to then; all the cities and seasons and casual passions of his days had now to be looked at in a new and elusive light. He did not know if he was equal to the task. He was aware of the dangers of the reductive fallacy[④] and, he hoped, strong enough not to drift into the graceful decadence of an enervated fatalism. His had always been a vigorous, Italian sort of pessimism: like Machiavelli[⑤], he allowed the forces of *virtù and fortuna*[⑥] to be about 50/50; but the equations now introduced a random factor which he found himself afraid to calculate." Around him loomed vague hothouse shapes; the pitifully small heart fluttered against his own. Counterpointed against his words the girl heard the chatter of birds and fitful car honkings scattered along the

---

① Josiah Willard Gibbs：吉布斯(1839—1903)，美国物理学家，曾用一些统计学公式表示物质向熵的运动。

② Rudolph Clausius：克劳修斯(1822—1888)，德国物理学家，提出了熵的概念。

③ Ludwig Boltzman：玻尔兹曼(1844—1906)，奥地利物理学家，提出了关于分子温度与能量比例的定律，认为温度越高，能量越大。

④ reductive fallacy：将复杂的问题简化成过分容易、简单的问题的错误。

⑤ Niccolò Machiavelli：马基雅弗利(1469—1527)，意大利外交家和政治理论家，他的著作《君主论》(*The Prince*, 1513)为统治者出谋划策，对人类表现了悲观看法。

⑥ *virtù and fortuna*：意大利语：美德和机会。

wet morning and Earl Bostic's alto rising in occasional wild peaks through the floor. The architectonic purity of her world was constantly threatened by such hints of anarchy: gaps and excrescences and skew lines, and a shifting or tilting of planes to which she had continually to readjust lest the whole structure shiver into a disarray of discrete and meaningless signals. Callisto had described the process once as a kind of "feedback": she crawled into dreams each night with a sense of exhaustion, and a desperate resolve never to relax that vigilance. Even in the brief periods when Callisto made love to her, soaring above the bowing of taut nerves in haphazard double-stops① would be the one singing string of her determination.

"Nevertheless," continued Callisto, "he found in entropy or the measure of disorganization for a closed system an adequate metaphor to apply to certain phenomena in his own world. He saw, for example, the younger generation responding to Madison Avenue with the same spleen his own had once reserved for Wall Street: and in American 'consumerism' discovered a similar tendency from the least to the most probable, from differentiation to sameness, from ordered individuality to a kind of chaos. He found himself, in short, restating Gibb's prediction in social terms, and envisioned a heat-death for his culture in which ideas, like heat-energy, would no longer be transferred, since each point in it would ultimately have the same quantity of energy; and intellectual motion would, accordingly, cease." He glanced up suddenly. "Check it now," he said. Again she rose and peered out at the thermometer. "37," she said. "The rain has stopped." He bent his head quickly and held his lips against a quivering wing. "Then it will change soon," he said, trying to keep his voice firm.

Sitting on the stove Saul was like any big rag doll that a kid has been taking out some incomprehensible rage on. "What happened," Meatball said. "If you feel like talking, I mean."

"Of course I feel like talking," Saul said. "One thing I did, I slugged her."

"Discipline must be maintained."

"Ha, ha. I wish you'd been there. Oh Meatball, it was a lovely fight. She ended up throwing a *Handbook of Chemistry and Physics* at me, only it missed and went through the window, and when the glass broke I reckon something in her broke too. She stormed out of the house crying, out in the rain. No raincoat or anything."

"She'll be back."

---

① double-stops：用乐器上相近的两根弦同时演奏两个曲调。

"No."

"Well." Soon Meatball said: "It was something earth-shattering, no doubt. Like who is better, Sal Mineo or Ricky Nelson."

"What it was about," Saul said, "was communication theory. Which of course makes it very hilarious."

"I don't know anything about communication theory."

"Neither does my wife. Come right down to it, who does? That's the joke."

When Meatball saw the kind of smile Saul had on his face he said: "Maybe you would like tequila or something."

"No. I mean, I'm sorry. It's a field you can go off the deep end in, is all. You get where you're watching all the time for security cops: behind bushes, around corners. MUFFET is top secret."

"Wha."

"Multi-unit factorial field electronic tabulator."

"You were fighting about that."

"Miriam has been reading science fiction again. That and *Scientific American*. It seems she is, as we say, bugged at this idea of computers acting like people. I made the mistake of saying you can just as well turn that around, and talk about human behavior like a program fed into an IBM machine."

"Why not," Meatball said.

"Indeed, why not. In fact it is sort of crucial to communication, not to mention information theory. Only when I said that she hit the roof. Up went the balloon. And I can't figure out *why*. If anybody should know why, I should. I refuse to believe the government is wasting taxpayers' money on me, when it has so many bigger and better things to waste it on."

Meatball made a mouse[①]. "Maybe she thought you were acting like a cold, dehumanized amoral scientist type."

"My god," Saul flung up an arm. "Dehumanized. How much more human can I get? I worry, Meatball, I do. There are Europeans wandering around North Africa these days with their tongues torn out of their heads because those tongues have spoken the wrong words. Only the Europeans thought they were the right words."

"Language barrier," Meatball suggested.

Saul jumped down off the stove. "That," he said, angry, "is a good candidate

---

① made a mouse：扮鬼脸。

for sick joke of the year. No, ace, it is *not* a barrier. If it is anything it's a kind of leakage. Tell a girl: 'I love you.' No trouble with two-thirds of that, it's a closed circuit. Just you and she. But that nasty four-letter word in the middle, *that's* the one you have to look out for. Ambiguity. Redundancy. Irrelevance, even. Leakage. All this is noise. Noise screws up your signal, makes for disorganization in the circuit."

Meatball shuffled around. "Well, now, Saul," he muttered, "you're sort of, I don't know, expecting a lot from people. I mean, you know. What it is is, most of the things we say, I guess, are mostly noise."

"Ha! Half of what you just said, for example."

"Well, you do it too."

"I know." Saul smiled grimly. "It's a bitch, ain't it."

"I bet that's what keeps divorce lawyers in business. Whoops."

"Oh I'm not sensitive. Besides," frowning, "you're right. You find I think that most 'successful' marriages—Miriam and me, up to last night—are sort of founded on compromises. You never run at top efficiency, usually all you have is a minimum basis for a workable thing. I believe the phrase is Togetherness."

"Aarrgghh."

"Exactly. You find that one a bit noisy, don't you. But the noise content is different for each of us because you're a bachelor and I'm not. Or wasn't. That hell with it."

"Well sure," Meatball said, trying to be helpful, "you were using different words. By 'human being' you meant something that you can look at like it was a computer. It helps you think better on the job or something. But Miriam meant something entirely—"

"The hell with it."

Meatball fell silent. "I'll take that drink," Saul said after a while.

The card game had been abandoned and Sandor's friends were slowly getting wasted on tequila. On the living room couch, one of the coeds and Krinkles were engaged in amorous conversation. "No," Krinkles was saying, "no, I can't put Dave[①] down. In fact I give Dave a lot of credit, man. Especially considering his accident and all." The girl's smile faded. "How terrible," she said. "What accident?" "Hadn't you heard?" Krinkles said. "When Dave was in the army, just a

---

① Dave Brubeck：布鲁贝克(1920—   )，美国爵士乐钢琴家。

258

private E-2, they sent him down to Oak Ridge① on special duty. Something to do with the Manhattan Project. He was handling hot stuff one day and got an overdose of radiation. So now he's got to wear lead gloves all the time." She shook her head sympathetically. "What an awful break for a piano-player."

Meatball had abandoned Saul to a bottle of tequila and was about to go to sleep in a closet when the front door flew open and the place was invaded by five enlisted personnel of the U.S. Navy, all in varying stages of abomination. "This is the place," shouted a fat, pimply seaman apprentice who had lost his white hat. "This here is the hoorhouse that chief was telling us about." A stringy-looking 3rd class boatswain's mate pushed him aside and cased the living room. "You're right, Slab," he said. "But it don't look like much, even for Stateside. I seen better tail in Naples, Italy." "How much, hey," boomed a large seaman with adenoids, who was holding a Mason jar full of white lightning②. "Oh, my god," said Meatball.

Outside the temperature remained constant at 37 degrees Fahrenheit. In the hothouse Aubade stood absently caressing the branches of a young mimosa, hearing a motif of sap-rising, the rough and unresolved anticipatory theme of those fragile pink blossoms which, it is said, insure fertility. That music rose in a tangled tracery: arabesques of order competing fugally with the improvised discords of the party downstairs, which peaked sometimes in cusps and ogees of noise. That precious signal-to-noise ratio, whose delicate balance required every calorie of her strength, seesawed inside the small tenuous skull as she watched Callisto, sheltering the bird. Callisto was trying to confront any idea of the heat-death now, as he nuzzled the feathery lump in his hands. He sought correspondences. Sade③, of course. And Temple Drake④, gaunt and hopeless in her little park in Paris, at the end of *Sanctuary*. Final equilibrium. *Nightwood*⑤. And the tango. Any tango, but more than any perhaps the sad sick dance in Stravinsky's *L' Histoire du Soldat*.⑥ He thought back: what had tango music been for them after the war,

---

① Oak Ridge：田纳西州中部的一个城市，制造原子弹的曼哈顿计划所用的放射性材料就是在这里准备的。
② white lightning：(美俚)违法自制的威士忌酒。
③ The Marquis de Sade：萨德(1740—1814)，法国作家，其著作多描写性变态。
④ Temple Drake：美国作家福克纳(William Faulkner, 1897—1962)的小说《圣殿》(Sanctuary, 1931)里的人物。小说结尾，她已经堕落，坐在巴黎的卢森堡花园里。
⑤ *Nightwood*：美国作家巴恩斯(Djuna Barnes, 1892—1982)的小说，写20世纪20年代移居巴黎的颓废美国人的生活。
⑥ *L' Histoire du soldat*：(法语)《士兵的故事》。俄国作曲家斯特拉文斯基(Igor Fyodorovich Stravinsky, 1882—1971)的音乐作品。

what meanings had he missed in all the stately coupled automatons in the *cafés-dansants*①, or in the metronomes which had ticked behind the eyes of his own partners? Not even the clean constant winds of Switzerland could cure the *grippe espagnole*②: Stravinsky had had it, they all had had it. And how many musicians were left after Passchendaele, after the Marne③? It came down in this case to seven: violin, double-bass. Clarinet, bassoon. Cornet, trombone. Tympani. Almost as if any tiny troupe of saltimbanques④ had set about conveying the same information as a full pit-orchestra⑤. There was hardly a full complement left in Europe. Yet with violin and tympani Stravinsky had managed to communicate in that tango the same exhaustion, the same airlessness one saw in the slicked-down youths who were trying to imitate Vernon Castle⑥, and in their mistresses, who simply did not care. *Ma maîtresse*⑦. Celeste. Returning to Nice after the second war he had found that café replaced by a perfume shop which catered to American tourists. And no secret vestige of her in the cobblestones or in the old pension⑧ next door; no perfume to match her breath heavy with the sweet Spanish wine she always drank. And so instead he had purchased a Henry Miller novel and left for Paris, and read the book on the train so that when he arrived he had been given at least a little forewarning. And saw that Celeste and the others and even Temple Drake were not all that had changed. "Aubade," he said, "my head aches." The sound of his voice generated in the girl an answering scrap of melody. Her movement toward the kitchen, the towel, the cold water, and his eyes following her formed a weird and intricate canon; as she placed the compress on his forehead his sigh of gratitude seemed to signal a new subject, another series of modulations.

"No," Meatball was still saying, "no, I'm afraid not. This is not a house of ill repute. I'm sorry, really I am." Slab was adamant. "But the chief said," he kept repeating. The seaman offered to swap the moonshine for a good piece. Meatball looked around frantically, as if seeking assistance. In the middle of the

---

① cafés-dansants：(法语)舞厅。
② grippe espagnole：(法语)西班牙流感，为1918年的大流感所起的名称。
③ 比利时的帕申代尔(Passchendaele)村和法国的马恩(Marne)河流域，都是第一次世界大战的战场。
④ saltimbanques：(法语)表演者，小丑。
⑤ pit-orchestra：在乐池里演奏的管弦乐团。
⑥ Vernon Castle：卡索耳 (1887—1918)，英裔舞蹈家，第一次世界大战前在美国和欧洲极受欢迎。
⑦ Ma maîtresse：(法语)My mistress。
⑧ the old pension：欧洲大陆国家提供膳宿的公寓或小旅馆。

room, the Duke di Angelis quartet were engaged in a historic moment. Vincent was seated and the others standing: they were going through the motions of a group having a session, only without instruments. "I say," Meatball said. Duke moved his head a few times, smiled faintly, lit a cigarette, and eventually caught sight of Meatball. "Quiet, man," he whispered. Vincent began to fling his arms around, his fists clenched; then, abruptly, was still, then repeated the performance. This went on for a few minutes while Meatball sipped his drink moodily. The navy had withdrawn to the kitchen. Finally at some invisible signal the group stopped tapping their feet and Duke grinned and said, "At least we ended together."

Meatball glared at him. "I say," he said. "I have this new conception, man," Duke said. "You remember your namesake. You remember Gerry①."

"No," said Meatball. "I'll remember April, if that's any help."

"As a matter of fact," Duke said, "it was Love for Sale. Which shows how much you know. The point is, it was Mulligan, Chet Baker and that crew, way back then, out yonder. You dig?"

"Baritone sax," Meatball said. "Something about a baritone sax."

"But no piano, man. No guitar. Or accordion. You know what that means."

"Not exactly," Meatball said.

"Well first let me just say, that I am no Mingus, no John Lewis②. Theory was never my strong point. I mean things like reading were always difficult for me and all—"

"I know," Meatball said drily. "You got your card③ taken away because you changed key on Happy Birthday at a Kiwanis Club picnic."

"Rotarian. But it occurred to me, in one of these flashes of insight, that if that first quartet of Mulligan's had no piano, it could only mean one thing."

"No chords," said Paco, the baby-faced bass.

"What he is trying to say," Duke said, "is no root chords④. Nothing to listen to while you blow a horizontal line. What one does in such a case is, one *thinks* the roots."

A horrified awareness was dawning on Meatball. "And the next logical ex-

---

① Gerry Mulligan：格里(1929—1996)，美国爵士乐萨克斯管吹奏者。
② Charlie Mingus：明戈斯(1929—1979)，美国低音提琴家和作曲家。刘易斯(John Lewis, 1920—)，美国钢琴家和作曲家。
③ card：音乐家工会会员证。
④ root chords：一首乐曲的和声基音。

tension," he said.

"Is to think everything," Duke announced with simple dignity. "Roots, line, everything."

Meatball looked at Duke, awed. "But," he said.

"Well," Duke said modestly, "there are a few bugs to work out."

"But," Meatball said.

"Just listen," Duke said. "You'll catch on." And off they went again into orbit, presumably somewhere around the asteroid belt. After a while Krinkles made an embouchure① and started moving his fingers and Duke clapped his hand to his forehead. "Oaf!" he roared. "The new head② we're using, you remember, I wrote last night?" "Sure," Krinkles said, "the new head. I come in on the bridge. All your heads I come in then." "Right," Duke said. "So why—" "Wha," said Krinkles, "16 bars, I wait, I come in—" "16?" Duke said. "No. No, Krinkles. Eight you waited. You want me to sing it? A cigarette that bears a lipstick's traces, an airline ticket to romantic places." Krinkles scratched his head. "These Foolish Things, you mean." "Yes," Duke said, "yes, Krinkles. Bravo." "Not I'll Remember April," Krinkles said. "*Minghe morte*,"③ said Duke. "I *figured* we were playing it a little slow," Krinkles said. Meatball chuckled. "Back to the old drawing board," he said. "No, man," Duke said, "back to the airless void." And they took off again, only it seemed Paco was playing in G sharp while the rest were in E flat, so they had to start all over.

In the kitchen two of the girls from George Washington and the sailors were singing Let's All Go Down and Piss on the Forrestal④. There was a two-handed, bilingual *morra*⑤ game on over by the icebox. Saul had filled several paper bags with water and was sitting on the fire escape, dropping them on passersby in the street. A fat government girl in a Bennington sweatshirt, recently engaged to an ensign attached to the Forrestal, came charging into the kitchen, head lowered, and butted Slab in the stomach. Figuring this was as good an excuse for a fight as any, Slab's buddies piled in. The *morra* players were nose-to-nose, screaming *trios, sette*⑥ at the tops of their lungs. From the shower the girl Meatball had tak-

---

① embouchure：演奏管乐器的口型。
② the new head：一首乐曲的开头部分或引子。
③ Minghe morte：(意大利粗俗俚语)Dead prick。
④ the Forrestal：美国航空母舰，以美国国防部长福雷斯特尔(James Forrestal, 1892—1949)的名字命名。
⑤ morra：意大利游戏，由一个参与者猜另一参与者竖起几个手指头。
⑥ trios, sette：(意大利语)三、七。

en out of the sink announced that she was drowning. She had apparently sat on the drain and the water was now up to her neck. The noise in Meatball's apartment had reached a sustained, ungodly crescendo.

Meatball stood and watched, scratching his stomach lazily. The way he figured, there were only about two ways he could cope: (a) lock himself in the closet and maybe eventually they would all go away, or (b) try to calm everybody down, one by one. (a) was certainly the more attractive alternative. But then he started thinking about that closet. It was dark and stuffy and he would be alone. He did not feature being alone. And then this crew off the good ship Lollipop or whatever it was might take it upon themselves to kick down the closet door, for a lark. And if that happened he would be, at the very least, embarrassed. The other way was more a pain in the neck, but probably better in the long run.

So he decided to try and keep his lease-breaking party from deteriorating into total chaos: he gave wine to the sailors and separated the *morra* players; he introduced the fat government girl to Sandor Rojas, who would keep her out of trouble; he helped the girl in the shower to dry off and get into bed; he had another talk with Saul; he called a repairman for the refrigerator, which someone had discovered was on the blink. This is what he did until nightfall, when most of the revellers had passed out and the party trembled on the threshold of its third day.

Upstairs Callisto, helpless in the past, did not feel the faint rhythm inside the bird begin to slacken and fail. Aubade was by the window, wandering the ashes of her own lovely world; the temperature held steady, the sky had become a uniform darkening gray. Then something from downstairs—a girl's scream, an overturned chair, a glass dropped on the floor, he would never knew what exactly—pierced that private time-warp and he became aware of the faltering, the constriction of muscles, the tiny tossings of the bird's head; and his own pulse began to pound more fiercely, as if trying to compensate. "Aubade," he called weakly, "he's dying." The girl, flowing and rapt, crossed the hothouse to gaze down at Callisto's hands. The two remained like that, poised, for one minute, and two, while the heartbeat ticked a graceful diminuendo down at last into stillness. Callisto raised his head slowly. "I held him," he protested, impotent with the wonder of it, "to give him the warmth of my body. Almost as if I were communicating life to him, or a sense of life. What has happened? Has the transfer of heat ceased to work? Is there no more... " He did not finish.

"I was just at the window," she said. He sank back, terrified. She stood a moment more, irresolute; she had sensed his obsession long ago, realized somehow that that constant 37 was now decisive. Suddenly then, as if seeing the single and unavoidable conclusion to all this she moved swiftly to the window before Callisto could speak;   tore away the drapes and smashed out the glass with two exquisite hands which came away bleeding and glistening with splinters;   and turned to face the man on the bed and wait with him until the moment of equilibrium was reached,   when 37 degrees Fahrenheit should prevail both outside and inside,   and forever,   and the hovering,   curious dominant of their separate lives should resolve into a tonic of darkness① and the final absence of all motion.

尽管品钦说《熵》(1960)走的是主题先行的路子,违背艺术创作的规律,他本人不太喜欢它,但它一直是品钦最受批评界关注的短篇小说,故事所表现的熵这一主题对于理解他的全部作品具有重要意义。

故事以多种方式强调了熵这一主题,引导读者从熵的角度看待日常生活中的衰颓。在通信理论中,熵指噪音大于信号时必然发生的误解和交流失败。这种情况恰好就发生在《熵》里的一个聚会上。在住在公寓房楼下的马利根(Mulligan)所举行的这个违反租约的聚会上,有人吵闹,甚至打起架来。面对这种情况,马利根"只有两种应付的办法:(a)把自己锁在壁橱里,也许最终他们都会走掉,或者(b)试着让大家平静下来,逐个地"。为了不让他的聚会"恶化成一片混乱",马利根采取了后一种办法,使秩序得到了一些恢复。尽管熵意味着这一秩序不会持久,但马利根的努力在道德上还是可嘉的。

楼上的卡利斯托(Callisto)住在一套"温室"般的房子里,房子里发生的事件与热力学意义上的熵有关。在热力学中,熵指热量必然由高温物体流向低温物体,从而使温差在一定时间内消失,发生"热的死亡"。虽然卡利斯托知道熵会使生命耗尽,要努力加以阻止,但他的所作所为却是在加速这一进程。故事写了他在努力温暖一只病鸟,想使它恢复健康,但这只鸟不久就死了,令人怀疑他接触鸟的手是否使鸟的热量过早地流失了。卡利斯托在暖鸟的同时,也在向女友欧芭德(Aubade)口授自我放纵的经历,试图通过撰写自传为必然走向熵或衰竭的生活提供某种秩序。如果说马利根的麻烦是由于能量太多而控制太少,那么卡利斯托的麻烦就是由于能量太少而控制太多。

小说结尾似乎把熵表现成了世界末日,但它的视点却是通过卡利斯托的思想来聚焦的。卡利斯托坚持认为温度必须保持不变,结果将自己封闭了起来。是欧芭德打碎了玻璃,敞开了系统,使交流成为可能。在这开放而又含糊的结尾里,一直困扰卡

---

① resolve into a tonic darkness:返回原来的黑暗。音乐中的主音(tonic)就是最初的音调;乐曲要返回(或转换成)这一音调。

利斯托的问题并没有得到彻底的解决。

思考题

1. What is the appropriateness of the story's epigraph?
2. What similarities and differences exist between the happenings downstairs and upstairs? What changes take place? What remains the same?
3. How does the author organize the happenings in different places? What effects may come out of this organization?
4. What are we to make of the story's conclusion? Is it optimistic, pessimistic, or simply ambivalent and inconclusive?

推荐作品

The Crying of Lot 49 (1966)
Gravity's Rainbow (1973)
Mason & Dixon (1997)

参考资料

Berressem, Hanjo. *Pynchon's Poetics: Interfacing Theory and Text*. Urbana: U of Illinois P, 1993.

Chambers, Judith. *Thomas Pynchon*. New York: Twayne, 1992.

Hite, Molly. *Ideas of Order in the Novels of Thomas Pynchon*. Columbus: Ohio State UP, 1983.

O'Donnell, Patrick, ed. *New Essays on The Crying of Lot 49*. Beijing: Peking UP; Cambridge UP, 2006.

第十五单元
Maxine Hong Kingston
(1940—   )
汤亭亭

作者简介

汤亭亭,华裔女作家,出生于美国加利福尼亚,祖籍广东新会。儿时,她从母亲那里听到许多有关中国的神话和传说、中国风俗习惯,以及祖先飘洋过海、寻找美国梦的传奇经历。她后来对这些故事题材进行了大胆改写,以丰富的文学想象力,创作了三部长篇小说。虽然她对中国神话和传说的改写引起了不小的争议,但她蜚声美国文坛却是一个不争的事实。她的第一部作品《女勇士》(The Woman Warrior: Memoirs of a Girlhood among Ghosts,又译《女战士》),自1976年出版后,在美国多次获奖。该作品以独特的叙述视角和手法、丰富的文化形象和奇特的故事内容震撼了美国文坛,被翻译成20多种文字。1995年,根据该作品改编的电视剧被评为该年度的美国最佳电视剧。1980年出版的第二部作品《中国佬》(China Men,又译《金山华人》),以及1989年出版的第三部作品《孙行者》(Tripmaster Monkey: His Fake Book),也都获得不同的文学奖项和不同程度的好评。这三部作品奠定了汤婷婷在当代亚裔作家群中的领先地位,也使她成为进入美国主流的亚裔女作家。她的小说被各种文选收录,作为当代美国文学、女性研究、族裔研究等课程的必读教材,成为美国大学讲坛上讲授最多、大学生阅读最多的作品之一。

除了长篇创作,她还发表了不少散文、随笔和诗歌,例如散文集《夏威夷之夏》(Hawaii One Summer, 1987)、随笔《穿过黑幕》(Through the Black Curtain, 1988)。她的最新作品包括诗集《当诗人》(To Be The Poet, 2002)以及反战长篇小说《第五和平书》(The Fifth Book of Peace, 2003)等。她是目前美国最有实力的女作家之一。

作品

The Woman Warrior
A Song for a Barbarian Reed Pipe①

    ...

    Maybe that's why my mother cut my tongue. She pushed my tongue up and

---

① 选篇出自汤亭亭《女勇士》的最后一个部分"羌笛之歌"。

sliced the frenum. Or maybe she snipped it with a pair of nail scissors. I don't remember her doing it, only her telling me about it, but all during childhood I felt sorry for the baby whose mother waited with scissors or knife in hand for it to cry—and then, when its mouth was wide open like a baby bird's, cut. The Chinese say "a ready tongue is an evil."

I used to curl up my tongue in front of the mirror and tauten my frenum into a white line, itself as thin as a razor blade. I saw no scars in my mouth. I thought perhaps I had had two frena, and she had cut one. I made other children open their mouths so I could compare theirs to mine. I saw perfect pink membranes stretching into precise edges that looked easy enough to cut. Sometimes I felt very proud that my mother committed such a powerful act upon me. At other times I was terrified—the first thing my mother did when she saw me was to cut my tongue.

"Why did you do that to me, Mother?"

"I told you."

"Tell me again."

"I cut it so that you would not be tongue-tied. Your tongue would be able to move in any language. You'll be able to speak languages that are completely different from one another. You'll be able to pronounce anything. Your frenum looked too tight to do those things, so I cut it."

"But isn't 'a ready tongue an evil'?"

"Things are different in this ghost[①] country."

"Did it hurt me? Did I cry and bleed?"

"I don't remember. Probably."

She didn't cut the other children's. When I asked cousins and other Chinese children whether their mothers had cut their tongues loose, they said, "What?"

"Why didn't you cut my brothers' and sisters' tongues?"

"They didn't need it."

"Why not? Were theirs longer than mine?"

"Why don't you quit blabbering and get to work?"

If my mother was not lying she should have cut more, scraped away the rest of the frenum skin, because I have a terrible time talking. Or she should not have cut at all, tampering with my speech. When I went to kindergarten and had to

---

① ghost: 这里指"洋鬼子"。

speak English for the first time, I became silent. A dumbness—a shame—still cracks my voice in two, even when I want to say "hello" casually, or ask an easy question in front of the check-out counter, or ask directions of a bus driver. I stand frozen, or I hold up the line with the complete, grammatical sentence that comes squeaking out at impossible length. "What did you say?" says the cab driver, or "Speak up," so I have to perform again, only weaker the second time. A telephone call makes my throat bleed and takes up that day's courage. It spoils my day with self-disgust when I hear my broken voice come skittering out into the open. It makes people wince to hear it. I'm getting better, though. Recently I asked the postman for special issue stamps; I've waited since childhood for postmen to give me some of their own accord. I am making progress, a little every day.

My silence was thickest—total—during the three years that I covered my school paintings with black paint. I painted layers of black over houses and flowers and suns, and when I drew on the blackboard, I put a layer of chalk on top. I was making a stage curtain, and it was the moment before the curtain parted or rose. The teachers called my parents to school, and I saw they had been saving my pictures, curling and cracking, all alike and black. The teachers pointed to the pictures and looked serious, talked seriously too, but my parents did not understand English. ("The parents and teachers of criminals were executed," said my father.) My parents took the pictures home. I spread them out (so black and full of possibilities) and pretended the curtains were swinging open, flying up, one after another, sunlight underneath, mighty operas.

During the first silent year I spoke to no one at school, did not ask before going to the lavatory, and flunked kindergarten. My sister also said nothing for three years, silent in the playground and silent at lunch. There were other quiet Chinese girls not of our family, but most of them got over it sooner than we did. I enjoyed the silence. At first it did not occur to me I was supposed to talk or to pass kindergarten. I talked at home and to one or two of the Chinese kids in class. I made motions and even made some jokes. I drank out of a toy saucer when the water spilled out of the cup, and everybody laughed, pointing at me, so I did it some more. I didn't know that Americans don't drink out of saucers.

I liked the Negro students (Black Ghosts) best because they laughed the loudest and talked to me as if I were a daring talker too. One of the Negro girls had her mother coil braids over her ears Shanghai-style like mine; we were Shanghai twins except that she was covered with black like my paintings. Two Negro kids enrolled in Chinese school, and the teachers gave them Chinese names. Some Negro kids walked me to school and home, protecting me from the Japanese kids, who hit me and chased me and stuck gum in my ears. The Japanese kids were noisy and tough. They appeared one day in kindergarten, released from concentration camp, which was a tic-tac-toe mark, like barbed wire, on the map.

It was when I found out I had to talk that school became a misery, that the silence became a misery. I did not speak and felt bad each time that I did not speak. I read aloud in first grade, though, and heard the barest whisper with little squeaks come out of my throat. "Louder," said the teacher, who scared the voice away again. The other Chinese girls did not talk either, so I knew the silence had to do with being a Chinese girl.

Reading out loud was easier than speaking because we did not have to make up what to say, but I stopped often, and the teacher would think I'd gone quiet again. I could not understand "I." The Chinese "I" has seven strokes, intricacies. How could the American "I," assuredly wearing a hat like the Chinese, have only three strokes, the middle so straight? Was it out of politeness that this writer left off strokes the way a Chinese has to write her own name small and crooked? No, it was not politeness; "I" is a capital and "you" is lower-case. I stared at that middle line and waited so long for its black center to resolve into tight strokes and dots that I forgot to pronounce it. The other troublesome word was "here," no strong consonant to hang on to, and so flat, when "here" is two mountainous ideographs. The teacher, who had already told me every day how to read "I" and "here," put me in the low corner under the stairs again, where the noisy boys usually sat.

When my second grade class did a play, the whole class went to the auditorium except the Chinese girls. The teacher, lovely and Hawaiian, should have understood about us, but instead left us behind in the classroom. Our voices were too soft or nonexistent, and our parents never signed the permission slips anyway. They never signed anything unnecessary. We opened the door a crack and peeked out, but closed it again quickly. One of us (not me) won every spelling bee, though.

I remember telling the Hawaiian teacher, "We Chinese can't sing 'land

where our fathers died.'" She argued with me about politics, while I meant because of curses. But how can I have that memory when I couldn't talk? My mother says that we, like the ghosts, have no memories.

After American school, we picked up our cigar boxes, in which we had arranged books, brushes, and an inkbox neatly, and went to Chinese school, from 5:00 to 7:30 p.m. There we chanted together, voices rising and falling, loud and soft, some boys shouting, everybody reading together, reciting together and not alone with one voice. When we had a memorization test, the teacher let each of us come to his desk and say the lesson to him privately, while the rest of the class practiced copying or tracing. Most of the teachers were men. The boys who were so well behaved in the American school played tricks on them and talked back to them. The girls were not mute. They screamed and yelled during recess, when there were no rules; they had fist-fights. Nobody was afraid of children hurting themselves or of children hurting school property. The glass doors to the red and green balconies with the gold joy symbols were left wide open so that we could run out and climb the fire escapes. We played capture-the-flag in the auditorium, where Sun Yat-sen① and Chiang Kai-shek's② pictures hung at the back of the stage, the Chinese flag on their left and the American flag on their right. We climbed the teak ceremonial chairs and made flying leaps off the stage. One flag headquarters was behind the glass door and the other on stage right. Our feet drummed on the hollow stage. During recess the teachers locked themselves up in their office with the shelves of books, copybooks, inks from China. They drank tea and warmed their hands at a stove. There was no play supervision. At recess we had the school to ourselves, and also we could roam as far as we could go—downtown, Chinatown stores, home—as long as we returned before the bell rang.

At exactly 7:30 the teacher again picked up the brass bell that sat on his desk and swung it over our heads, while we charged down the stairs, our cheering magnified in the stairwell. Nobody had to line up.

Not all of the children who were silent at American school found voice at Chinese school. One new teacher said each of us had to get up and recite in front of the class, who was to listen. My sister and I had memorized the lesson perfectly. We said it to each other at home, one chanting, one listening. The teacher called on my sister to recite first. It was the first time a teacher had called on the

---

① Sun Yat-sen：孙逸仙,孙中山的字。
② Chiang Kai-shek：蒋介石。

second-born to go first. My sister was scared. She glanced at me and looked away; I looked down at my desk. I hoped that she could do it because if she could, then I would have to. She opened her mouth and a voice came out that wasn't a whisper, but it wasn't a proper voice either. I hoped that she would not cry, fear breaking up her voice like twigs underfoot. She sounded as if she were trying to sing though weeping and strangling. She did not pause or stop to end the embarrassment. She kept going until she said the last word, and then she sat down. When it was my turn, the same voice came out, a crippled animal running on broken legs. You could hear splinters in my voice, bones rubbing jagged against one another. I was loud, though. I was glad I didn't whisper. There was one little girl who whispered.

You can't entrust your voice to the Chinese, either; they want to capture your voice for their own use. They want to fix up your tongue to speak for them. "How much less can you sell it for?" we have to say. Talk the Sales Ghosts down. Make them take a loss.

We were working at the laundry when a delivery boy came from the Rexall drugstore around the corner. He had a pale blue box of pills, but nobody was sick. Reading the label we saw that it belonged to another Chinese family, Crazy Mary's family. "Not ours," said my father. He pointed out the name to the Delivery Ghost, who took the pills back. My mother muttered for an hour, and then her anger boiled over. "That ghost! That dead ghost! How dare he come to the wrong house?" She could not concentrate on her marking and pressing. "A mistake! Huh!" I was getting angry myself. She fumed. She made her press crash and hiss. "Revenge. We've got to avenge this wrong on our future, on our health, and on our lives. Nobody's going to sicken my children and get away with it." We brothers and sisters did not look at one another. She would do something awful, something embarrassing. She'd already been hinting that during the next eclipse we slam pot lids together to scare the frog from swallowing the moon. (The word for "eclipse" is *frog-swallowing-the-moon*.)① When we had not banged lids at the last eclipse and the shadow kept receding anyway, she'd said, "The villagers must be banging and clanging very loudly back home in China."

("On the other side of the world, they aren't having an eclipse, Mama. That's just a shadow the earth makes when it comes between the moon and the sun."

---

① The word for "eclipse" is *frog-swallowing-the-moon*.：汉语称"月蚀"为"蟾蜍吞月"。

"You're always believing what those Ghost Teachers tell you. Look at the size of the jaws!")

"Aha!" she yelled. "You! The biggest." She was pointing at me. "You go to the drugstore."

"What do you want me to buy, Mother?" I said.

"Buy nothing. Don't bring one cent. Go and make them stop the curse."

"I don't want to go. I don't know how to do that. There are no such things as curses. They'll think I'm crazy."

"If you don't go, I'm holding you responsible for bringing a plague on this family."

"What am I supposed to do when I get there?" I said, sullen, trapped. "Do I say, 'Your delivery boy made a wrong delivery'?"

"They know he made a wrong delivery. I want you to make them rectify their crime."

I felt sick already. She'd make me swing stinky censers around the counter, at the druggist, at the customers. Throw dog blood on the druggist. I couldn't stand her plans.

"You get reparation candy," she said. "You say, 'You have tainted my house with sick medicine and must remove the curse with sweetness.' He'll understand."

"He didn't do it on purpose. And no, he won't, Mother. They don't understand stuff like that. I won't be able to say it right. He'll call us beggars."

"You just translate." She searched me to make sure I wasn't hiding any money. I was sneaky and bad enough to buy the candy and come back pretending it was a free gift.

"Mymotherseztagimmesomecandy," I said to the druggist. Be cute and small. No one hurts the cute and small.

"What? Speak up. Speak English," he said, big in his white druggist coat.

"Tatatagimme somecandy."

The druggist leaned way over the counter and frowned. "Some free candy," I said. "Sample candy."

"We don't give sample candy, young lady," he said.

"My mother said you have to give us candy. She said that is the way the Chinese do it."

"What?"

"That is the way the Chinese do it."

"Do what?"

"Do things." I felt the weight and immensity of things impossible to explain to the druggist.

"Can I give you some money?" he asked.

"No, we want candy."

He reached into a jar and gave me a handful of lollipops. He gave us candy all year round, year after year, every time we went into the drugstore. When different druggists or clerks waited on us, they also gave us candy. They had talked us over. They gave us Halloween candy in December, Christmas candy around Valentine's day, candy hearts at Easter, and Easter eggs at Halloween. "See?" said our mother. "They understand. You kids just aren't very brave." But I knew they did not understand. They thought we were beggars without a home who lived in back of the laundry. They felt sorry for us. I did not eat their candy. I did not go inside the drugstore or walk past it unless my parents forced me to. Whenever we had a prescription filled, the druggist put candy in the medicine bag. This is what Chinese druggists normally do, except they give raisins. My mother thought she taught the Druggist Ghosts a lesson in good manners (which is the same word as "traditions").

My mouth went permanently crooked with effort, turned down on the left side and straight on the right. How strange that the emigrant villagers are shouters, hollering face to face. My father asks, "Why is it I can hear Chinese from blocks away? Is it that I understand the language? Or is it they talk loud?" They turn the radio up full blast to hear the operas, which do not seem to hurt their ears. And they yell over the singers that wail over the drums, everybody talking at once, big arm gestures, spit flying. You can see the disgust on American faces looking at women like that. It isn't just the loudness. It is the way Chinese sounds, chingchong ugly, to American ears, not beautiful like Japanese sayonara words with the consonants and vowels as regular as Italian. We make guttural peasant noise and have Ton Duc Thang names you can't remember. And the Chinese can't hear Americans at all; the language is too soft and western music unhearable. I've watched a Chinese audience laugh, visit, talk-story, and holler during a piano recital, as if the musician could not hear them. A Chinese-American, somebody's son, was playing Chopin[①], which has no punctuation, no cymbals,

---

[①] Chopin: 肖邦,波兰作曲家、钢琴家。

no gongs. Chinese piano music is five black keys. Normal Chinese women's voices are strong and bossy. We American-Chinese girls had to whisper to make ourselves American-feminine. Apparently we whispered even more softly than the Americans. Once a year the teachers referred my sister and me to speech therapy, but our voices would straighten out, unpredictably normal, for the therapists. Some of us gave up, shook our heads, and said nothing, not one word. Some of us could not even shake our heads. At times shaking my head no is more self-assertion than I can manage. Most of us eventually found some voice, however faltering. We invented an American-feminine speaking personality, except for that one girl who could not speak up even in Chinese school.

  She was a year older than I and was in my class for twelve years. During all those years she read aloud but would not talk. Her older sister was usually beside her; their parents kept the older daughter back to protect the younger one. They were six and seven years old when they began school. Although I had flunked kindergarten, I was the same age as most other students in our class; my parents had probably lied about my age, so I had had a head start and came out even. My younger sister was in the class below me; we were normal ages and normally separated. The parents of the quiet girl, on the other hand, protected both daughters. When it sprinkled, they kept them home from school. The girls did not work for a living the way we did. But in other ways we were the same.

  We were similar in sports. We held the bat on our shoulders until we walked to first base. (You got a strike only when you actually struck at the ball.) Sometimes the pitcher wouldn't bother to throw to us. "Automatic walk," the other children would call, sending us on our way. By fourth or fifth grade, though, some of us would try to hit the ball. "Easy out," the other kids would say. I hit the ball a couple of times. Baseball was nice in that there was a definite spot to run to after hitting the ball. Basketball confused me because when I caught the ball I didn't know whom to throw it to. "Me. Me," the kids would be yelling. "Over here." Suddenly it would occur to me I hadn't memorized which ghosts were on my team and which were on the other. When the kids said, "Automatic walk," the girl who was quieter than I kneeled with one end of the bat in each hand and placed it carefully on the plate. Then she dusted her hands as she walked to first base, where she rubbed her hands softly, fingers spread. She always got tagged out before second base. She would whisper-read but not talk. Her whisper was as soft as if she had no muscles. She seemed to be breathing from a distance. I heard no anger or tension.

　　I joined in at lunchtime when the other students, the Chinese too, talked about whether or not she was mute, although obviously she was not if she could read aloud. People told how *they* had tried *their* best to be friendly. *They* said hello, but if she refused to answer, well, they didn't see why they had to say hello anymore. She had no friends of her own but followed her sister everywhere, although people and she herself probably thought I was her friend. I also followed her sister about, who was fairly normal. She was almost two years older and read more than anyone else.

　　I hated the younger sister, the quiet one. I hated her when she was the last chosen for her team and I, the last chosen for my team. I hated her for her China doll hair cut. I hated her at music time for the wheezes that came out of her plastic flute.

　　One afternoon in the sixth grade (that year I was arrogant with talk, not knowing there were going to be high school dances and college seminars to set me back), I and my little sister and the quiet girl and her big sister stayed late after school for some reason. The cement was cooling, and the tetherball poles made shadows across the gravel. The hooks at the rope ends were clinking against the poles. We shouldn't have been so late; there was laundry work to do and Chinese school to get to by 5:00. The last time we had stayed late, my mother had phoned the police and told them we had been kidnapped by bandits. The radio stations broadcast our descriptions. I had to get home before she did that again. But sometimes if you loitered long enough in the schoolyard, the other children would have gone home and you could play with the equipment before the office took it away. We were chasing one another through the playground and in and out of the basement, where the playroom and lavatory were. During air raid drills (it was during the Korean War, which you knew about because every day the front page of the newspaper printed a map of Korea with the top part red and going up and down like a window shade), we curled up in this basement. Now everyone was gone. The playroom was army green and had nothing in it but a long trough with drinking spigots in rows. Pipes across the ceiling led to the drinking fountains and to the toilets in the next room. When someone flushed you could hear the water and other matter, which the children named, running inside the big pipe above the drinking spigots. There was one playroom for girls next to the girls' lavatory and one playroom for boys next to the boys' lavatory. The stalls were open and the toilets had no lids, by which we knew that ghosts have no sense of shame or privacy.

Inside the playroom the lightbulbs in cages had already been turned off. Daylight came in x-patterns through the caging at the windows. I looked out and, seeing no one in the schoolyard, ran outside to climb the fire escape upside down, hanging on to the metal stairs with fingers and toes.

I did a flip off the fire escape and ran across the school-yard. The day was a great eye, and it was not paying much attention to me now. I could disappear with the sun; I could turn quickly sideways and slip into a different world. It seemed I could run faster at this time, and by evening I would be able to fly. As the afternoon wore on we could run into the forbidden places—the boys' big yard, the boys' playroom. We could go into the boys' lavatory and look at the urinals. The only time during school hours I had crossed the boys' yard was when a flatbed truck with a giant thing covered with canvas and tied down with ropes had parked across the street. The children had told one another that it was a gorilla in captivity; we couldn't decide whether the sign said "Trail of the Gorilla" or "Trial of the Gorilla." The thing was as big as a house. The teachers couldn't stop us from hysterically rushing to the fence and clinging to the wire mesh. Now I ran across the boys' yard clear to the Cyclone fence and thought about the hair that I had seen sticking out of the canvas. It was going to be summer soon, so you could feel that freedom coming on too.

I ran back into the girls' yard, and there was the quiet sister all by herself. I ran past her, and she followed me into the girls' lavatory. My footsteps rang hard against cement and tile because of the taps I had nailed into my shoes. Her footsteps were soft, padding after me. There was no one in the lavatory but the two of us. I ran all around the rows of twenty-five open stalls to make sure of that. No sisters. I think we must have been playing hide-and-go-seek. She was not good at hiding by herself and usually followed her sister; they'd hide in the same place. They must have gotten separated. In this growing twilight, a child could hide and never be found.

I stopped abruptly in front of the sinks, and she came running toward me before she could stop herself, so that she almost collided with me. I walked closer. She backed away, puzzlement, then alarm in her eyes.

"You're going to talk," I said, my voice steady and normal, as it is talking to the familiar, the weak, and the small. "I am going to make you talk, you sissy-girl." She stopped backing away and stood fixed.

I looked into her face so I could hate it close up. She wore black bangs, and her cheeks were pink and white. She was baby soft. I thought that I could put my thumb on her nose and push it bonelessly in, indent her face. I could poke dimples into her cheeks. I could work her face around like dough. She stood still, and I did not want to look at her face anymore; I hated fragility. I walked around her, looked her up and down the way the Mexican and Negro girls did when they fought, so tough. I hated her weak neck, the way it did not support her head but let it droop; her head would fall backward. I stared at the curve of her nape. I wished I was able to see what my own neck looked like from the back and sides. I hoped it did not look like hers; I wanted a stout neck. I grew my hair long to hide it in case it was a flower-stem neck. I walked around to the front of her to hate her face some more.

I reached up and took the fatty part of her cheek, not dough, but meat, between my thumb and finger. This close, and I saw no pores. "Talk," I said. "Are you going to talk?" Her skin was fleshy, like squid out of which the glassy blades of bones had been pulled. I wanted tough skin, hard brown skin. I had callused my hands; I had scratched dirt to blacken the nails, which I cut straight across to make stubby fingers. I gave her face a squeeze. "Talk." When I let go, the pink rushed back into my white thumbprint on her skin. I walked around to her side. "Talk!" I shouted into the side of her head. Her straight hair hung, the same all these years, no ringlets or braids or permanents. I squeezed her other cheek. "Are you? Huh? Are you going to talk?" She tried to shake her head, but I had hold of her face. She had no muscles to jerk away. Her skin seemed to stretch. I let go in horror. What if it came away in my hand? "No, huh?" I said, rubbing the touch of her off my fingers. "Say 'No.' then," I said. I gave her another pinch and a twist. "Say 'No.'" She shook her head, her straight hair turning with her head, not swinging side to side like the pretty girls'. She was so neat. Her neatness bothered me. I hated the way she folded the wax paper from her lunch; she did not wad her brown paper bag and her school papers. I hated her clothes—the blue pastel cardigan, the white blouse with the collar that lay flat over the cardigan, the homemade flat, cotton skirt she wore when everybody else was wearing flared skirts. I hated pastels; I would wear black always. I squeezed again, harder, even though her cheek had a weak rubbery feeling I did not like. I squeezed one cheek, then the other, back and forth until the tears ran out of her eyes as if I had pulled

them out. "Stop crying," I said, but although she habitually followed me around, she did not obey. Her eyes dripped; her nose dripped. She wiped her eyes with her papery fingers. The skin on her hands and arms seemed powdery-dry, like tracing paper, onion skin. I hated her fingers. I could snap them like breadsticks. I pushed her hands down. "Say 'Hi,'" I said. "'Hi.' Like that. Say your name. Go ahead. Say it. Or are you stupid? You're so stupid, you don't know your own name, is that it? When I say, 'What's your name?' you just blurt it out, o.k.? What's your name?" Last year the whole class had laughed at a boy who couldn't fill out a form because he didn't know his father's name. The teacher sighed, exasperated, and was very sarcastic, "Don't you notice things? What does your mother call him?" she said. The class laughed at how dumb he was not to notice things. "She calls him father of me," he said. Even we laughed, although we knew that his mother did not call his father by name, and a son does not know his father's name. We laughed and were relieved that our parents had had the foresight to tell us some names we could give the teachers. "If you're not stupid," I said to the quiet girl, "what's your name?" She shook her head, and some hair caught in the tears; wet black hair stuck to the side of the pink and white face. I reached up (she was taller than I) and took a strand of hair. I pulled it. "Well, then, let's honk your hair," I said. "Honk. Honk." Then I pulled the other side—"ho-o-n-nk"—a long pull; "ho-o-n-n-nk"—a longer pull. I could see her little white ears, like white cutworms curled underneath the hair. "Talk!" I yelled into each cutworm.

I looked right at her. "I know you talk," I said. "I've heard you." Her eyebrows flew up. Something in those black eyes was startled, and I pursued it. "I was walking past your house when you didn't know I was there. I heard you yell in English and in Chinese. You weren't just talking. You were shouting. I heard you shout. You were saying, 'Where are you?' Say that again. Go ahead, just the way you did at home." I yanked harder on the hair, but steadily, not jerking. I did not want to pull it out. "Go ahead. Say, 'Where are you?' Say it loud enough for your sister to come. Call her. Make her come help you. Call her name. I'll stop if she comes. So call. Go ahead."

She shook her head, her mouth curved down, crying. I could see her tiny white teeth, baby teeth. I wanted to grow big strong yellow teeth. "You do have a tongue," I said. "So use it." I pulled the hair at her temples, pulled the tears out of her eyes. "Say, 'Ow,'" I said. "Just 'Ow.' Say, 'Let go.' Go ahead. Say it. I'll honk you again if you don't say, 'Let me alone.' Say, 'Leave me alone,' and I'll let you go. I will. I'll let go if you say it. You can stop this anytime you want to, you know. All you have to do is tell me to stop. Just say, 'Stop.' You're just asking for it, aren't you? You're just asking for another honk. Well then, I'll have to give you another honk. Say, 'Stop.'" But she didn't. I had to pull again and again.

Sounds did come out of her mouth, sobs, chokes, noises that were almost words. Snot ran out of her nose. She tried to wipe it on her hands, but there was too much of it. She used her sleeve. "You're disgusting," I told her. "Look at you, snot streaming down your nose, and you won't say a word to stop it. You're such a nothing." I moved behind her and pulled the hair growing out of her weak neck. I let go. I stood silent for a long time. Then I screamed, "Talk!" I would scare the words out of her. If she had had little bound feet, the toes twisted under the balls, I would have jumped up and landed on them—crunch!—stomped on them with my iron shoes. She cried hard, sobbing aloud. "Cry, 'Mama,'" I said. "Come on. Cry, 'Mama.' Say, 'Stop it.'"

I put my finger on her pointed chin. "I don't like you. I don't like the weak little toots you make on your flute. Wheeze. Wheeze. I don't like the way you don't swing at the ball. I don't like the way you're the last one chosen. I don't like the way you can't make a fist for tetherball. Why don't you make a fist? Come on. Get tough. Come on. Throw fists." I pushed at her long hands; they swung limply at her sides. Her fingers were so long, I thought maybe they had an extra joint. They couldn't possibly make fists like other people's. "Make a fist," I said. "Come on. Just fold those fingers up; fingers on the inside, thumbs on the outside. Say something. Honk me back. You're so tall, and you let me pick on you."

"Would you like a hanky? I can't get you one with embroidery on it or crocheting along the edges, but I'll get you some toilet paper if you tell me to. Go ahead. Ask me. I'll get it for you if you ask." She did not stop crying. "Why don't you scream, 'Help'?" I suggested. "Say, 'Help.' Go ahead." She cried on. "O.K. O.K. Don't talk. Just scream, and I'll let you go. Won't that feel good? Go ahead. Like this." I screamed, not too loudly. My voice hit the tile and rang it as if I had thrown a rock at it. The stalls opened wider and the toilets wider and darker. Shadows leaned at angles I had not seen before. It was very late. Maybe a janitor

had locked me in with this girl for the night. Her black eyes blinked and stared, blinked and stared. I felt dizzy from hunger. We had been in this lavatory together forever. My mother would call the police again if I didn't bring my sister home soon. "I'll let you go if you say just one word," I said. "You can even say, 'a' or 'the,' and I'll let you go. Come on. Please." She didn't shake her head anymore, only cried steadily, so much water coming out of her. I could see the two duct holes where the tears welled out. Quarts of tears but no words. I grabbed her by the shoulder. I could feel bones. The light was coming in queerly through the frosted glass with the chicken wire embedded in it. Her crying was like an animal's—a seal's—and it echoed around the basement. "Do you want to stay here all night?" I asked. "Your mother is wondering what happened to her baby. You wouldn't want to have her mad at you. You'd better say something." I shook her shoulder. I pulled her hair again. I squeezed her face. "Come on! Talk! Talk! Talk!" She didn't seem to feel it anymore when I pulled her hair. "There's nobody here but you and me. This isn't a classroom or a playground or a crowd. I'm just one person. You can talk in front of one person. Don't make me pull harder and harder until you talk." But her hair seemed to stretch; she did not say a word. "I'm going to pull harder. Don't make me pull anymore, or your hair will come out and you're going to be bald. Do you want to be bald? You don't want to be bald, do you?"

Far away, coming from the edge of town, I heard whistles blow. The cannery was changing shifts, letting out the afternoon people, and still we were here at school. It was a sad sound—work done. The air was lonelier after the sound died.

"Why won't you talk?" I started to cry. What if I couldn't stop, and everyone would want to know what happened? "Now look what you've done," I scolded. "You're going to pay for this. I want to know why. And you're going to tell me why. You don't see I'm trying to help you out, do you? Do you want to be like this, dumb (do you know what dumb means?), your whole life? Don't you ever want to be a cheerleader①? Or a pompon girl②? What are you going to do for a living? Yeah, you're going to have to work because you can't be a housewife. Somebody has to marry you before you can be a housewife. And you, you are a plant. Do you know that? That's all you are if you don't talk. If you don't talk, you can't have a personality. You'll have no personality and no hair. You've got

---

① cheerleader：(体育比赛时的)啦啦队队长。
② pompon girl：擅长交际的女孩。

to let people know you have a personality and a brain. You think somebody is going to take care of you all your stupid life? You think you'll always have your big sister? You think somebody's going to marry you, is that it? Well, you're not the type that gets dates, let alone gets married. Nobody's going to notice you. And you have to talk for interviews, speak right up in front of the boss. Don't you know that? You're so dumb. Why do I waste my time on you?" Sniffling and snorting, I couldn't stop crying and talking at the same time. I kept wiping my nose on my arm, my sweater lost somewhere (probably not worn because my mother said to wear a sweater). It seemed as if I had spent my life in that basement, doing the worst thing I had yet done to another person. "I'm doing this for your own good," I said. "Don't you dare tell anyone I've been bad to you. Talk. Please talk."

I was getting dizzy from the air I was gulping. Her sobs and my sobs were bouncing wildly off the tile, sometimes together, sometimes alternating. "I don't understand why you won't say just one word," I cried, clenching my teeth. My knees were shaking, and I hung on to her hair to stand up. Another time I'd stayed too late, I had had to walk around two Negro kids who were bonking each other's head on the concrete. I went back later to see if the concrete had cracks in it. "Look. I'll give you something if you talk. I'll give you my pencil box. I'll buy you some candy. O.K.? What do you want? Tell me. Just say it, and I'll give it to you. Just say, 'yes,' or, 'O.K.,' or, 'Baby Ruth.'" But she didn't want anything.

I had stopped pinching her cheek because I did not like the feel of her skin. I would go crazy if it came away in my hands. "I skinned her," I would have to confess.

Suddenly I heard footsteps hurrying through the basement, and her sister ran into the lavatory calling her name. "Oh, there you are," I said. "We've been waiting for you. I was only trying to teach her to talk. She wouldn't cooperate, though." Her sister went into one of the stalls and got handfuls of toilet paper and wiped her off. Then we found my sister, and we walked home together. "Your family really ought to force her to speak," I advised all the way home. "You mustn't pamper her."

The world is sometimes just, and I spent the next eighteen months sick in bed with a mysterious illness. There was no pain and no symptoms, though the middle line in my left palm broke in two. Instead of starting junior high school, I lived like the Victorian recluses I read about. I had a rented hospital bed in the living room, where I watched soap operas on t.v., and my family cranked me up and down. I saw no one but my family, who took good care of me. I could have no visitors, no other relatives, no villagers. My bed was against the west window, and I watched the seasons change the peach tree. I had a bell to ring for help. I used a bedpan. It was the best year and a half of my life. Nothing happened.

But one day my mother, the doctor, said, "You're ready to get up today. It's time to get up and go to school." I walked about outside to get my legs working, leaning on a staff I cut from the peach tree. The sky and trees, the sun were immense —no longer framed by a window, no longer grayed with a fly screen. I sat down on the sidewalk in amazement—the night, the stars. But at school I had to figure out again how to talk. I met again the poor girl I had tormented. She had not changed. She wore the same clothes, hair cut, and manner as when we were in elementary school, no make-up on the pink and white face, while the other Asian girls were starting to tape their eyelids. She continued to be able to read aloud. But there was hardly any reading aloud anymore, less and less as we got into high school.

I was wrong about nobody taking care of her. Her sister became a clerk-typist and stayed unmarried. They lived with their mother and father. She did not have to leave the house except to go to the movies. She was supported. She was protected by her family, as they would normally have done in China if they could have afforded it, not sent off to school with strangers, ghosts, boys.

We have so many secrets to hold in. Our sixth grade teacher, who liked to explain things to children, let us read our files. My record shows that I flunked kindergarten and in first grade had no IQ—a zero IQ[①]. I did remember the first grade teacher calling out during a test, while students marked X's on a girl or a boy or a dog, which I covered with black. First grade was when I discovered eye control; with my seeing I could shrink the teacher down to a height of one inch, gesticulating and mouthing on the horizon. I lost this power in sixth grade for lack of practice, the teacher a generous man. "Look at your family's old addresses and think about how you've moved," he said. I looked at my parents' aliases and their birthdays, which variants I knew. But when I saw Father's occupations I exclaimed, "Hey, he wasn't a farmer, he was a ..." He had been a gambler. My throat cut off the word—silence in front of the most understanding teacher. There

---

① IQ: intelligence quotient。

were secrets never to be said in front of the ghosts, immigration secrets whose telling could get us sent back to China.

...

作品赏析

《女勇士》是一部回忆录式的成长小说。全书分五个部分："无名女人"、"白虎山峰"、"巫医"、"西宫门外"、"羌笛之歌"。每个部分都有一位女主角，都与叙述者的成长有关。在前三部分中，叙述者"我"记述了儿时从妈妈那里听到的几个故事：在中国老家，她的姑姑因为"私通"，分娩的当天被村里人抄了家，抱着婴儿跳进家中的水井，从此，她的名字成为家族中的忌讳；作者想象自己成为故事中的花木兰，进白虎山修炼15年，然后带兵打仗报了国仇家恨，回到故乡成了英雄；母亲英兰年轻时是一个勇敢而独立的女性，她在旧中国有过学医和行医的经历，而且还有过捉鬼和招魂的大胆之举。第四、第五部分是叙述者本人的讲述。第四部分讲的是英兰得知妹妹月兰的丈夫在美国又结了婚，便把在香港的月兰"偷渡"到美国讨回她的权利；但软弱的月兰没有胆量面对丈夫，也不能适应美国的生活环境，最后病死在疯人院。第五部分，追述了叙述者童年的生活经历。叙述者的童年是在压抑和困惑中度过的。不过，她现在终于打破了沉默，像在异国他乡生活13年的女诗人蔡琰那样，用文学形式表达了自己的心声。全书以蔡琰的故事结尾，寓意深长。

该作品以"讲故事"的形式，通过充满想象力的虚构与简洁的白描，集中表现一个生活在美国唐人街华人圈中的小女孩在两种相互矛盾的文化影响下，从内心混乱、不知所措到怀疑和反抗，再到寻求自我和定位的成长过程，反映了华裔美国人在东西文化冲突中的困境和痛苦，以及在双重文化背景下努力构建新的自我与文化认同的艰难历程。该作品侧重描写了女性在权力不平等社会中的失落和挣扎、沉默和反抗，抒发了她对旧中国男权压迫的愤恨。该小说具有较强的可读性和艺术性。题材涉及文化冲突、移民处境、女性经验、母女关系、个人成长与历史叙述等诸多方面，可从不同角度阅读它。作者打破了传说与现实、虚构与历史的界限，将多种风格相结合，采用多元的叙述视角，灵活转换的时空，使作品充满了传奇色彩和异国情调。其创作思想、主题和手法对其他华裔作家产生了重要的影响。

需要指出的是，《女勇士》是一本主要面向西方读者的书。作为一个在美国文化氛围中长大的华裔，汤婷婷对中国文化有着与我们不同的视角，而且也难免受到美国主流文化认知范式的影响。汤亭亭在一次采访中强调了其美国属性。她说："实际上，我作品中的美国味儿要比中国味儿多得多。我觉得不论是写我自己还是写其他华人，我都是在写美国人。……虽然我写的人物有着让人感到陌生的中国记忆，但他们是美国人。再说我的创作是美国文学的一部分……评论家们还不了解我的文学创作其实是美国文学的另一个传统。"对于指责她歪曲中国神话的批评，她说："把神话带到大洋彼岸的人成了美国人，同样，神话也成了美国神话。我写的神话是新的、美

国的神话。"的确,她笔下的花木兰、关公等已不是中国传统文化中的人物形象了,而是有独特个性的华裔美国版的人物形象。

思考题

1. What do you think about the image of the barbarian used in the narrative?
2. Are there any similarities and differences between the narrator and the character, Ts'ai Yen?
3. Why does Kingston describe the Chinese children as silent at the American school but loud at the Chinese school?
4. What is the importance of the figure of the silent character in the narrative? Can you relate this figure to the dual themes of keeping silence and breaking silence?
5. In what ways does the young narrator attempt to reconcile Chinese and American cultural pressures within her developing sense of personal identity?

推荐作品

China Men (1980)
Tripmaster Monkey: His Fake Book (1989)
The Fifth Book of Peace (2003)

参考资料

Bruccoli, Matthew J. and Layman Richard, eds. *The Woman Warrior and China Men*. Farmington Hills: The Gale Group, 2001.

Lim, Shirley Geok-lin, ed. *Approaches to Teaching Kingston's The Woman Warrior*. New York: Modern Language Association of America, 1991.

Wong, Sau-ling Cynthia, ed. *Maxine Hong Kingston's The Woman Warrior: A Casebook*. New York and Oxford: Oxford UP, 1999.

第十六单元
Leslie Marmon Silko
(1948—)

莱丝莉·摩门·西尔柯

作者简介

莱丝莉·摩门·西尔柯，美国印第安女作家，出生于新墨西哥北部拉古那地区一个印第安部落的保留地，具有白人、墨西哥人、印第安人的混合血统。1969年毕业于新墨西哥大学英语系并开始攻读法学，1971年"弃法从文"，开始写作生涯。1977年，第一部长篇小说《仪式》(Ceremony)出版，获得评论界的高度评价，被公认为美国当代最优秀的小说之一。作品将诗歌和叙事相结合，描写一个混血的土著印第安人在经历第二次世界大战的恐惧和绝望后返回保留地、在寻觅印第安历史和传统的过程中获得新生。该作品是迄今已发现的由美国土著女作家发表的第一部小说。1981年，短篇小说和诗歌集《讲故事的人》(Storyteller)的出版进一步奠定了西尔柯在美国文学史上的重要地位。该作品将自传、历史、神话、摄影与诗歌和小说融合为一体，突出表现了作者对各种文学体裁的大胆探索和实验。其他主要作品包括诗歌集《拉古那地区的女人》(Laguna Pueblo Woman, 1974)，短篇小说集《西部故事》(Western Stories, 1980)，书信集《蕾丝的纤巧和力量》(Delicacy and Strength of Lace, 1985)，叙事和摄影作品集《圣水》(Sacred Water: Narratives and Pictures, 1993)，《雨》(Rain, 1996)，散文集《黄女》(Yellow Woman and a Beauty of the Spirit, 1996)以及长篇小说《死者的历书》(Almanac of the Dead: A Novel, 1991)，《沙丘里的庭院》(Gardens in the Dunes, 1999)等。其中，《死者的历书》尤其值得注意。这是一部历经10年完成的巨著，揭示了几百年以来美洲殖民主义所造成的各种后果，具有很强的批判性。

作家成功地将西方小说传统与美国印第安口头文学传统结合在一起，再现了当代印第安人生活的方方面面：保护民族传统的重要性、语言和文学在民族文化遗产中的重要地位、人与土地的密切联系、民族权益及文化归属、印第安人遭受贫困与不公的生活现状及其顽强的生存精神、不同文化的相互影响和相互融合等，对当代美国文坛产生了很大影响。她因此获得多项文学奖（其中包括美国土著作家终身成就奖），并荣获"活的文化遗产"称号。

Lullaby

The sun had gone down but the snow in the wind gave off its own light. It came in thick tufts like new wool—washed before the weaver spins it. Ayah reached out for it like her own babies had, and she smiled when she remembered how she had laughed at them. She was an old woman now, and her life had become memories. She sat down with her back against the wide cottonwood tree, feeling the rough bark on her back bones; she faced east and listened to the wind and snow sing a high-pitched Yeibechei① song. Out of the wind she felt warmer, and she could watch the wide fluffy snow fill in her tracks, steadily, until the direction she had come form was gone. By the light of the snow she could see the dark outline of the big arroyo a few feet away. She was sitting on the edge of Cebolleta Creek, where in the springtime the thin cows would graze on grass already chewed flat to the ground. In the wide deep creek bed where only a trickle of water flowed in the summer, the skinny cows would wander, looking for new grass along winding paths splashed with manure.

Ayah pulled the old Army blanket over her head like a shawl. Jimmie's blanket—the one he had sent to her. That was a long time ago and the green wool was faded, and it was unraveling on the edges. She did not want to think about Jimmie. So she thought about the weaving and the way her mother had done it. On the tall wooden loom set into the sand under a tamarack② tree for shade. She could see it clearly. She had been only a little girl when her grandma gave her the wooden combs to pull the twigs and burrs from the raw, freshly washed wool. And while she combed the wool, her grandma sat beside her, spinning a silvery strand of yarn around the smooth cedar spindle. Her mother worked at the loom with yarns dyed bright yellow and red and gold. She watched them dye the yarn in boiling black pots full of beeweed petals, juniper berries, and sage. The blankets her mother made were soft and woven so tight that rain rolled off them like birds' feathers. Ayah remembered sleeping warm on cold windy nights, wrapped in her

---

① Yeibechei：印第安纳瓦霍人用于驱除病魔的一首夜曲。
② tamarack：美洲落叶松。

mother's blankets on the hogan's① sandy floor.

The snow drifted now, with the northwest wind hurling it in gusts. It drifted up around her black overshoes—old ones with little metal buckles②. She smiled at the snow which was trying to cover her little by little. She could remember when they had no black rubber overshoes; only the high buckskin leggings③ that they wrapped over their elkhide moccasins④. If the show was dry or frozen, a person could walk all day and not get wet; and in the evenings the beams of the ceiling would hang with lengths of pale buckskin leggings, drying out slowly.

She felt peaceful remembering. She didn't feel cold any more. Jimmie's blanket seemed warmer than it had ever been. And she could remember the morning he was born. She could remember whispering to her mother, who was sleeping on the other side of the hogan, to tell her it was time now. She did not want to wake the others. The second time she called to her, her mother stood up and pulled on her shoes; she knew. They walked to the old stone hogan together, Ayah walking a step behind her mother. She waited alone, learning the rhythms of the pains while her mother went to call the old woman to help them. The morning was already warm even before dawn and Ayah smelled the bee flowers blooming and the young willow growing at the springs. She could remember that so clearly, but his birth merged into the births of the other children and to her it became all the same birth. They named him for the summer morning and in English they called him Jimmie.

It wasn't like Jimmie died. He just never came back, and one day a dark blue sedan with white writing on its doors pulled up in front of the boxcar shack where the rancher let the Indians live. A man in a khaki uniform trimmed in gold gave them a yellow piece of paper and told them that Jimmie was dead. He said the Army would try to get the body back and then it would be shipped to them; but it wasn't likely because the helicopter had burned after it crashed. All of this was told to Chato because he could understand English. She stood inside the doorway holding the baby while Chato listened. Chato spoke English like a white man and he spoke Spanish too. He was taller than the white man and he stood straighter too. Chato didn't explain why; he just told the military man they could

---

① hogan:北美西南部印第安人(尤其是纳瓦霍族人)用圆木垒成上覆泥土的六边形泥屋,户门朝东。
② buckle:鞋上的扣形饰物。
③ buckskin leggings:用鹿皮做成的绑腿。
④ elkhide moccasins:北美印第安人穿的用鹿皮制的无后跟软底鞋。

keep the body if they found it. The white man looked bewildered; he nodded his head and he left. Then Chato looked at her and shook his head, and then he told her, "Jimmie isn't coming home anymore," and when he spoke, he used the words to speak of the dead. She didn't cry then, but she hurt inside with anger. And she mourned him as the years passed, when a horse fell with Chato and broke his leg, and the white rancher told them he wouldn't pay Chato until he could work again. She mourned Jimmie because he would have worked for his father then; he would have saddled the big bay horse and ridden the fence lines each day, with wire cutters and heavy gloves, fixing the breaks in the barbed wire and putting the stray cattle back inside again.

She mourned him after the white doctors came to take Danny and Ella away. She was at the shack alone that day they came. It was back in the days before they hired Navajo women to go with them as interpreters. She recognized one of the doctors. She had seen him at the children's clinic at Cañoncito about a month ago. They were wearing khaki uniforms and they waved papers at her and a black ball-point pen, trying to make her understand their English words. She was frightened by the way they looked at the children, like the lizard watches the fly. Danny was swinging on the tire swing on the elm tree behind the rancher's house, and Ella was toddling around the front door, dragging the broomstick horse Chato made for her. Ayah could see they wanted her to sign the papers, and Chato had taught her to sign her name. It was something she was proud of. She only wanted them to go, and to take their eyes away from her children.

She took the pen from the man without looking at his face and she signed the papers in three different places he pointed to. She stared at the ground by their feet and waited for them to leave. But they stood there and began to point and gesture at the children. Danny stopped swinging. Ayah could see his fear. She moved suddenly and grabbed Ella into her arms; the child squirmed, trying to get back to her toys. Ayah ran with the baby toward Danny; she screamed for him to run and then she grabbed him around his chest and carried him too. She ran south into the foothills of juniper trees and black lava rock. Behind her she heard the doctors running, but they had been taken by surprise, and as the hills became steeper and the cholla cactus① were thicker; they stopped. When she reached the top of the hill, she stopped to listen in case they were circling around her. But in a

---

① cholla cactus: 仙人掌。

few minutes she heard a car engine start and they drove away. The children had been too surprised to cry while she ran with them. Danny was shaking and Ella's little fingers were gripping Ayah's blouse.

She stayed up in the hills for the rest of the day, sitting on a black lava boulder in the sunshine where she could see for miles all around her. The sky was light blue and cloudless, and it was warm for late April. The sun warmth relaxed her and took the fear and anger away. She lay back on the rock and watched the sky. It seemed to her that she could walk into the sky, stepping through clouds endlessly. Danny played with little pebbles and stones, pretending they were birds eggs and then little rabbits. Ella sat at her feet and dropped fistfuls of dirt into the breeze, watching the dust and particles of sand intently. Ayah watched a hawk soar high above them, dark wings gliding; hunting or only watching, she did not know. The hawk was patient and he circled all afternoon before he disappeared around the high volcanic peak the Mexicans called Guadalupe.

Late in the afternoon, Ayah looked down at the gray boxcar shack with the paint all peeled from the wood; the stove pipe on the roof was rusted and crooked. The fire she had built that morning in the oil drum stove had burned out. Ella was asleep in her lap now and Danny sat close to her, complaining that he was hungry; he asked when they would go to the house. "We will stay up here until your father comes," she told him, "because those white men were chasing us." The boy remembered then and he nodded at her silently.

If Jimmie had been there he could have read those papers and explained to her what they said. Ayah would have known then, never to sign them. The doctors came back the next day and they brought a BIA[①] policeman with them. They told Chato they had her signature and that was all they needed. Except for the kids. She listened to Chato sullenly; she hated him when he told her it was the old woman who died in the winter, spitting blood; it was her old grandma who had given the children this disease. "They don't spit blood," she said coldly. "The whites lie." She held Ella and Danny close to her, ready to run to the hills again. "I want a medicine man first," she said to Chato, not looking at him. He shook his head. "It's too late now. The policeman is with them. You signed the paper." His voice was gentle.

It was worse than if they had died: to lose the children and to know that

---

① BIA: U. S. Bureau of Indian Affairs: 美国印第安人事务局。

somewhere, in a place called Colorado, in a place full of sick and dying strangers, her children were without her. There had been babies that died soon after they were born, and one that died before he could walk. She had carried them herself, up to the boulders and great pieces of the cliff that long ago crashed down from Long Mesa; she laid them in the crevices of sandstone and buried them in fine brown sand with round quartz pebbles that washed down the hills in the rain. She had endured it because they had been with her. But she could not bear this pain. She did not sleep for a long time after they took her children. She stayed on the hill where they had fled the first time, and she slept rolled up in the blanket Jimmie had sent her. She carried the pain in her belly and it was fed by everything she saw: the blue sky of their last day together and the dust and pebbles they played with; the swing in the elm tree and broomstick horse choked life from her. The pain filled her stomach and there was no room for food or for her lungs to fill with air. The air and the food would have been theirs.

She hated Chato, not because he let the policeman and doctors put the screaming children in the government car, but because he had taught her to sign her name. Because it was like the old ones always told her about learning their language or any of their ways: it endangered you. She slept alone on the hill until the middle of November when the first snows came. Then she made a bed for herself where the children had slept. She did not lie down beside Chato again until many years later, when he was sick and shivering and only her body could keep him warm. The illness came after the white rancher told Chato he was too old to work for him anymore, and Chato and his old woman should be out of the shack by the next afternoon because the rancher had hired new people to work there. That had satisfied her. To see how the white man repaid Chato's years of loyalty and work. All of Chato's fine-sounding English talk didn't change things.

It snowed steadily and the luminous light from the snow gradually diminished into the darkness. Somewhere in Cebolleta a dog barked and other village dogs joined with it. Ayah looked in the direction she had come, from the bar where Chato was buying the wine. Sometimes he told her to go on ahead and wait; and then he never came. And when she finally went back looking for him, she would find him passed out at the bottom of the wooden steps to Azzie's Bar. All the wine would be gone and most of the money too, from the pale blue check that came to them once a month in a government envelope. It was then that she would look at his face and his hands, scarred by ropes and the barbed wire of all those years, and she would think, this man is a stranger; for forty years she had smiled at him and cooked his food, but he remained a stranger. She stood up again, with the snow almost to her knees, and she walked back to find Chato.

It was hard to walk in the deep snow and she felt the air burn in her lungs. She stopped a short distance from the bar to rest and readjust the blanket. But this time he wasn't waiting for her on the bottom step with his old Stetson hat pulled down and his shoulders hunched up in his long wool overcoat.

She was careful not to slip on the wooden steps. When she pushed the door open, warm air and cigarette smoke hit her face. She looked around slowly and deliberately, in every corner, in every dark place that the old man might find to sleep. The bar owner didn't like Indians in there, especially Navajos, but he let Chato come in because he could talk Spanish like he was one of them. The men at the bar stared at her, and the bartender saw that she left the door open wide. Snowflakes were flying inside like moths and melting into a puddle on the oiled wood floor. He motioned to her to close the door, but she did not see him. She held herself straight and walked across the room slowly, searching the room with every step. The snow in her hair melted and she could feel it on her forehead. At the far corner of the room, she saw red flames at the mica window of the old stove door; she looked behind the stove just to make sure. The bar got quiet except for the Spanish polka music playing on the jukebox. She stood by the stove and shook the snow from her blanket and held it near the stove to dry. The wet wool smell reminded her of new-born goats in early March, brought inside to warm near the fire. She felt calm.

In past years they would have told her to get out. But her hair was white now and her face was wrinkled. They looked at her like she was a spider crawling slowly across the room. They were afraid; she could feel the fear. She looked at their faces steadily. They reminded her of the first time the white people brought her children back to her that winter. Danny had been shy and hid behind the thin white woman who brought them. And the baby had not known her until Ayah took her into her arms, and then Ella had nuzzled close to her as she had when she was nursing. The blonde woman was nervous and kept looking at a dainty gold watch on her wrist. She sat on the bench near the small window and watched the dark snow clouds gather around the mountains; she was worrying about the unpaved road. She was frightened by what she saw inside too: the strips of venison drying on a rope across the ceiling and the children jabbering excitedly in a language she did not know. So they stayed for only a few hours. Ayah watched the government car disappear down the road and she knew they were already being weaned from these lava hills and from this sky. The last time they came was in early June, and Ella stared at her the way the men in the bar were now staring. Ayah did not try to pick her up; she smiled at her instead and spoke cheerfully to Danny. When he tried to answer her, he could not seem to remember and he spoke English words with the Navajo①. But he gave her a scrap of paper that he had found somewhere and carried in his pocket; it was folded in half, and he shyly looked up at her and said it was a bird. She asked Chato if they were home for good this time. He spoke to the white woman and she shook her head. "How much longer?" he asked, and she said she didn't know; but Chato saw how she stared at the boxcar shack. Ayah turned away then. She did not say good-bye.

She felt satisfied that the men in the bar feared her. Maybe it was her face and the way she held her mouth with teeth clenched tight, like there was nothing anyone could do to her now. She walked north down the road, searching for the old man. She did this because she had the blanket, and there would be no place for him except with her and the blanket in the old adobe barn near the arroyo. They always slept there when they came to Cebolleta. If the money and the wine were gone, she would be relieved because then they could go home again; back to the old hogan with a dirt roof and rock walls where she herself had been born. And the next day the old man could go back to the few sheep they still had, to follow along behind them, guiding them, into dry sandy arroyos where sparse grass grew. She knew he did not like walking behind old ewes when for so many years he rode big quarter horses② and worked with cattle. But she wasn't sorry for him; he should have known all along what would happen.

There had not been enough rain for their garden in five years; and that was when Chato finally hitched a ride into the town and brought back brown boxes of rice and sugar and big tin cans of welfare peaches. After that, at the first of the month they went to Cebolleta to ask the postmaster for the check; and then Chato would go to the bar and cash it. They did this as they planted the garden every May, not because anything would survive the summer dust, but because it was time to do this. The journey passed the days that smelled silent and dry like the

---

① Navajo：纳瓦霍人，美国最大的印第安部落。现散居在美国新墨西哥州、亚利桑那州、犹他州。
② quarter horse：夸特马，善于短距离冲刺，原用于1/4英里比赛。

caves above the canyon with yellow painted buffaloes on their walls.

  He was walking along the pavement when she found him. He did not stop or turn around when he heard her behind him. She walked beside him and she noticed how slowly he moved now. He smelled strong of woodsmoke and urine. Lately he had been forgetting. Sometimes he called her by his sister's name and she had been gone for a long time. Once she had found him wandering on the road to the white man's ranch, and she asked him why he was going that way; he laughed at her and said, "You know they can't run that ranch without me," and he walked on determined, limping on the leg that had been crushed many years before. Now he looked at her curiously, as if for the first time, but he kept shuffling along, moving slowly along the side of the highway. His gray hair had grown long and spread out on the shoulders of the long overcoat. He wore the old felt hat pulled down over his ears. His boots were worn out at the toes and he had stuffed pieces of an old red shirt in the holes. The rags made his feet look like little animals up to their ears in snow. She laughed at his feet; the snow muffled the sound of her laugh. He stopped and looked at her again. The wind had quit blowing and the snow was falling straight down; the southeast sky was beginning to clear and Ayah could see a star.

  "Let's rest awhile," she said to him. They walked away from the road and up the slope to the giant boulders that had tumbled down from the red sandrock mesa throughout the centuries of rainstorms and earth tremors. In a place where the boulders shut out the wind, they sat down with their backs against the rock. She offered half of the blanket to him and they sat wrapped together.

  The storm passed swiftly. The clouds moved east. They were massive and full, crowding together across the sky. She watched them with the feeling of horses—steely blue-gray horses startled across the sky. The powerful haunches pushed into the distances and the tail hairs streamed white mist behind them. The sky cleared. Ayah saw that there was nothing between her and the stars. The light was crystalline. There was no shimmer, no distortion through earth haze. She breathed the clarity of the night sky; she smelled the purity of the half moon and the stars. He was lying on his side with his knees pulled up near his belly for warmth. His eyes were closed now, and in the light from the stars and the moon, he looked young again.

  She could see it descend out of the night sky: an icy stillness from the edge of the thin moon. She recognized the freezing. It came gradually, sinking snowflake by snowflake until the crust was heavy and deep. It had the strength of the stars in Orion, and its journey was endless. Ayah knew that with the wine he would sleep. He would not feel it. She tucked the blanket around him, remembering how it was when Ella had been with her; and she felt the rush so big inside her heart for the babies. And she sang the only song she knew to sing for babies. She could not remember if she had ever sung it to her children, but she knew that her grandmother had sung it and her mother had sung it:

> The earth is your mother,
>   she holds you.
> The sky is your father,
>   he protects you.
> Sleep,
> sleep.
> Rainbow is your sister,
>   she loves you.
> The winds are your brothers,
>   they sing to you.
> Sleep,
> Sleep.
> We are together always
> We are together always
> There never was a time
> when this
> was not so.

《摇篮曲》是西尔柯短篇小说集《讲故事的人》中的一个名篇，1974年发表于《芝加哥书评》并获奖，1975年被选入《美国最佳短篇小说选》。故事发生一个冬天的晚上，一个叫阿雅的印第安老妇人一边到酒吧去寻找丈夫，一边回忆自己一生的经历：大儿子在为政府军队服役时死了，剩下的两个未成年孩子也被白人带走了——虽然他们后来回来看过她两次，但他们和她越来越疏远。失去孩子后，丈夫又被白人农场主榨干油水后解雇。失业后的丈夫变得颓废绝望，经常用酒精来麻痹自己。他们现在又老又穷，靠政府一点可怜的救济生活。失去两个孩子使她对白人的态度由害怕变成了愤怒，也使她对丈夫产生怨恨和隔膜，因为是他教她用英文签名，使她在白人的欺骗下签了让白人带走孩子的文件。当阿雅回忆一生的不幸遭遇时，让她悲伤的不仅是因为她失去了自己的孩子,而且还因为她的民族正在失去自己的传统和语言。不过,她的回忆并不都是痛苦的。她在回忆往事时,也会想起自己儿时与祖母和母亲的亲密关系,想起当年祖母和母亲编织毯子的美好时光,这一甜蜜回忆给予她极大的慰藉和力量。像西尔柯笔下的许多女性人物一样,阿雅坚强而沉着,具有大地母亲一般的胸怀。她后来宽恕了丈夫并陪伴他走完人生的最后路程。故事以一首摇篮曲结束,表达了她对孩子的思念、对祖母和母亲的怀念,也反映了印第安文化对人与大自然和谐关系的强调。作品采用第三人称叙述视角,故事情节主要由老妇人对往事的回忆和感受组成,再现了印第安人文化与白人文化的冲突、印第安人遭受歧视和压迫的历史,以及他们顽强生存的勇气和尊严,而这也是西尔柯创作中的一贯主题。作品语言通俗易懂,描写细致生动,体现了作家将传统和现代、叙事和诗歌融为一体的创作风格。

 思考题

1. Discuss the structure of "Lullaby". Is it linear or cyclic?
2. How does the story impress you?
3. What criticisms of the American society are implied in the story?
4. What Navajo cultural values are evident in the story?

 推荐作品

Ceremony (1977)

"Storyteller" (1981)

"Yellow Woman" (1996)

参考资料

Bernett, Louise K. and James L. Thorsen, eds. *Leslie Marmon Silko: A Collection of Critical Essays*. Albuquerque: U of New Mexico P, 1999.

Porter, Joy and Kenneth M. Roemer, eds. *The Cambridge Companion to Native American Literature*. Cambridge: Cambridge UP, 2005.

Salyer, Gregory. *Leslie Marmon Silko*. New York: Twayne Publishers, 1997.

第十七单元
Robert Penn Warren
(1905—1989)
罗伯特·潘·沃伦

作者简介

罗伯特·潘·沃伦出生于美国南方肯塔基州托德县的格思里市，1921年进入田纳西州的范德比尔特大学，在学期间师从约翰·克罗·兰塞姆(John Crowe Ransom)，与艾伦·泰特(Allen Tate)一起成为极力维护美国南方农业社会传统价值观的"逃亡者"诗派(Fugitives)的最年轻成员，后来又到加利福尼亚大学攻读研究生，此后相继在耶鲁大学、牛津大学深造，1930年在牛津取得文学博士学位。

沃伦在小说、诗歌、散文、文艺理论、教育乃至政治方面都做出了卓越的贡献，是美国历史上唯一获得过普利策诗歌和小说双奖项的作家：作为诗人，出版过16册诗集，在1986年成为首位美国"桂冠诗人"，凭借诗集《诺言：1954—1956年的诗歌》(*Promises, Poems 1954—1956*, 1957)和诗集《此时彼时：1976—1978年的诗歌》(*Now and Then: Poems, 1976—1978*, 1982)两次获得普利策诗歌奖；作为小说家，他出版了10部小说，其中最负盛名的《国王的人马》(*All the King's Men*, 1946)为他赢得了普利策小说奖。1935年，沃伦与克林斯·布鲁克斯(Cleanth Brooks)等人创办《南方评论》(*Southern Review*)杂志，成为现代美国最重要的文艺批评流派——"新批评"学派(New Critics)的代表人物之一。1938年，他与C.布鲁克斯合写《理解诗歌》(*Understanding Poetry*)一书，对美国学院里的诗歌研究产生了深远影响。上世纪80年代，沃伦曾多次获得诺贝尔文学奖提名。他被看成是福克纳之后美国南方文学中最优秀的代表人物。

在诗歌创作上，沃伦早期深受T.S.艾略特等现代派诗人和17世纪玄学派诗人的影响，注重古典主义诗歌传统的借鉴和诗歌创作技巧的创新实验。20世纪三四十年代，由于沃伦将大量的时间和精力投入了小说写作与文学评论之中，诗歌创作一度中断，继1944年发表《诗选：1923—1943》(*Selected Poems: 1923—1943*)后，直到1953年才推出下一部诗集《龙的兄弟》(*Brother to Dragon*，又译《与龙为伍》)，随后又有不下十二部诗集相继出版。布鲁姆于1998年为《罗伯特·潘·沃伦诗歌全集》(*The Collected Poems of Robert Penn Warren*)所作序言指出，从1922年到1966年，艾略特对沃伦的诗歌创作的影响在形式、风格和观点等方面都有深刻的体现，这在很大程度上约束了他的个性发挥。过渡性的诗集——《诺言》(1957)、《你，皇帝们，及其他：1957—1960的诗歌》(*You, Emperors, and Others: Poems 1957—1960*, 1960)，和《诗选：新诗和旧诗,1923—1966》(Selected Poems New and Old: 1923—1966, 1966)——仍然处于艾略特的影响之下。从《化身》(Incarnations, 1968)和随后的《奥都本：一个幻象》(Audubon: A Vision,1969)开始,沃伦的后期诗风有了明显的改变,以其刻意的艺术技巧形成了"硬朗的、如谜的、真实的"个性化新风格。总体看来,通过诗歌认识自我和世界,在自然主义的语境中寻求宇宙的意义,——这个理念贯穿沃伦诗歌创作的始终,激发了诗人的创作热情和灵感,构成其想象力的丰富源泉。

作　品

Evening Hawk

From plane of light to plane①, wings dipping through
Geometries and orchids that the sunset builds,
Out of the peak's black angularity② of shadow, riding
The last tumultuous avalanche③ of
Light above pines and the guttural gorge④,
The hawk comes.

　　　　His wing
Scythes⑤ down another day, his motion
Is that of the honed⑥ steel-edge, we hear
The crashless fall of stalks of Time⑦.

The head of each stalk is heavy with the gold of our error.

Look! Look! he is climbing the last light
Who knows neither Time nor error, and under
Whose eye, unforgiving, the world, unforgiven, swings

---

① plane：平面。
② angularity：角状，棱角分明。
③ tumultuous avalanche：喧嚣的雪崩。
④ guttural gorge：guttural，喉状的。这里指幽深的山谷。
⑤ scythe：用长柄大镰刀砍。
⑥ honed：用磨刀石磨得锋利的。
⑦ stalk：植物的茎秆。
⑧ 这里的 who, whose 从句都是用来修饰前面的代词 he,指山鹰。

Into shadow.⑧
　　　　　　Long now,
The last thrush is still, the last bat
Now cruises in his sharp hieroglyphics①. His wisdom
Is ancient, too, and immense. The star
Is steady, like Plato②, over the mountain.

If there were no wind we might, we think, hear
The earth grind on its axis, or history
Drip in darkness like a leaking pipe in the cellar.

作品赏析　　本诗开篇唤起了贯穿沃伦的诗歌创作始终、反复出现于不同诗作的山鹰意象。山鹰意象与落日相伴，乘风而上。本诗第一节勾勒出一个光与影层叠相映、动与静相得益彰的山林夕照图景：夕阳的光线交织出各种几何图形和兰花图案，映衬着暗影里山峰那黑黢黢的棱角。诗人将夕照的最后光线比喻成在松林和幽深山谷上方喧嚣而下的一阵雪崩，而山鹰正是乘着这道光柱，从暗影里冲出来，振翅向上穿过层叠的光影，呼啸着打破了画面的静止。山鹰的翅膀被比作收割时光的锋利镰刀，时间则被喻为植物的茎秆，在镰刀的挥动之间无声地倒下。

接下来是沃伦的经典名句：金色的麦穗沉甸甸地坠满我们曾经犯下的错误。对于世人来说，流逝的是时光，收获的却是错误。诗句中表达了山鹰超越时空的冷峻无情：山鹰循光而上，世界遁入暗影。这里，山鹰被作了拟人化处理：它既不懂得时光，也意识不到错误，从而就没有宽恕可言——它不会宽恕尘世的错误，并且弃未得到宽恕的尘世而去。

暮色渐浓，画眉早已不再作声，蝙蝠缓慢飞行，在空中画着轮廓分明的象形文字，似乎体现着一种古老而广袤的智慧。相应地，空中恒久不变的星辰被比作柏拉图，散发出哲人睿智的平和。最后三行诗句用听觉意象形象地表达了诗人的时空意识和焦虑感：地球围绕轴心转动，发出沉重的转动声；历史在黑暗中不断流逝，滴答作响。

如哈罗德·布鲁姆所指出，山鹰是沃伦诗歌里反复出现的一个重要意象。尽管评论家对此作出了不同的解读，从而极大地拓展了它的阐释空间，但是，该诗中的山鹰意象无疑代表着一种超越时空的自然力量，集中体现了诗人充满矛盾的宇宙观和世界观。

---

① cruise：巡游，缓慢悠然地飞行；hieroglyphics：象形文字。
② Plato：柏拉图(427—347BC)，古希腊哲学家。

思考题

1. Identify the images from the poem and explain how each acquires significance as the picture unfolds.
2. Analyze the symbolic meaning(s) of the dominant image—the evening hawk.
3. What kind of view(s) is conveyed in this poem with regard to history and the universe?

推荐作品

"Mortal Limit" (1985)

Understanding Poetry (1938) (与 Cleanth Brooks 合著)

All the King's Men (1946)

参考资料

Burt, J. *Selected Poems of Robert Penn Warren*. Baton Rouge: Louisiana State UP, 2001.

Blotner, J. L. *Robert Penn Warren: A Biography*. New York: Random House, 1997.

Nakadate, N., ed. *Robert Penn Warren: Critical Perspectives*. Lexington, KY.: UP of Kentucky, 1981.

John Ashbery
(1927—   )

约翰·阿什贝利

作者简介

约翰·阿什贝利,美国后现代诗歌代表人物之一。生于纽约州罗切斯特。1949年毕业于哈佛大学,1951年获哥伦比亚大学硕士学位,1953年出版第一部诗集《图兰朵及其他诗歌》(*Turandot and Other Poems*),1955年作为富布莱特访问学者赴法国,逗留期间为《先驱论坛报》和《艺术新闻》撰稿,1965年回到纽约,1974年起在大学任教。

阿什贝利与弗兰克·奥哈拉(Frank O'Hara)、肯尼思·柯克(Kenneth Koch)同为纽约派(New York Poets)核心人物。该派是一个以地域为基础的松散组合,其成员风格各有不同;总体来说,被归于超现实主义流派,通常以诗作中的大众意象、超现实主义思维方式和积极向上的幽默感著称。阿什贝利的诗歌被评论家称作"诗歌的诗歌",主题多是关于诗歌本身的;关注的焦点不是经验本身,而是经验渗透意识的方式,旨在揭示甚至颠覆意义建构的人为性。阿什贝利一度深受美国现代派诗人华莱士·史蒂文斯(Wallace Stevens, 1879—1955)诗风的影响,其诗歌充满了哲性思考。尽管作品经常取材于浪漫主义传统题材,其视角和处理手法却往往前卫,常常与抽象表现主义绘画有异曲同工之处。

阿什贝利既受实验派艺术家推崇,又能得到学院派批评家认可,这在现当代诗人中是不多见的。其诗集《凸面镜中的自画像》(*Self-Portrait in a Convex Mirror*, 1975)获得美国国家图书奖、普利策奖和全美批评界奖。著名批评家布鲁姆夸赞诗人"把包括惠特曼、迪金森、史蒂文斯、哈特·克兰的美国的严肃性连接起来,从而实现了爱默生对于美国文学自治的幻想的预言"(王家新等编:《二十世纪外国诗人如是说》,河南人民出版社,1992年,第559页)。以下诗歌选自另一部重要诗集《休闲日》(又译《船屋的日子》,*Houseboat Days*, 1977)。

第十七单元

And Ut Pictura Poesis① Is Her Name

You can't say it that way anymore.
Bothered about beauty you have to
Come out into the open, into a clearing②,
And rest. Certainly whatever funny happens to you
Is OK. To demand more than this would be strange
Of you, you who have so many lovers,
People who look up to you and are willing
To do things for you, but you think
It's not right, that if they really knew you...
So much for self-analysis③. Now,
About what to put in your poem-painting:
Flowers are always nice, particularly delphinium④.
Names of boys you once knew and their sleds,
Skyrockets⑤ are good—do they still exist?
There are a lot of other things of the same quality
As those I've mentioned. Now one must
Find a few important words, and a lot of low-keyed⑥,
Dull-sounding ones. She approached me
About buying her desk. Suddenly the street was
Bananas and the clangor⑦ of Japanese instruments.
Humdrum testaments⑧ were scattered around. His head
Locked into mine. We were a seesaw⑨. Something

---

① Ut Pictura Poesis：（拉）u.p.p., "as is painting so is poetry"（Horace, *Ars Poetica*）。公元前 1 世纪罗马著名诗人贺拉斯在《诗论》中提出的"诗歌绘画性"概念。
② clearing：空地，相当于前面的 open 一词。
③ self-analysis：自我分析，这里指的是诗中称呼的"你"，应为带给诗人创作灵感的缪斯女神。
④ skyrocket：流星焰火。
⑤ delphinium：飞燕草，翠雀花，在这里取其读音，并无特别意义。
⑥ low-keyed：低调的，有节制的。
⑦ clangor：连续的铿锵声，丁当声。
⑧ Humdrum testaments：平淡乏味的遗嘱。
⑨ seesaw：跷跷板。该意象在这里暗示现实的纷纭多变性对个体意识造成的冲击。

Ought to be written about how this① affects
You when you write poetry:
The extreme austerity② of an almost empty mind
Colliding with the lush, Rousseau-like foliage③ of its desire to communicate
Something between breaths, if only for the sake
Of others and their desire to understand you and desert you
For other centers of communication④, so that understanding
May begin, and in doing so be undone⑤.

  这里所选的诗作集中体现了诗人对诗歌创作原则的反思。本诗开篇提出的问题是：在现代语境下，"诗歌绘画性"的古典主义诗歌理念已变得不再适用。首先，在题材上，诗歌需要开诚布公地讲述日常发生的趣事，一贯受人仰视的缪斯女神不得不走下神坛，其凡性得到强化。其次，作为传统诗歌要素的浪漫意象遭到质疑，日常生活的平凡事件和琐碎细节被纳入诗歌创作中。另外，在语言上，低调、沉闷的词语多于华丽的词藻，诗歌风格变得朴素平实。但是，极其空洞平淡的头脑与内涵丰富的交流欲望之间产生了强烈的反差。最后四行诗句表达了诗人在当下语境中的尴尬处境：诗人具有强烈的倾诉欲望，以便得到他人的理解并且满足他人了解自己的愿望；可是，一旦理解，对方就会弃之而去。在这个互动过程中，理解与消解几乎同时发生，其中暗含了对当时盛行的解构主义思潮的应和。

  宇宙的多变性（mutability）以及人类自我意识的多元流动性作为英国文艺复兴和美国超验主义时期的中心主题，也是阿什贝利在诗歌创作中反复思考的一个问题。对他来说，现实是充满变数的意识碎片之组合，而非切实固定的整体，因此，其诗作也就相应地折射出关于这种现实的记忆、印象、欲望碎片及其流动多变性。有评论说"在阅读阿什贝利的作品时，你偶然在这里那里抓住一些清晰的意义，但它们很快就转变成别的陌生的东西，或者迅速消失、融化。"线性时间模式的破坏、传统认知秩序的颠覆、意义的随机性、反讽语气等特点都是造成阿什贝利的诗歌晦涩难懂的原因，这些特点可在本诗中窥见一斑，值得深刻探讨。

---

  ① 这里 this 一词指的是上述所有这些日常生活的琐碎细节，诗人在此提出的问题是：它们是如何影响诗歌创作的。
  ② austerity：严格，朴素。
  ③ lush：繁茂的，郁郁葱葱的；foliage：树叶。该意象在此与空虚乏味的头脑形成对照，用来比喻强烈的交流欲望。Rousseau：皮埃尔·卢梭(1812—1867)，法国风景画家，巴比松画派主要人物之一，该画派诞生于巴黎南郊约50公里处紧挨着枫丹白露森林的一个村落，活跃于19世纪30—40年代，主张描绘具有民族特色的法国农村自然风景。
  ④ other centers of communication：其他交流中心，指具有不同特性的其他意识主体。
  ⑤ undone：未完成，消解。

思考题

1. The poet sets in contrast two kinds of artistic ideals in this poem. What are they?
2. In illustrating the contemporary poetic practices, who is the speaker addressing? What kind of tone is conveyed, didactic or ironic or whatsoever?
3. What do you make of the last four lines?

推荐作品

"The Painter" (1956)

"Self-Portrait in a Convex Mirror" (1975)

"Chinese Whispers: Poems" (2002)

参考资料

Herd, David. *John Ashbery & American Poetry*. New York: Farrar, Straus, and Giroux, 2001.

Lehman, D. *Beyond Amazement: New Essays on John Ashbery*. Ithaca, NY: Cornell UP, 1980.

Shapiro, D. *John Ashbery: An Introduction to the Poetry*. New York: Columbia UP, 1979.

Robert Pinsky
(1940—   )

罗伯特·平斯基

作者简介

　　罗伯特·平斯基生于美国新泽西州,在斯坦福大学获硕士、博士学位。诗歌《悲伤与欢愉》(*Sadness and Happiness*, 1975)用节奏明快的语言勾勒出美国寻常百姓生活的各个侧面,象征"美国诗歌步入充满信心的新时代"。长诗《对美国的一种解释》(*An Explanation of America*, 1980)一反传统诗歌创作手法,回顾美国的历史进程,在诗歌末尾借用12岁女孩的视角揭示商业文化使童趣消失殆尽的残酷现实。《我的心史》(*History of My Heart*, 1985)以诗人回忆其家庭庆祝圣诞节为开端,用冷峻的目光审视这个家庭所经历的酸甜苦辣,并融入他对政治、社会与哲学等问题的思考。该诗获美国诗歌学会设的威廉·卡洛斯·威廉斯奖。1996年出版的《想象中的车轮:新旧诗选》(*The Figured Wheel: New and Collected Poems 1966—1996*, 又译《花车巨轮》),用丰富的想象力展现遍及美国城乡、贫富阶层、男女老少、各色人种的"车轮",再次深刻体现出平斯基作为诗人兼评论家的创新和深邃。该诗集1997年获普里策诗歌奖提名。1997年至2000年,平斯基成为美国历史上第一位连任三届的桂冠诗人。在任桂冠诗人期间,平斯基与人合编《美国最受欢迎的诗歌:最受欢迎的诗歌项目选集》(*Americans' Favorite Poems: The Favorite Poem Project Anthology*, 1999),通过摄像和录音为美国人喜爱的诗歌留下宝贵资料,平斯基认为这种记录具有重要价值,"记录了我们的现在,为未来的教育树立了典范,并见证了或许忽略现有文化的这一事实。"2000年出版的诗集《泽西雨》(*Jersey Rain*)汇集平斯基对各种科技发明的感悟与思考。平斯基的译作《但丁的地狱》(*The Inferno of Dante*)荣获美国诗歌学会的诗歌翻译奖。平斯基现担任网络周刊《石板色》(*Slate*)的诗歌编辑,并在波士顿大学讲授文学创作课程。平斯基诗歌的特点主要表现在:一、关注现代技术与诗歌创作的联系;二、对平凡人生的辩证思考;三、使用丰富多彩的典故;四、在继承诗歌传统的基础上有所创新。

To Television

Not a "window on the world"
But as we call you,
A box a **tube**①

Terrarium② of dreams and wonders.
Coffer③ of shades, **ordained**
Cotillion of phosphors
Or liquid crystal

Raster dance,
Quick one, little thief, escort
Of the dying and comfort of the sick, In a blue glow my father and little sister sat
Snuggled④ in one chair watching you
Their wife and mother was sick in the head
I scorned you and them as I scorned so much
Homey miracle, tub
Of acquiescence, vein of defiance.
Your patron in the **pantheon**⑤ would be **Hermes**

Now I like you best in a hotel room,
Maybe minutes
Before I have to face an audience: behind
The doors of the **armoire**⑥, box
Within a box—**Tom & Jerry**, or also brilliant

---

① tube：（美俚）电视。
② terrarium：陆栖小动物饲养箱。
③ coffer：保险箱。ordain：注定。cotillion：法国花式舞；早期法国交谊舞。phosphor：磷光体。raster：（电）光栅。
④ snuggle：偎依。
⑤ Pantheon：罗马万神殿。Hermes：(希神)赫尔墨斯(众神的使者，并为掌管疆界、道路、商业以及科学发明、辩才、幸运、灵巧之神，也是盗贼、赌徒的保护神)。
⑥ armoire：大型衣橱。Tom & Jerry：美国《猫和老鼠》动画片。Oprah Winfrey：美国著名黑人脱口秀女主持人。

And reassuring, **Oprah Winfrey**.

Thank you, for I watched, I watched
Sid Caesar① speaking French and Japanese not
Through knowledge but imagination,
His quickness, and Thank You, I watched live
Jackie Robinson② stealing

Home, the image—O strung shell—enduring
Fleeter than light like these words we
Remember in, they too winged
At the helmet and ankles.

"致电视"选自《泽西雨》,是诗人关注科技发明与诗歌创作之间关系的一个例证。诗人对电视的态度似难以捉摸:富有哲理的话语让读者领略到电视具有白衣天使的功效,"陪伴垂危的人,安抚卧榻的病人"("escort of the dying and comfort of the sick")。然而,诗人对电视的态度并非完全赞赏,电视作为大众媒体固然已成为人类生活不可或缺的一部分并且能改善人类生活,但它是否展示生活的真谛,诗人对此表示怀疑。诗人随即将电视与古希腊神话人物联系起来,一方面使读者认识到高科技发展如此迅猛以至于想象中的神话人物特征已成为现实,另一方面又暗示大众对电视到了顶礼膜拜的地步。电视传播速度之快,范围之广,堪称古罗马神话中的信神赫尔墨斯。电视为广大观众提供各种层次的娱乐节目,男女老少都成为电视的俘虏。诗人巧妙地将电视媒体切换到文字媒介,画龙点睛地突出了本诗的核心:诗的语言犹如头盔和双脚都长有双翼、科学与发明的象征的信神赫尔墨斯;与转瞬即逝的电视节目相比,诗歌将流芳千古,会真正深入人心。正如平斯基1999年在斯坦福大学毕业典礼上所讲,"诗歌的媒介就是人的声音。根据这种媒介的本质,诗歌就要与大众艺术保持平衡"。"致电视"借助电视这一娱乐媒介抒发诗人力图普及诗歌这一美好愿望,恰恰印证了诗人藉助网络技术让诗歌进入百姓人家这一事实。

---

① Sid Caesar:美国著名喜剧家,擅长模仿外国语言。
② Jackie Robinson:美国著名黑人棒球明星。

思考题

1. What does "a window on the world" suggest about television?
2. How can television be the "escort of the dying and the comfort of the sick"?
3. For what reason do you think the speaker scorns the father and the little sister?
4. What relevance does television bear to Hermes?
5. Is there any purpose in the speaker's listing of so many celebrities?
6. Describe the poet's attitude toward television.

 推荐作品

An Explanation of America (1980)
The Figured Wheel: New and Collected Poems 1966—1996 (1996)
History of My Heart (1985)

参考资料

Matthias, John. *Five American Poets: Robert Hass, John Matthias, James McMichael, John Peck, Robert Pinsky*. New York: Persea Books, 1981.

Pinsky, Robert. *Democracy, Culture and the Voice of Poetry*. Princeton, N. J.: Princeton UP, 2002.

Rita Dove
(1952—   )

丽塔·达夫

作者简介

丽塔·达夫,美国黑人女诗人,生于俄亥俄州,衣阿华大学获美术硕士学位。出版的诗集有《街角的黄房子》(*The Yellow House on the Corner*, 1980)、《博物馆》(*Museum*, 1983)、《托马斯和比尤拉》(*Thomas and Beulah*, 1986),其中《托马斯和比尤拉》于1987年获普利策诗歌奖,是继格温德琳·布鲁克斯(Gwendolyn Brooks)1950年获普利策诗歌奖后第二个获此殊荣的美国黑人诗人。1993年,达夫成为美国历史上最年轻的桂冠诗人,也是第一位黑人桂冠诗人,并连任两届。不过,达夫并不情愿被贴上美国黑人诗人的标签,她将自己首先定位为诗人,认为诗歌创作与种族无关。在担任桂冠诗人期间,达夫积极组织各种与诗歌相关的活动,倡导儿童阅读诗歌,为普及诗歌教育做出了贡献;此外,达夫还组织作家们从艺术角度研究非洲移民社群。达夫的诗歌语言质朴无华,将抒情与叙事有机结合起来,主题涵盖微观的生活事件与宏观的历史事件,以个人情感、家庭关系、历史事件、古代神话等相互交融为特点。正如达夫曾说过的,"个人的与历史的同样重要"。《托马斯和比尤拉》通过描写诗人外祖父母的生活历程生动呈现出南方农村黑人移居北方城市的历史画卷。《母爱》(*Mother Love*, 1995)是诗人对希腊神话人物得墨忒耳(Demeter)、珀尔塞弗涅(Persephone)以及冥王(Hades)的现代阐释,诗人根据这一神话框架用十四行诗传达出母爱的局限性以及母女之间相互依赖又相互独立的复杂关系。《与罗莎·帕克斯乘坐公共汽车》(*On the Bus with Rosa Parks*, 1999)诗集中的诗歌巧妙地将现代人纳入历史时空,既有对历史的体验,又有对人生的思考。最近出版的诗集有《美式平滑》(*American Smooth*, 2004)。达夫认为"诗歌是最精炼和最有力的语言"。因此,她的诗歌简洁明快,语颇隽永,耐人寻味。

My Mother Enters the Work Force

The path to ABC Business School
was paid for by a lucky sign:
Alterations[①]**, Qualified Seamstress Inquire Within**[②].
Tested on Sleeves, hers
never **puckered**[③] - - **puffed or sleek**,
Leg o'[④] **or Raglan** - -
they barely needed the damp cloth
to steam them perfect.

Those were the afternoons. Evenings
she took in **piecework**, the **treadle machine**[⑤]
with its locomotive **whir**
traveling the lit path of the needle
through **quicksand taffeta**[⑥]
or velvet deep as a forest.
And now and now sang the treadle,
I know, I know....
And then it was day again, all morning
at the office machines, their clack and chatter
another journey—rougher,
that would go on forever
until she could break a hundred words
with no errors—ah, and then
no more postponed groceries,
and that blue pair of shoes!

---

① alteration：对衣服做的改动。
② Qualified Seamstress Inquire Within：优秀女裁缝，欢迎咨询。
③ puckered：折成褶的。puffed：泡泡袖。sleek：平整的。
④ leg o'：leg-of-mutton 一头宽一头窄的，近似三角形的。raglan：套袖的，插肩袖的。
⑤ piecework：计件工作。treadle machine：脚踏缝纫机。
⑥ quicksand taffeta：如流沙般的塔夫绸。

 "我母亲加入劳动大军"是首叙事兼抒情诗,该诗通过简练的叙事引出"我"对母亲的敬仰和同情。第一节中的"幸运招牌"("lucky sign")可谓一举三得:首先,流露出母亲的自豪("Qualified Seamstress");其次,表达出"我"对母亲自力更生精神的敬意;最后,却悄无声息地将注意力从这块令人陶醉的"幸运招牌"转移到母亲自己的穿戴上。这一颇具反讽意义的转折将贫富不均的阶级差异前景化。第二节用丰富的感官意象和拟人手法再现母亲挑灯夜战的情景:脚踏缝纫机嗡嗡作响暗喻"流沙塔夫绸"("quicksand taffeta")与明喻"天鹅绒深似森林"("velvet deep as a forest")比喻这些布料几将母亲吞没,从而呈现母亲不堪重负的情形。诗人还通过拟人法进一步强化读者对"我"母亲的同情:踏板缝纫机的声音犹如雇主不容置疑的催促,"马上,马上"("And now and now"),"我"母亲疲惫不堪的应答,"我明白,我明白"("I know, I know")。第三节中的听觉与视觉意象巧妙结合,深刻再现母亲作为工人阶级一员含辛茹苦、单调乏味的现实生活。譬如,母亲敲打字机的嗒嗒声("clack and chatter")与上一节缝纫机发出的嗡嗡声遥相呼应,母亲的生命似乎注定在机器轰鸣声中日渐消耗。然而,诗人笔锋突转,随之出现的"那双蓝鞋子!"("that blue pair of shoes!")饱含母亲的期盼和乐观心态。全诗从细处着手,用精炼而有力的语言和丰富多彩的意象婉转表达出"我"对母亲的敬佩之情。正如诗人所说,"我情愿探索最亲密的时刻,那些和我们生活紧密相连的更微小、更晶莹剔透的细节。"

思考题

1. How do you understand "lucky sign"?
2. Why do you think "Those were the afternoons" is followed by "Evenings..."?
3. In what ways are "traveling" (in the second stanza) and "another journey" (in the third stanza) significant?
4. Describe the differences between "my" mother's sewing work and typing work. Why is the latter a "rougher" journey?
5. Explain the function of "ah, and then" in the last stanza.
6. State the reason why the poet entitles the poem "My Mother Enters the Work Force."

American Smooth (2004)
On the Bus with Rosa Parks (1999)
Grace Notes (1987)

参考资料

Ingersoll, Earl G., ed. *Conversations with Rita Dove.* Jackson: UP of Mississippi, 2003.

Therese, Steffen. *Crossing Color: Transcultural Space and Place in Rita Dove's Poetry, Fiction, and Drama.* New York: Oxford UP, 2001.

Robert Bly
(1926—   )
罗伯特·布莱

作者简介

　　罗伯特·布莱生于明尼苏达州,祖籍挪威。1944 年加入海军并服役两年,1947 年在明尼苏达圣奥拉夫学院学习一年后转至哈佛大学,在哈佛大学期间经常参加文学创作讨论。1956 年在挪威从事诗歌翻译期间,发现众多诸如智利诗人聂鲁达(Pablo Neruda)等杰出诗人并不为美国读者所熟悉,于是经过努力创办了诗歌翻译的文学杂志,如《五十年代》(The Fifties)、《六十年代》(The Sixties)和《七十年代》(The Seventies),翻译并介绍了许多著名诗歌作品。1966 年与人合建美国作家反对越南战争组织,并多次领导反越战活动。诗歌《人体之光》(The Light Around the Body, 1967)获美国国家图书奖。该诗集反映了布莱反越战的坚定立场,他通过借鉴 17 世纪德国哲学家雅各布·贝姆的"内在"和"外在"思想,指出完整和谐的人生不应有战争,对越南战争是如何源自美国人内心进行了探索。布莱认为,人体之光只有在征服战争、治愈心灵之后才会出现。《黑衣男子回头》(The Man in the Black Coat Turns, 1981)和《在两个世界爱一个女人》(Loving a Woman in Two Worlds, 1985)分别体现出布莱的"男性意识"和"女性意识",前者主要探索父子关系,后者试图阐释男女两性间复杂关系的发展过程。布莱不仅创作诗歌,而且研究人尤其是男性的心理。评论家指出,布莱是"席卷美国文化革新运动的催化剂。"《铁约翰:一本有关男人的书》(Iron John: A Book About Men, 1990)中,布莱根据格林童话同名故事追溯男性英雄的成长历程,深入探究当代美国男性的困惑,出版后畅销全球。《同胞社会》(The Sibling Society, 1996)是继《铁约翰:一本有关男人的书》之后的又一本探索男性意识的书,布莱认为当代美国男性处于"青少年"时期,在失去父辈指导后无法承担社会责任。罗伯特·布莱是美国诗歌深层意象运动的代表诗人,他认为,"意象与图画的区别在于,意象是想象力的自然表达,无法来自现实世界,也无法返回现实世界。它是一种源于想象力的动物。"布莱主张发挥想象力,借助深层意象,在"心理跳跃"("psychic leaps")中通过大脑中有意识和无意识两部分来完成诗歌创作。深层意象运动将弗洛伊德、容格的精神分析理论引入诗歌创作,极大推动了美国诗歌的发展。

The Buried Train

Tell me about the train that people say got buried
By the **avalanche**① —was it snow? —It was
In Colorado, and no one saw it happen.
There was smoke from the engine curling up
Lightly through fir tops, and the engine sounds.
There were all those people reading - - some
From **Thoreau**②, some from **Henry Ward Beecher**③.
And the engineer smoking and putting his head out.
I wonder when that happened. Was it after
High School, or was it the year we were two?
We entered this narrow place, and we heard the sound
Above us—the train couldn't move fast enough.
It isn't clear what happened next. Are you and I
Still sitting there in the train, waiting for the lights
To go on? Or did the real train get really buried;
So at night a ghost train comes out and keeps going...

该诗出自《黑衣男子回头》，通过深层意象"被埋的火车"揭示出现代美国生活的世态炎凉。"被埋的火车"这一深层意象本应让人们对这场灾难产生恐惧，对受难者产生同情，然而第一节中事无巨细、不含任何感情色彩的客观描述——There was smoke from the engine curling up / Lightly through fir tops, and the engine sounds. / There were all those people reading——直接反映出描述者的袖手旁观，更强化了遇难者的孤独无助，这种反讽效果不仅折射出诗人的洞察力，而且烘托出诗人的愤懑。第二节，诗人通过让"我们"介入（"We entered this narrow place, and we heard the sound"），进一步缩短"我们"与灾难之间的距离。令诗人痛心的是，这种亲密接触非但没有加强人与人之间的

---

① avalanche：雪崩。
② Thoreau：梭罗(1817—1862)，美国作家，超验主义运动的代表人物，主张回归自然，反对蓄奴制和美国对墨西哥的战争。代表作为《沃尔登湖》。
③ Henry Ward Beecher：比彻(1813—1887)，美国基督教公理会自由派牧师、废奴运动领袖，主张妇女参政，赞成进化论。

联系,反而更加突出人与人之间的隔离。"被埋的火车"俨然是现代人的心灵荒原,人类心中膨胀着自我,对同类的灾难视而不见,听而不闻,宛如被埋的火车。诗人采用"被埋的火车"这一深层意象,分别从想象中的旁观者与想象中的亲历者这两个角度对"你和我"漠不关心以及由此产生的隔离感进行细致披露。诗人采用问句邀请读者对个人的行为进行思考,从中可窥见诗人诚恳希望大家从自身做起,互相关心,共同创造和谐生活。至此,该诗实现了"心理飞跃"。这首诗由表及里,用忧郁的笔触传达了诗人对美国文化的忧虑。

思考题

1. Dash is used three times in this poem. What are its effects?
2. What do the allusions to Thoreau and Henry Ward Beecher imply?
3. Why do you think the engineer is seen "smoking and putting his head out"?
4. To whom do you think "I" pose the question of "Was it after High School, or was it the year we were two?"
5. What does "the ghost train" suggest?
6. Describe the similarities and differences between Imagist poems and Deep Image poems.

推荐作品

Iron John: A Book about Men (1990)
The Light Around the Body (1991)
Loving a Woman in Two Worlds (1985)

参考资料

Davis, William V., ed. *Critical Essays on Robert Bly.* New York: Maxwell Macmillan International, 1992.

Wadden, Paul. *The Rhetoric of Self in Robert Bly and Adrienne Rich: Doubling and the Holotropic Urge.* New York: P. Lang, Publishers, 2003.

White, Terry, ed. *The Sibling Society: Papers Presented at the Robert Bly Colloquium.* Lanham, Md.: UP of America, 2000.

Gary Soto
(1952—   )
加里·索托

 作者简介

  加里·索托，美籍墨西哥人后裔，出生在富饶的加利福尼亚州圣约魁谷弗雷斯诺市的一个工人阶级家庭，早年受过良好的教育，受到普利策奖诗人菲利普·莱文(Philip Levine)的影响对文学产生兴趣，1973年在《爱荷华评论》(Iowa Review)上发表首篇诗作，1977年出版首部诗集《圣约魁谷要素》(The Elements of San Joaquin)，同年开始任教于加州大学伯克利分校，至今获得过包括古根海姆奖和美国诗人协会奖在内的多个重要诗歌奖项，是入选《诺顿现代诗选》的诗人中最年轻的一位。1995年，索托凭诗集《新诗精选》(New and Selected Poems)获得洛杉矶时报图书奖和美国国家图书奖两项提名奖。

  索托诗风平易朴实，创作中往往以童年时代所熟悉的场所和少数族裔的生活经历为素材，加州弗雷斯诺的街道和他自己的家庭成员经常出现在作品中。"失去"(loss)被看作记忆的一个必不可少的成分。虽然索托笔下的墨西哥裔美国家庭多半经济拮据窘迫，面临诸多生活难题，但是，他仅仅着眼于问题及其解决方法，并非表达怨天尤人的消极情绪。其作品集中反映丰富多彩的民族文化，强调以家庭为核心的价值观，有助于美国社会消除历史上墨西哥人懒惰的负面形象，树立健康积极的少数族裔形象，并且为后殖民主义研究提供了颇为有效的文本参照。

作品 一

Mexicans Begin Jogging

At the factory I worked
In the fleck of rubber①, under the press②
Of an oven yellow with flame,
Until the border patrol③ opened

---
① fleck of rubber: 橡胶颗粒。
② press: 熨烫。
③ border patrol: 边境巡逻队，专门负责追查遭返非法越界人员。

Their vans and my boss waved for us to run.
"Over the fence①, Soto," he shouted,
And I shouted that I was American.
"No time for lies," he said, and pressed
A dollar in my palm, hurrying me
Through the back door.

Since I was on his time②, I ran
And became the wag to a short tail of Mexicans—③
Ran past the amazed crowds that lined
The street and blurred like photographs, in rain.
I ran from that industrial road to the soft
Houses where people paled at the turn of an autumn sky④.
What could I do but yell *vivas*⑤
To baseball, milkshakes, and those sociologists
Who would clock me⑥
As I jog into the next century
On the power of a great, silly grin⑦.

How Things Work

Today it's going to cost us twenty dollars
To live. Five for a softball⑧. Four for a book,

---

① Over the fence：跳过栅栏。

② Since I was on his time：在他的工作时间里。由于"我"是受雇于老板，所以只好奉命开始奔跑。

③ the wag to a short tail of Mexicans：在美国的白人主流社会中，作为少数族裔的墨西哥移民（合法或非法）被边缘化。诗人在这里将其比作动物躯干以外的一条短短的尾巴，"我"这个个体则在奔跑中引起了这条短尾的摆动。

④ the soft / Houses where people paled at the turn of an autumn sky：这里指贫民住宅区。按照字面的意思，房屋在雨中变得松软，人们在秋凉的天气中变得面色苍白。诗人通过这两个意象暗示了少数族裔贫民居住条件的恶劣和生活的窘迫。

⑤ viva：意大利、西班牙语中"万岁"的欢呼，欢呼声。

⑥ baseball, milkshakes, and those sociologists / Who would clock me：棒球和奶昔都是美国中产阶级大众文化的代表；更具讽刺意味的是，那些社会学家理应对少数族裔的现状了如指掌，却无力改变，只能一味用计时等方法采集数据。

⑦ On the power of a great, silly grin：傻乎乎地咧嘴大笑，表示一种处事态度。意思是，促使"我"继续奔跑前行的力量唯有装傻充愣，自欺欺人。

⑧ softball：垒球。这里指一场垒球比赛。

A handful of ones for coffee and two sweet rolls①,
Bus fare, rosin② for your mother's violin.
We're completing our task. The tip I left
For the waitress filters down③
Like rain, wetting the new roots of a child④,
Perhaps, a belligerent cat⑤ that won't let go
Of a balled sock⑥ until there's chicken to eat.
As far as I can tell, daughter, it works like this:
You buy bread from a grocery, a bag of apples
From a fruit stand, and what coins
Are passed on helps others buy pencils, glue,
Tickets to a movie in which laughter
Is thrown into their faces.⑦
If we buy goldfish, someone tries on a hat.
If we buy crayons, someone walks home with a broom.
A tip, a small purchase⑧ here and there,
And things just keep going. I guess.

与其家庭背景和成长经历相对应，索托的诗歌创作有两个主要特征：

其一是鲜明的自传体特性，尤其是他的种族和群体意识。诗人的工人阶级出身和少数族裔身份赋予了他独特的文化视角以及对边缘群体所处困境的敏锐感知力和为受压迫人群代言的强烈责任感。他曾这样明确表述过自己的政治立场："我信奉穷人的文化。"

可以说，这个特征在前一首诗里得以集中体现。开篇三行诗句交代了"我"身处的恶劣工作环境：空气中悬浮着橡胶颗粒，炉火烧得正旺，热浪逼人。随后，边境巡逻人员的到来打断了单调的工作，老板招呼工人们赶快逃跑，以免这些人被作为非法

---

① sweet rolls：甜面包卷。
② rosin：松香。
③ filter down：逐渐渗透。此处采用"陌生化"技巧，将付小费与细雨的意象联系起来，表示尽管微不足道，却由于连绵不断而产生累积效应，达到"润物细无声"的效果。对于付费者来说，累计起来，这会是一笔不小的开支。
④ wetting the new roots of a child：打湿一个孩子新生的毛发。暗指小费的去向：一方付出的小费很可能会帮助对方养育一个孩子。
⑤ a belligerent cat：执拗的猫。
⑥ a balled sock：卷成一团的袜子。
⑦ Tickets to a movie in which laughter / Is thrown into their faces：在电影中，人们享受到难得的欢笑。这里的动词"抛撒"代表了诗人对商业化社会娱乐活动的一种讽刺态度，花钱买到的快乐被轻率而粗暴地掷到人们的脸上去。
⑧ a small purchase：购物的小笔开支。

移民抓获而给自身带来麻烦。"我"也在其中,老板不理会"我"是合法公民的辩解,硬塞给"我"一美元,命令"我"跑。在雨中,"我"从工业区一直穿越少数族裔贫民窟,心中苦楚,却只能依靠傻乎乎咧嘴大笑的力量活下去。

其二则是生动的日常生活题材和朴素的生活口语。诗人擅长从熟悉的日常生活场景中提炼素材,具有将司空见惯的庸常事件化入诗歌语境的高超技巧。这里所选的两首短诗分别集中体现了上述特征。特别值得注意的是,与美国诗歌传统相符,诗中的主要意象多半取自于自然;然而,与经典主流诗风相异,自然意象并非旨在营造超脱尘世的美感,而是为了强化生活艰辛的主题。

后一首短诗借助于日常生活场景,采用了口语体语言,读来通俗平实,琅琅上口。开篇所直接称呼的"我们"以及第四行所指的"你"到第十行才得到具体化处理:该诗是一名父亲对女儿所讲的心里话。随之,语境也得以具体化,即父亲带年幼的女儿一起出发去逛街购物,前五行相当于列举了当天的开销预算清单(看球赛、买书、喝咖啡、吃甜点、乘坐公共汽车、买母亲拉小提琴用的松香,总共二十美元),从中可以推知这是一个普通的美国中产阶级家庭。诗句通过可以为孩童所接受的一连串具体而浅显的实例解释了消费社会人类生存链条的运作方式,这其中体现了人际间紧密的相互依存关系,颇具朴素的哲理性。

思考题

1. What is the Mexican immigrants' situation in the American context? How is ethnic identity constructed in the first poem?

2. What kind of attitude toward life does "a great, silly grin" indicate? What does the first poem imply about the illegal immigrants' pursuit of the American dream?

3. Describe the specific view of human life and relationship the father imparts to his daughter in the second poem.

推荐作品

Living Up the Street: Narrative Recollections (1985)
New and Selected Poems (1995)
"Like Mexicans" (2000)

参考资料

Orr, Tamra. *Gary Soto*. New York: Rosen Publishing Group, 2005.

Adrienne Rich
(1929—   )

艾德里安娜·里奇

作者简介

艾德里安娜·里奇生于美国马里兰州巴尔的摩的一个上中层家庭，出生在一家黑人区的医院；父亲有犹太人血统，等待多年也得不到约翰霍普金斯大学的教授职位；祖父留下的遗物包括一支象牙长笛、一只金怀表和一本希伯来语的祷告书。这些都在里奇追溯个人历史的诗歌里有所反映。1951年，里奇毕业于拉德克利夫学院，同年凭诗集《世事一沧桑》(A Change of World)获得耶鲁年轻诗人奖。作为评委之一的"现代派"诗人W.H.奥顿(W. H. Auden)在为其诗集所写的序言中评论道："呈现在读者面前的这些诗有着整洁谦逊的衣着，言说从容平静而不含混，尊重长辈而不畏缩，并且没有谎言：这对于第一部诗集来说，已经相当不俗了。"字里行间多少暴露了男性轻视女性的文化沙文主义心态。

1953年不顾家人的反对与哈佛大学经济学教授、德系东正教教徒阿尔弗雷德·康拉德结婚，随后生了三个儿子，完全沦为家庭主妇。经过八年之久的沉默，里奇于1963年出版了诗集《儿媳妇的快照》(Snapshots of a Daughter-in-Law)，倾诉了具有创造力的女性受到压抑的愤懑。1969年和1971年分别出版诗集《传单》(Leaflets: Poems 1965—1968)和《改变的意志》(The Will to Change: Poems 1968—1970)。里奇在诗歌和散文创作中反映了女性以及女同性恋者在父权社会的成长经历和自我意识觉醒过程，并且将艺术创作与政治行动有效地结合起来，成为了20世纪美国激进女权主义的艺术代言人。她写于1971年的著名论文《当我们死人醒来时：作为再修正的写作》(When We Dead Awaken: Writing as Re-Vision)和1978年的《强制的异性恋与同性恋的经验》(Compulsory Heterosexuality and Lesbian Existence)可谓当代女性主义思想的代表作。1974—1976年间创作的组诗《二十一首恋歌》(Twenty-One Love Poems)以她与米雪儿·克利芙(Michelle Cliff)之间从隐秘走向公开的同性恋情为主题，是她从女性主义诗人转向女性主义/同性恋诗人的标志性作品。

里奇的诗歌作品曾多次获奖，曾凭借1973年出版的诗集《潜入沉船》(Diving into the Wreck)与金斯堡(Allen Ginsberg, 1926—1997)分享1974年的美国国家图书奖。作品中表现了她在这个阶段把"雌雄同体(androgyny)"看作父权制社会中两性关系调和的理想状态的女性主义思想。以下作品就是出自这个诗集。

Diving into the Wreck

First having read the book of myths,
and loaded the camera,
and checked the edge of the knife-blade,
I put on
the body-armor of black rubber
the absurd flippers
the grave and awkward mask①.
I am having to do this
not like Cousteau② with his
assiduous team
aboard the sun-flooded schooner③
but here alone.

There is a ladder.
The ladder is always there
hanging innocently
close to the side of the schooner.
We know what it is for,
we who have used it.
Otherwise
it's a piece of maritime floss④
some sundry⑤ equipment.

I go down.

---

① the body-armor of black rubber / the grave and awkward mask / the absurd flippers：黑橡胶的盔甲、脚蹼和面罩构成了全套的潜水用品。
② Cousteau：科斯特，指雅克·科斯特(1910—)，法国水下探险家、作家。
③ schooner：斯库纳纵帆船，两桅纵帆船。
④ maritime floss：海上漂浮物，絮状浮渣。
⑤ sundry：各式各样的。

Rung after rung① and still
the oxygen immerses me
the blue light
the clear atoms
of our human air.
I go down.
My flippers cripple② me,
I crawl like an insect down the ladder
and there is no one
to tell me when the ocean
will begin.

First the air is blue and then
it is bluer and then green and then
black I am blacking out③ and yet
my mask is powerful
it pumps my blood with power
the sea is another story
the sea is not a question of power
I have to learn alone
to turn my body without force
in the deep element④.

And now: it is easy to forget
what I came for
among so many who have always
lived here
swaying their crenellated⑤ fans
between the reefs⑥
and besides

---

① rung：梯子的横档，梯级。
② cripple：使行动不便。
③ black out：昏过去。
④ element：自然环境，此处指海洋。
⑤ crenellated：锯齿状的。
⑥ reef：暗礁，珊瑚礁。

you breathe differently down here.

I came to explore the wreck.
The words are purposes.
The words are maps.
I came to see the damage that was done
and the treasures that prevail①.
I stroke the beam of my lamp
slowly along the flank②
of something more permanent
than fish or weed

the thing I came for:
the wreck and not the story of the wreck
the thing itself and not the myth
the drowned face always staring
toward the sun
the evidence of damage
worn by salt and sway into this threadbare③ beauty
the ribs of the disaster
curving their assertion
among the tentative haunters④.

This is the place.
And I am here, the mermaid whose dark hair
streams black, the merman in his armored body⑤
We circle silently
about the wreck
we dive into the hold⑥.

---

① prevail：盛行，占优势，这里指到处都是。
② beam：横梁；flank：侧翼，侧面。
③ threadbare：磨破了的，陈旧的，陈腐的。
④ the ribs of the disaster／curving their assertion／among the tentative haunters：灾难的肋骨／在暂时的逗留者中／弯曲地倾诉着。
⑤ mermaid、merman：美人鱼、雄人鱼，此指男女遇难者的尸体，前者长发飘扬，后者遍身盔甲。
⑥ hold：船舱。

I am she: I am he

whose drowned face sleeps with open eyes
whose breasts still bear the stress
whose silver, copper, vermeil① cargo lies
obscurely② inside barrels
half-wedged③ and left to rot
we are the half-destroyed instruments
that once held to a course④
the water-eaten log
the fouled compass

We are, I am, you are
by cowardice or courage
the one who find our way
back to this scene
carrying a knife, a camera
a book of myths
in which
our names do not appear.

这首诗是里奇20世纪70年代诗歌的代表作,表达了诗人对女性命运的关注。首先,如玛格丽特·阿特伍德所说,"沉船"意象象征着"为世人遗忘的神话,特别是关于男女两性的神话"的残骸。诗歌开篇,"我"有备而来,带着一本神话书,而在诗歌结尾处,诗人指出,这是"一本没有我们名字的神话书"。值得注意的是,与男性探险家科斯特不同,"我"没有群体的协助,而是独自一人踏上这段充满未知的旅程:"那里无人告诉我/海洋何时/开始";"我必须独自学习/在深沉的海洋中/不费力地转身"。同时,"我"也是抱着特定目标而来,即:亲自搜集证据,以期发现事情的真相——尽管"词语是我的目标/词语是地图","我"却并不迷信文字,因为"我为它而来:/是沉船而非沉船的故事/是事物本身而非神话"。结果,"我"看到了死去的同类,与他们相融合,从而获得了跨越时空的群体归属感和历史观。

---

① vermeil:朱砂红。
② obscurely:隐现地,朦胧地。
③ half-wedged:半楔入的。
④ course:航线,特定的行程。

从诗人特有的女性主义立场出发,"沉船"的意象承载了父权社会中被埋没的女性史。相应地,"潜入沉船"是一个象征性行动,集中体现了整个诗集的"探寻"(quest)主题。在一定程度上,潜水的过程正是女性个体发掘历史,唤醒沉睡的自我的过程。里奇信奉诗歌改变生活乃至带来社会变革的功用,而该诗恰好代表了20世纪六七十年代女权主义者发掘湮没的妇女史、女性文学史的积极行动倡议和艺术创作理念。

思考题

1. What does the wreck symbolize? And what about the act of diving?
2. What message does the lines "the thing I came for: / the wreck and not the story of the wreck / the thing itself and not the myth" communicate?
3. Why do "I" identify with the mermaid and the merman at once? Who do you think "we" are toward the end of the poem?

推荐作品

"Aunt Jennifer's Tigers" (1951)

"When We Dead Awaken: Writing as Re-Vision" (1971)

"Compulsory Heterosexuality and Lesbian Existence" (1980)

参考资料

Cooper, Jane R. *Reading Adrienne Rich: Reviews and Re-Visions, 1951–1981.* Ann Arbor: U of Michigan P, 1984.

Gelpi, Barbara Charlesworth, and Albert Gelpi, eds. *Adrienne Rich's Poetry: A Norton Critical Edition.* New York: WW Norton, 1975.

---. *Adrienne Rich's Poetry and Prose.* New York: WW Norton, 1993.

第十八单元
David Alan Mamet
(1947—)
大卫·艾伦·马麦特

作者简介

　　大卫·马麦特(1947—   )，美国剧作家、电影剧本作家和导演。他出生于芝加哥，到佛蒙特州的戈达德学院读完大学后又回到芝加哥。他在好几家工厂和一家房地产经纪公司工作过，也做过出租车司机，这些经历都反映在他的剧作中。20 世纪 70 年代，他最早的几部剧作《鸭子变奏曲》(1972)、《芝加哥的性错乱》(1974；电影 1986，改名为《关于昨夜》)、《美国水牛》(1976；电影 1996)等在"外百老汇"上演，使他成为美国当代最有影响的剧作家之一。他以后的剧作包括：《剧院里的生活》(1977)，《埃德蒙》(1982；电影 2005)，《快点耕耘》(1987)，《格林格里·葛兰·罗斯》(1983；电影 1992)，《奥里安娜》(1993；电影 1994)，《密码》(1995)，《老街区》(1997)，《波士顿婚姻》(1999)等。

　　马麦特擅长描写社会下层(包括中产阶级下层)孤单无助的人物，他们拙于表达，时有暴力或者欺诈行为。他笔下的人物包括推销员、无业游民和街头无赖；他们以不同的方式追寻着"美国梦"，但大多以失败告终。他们生活在一个世风日下的社会，而他们自己也是造成这一道德荒原的罪魁祸首。马麦特的戏剧语言具有极为独特的风格，被称为"马麦特式的语言"(Mametspeak)。这种语言具有生活和街头语言的节奏和风格，既粗俗猥亵，又简洁明快，富有诗意；马麦特的剧作甚至简洁到没有任何舞台说明。

　　在美国，以百老汇为基地、以少数"严肃艺术家"为代表的主流戏剧时代似乎已经完结；取而代之的是外百老汇(Off Broadway)、外外百老汇(Off Off Broadway)、地区剧院(regional theaters)，以及剧作家、电影剧本作家、导演、演员等各显身手的"后现代"戏剧。在这样一个时代，马麦特是一位将以上诸种成分、诸多角色集于一身的重要人物。作为电影编剧，马麦特不仅将自己的剧作《美国水牛》、《埃德蒙》、《格林格里·葛兰·罗斯》、《奥里安娜》等改编为电影剧本，而且还改编了多部小说，其中包括：《邮差总按两次铃》(1981)、《判决》(1982)、《摇尾狗》(1997)、《汉尼拔》(2001)等。他还创作了多部电影剧本，其中又有数部由他自己亲自执导，搬上电影屏幕，例如《赌场》(1987)、《杀人拼图》(1991)、《西班牙囚犯》(1998)、《欲望小镇》(2000)、《圣犬珍妮：拯救法兰西的狗》(摄制中，预计 2007 年上映)等。马麦特也曾在影片中担任角色。将戏剧与电影结合起来，将创作与改编结合起来。这也许正是"后戏剧"时代和数码时代

的典型特点。

Oleanna
ACT ONE

JOHN *is talking on the phone*. CAROL *is seated across the desk from him*.

JOHN (*on phone*): And what about the land. (*Pause*) The land. And what about the land? (*Pause*) What about it? (*Pause*) No. I don't understand. Well, yes, I'm I'm... no, I'm *sure* it's signif... I'm sure it's significant. (*Pause*) Because it's significant to mmmmmm... did you call Jerry? (*Pause*) Because... no, no, no, no, no. What did they say...? Did you speak to the *real* estate... where *is* she...? Well, well, all right. Where are her notes? Where are the notes we took with her? (*Pause*) I thought you were? No. No, I'm sorry, I didn't mean that, I just thought that I saw you, when we were there... what...? I thought I saw you with a *pencil*. WHY NOW? Is what I'm say... well, that's why I say "call Jerry." Well, I can't right now, be... no, I didn't schedule any... Grace: *I didn't*... I'm well aware... Look: Look. Did you call Jerry? Will you call Jerry...? Because I can't now. I'll be there, I'm sure I'll be there in fifteen, in twenty. I intend to. No, we aren't *going* to lose the, we aren't *going* to lose the house. Look: look, I'm not minimizing it. The "easement." Did she say "easement"? (*Pause*) What did she *say*; is it a "term of art," are we *bound* by it... I'm sorry... (*Pause*) are: we: yes. *Bound* by... Look: (*He checks his watch.*) before the other side *goes home*, all right? "a term of art[①]." Because: that's right (*Pause*) The yard for the boy. Well, that's the whole... Look: I'm going to meet you there... (*He checks his watch.*) Is the realtor there? All right, tell her

---

[①] a term of art: 专门术语。在电话里，约翰提到房地产经纪人(realtor)使用了一些"专门术语"，其中包括"easement"(地役权；在他人土地上的通行权)。卡罗尔对此甚为好奇，询问"专门术语"是什么意思。但约翰并不想回答这一与她的功课无关的问题，所以居高临下地反问："这就是你想谈的事情？"随后，他感到自己的态度有些生硬，所以又词不达意地进行了解释。剧中，"专门术语"是"话语权"的最重要内容：卡罗尔先是被学术的"专门术语"拒之门外，后来又因为女权的话语而掌控了权力。

to show you the basement again. Look at the *this* because... Bec... I'm leaving in, I'm leaving in ten or fifteen... Yes. No, no, I'll meet you at the new... That's a good. If he thinks it's necc... you tell Jerry to meet... All right? We *aren't* going to lose the deposit. All right? I'm sure it's going to be... (*Pause*) I hope so. (*Pause*) I love you, too. (*Pause*) I love you, too. As soon as... I will.

(He hangs up.) (*He bends over the desk and makes a note.*) (*He looks up.*) (*To* CAROL:) I'm sorry...

CAROL: (*Pause*) What is a "term of art"?

JOHN: (*Pause*) I'm sorry...?

CAROL: (*Pause*) What is a "term of art"?

JOHN: Is that what you want to talk about?

CAROL: ...to talk about...?

JOHN: Let's take the mysticism out of it, shall we? Carol? (*Pause*) Don't you think? I'll tell you: when you have some "thing." Which must be broached. (*Pause*) Don't you think...? (*Pause*)

CAROL: ...don't I think...?

JOHN: Mmm?

CAROL: ...did I...?

JOHN: ...what?

CAROL: Did... did I... did I say something wr...

JOHN: (*Pause*) No. I'm sorry. No. You're right. I'm very sorry. I'm somewhat rushed. As you see. I'm sorry. You're right. (*Pause*) What is a "term of art"? It seems to mean a *term*, which has come, through its use, to mean something *more specific* than the words would, to someone *not acquainted* with them... indicate. That, I believe, is what a "term of art," would mean. (*Pause*)

CAROL: You don't know what it means...?

JOHN: I'm not sure that I know what it means. It's one of those things, perhaps you've had them, that, you look them up, or have someone explain them to you, and you say "aha," and, you immediately *forget* what...

CAROL: You don't do that.

JOHN: ...I...?

CAROL: You don't do...

JOHN: ...I don't, what...?

CAROL: ...for...

JOHN: ...I don't for...

CAROL: ...no...

JOHN: ...forget things? Everybody does that.

CAROL: No, they don't.

JOHN: They don't...

CAROL: No.

JOHN: (*Pause*) No. Everybody does that.

CAROL: Why would they do that...?

JOHN: Because. I don't know. Because it doesn't interest them.

CAROL: No.

JOHN: I think so, though. (*Pause*) I'm sorry that I was distracted.

CAROL: You don't have to say that to me.

JOHN: You paid me the compliment, or the "obeisance" —all right— of coming in here... All right. *Carol*. I find that I am at a *standstill*. I find that I...

CAROL: ...what...

JOHN: ...one moment. In regard to your... to your...

CAROL: Oh, oh. You're buying a new house!

JOHN: No, let's get on with it.

CAROL: "get on"? (*Pause*)

JOHN: I know how... *believe* me. I know how... potentially *humiliating* these... I have no desire to... I have no desire other than to help you. But: (*He picks up some papers on his desk.*) I won't even say "but." I'll say that as I go back over the...

CAROL: I'm just, I'm just trying to...

JOHN: ...no, it will not do.

CAROL: ...what? What will...?

JOHN: No. I see, I see what you, it... (*He gestures to the papers.*) but your work...

CAROL: I'm just: I sit in class I... (*She holds up her notebook.*) I take notes...

JOHN (*simultaneously with "notes"*): Yes, I understand. What I am trying to *tell* you is that some, some basic...

CAROL:	...I...
JOHN:	...one moment: some basic missed communi...
CAROL:	I'm doing what I'm told. I bought your book, I read your...
JOHN:	No, I'm sure you...
CAROL:	No, no, no. I'm doing what I'm told. It's *difficult* for me. It's *difficult*...
JOHN:	...but...
CAROL:	I don't... lots of the *language*...
JOHN:	...please...
CAROL:	The *language*, the "things" that you say...
JOHN:	I'm sorry. No. I don't think that that's true.
CAROL:	It *is* true. I...
JOHN:	I think...
CAROL:	It *is* true.
JOHN:	...I...
CAROL:	Why would I...?
JOHN:	I'll tell you why: you're an incredibly bright girl.
CAROL:	...I...
JOHN:	You're an incredibly... you have no problem with the... Who's kidding who?
CAROL:	...I...
JOHN:	No. No. I'll tell you why. I'll tell... I think you're *angry*, I...
CAROL:	...why would I...
JOHN:	...wait one moment. I...
CAROL:	It *is* true. I have *problems*...
JOHN:	...every...
CAROL:	...I come from a different *social*...
JOHN:	...ev...
CAROL:	a different economic...
JOHN:	...Look:
CAROL:	No. I: when I *came* to this school:
JOHN:	Yes. Quite... (*Pause*)
CAROL:	...does that mean nothing...?
JOHN:	...but look: look...

CAROL: ...I...

JOHN: (*Picks up paper.*) Here: Please: Sit down. (*Pause*) Sit down. (*Reads from her paper.*) "I think that the ideas contained in this work express the author's feelings in a way that he intended, based on his results." What can that mean? Do you see? What...

CAROL: I, the best that I...

JOHN: I'm saying, that perhaps this course...

CAROL: No, no, no, you can't, you can't... I have to...

JOHN: ...how...

CAROL: ...I have to pass it...

JOHN: Carol, I:

CAROL: I *have* to pass this course, I...

JOHN: Well.

CAROL: ...don't you...

JOHN: Either the...

CAROL: ...I...

JOHN: ...either the, I... either the *criteria* for judging progress in the class are...

CAROL: No, no, no, no, I have to pass it.

JOHN: Now, look: I'm a human being, I...

CAROL: I did what you told me. I did, I did everything that, I read your *book*, you told me to buy your book and read it. Everything you *say* I... (*She gestures to her notebook.*) (*The phone rings.*) I do. ...Ev...

JOHN: ...look:

CAROL: ...everything I'm told...

JOHN: Look. Look. I'm not your *father*. (*Pause*)

CAROL: What?

JOHN: I'm.

CAROL: Did I say you were my father?

JOHN: ...no...

CAROL: Why did you say that...?

JOHN: I...

CAROL: ...why...?

JOHN: ...in class I... (*He picks up the phone.*) (*Into phone:*) Hello. I can't talk now. Jerry? Yes? I underst... I can't talk now. I know... I know... Jerry. I can't *talk* now. Yes, I. Call me back in... Thank you. (*He hangs up.*) (*To* CAROL:) What do you want me to do? We are two people, all right? Both of whom have subscribed to...

CAROL: No, no...

JOHN: ...certain arbitrary...

CAROL: No. You have to help me.

JOHN: Certain institutional... you tell me what you want me to do... You tell me what you want me to...

CAROL: How can I go back and tell them the *grades* that I...

JOHN: ...what can I do...?

CAROL: *Teach me. Teach me.*

JOHN: ...I'm trying to teach you.

CAROL: I read your book. I read it. I don't under...

JOHN: ...you don't understand it.

CAROL: No.

JOHN: Well, perhaps it's not well *written*...

CAROL (*simultaneously with* "written"): No. No. No. I want to *understand* it.

JOHN: What don't you understand? (*Pause*)

CAROL: *Any* of it. What you're trying to say. When you talk about...

JOHN: ...yes...? (*She consults her notes.*)

CAROL: "Virtual warehousing of the young"...

JOHN: "Virtual warehousing of the young." If we artificially prolong adolescence...①

CAROL: ...and about "The Curse of Modern Education."

JOHN: ...well...

CAROL: I don't...

JOHN: Look. It's just a *course*, it's just a *book*, it's just a...

CAROL: No. No. There are *people* out there. People who came *here*. To know something they didn't *know*. Who *came* here. To be helped. To be *helped*. So someone would *help* them. To *do* something. To *know* something. To get, what do they say? "To get on in the world."

---

① 约翰试图解释卡罗尔无法理解的书中内容和术语："Virtual warehousing of the young"的意思就是"人为延长青春期"。

How can I do that if I don't, if I fail? But I don't *understand*. I don't *understand*. I don't understand what anything means... and I walk around. From morning 'til night: with this one thought in my head. I'm *stupid*.

JOHN: No one thinks you're stupid.

CAROL: No? What am I...?

JOHN: I...

CAROL: ...what am I, then?

JOHN: I think you're angry. Many people are. I have a *telephone* call that I have to make. And an *appointment*, which is rather *pressing*; though I sympathize with your concerns, and though I wish I had the time, this was not a previously scheduled meeting and I...

CAROL: ...you think I'm nothing...

JOHN: ...have an appointment with a *realtor*, and with my wife and...

CAROL: You think that I'm stupid.

JOHN: No. I certainly don't.

CAROL: You said it.

JOHN: No. I did not.

CAROL: You did.

JOHN: When?

CAROL: ...you...

JOHN: No. I never did, or never would say that to a student, and...

CAROL: You said, "What can that mean?" (*Pause*) "What can that mean?"... (*Pause*)

JOHN: ...and what did that mean to you...?

CAROL: That meant I'm stupid. And I'll never learn. That's what that meant. And you're right.

JOHN: ...I...

CAROL: But then. But then, what am I doing here...?

JOHN: ...if you thought that I...

CAROL: ...when nobody wants me, and...

JOHN: ...if you interpreted...

CAROL: Nobody *tells* me anything. And I *sit* there... in the *corner*. In the *back*. And everybody's talking about "this" all the time. And "concepts," and "precepts" and, and, and, and, and, WHAT IN THE WORLD ARE YOU *TALKING* ABOUT? And I read your book. And they said, "Fine, go in that class." Because you talked about responsibility to the young. I DON'T KNOW WHAT IT MEANS AND I'M *FAILING*...

JOHN: May...

CAROL: No, you're right. "Oh, hell." I failed. Flunk me out of it. It's garbage. Everything I do. "The ideas contained in this work express the author's feelings." That's right. That's right. I know I'm stupid. I know what I am. (*Pause*) I know what I am, Professor. You don't have to tell me. (*Pause*) It's pathetic. Isn't it?

JOHN: ...Aha... (*Pause*) Sit down. Sit down. Please. (*Pause*) Please sit down.

CAROL: Why?

JOHN: I want to talk to you.

CAROL: Why?

JOHN: Just sit down. (*Pause*) Please. Sit down. Will you, please...? (*Pause. She does so.*) Thank you.

CAROL: What?

JOHN: I want to tell you something.

CAROL: (*Pause*) What?

JOHN: Well, I know what you're talking about.

CAROL: No. You don't.

JOHN: I think I do. (*Pause*)

CAROL: How can you?

JOHN: I'll tell you a story about myself. (*Pause*) Do you mind? (*Pause*) I was raised to think myself stupid. That's what I want to tell you. (*Pause*)

CAROL: What do you mean?

JOHN: Just what I said. I was brought up, and my earliest, and most persistent memories are of being told that I was stupid. "You have such *intelligence*. Why must you behave so *stupidly*?" Or, "Can't you *understand*? Can't you *understand*?" And I could *not* understand. I could *not* understand.

CAROL: What?

JOHN: The simplest problem. Was beyond me. It was a mystery.

CAROL: What was a mystery?

JOHN: How people learn. How *I* could learn. Which is what I've been speaking of in class. And of *course* you can't hear it. Carol. Of *course* you can't. (*Pause*) I used to speak of "real people," and wonder what the *real* people did. The *real* people. Who were they? *They* were the people other than myself. The *good* people. The *capable* people. The people who could do the things, I *could* not do: learn, study, retain... all that *garbage*—which is what I have been talking of in class, and that's *exactly* what I have been talking of—If you are told... Listen to this. If the young child is told he cannot understand. Then he takes it as a *description* of himself. What am I? I am *that which can not understand*. And I saw you out there, when we were speaking of the concepts of...

CAROL: I can't understand any of them.

JOHN: Well, then, that's *my* fault. That's not your fault. And that is not verbiage. That's what I firmly hold to be the truth. And I am sorry, and I owe you an apology.

CAROL: Why?

JOHN: And I suppose that I have had some *things* on my mind.... We're buying a *house*, and...

CAROL: People said that you were stupid...?

JOHN: Yes.

CAROL: When?

JOHN: I'll tell you when. Through my life. In my childhood; and, perhaps, they stopped. But I heard them continue.

CAROL: And what did they say?

JOHN: They said I was incompetent. Do you see? And when I'm tested the, the, the *feelings* of my youth about the *very subject of learning* come up. And I... I become, I feel "unworthy," and "unprepared."...

CAROL: ...yes.

JOHN: ...eh?

CAROL: ...yes.

JOHN: And I feel that I must fail. (*Pause*)

CAROL: ...but then you *do* fail. (*Pause*) You have to. (*Pause*) Don't you?

JOHN: A *pilot*. Flying a plane. The pilot is flying the plane. He thinks: Oh, my *God*, my mind's been drifting! Oh, my God! What kind of a cursed imbecile am I, that I, with this so precious cargo of *Life* in my charge, would allow my attention to wander. Why was I born? How deluded are those who put their trust in me,... et cetera, so on, and he crashes the plane.

CAROL: (*Pause*) He could just...

JOHN: That's right.

CAROL: He could say:

JOHN: My attention *wandered* for a moment...

CAROL: ...uh huh...

JOHN: I had a *thought* I did not like... but now:

CAROL: ...but now it's...

JOHN: That's what I'm telling you. It's time to put my attention... see: it is not: this is what I learned. It is Not Magic. Yes. Yes. *You*. You are going to be frightened. When faced with what may or may not be but which you are going to perceive as a test. You will become frightened. And you will say: "I am incapable of..." and everything *in* you will think these two things. "I must. But I can't." And you will think: Why was I born to be the laughingstock of a world in which everyone is better than I? In which I am entitled to nothing. Where I can not learn. (*Pause*)

CAROL: Is that... (*Pause*) Is that what I have...?

JOHN: Well. I don't know if I'd put it that way. Listen: I'm talking to you as I'd talk to my son. Because that's what I'd like him to have that I never had. I'm talking to you the way I wish that someone had talked to me. I don't know how to do it, other than to be *personal*,... but...

CAROL: Why would you want to be personal with me?

JOHN: Well, you see? That's what I'm saying. We can only interpret the behavior of others through the screen we... (*The phone rings.*) Through... (*To phone:*) Hello...? (*To* CAROL:) Through the screen we create. (*To phone:*) Hello. (*To* CAROL:) Excuse me a moment.

(*To phone:*) Hello? No, I can't talk nnn... I know I did. In a few... I'm... is he coming to the... yes. I talked to him. We'll meet you at the No, because I'm with a *student*. It's going to be fff... This is important, too. I'm with a *student*, Jerry's going to... Listen: the sooner I get off, the sooner I'll be down, all right. I love you. Listen, listen, I said "I love you," it's going to work *out* with the, because I feel that it is, I'll be right down. All right? Well, then it's going to take as long as it takes. (*He hangs up.*) (*To* CAROL:) I'm sorry.

CAROL: What was that?

JOHN: There are some problems, as there usually are, about the final agreements for the new house.

CAROL: You're buying a new house.

JOHN: That's right.

CAROL: Because of your promotion.

JOHN: Well, I suppose that that's right.

CAROL: Why did you stay here with me?

JOHN: Stay here.

CAROL: Yes. When you should have gone.

JOHN: Because I like you.

CAROL: You like me.

JOHN: Yes.

CAROL: Why?

JOHN: Why? Well? Perhaps we're similar. (*Pause*) Yes. (*Pause*)

CAROL: You said "everyone has problems."

JOHN: Everyone has problems.

CAROL: Do they?

JOHN: Certainly.

CAROL: You do?

JOHN: Yes.

CAROL: What are they?

JOHN: Well. (*Pause*) Well, you're perfectly right. (*Pause*) If we're going to take off the Artificial *Stricture*, of "Teacher," and "Student,"[①] why should *my* own problems be any more a mystery than your own? Of

---

① the Artificial Stricture, of "Teacher," and "Student": "教师"和"学生"之间的人为限制。

|||||||course* I have problems. As you saw.

CAROL: ...with what?

JOHN: With my *wife*... with work...

CAROL: With work?

JOHN: Yes. And, and, perhaps my problems are, do you see? *Similar* to yours.

CAROL: Would you tell me?

JOHN: All right. (*Pause*) I came *late* to teaching. And I found it Artificial. The notion of "I know and you do not"; and I saw an *exploitation* in the education process. I told you. I hated school, I hated teachers. I hated everyone who was in the position of a "boss" because I *knew*— I didn't *think*, mind you, I *knew* I was going to fail. Because I was a fuckup. I was just no goddamned good. When I… late in life… (*Pause*) When I *got out from under*... when I worked my way out of the need to fail. When I...①

CAROL: How do you do that? (*Pause*)

JOHN: You have to look at what you are, and what you feel, and how you act. And, finally, you have to look at how you act. And say: If that's what I *did*, that must be how I think of myself.

CAROL: I don't understand.

JOHN: If I fail all the time, it must be that I think of myself as a failure. If I do not want to think of myself as a failure, perhaps I should begin by *succeeding* now and again. Look. The tests, you see, which you encounter, in school, in college, in life, were designed, in the most part, for idiots. By *idiots*. There is no need to fail at them. They are not a test of your worth. They are a test of your ability to retain and spout back misinformation. Of *course* you fail them. They're *nonsense*. And I...

CAROL: ...no...

JOHN: Yes. They're *garbage*. They're a *joke*. Look at me. Look at me. The Tenure Committee. The Tenure Committee. Come to judge me. The Bad Tenure Committee. The "Test." Do you see? They put me to

---

① 为了帮助卡罗尔，约翰试图表现得与她完全平等。所以，他不仅告诉卡罗尔他过去受到过歧视，现在正在遭受现行制度的折磨，而且为了套近乎，他还使用了本剧中少见的脏字。但这其实表现了他的自我中心主义：他没有直接讨论卡罗尔的问题，而是变成了倾诉和抱怨的一方，希望以此与对方沟通。

	the test. Why, they had people voting on me I wouldn't employ to wax my car. And yet, I go before the Great Tenure Committee, and I have an urge, to *vomit*, to, to, to puke my *badness* on the table, to show them: "I'm not good. Why would you pick *me*?"
CAROL:	They granted you tenure.
JOHN:	Oh no, they announced it, but they haven't *signed*. Do you see? "At any moment..."
CAROL:	...mmm...
JOHN:	"They might not *sign*"... I might not... the *house* might not go through... Eh? Eh? They'll find out my "dark secret." (*Pause*)
CAROL:	...what is it...?
JOHN:	There *isn't* one. But *they* will find an index of my badness...
CAROL:	Index?
JOHN:	A "...pointer." A "Pointer." You see? Do you see? I *understand* you. I. Know. That. Feeling. Am I entitled to my job, and my nice *home*, and my *wife*, and my *family*, and so on. This is what I'm saying: That theory of education which, that *theory*:
CAROL:	I... I... (*Pause*)
JOHN:	What?
CAROL:	I...
JOHN:	What?
CAROL:	I want to know about my grade. (*Long pause*)
JOHN:	Of course you do.
CAROL:	Is that bad?
JOHN:	No.
CAROL:	Is it bad that I asked you that?
JOHN:	No.
CAROL:	Did I upset you?
JOHN:	No. And I apologize. Of *course* you want to know about your grade. And, of course, you can't concentrate on anyth... (*The telephone starts to ring.*) Wait a moment.
CAROL:	I should go.
JOHN:	I'll make you a deal.
CAROL:	No, you have to...

JOHN: Let it ring. I'll make you a deal. You stay here. We'll start the whole course over. I'm going to say it was not you, it was I who was not paying attention. We'll start the whole course over. Your grade is an "A." Your final grade is an "A." (*The phone stops ringing.*)

CAROL: But the class is only half over...

JOHN (*simultaneously with* "over"): Your grade for the whole term is an "A." If you will come back and meet with me. A few more times. Your grade's an "A." Forget about the paper. You didn't like it, you didn't like writing it. It's not important. What's important is that I awake your interest, if I can, and that I answer your questions. Let's start over.① (*Pause*)

CAROL: Over. With what?

JOHN: Say this is the beginning.

CAROL: The beginning.

JOHN: Yes.

CAROL: Of what?

JOHN: Of the class.

CAROL: But we can't start over.

JOHN: I say we can. (*Pause*) I say we can.

CAROL: But I don't believe it.

JOHN: Yes, I know that. But it's true. What is The Class but you and me? (*Pause*)

CAROL: There are rules.

JOHN: Well. We'll break them.

CAROL: How can we?

JOHN: We won't tell anybody.

CAROL: Is that all right?

JOHN: I say that it's fine.

CAROL: Why would you do this for me?

JOHN: I like you. Is that so difficult for you to...

CAROL: Um...

JOHN: There's no one here but you and me. (*Pause*)

---

① 约翰决定完全抛开学校的规则,这表现出他对于自己权力的自信。但约翰的"权力"恰恰是"规则"赋予的;破坏了规则,约翰便丧失了他"控制"卡罗尔的权力。

CAROL: All right. I did not understand. When you referred...
JOHN: All right, yes?
CAROL: When you referred to hazing.
JOHN: Hazing.
CAROL: You wrote, in your book. About the comparative... in the comparative... (*She checks her notes.*)
JOHN: Are you checking your notes...?
CAROL: Yes.
JOHN: Tell me in your own...
CAROL: I want to make sure that I have it right.
JOHN: No. Of course. You want to be exact.
CAROL: I want to know everything that went on.
JOHN: ...that's good.
CAROL: ...so I...
JOHN: That's very good. But I was suggesting, many times, that that which we wish to retain is retained oftentimes, I think, *better* with less expenditure of effort.
CAROL: (*Of notes*) Here it is: you wrote of *hazing*.
JOHN: ...that's correct. Now: I said "hazing." It means ritualized annoyance.① We shove this book at you, we say read it. Now, you say you've read it? I think that you're *lying*. I'll *grill* you, and when I find you've lied, you'll be disgraced, and your life will be ruined. It's a sick game. Why do we do it? Does it educate? In no sense. Well, then, what is higher education? It is something-other-than-useful.
CAROL: What is "something-other-than-useful?"
JOHN: It has become a ritual, it has become an article of faith②. That all must be subjected to, or to put it differently, that all are entitled to Higher Education. And my point...
CAROL: You disagree with that?
JOHN: Well, let's address that. What do you think?
CAROL: I don't know
JOHN: What do you think, though? (*Pause*)
CAROL: I don't know.

① 约翰解释"hazing"的意思是"仪式化的难为"。按他下面举的例子，教育正是这种对于学生的"仪式化的难为"。
② an article of faith: 一种信仰；一个信条。

JOHN: I spoke of it in class. Do you remember my example?
CAROL: Justice.
JOHN: Yes. Can you repeat it to me? (*She looks down at her notebook.*) Without your notes? I ask you as a favor to me, so that I can see if my idea was interesting.
CAROL: You said "justice"...
JOHN: Yes?
CAROL: ...that all are entitled... (*Pause*) I... I... I...
JOHN: Yes. To a speedy trial. To a fair trial. But they needn't be given a trial *at all* unless they stand accused. Eh? Justice is their right, should they choose to avail themselves of it, they should have a fair trial. It does not follow, of necessity, a person's life is incomplete without a trial in it. Do you see? My point is a confusion between equity and *utility* arose.① So we confound the usefulness of higher education with our, granted, right to equal access to the same. We, in effect, create a *prejudice* toward it, completely independent of...
CAROL: ...that it is prejudice that we should go to school?
JOHN: Exactly. (*Pause*)
CAROL: How can you say that? How...
JOHN: Good. Good. *Good*. That's right! Speak up! What is a prejudice? An unreasoned belief. We are all subject to it. None of us is not. When it is threatened, or opposed, we feel anger, and feel, do we not? As you do now. Do you not? Good.
CAROL: ...but how can you...
JOHN: ...let us examine. Good.
CAROL: How...
JOHN: Good. Good. When...
CAROL: I'M SPEAKING... (*Pause*)
JOHN: I'm sorry.
CAROL: How can you...

---

① My point is a confusion between equity and utility arose.:我的观点是出现了将平等与应用混为一谈的情况。他在下一句解释说:"我们将高等教育的用途与我们被赋予的平等享受高等教育的权利混为一谈。"联系到他前面举的"正义"的例子,说"这并不必然意味着未经历过审判,一个人的一生就不完整"。他的意思是:虽然人人都有受高等教育的权利,但这并不意味着高等教育有用,也并不意味着每一个人都必须接受"审讯"(Grill)似的考试和"仪式化的难为"。

JOHN: ...I beg your pardon.
CAROL: That's all right.
JOHN: I beg your pardon.
CAROL: That's all right.
JOHN: I'm sorry I interrupted you.
CAROL: That's all right.
JOHN: You were saying?
CAROL: I was saying... I was saying... (*She checks her notes.*) How can you say in a class. Say in a college class, that college education is prejudice?
JOHN: I said that our predilection for it...
CAROL: Predilection...
JOHN: ...you know what that means.
CAROL: Does it mean "liking"?
JOHN: Yes.
CAROL: But how can you say that? That College...
JOHN: ...that's my *job*, don't you know.
CAROL: What is?
JOHN: To provoke you.
CAROL: No.
JOHN: Oh. Yes, though.
CAROL: To provoke me?
JOHN: That's right.
CAROL: To make me mad?
JOHN: That's right. To force you...
CAROL: ...to make me mad is your job?
JOHN: To force you to... listen: (*Pause*) Ah. (*Pause*) When I was young somebody told me, —are you ready?—the rich copulate less often than the poor. But when they do, they take more of their clothes off. Years. Years, mind you, I would compare experiences of my own to this dictum, saying, aha, that fits the norm, or ah, this is a variation from it. What did it mean? Nothing. It was some jerk thing, some school kid told me that took up room inside my head. (*Pause*)

Somebody told *you*, and you hold it as an article of faith, that higher education is an unassailable good.　This notion is so dear to you that when I question it you become angry. Good. Good, I say. Are not those the very things which we should question?　I say college education, since the war, has become so a matter of course, and such a fashionable necessity, for those either of or aspiring *to* to①　the new vast middle class, that we *espouse* it, as a matter of right, and have ceased to ask, "What is it good for?" (*Pause*)

What might be some reasons for pursuit of higher education?
One: A love of learning.
Two: The wish for mastery of a skill.
Three: For economic betterment. (*Stops. Makes a note.*)

CAROL:　　I'm keeping you.
JOHN:　　One moment. I have to make a note...
CAROL:　　It's something that I said?
JOHN:　　No, we're buying a house.
CAROL:　　You're buying the new house.
JOHN:　　To go with the tenure. That's right. Nice *house*, close to the *private school*... (*He continues making his note.*)... We were talking of economic *betterment* (CAROL *writes in her notebook.*)... I was thinking of the School Tax. (*He continues writing.*) (*To himself:*)... *where is it written* that I have to send my child to public school.... Is it a law that I have to improve the City Schools at the expense of my own interest?　And,　is this not simply *The White Man's Burden*②? Good. And (*Looks up to* CAROL)... does this interest you?
CAROL:　　No. I'm taking notes...
JOHN:　　You don't have to take notes, you know, you can just listen.
CAROL:　　I want to make sure I remember it. (*Pause*)
JOHN:　　I'm not lecturing you, I'm just trying to tell you some things I think.
CAROL:　　What do you think?
JOHN:　　Should all kids go to college? Why...

---

① 因为这是两个人的对话,有停顿、重复的地方。在此,约翰重复了"to",以示强调。

② *The White Man's Burden*：原出处为英国小说家和诗人卢迪亚·吉卜林(Rudyard Kipling)在1899年写的一首诗。他在诗中敦促美国像英国和欧洲其他老牌帝国主义国家一样,担负起"帝国"的责任。"白人的负担"已被认为是种族主义和帝国主义的辞藻。约翰后来受到性别歧视和精英主义的指控;他在此无意地或者是玩世不恭地使用这一说法,颇具讽刺意味。

CAROL: (*Pause*) To learn.
JOHN: But if he does not learn.
CAROL: If the child does not learn?
JOHN: Then why is he in college? Because he was told it was his "right"?
CAROL: Some might find college instructive.
JOHN: I would hope so.
CAROL: But how do they feel? Being told they are wasting their time?
JOHN: I don't think I'm telling them that.
CAROL: You said that education was "prolonged and systematic hazing."
JOHN: Yes. It can be so.
CAROL: ...if education is so bad, why do you do it?
JOHN: I do it because I love it. (*Pause*) Let's... I suggest you look at the demographics, wage-earning capacity, college- and non-college-educated men and women, 1855 to 1980, and let's see if we can wring some worth from the statistics. Eh? And...
CAROL: No.
JOHN: What?
CAROL: I can't understand them.
JOHN: ...you...?
CAROL: ...the "charts." The *Concepts*, the...
JOHN: "Charts" are simply...
CAROL: When I leave here...
JOHN: Charts, do you see...
CAROL: No, I can't...
JOHN: You can, though.
CAROL: NO, NO—I DON'T UNDERSTAND. DO YOU SEE??? I DON'T UNDERSTAND...
JOHN: What?
CAROL: *Any* of it. *Any* of it. I'm *smiling* in class, I'm *smiling*, the whole time. What are you *talking* about? What is everyone *talking* about? I don't *understand*. I don't know what it *means*. I don't know what it means to *be* here... you tell me I'm intelligent, and then you tell me I should not be *here*, what do you *want* with me? What does it *mean*? Who should I *listen* to... I...

(*He goes over to her and puts his arm around her shoulder.*)

NO! (*She walks away from him.*)
JOHN: Sshhhh.
CAROL: No, I don't under...
JOHN: Sshhhhh.
CAROL: I don't know what you're *saying*...
JOHN: Sshhhhh. It's all right.
CAROL: ...I have no...
JOHN: Sshhhhh. Sshhhhh. Let it go a moment. (*Pause*) Sshhhhh... let it go. (*Pause*) Just let it go. (*Pause*) Just let it go. It's all right. (*Pause*) Sshhhhh. (*Pause*) I understand... (*Pause*) What do you feel?
CAROL: I feel bad.
JOHN: I know. It's all right.
CAROL: I... (*Pause*)
JOHN: What?
CAROL: I...
JOHN: What? Tell me.
CAROL: I don't understand you.
JOHN: I know. It's all right.
CAROL: I...
JOHN: What? (*Pause*) What? *Tell* me.
CAROL: I can't tell you.
JOHN: No, you must.
CAROL: I can't.
JOHN: No. Tell me. (*Pause*)
CAROL: I'm bad. (*Pause*) Oh, God. (*Pause*)
JOHN: It's all right.
CAROL: I'm...
JOHN: It's all right.
CAROL: I can't talk about this.
JOHN: It's all right. Tell me.
CAROL: Why do you want to know this?
JOHN: I don't want to know. I want to know whatever you...
CAROL: I always...
JOHN: ...good...
CAROL: I always... all my life... I have never told anyone this...

JOHN: Yes. Go on. (*Pause*) Go on.

CAROL: All of my life... (*The phone rings.*) (*Pause.* JOHN *goes to the phone and picks it up.*)

JOHN (*into phone*): I can't talk now. (*Pause*) What? (*Pause*) Hmm. (*Pause*) All right, I... I. Can't. Talk. Now. No, no, no, I *Know* I did, but... What? Hello. What? She *what*? She *can't*, she said the agreement is void? How, how is the agreement *void*? *That's Our House*. I have the *paper*; when we come down, next week, with the payment, and the paper, that house is... wait, wait, wait, wait, wait, wait, wait: Did Jerry... is Jerry there? (*Pause*) Is *she* there...? Does she have a *lawyer*...? How the *hell*, how the *Hell*. That is... it's a question, you said, of the *easement*. I don't underst... it's not the *whole agreement*. It's just the *easement*, why would she? Put, put, put, Jerry on. (*Pause*) Jer, *Jerry*: What the *Hell*... that's my *house*. That's... Well, I'm, no, no, no, I'm *not* coming ddd... List, *Listen, screw* her. You *tell* her. You, listen: I want you to take *Grace*, you take Grace, and get out of that house. You *leave* her there. Her and her lawyer, and you *tell* them, we'll see them in court next... no. No. Leave her there, leave her to *stew* in it: You tell her, we're *getting* that house, and we are going to... No. I'm *not* coming down. I'll be damned if I'll sit in the same rrr... the next, you tell her the next time I *see* her is in court... I... (*Pause*) What? (*Pause*) What? I don't understand. (*Pause*) Well, what about the house? (*Pause*) There isn't any problem with the hhh... (*Pause*) No, no, no, that's all right. All ri... All right... (*Pause*) Of course. Tha... Thank you. No, I will. Right away. (*He hangs up.*) (*Pause*)

CAROL: What is it? (*Pause*)

JOHN: It's a surprise party.

CAROL: It is.

JOHN: Yes.

CAROL: A party for you.

JOHN: Yes.

CAROL: Is it your birthday?

JOHN: No.

CAROL:	What is it?
JOHN:	The tenure announcement.
CAROL:	The tenure announcement.
JOHN:	They're throwing a party for us in our new house.
CAROL:	Your new house.
JOHN:	The house that we're buying.
CAROL:	You have to go.
JOHN:	It seems that I do.
CAROL:	(Pause) They're proud of you.
JOHN:	Well, there are those who would say it's a form of aggression.
CAROL:	What is?
JOHN:	A surprise.

《奥里安娜》涉及"政治正确"、"性骚扰"、"女权立场"等美国社会的敏感话题,所以曾引起很大争议。该剧开始时,大学教师约翰正在办公室与女学生卡罗尔谈话。卡罗尔性格忧郁、缺乏自信、拙于交流;她学习吃力,显然无法理解很多专业术语,也无法了解约翰的想法。约翰认为卡罗尔很聪明,但并未发挥出潜能,所以学习成绩很差。在谈话中,约翰不断接到妻子 Grace 和朋友 Jerry 的电话,谈论购买房屋和他本人申请终身教职(tenure)的事情。他对终身教职审批委员会的做法颇有微词,对整个高等教育也持批评态度。所以,他对卡罗尔的处境极为同情,并提出要帮助她。他说只要不告诉别人,他们两人就可以抛开规则,两人私下上课,据此重新给出成绩。约翰居高临下,完全掌控着学术权力,卡罗尔对此极为不满,而且她也对约翰用肢体语言表示亲近做出了她自己的判断。在女权组织的支持下,她控告约翰性骚扰、性别歧视、精英主义。在这之后,约翰与她又在办公室见面,要求她撤销指控。在沟通失败之后,卡罗尔拒绝了约翰的要求,并要离去。约翰试图阻止她离去,进而发生了肢体上的冲突。卡罗尔这时已通过女权话语掌控了权力,而约翰则反而处于弱势。她还威胁要对约翰提出殴打和强奸未遂的刑事指控;面对着这一切,约翰举起一把椅子,真的要砸向卡罗尔。但我们不知道这是惶恐之举,还是孤注一掷。

该剧上演前,恰逢劳伦斯·托马斯大法官任命听证会的风波。美国总统乔治·布什提名保守的非洲裔美国人劳伦斯·托马斯担任美国最高法院大法官;但在国会听证时,他以前的下属、俄克拉荷马大学法学女教授安妮塔·希尔却对他提出了性骚扰的指控。这使工作场合的性骚扰问题成为全美国关注的热点。马麦特否认因为该事件而创作《奥丽安娜》,但又承认在事件之后才将搁置已久的该剧最终完成。该剧反映了美国社会的热点问题,反映了"权力"和"支配话语"在"强势"和"弱势"群体之间的转移。但在更深的层面,该剧也反映了人与人之间的隔阂;尤其反映了在"权力"、

"性别政治"、"政治正确"等话语的侵蚀下,人类生存中的异化状态。

因为该剧以大学教育为背景,剧中人物大多有良好的教养,所以马麦特其他剧作中的粗鲁猥亵的语言在该剧中出现较少,这使该剧有异于剧作家的惯常风格。该剧的剧名也有象征意义:这是一位19世纪的挪威歌唱家试图在西宾夕法尼亚州建立的一个理想化的、井然有序的住宅区,但其计划以失败告终。所以,"《奥丽安娜》是一部关于失败了的乌托邦的剧作;是一个失败了的学术乌托邦的个案。"(马麦特语)

思考题

1. How does the telephone conversation interact with the conversation between John and Carol?
2. How does John deal with Carol's problem? What are his strategies?
3. Can any of John's language and gestures be interpreted as sexual harassment? Are they all proper?

Sexual Perversity in Chicago (1974)
American Buffalo (1976)
Glengarry Glen Ross (1983)

参考资料

Bigsby, Christopher, ed. *The Cambridge Companion to David Mamet*. Cambridge UP, 2004.

SparkNotes: Oleanna. Online ed. http:// www.sparknotes.com/drama/ oleanna/.

第十九单元
Joyce Carol Oates
(1938—)
乔伊斯·卡洛尔·欧茨

作者简介

乔伊斯·卡洛尔·欧茨，美国当代女小说家、学者、文学教授。出生于纽约州的一个工人阶级家庭，大学期间开始学习写作，短篇小说《在旧世界》(In the Old World)曾获女大学生小说创作比赛一等奖。1962年进入底特律大学任教，一边从事教学，一边进行文学创作。1967年随丈夫移居加拿大，在温莎大学教授英美文学、文学创作、心理学和当代世界文学等课程。1978年回到美国，当选为美国文学艺术院院士，此后在普林斯顿大学任驻校作家、客座教授，讲授文学创作。

欧茨是一位多产作家，自1963年出版首部短篇小说集《北门边》(By the North Gate)以来一直活跃于美国文坛，勤于笔耕，不断有作品问世。迄今为止已发表长篇小说四十余部，另著有多部短篇小说、诗歌、戏剧、随笔、文学评论等文集，同时也致力于时事议论文与侦探小说等通俗文类写作。1970年以长篇小说代表作《他们》(Them)获得美国国家图书奖，《人间乐园》(A Garden of Earthly Delights, 1966)等5部小说曾获得图书奖提名奖，《漆黑的水》(Black Water, 1992)等三部作品曾获得普利策提名奖，《大瀑布》(The Falls, 2004)获得2005年度法国费米纳文学奖。《我们是马尔瓦尼一家》(We Were the Mulvaneys, 1996)于2001年成为"奥普拉读书俱乐部"(Oprah's Book Club)的推荐书目，这使得欧茨首次荣登纽约时报畅销书排行榜首。凭借她多年非凡的文学成就，欧茨至今已两度获得诺贝尔文学奖提名。

欧茨的作品在整体上构成了一幅当代美国社会全景图，不仅深刻反映了美国社会各个阶层的现实生活，特别是中下层阶级和劳动阶层，而且触及到当代美国社会生活的多个领域，如学术界、法律界、宗教界、政坛，甚至涉足拳击、足球等体育题材。同时，她的表现手法求新多变，创作中大胆尝试多种文学体裁。欧茨特别擅长使用心理现实主义手法，以揭露现代美国社会的暴力行径和罪恶现象见长，其作品往往充满了怪诞和黑色幽默成分，而且大都围绕一个关于爱与暴力的主题。她认为，在一个物质极度丰富的社会，人们的精神世界却苍白贫瘠，商业化价值观轻而易举地弱化或取代了人们的道德伦理；因此，对人生意义和生命价值的追问在这个语境中就显得尤为重要。欧茨在创作中体现出对美国文化传统的尊重，马克·吐温、德莱塞、斯坦贝克等作家的批判现实主义对她的影响显而易见。在继承传统的同时，她更注重用多样化的艺术手法刻画人物内心世界。尽管她在某些作品中，娴熟地借鉴并运用了

心理分析、内心独白、意识流、象征主义、神秘主义等现代主义表现手法,但评论界普遍认为,欧茨的创作思想根基主要还是现实主义,因此她常被称作"具有巴尔扎克式雄心"的现实主义女作家。至今,年届七旬的欧茨仍然处于创作活跃期。

Where Are You Going, Where Have You Been?
*For Bob Dylan*①

    Her name was Connie. She was fifteen and she had a quick, nervous giggling habit of craning her neck to glance into mirrors or checking other people's faces to make sure her own was all right. Her mother, who noticed everything and knew everything and who hadn't much reason any longer to look at her own face, always scolded Connie about it. "Stop gawking② at yourself. Who are you? You think you're so pretty?" she would say. Connie would raise her eyebrows at these familiar old complaints and look right through her mother, into a shadowy③ vision of herself as she was right at that moment: she knew she was pretty and that was everything. Her mother had been pretty once too, if you could believe those old snapshots④ in the album, but now her looks were gone and that was why she was always after Connie.

    "Why don't you keep your room clean like your sister? How've you got your hair fixed—what the hell stinks? Hair spray? You don't see your sister using that junk."

    Her sister June was twenty-four and still lived at home. She was a secretary in the high school Connie attended, and if that wasn't bad enough—with her in the same building—she was so plain and chunky⑤ and steady that Connie had to hear her praised all the time by her mother and her mother's sisters. June did this, June did that, she saved money and helped clean the house and cooked and

---

    ① 鲍勃·迪伦(1941—),美国著名摇滚音乐家。其作品成为20世纪60年代反战和人权运动中的圣歌,促使60年代美国青年的大觉醒。60年代后期创作开始自我回归,具有宗教式的超脱感。70年代吸收了爵士乐和布鲁斯元素,歌词充满哲理性,带动了70年代的美国青年从狂热的叛逆情绪中逐渐安定下来,开始进行哲性反思。
    ② gawk:呆呆地看,凝视。
    ③ shadowy:模糊的,朦胧的。
    ④ snapshot:快照,便照。
    ⑤ chunky:矮胖的,结实的。

Connie couldn't do a thing, her mind was all filled with trashy① daydreams. Their father was away at work most of the time and when he came home he wanted supper and he read the newspaper at supper and after supper he went to bed. He didn't bother talking much to them, but around his bent head Connie's mother kept picking at her until Connie wished her mother was dead and she herself was dead and it was all over. "She makes me want to throw up sometimes," she complained to her friends. She had a high, breathless, amused voice that made everything she said sound a little forced, whether it was sincere or not②.

There was one good thing: June went places with girl friends of hers, girls who were just as plain and steady as she, and so when Connie wanted to do that her mother had no objections. The father of Connie's best girl friend drove the girls the three miles to town and left them at a shopping plaza so they could walk through the stores or go to a movie, and when he came to pick them up again at eleven he never bothered to ask what they had done.

They must have been familiar sights, walking around the shopping plaza in their shorts and flat ballerina slippers that always scuffed③ the sidewalk, with charm bracelets④ jingling on their thin wrists; they would lean together to whisper and laugh secretly if someone passed who amused or interested them. Connie had long dark blond hair that drew anyone's eye to it, and she wore part of it pulled up on her head and puffed out⑤ and the rest of it she let fall down her back. She wore a pull-over jersey blouse that looked one way when she was at home and another way when she was away from home. Everything about her had two sides to it, one for home and one for anywhere that was not home: her walk, which could be childlike and bobbing⑥, or languid enough to make anyone think she was hearing music in her head; her mouth, which was pale and smirking⑦ most of the time, but bright and pink on these evenings out; her laugh, which was cynical and drawling⑧ at home—"Ha, ha, very funny,"—but high-pitched and nervous

---

① trashy：无用的，无价值的。
② a high, breathless, amused voice that made everything she said sound a little forced, whether it was sincere or not：她声音高亢，兴冲冲的，而且上气不接下气，使得她所说的话不管真诚与否，听起来总有点做作。
③ scuff：摩擦，以足擦地。
④ charm bracelets：护身符手镯。
⑤ puffed out：（头发）蓬松的。
⑥ bobbing：（走路）轻快活泼的。
⑦ smirk：傻笑，得意地笑。
⑧ drawling：慢吞吞的，有气无力的。

anywhere else, like the jingling of the charms on her bracelet.

Sometimes they did go shopping or to a movie, but sometimes they went across the highway, ducking① fast across the busy road, to a drive-in restaurant② where older kids hung out. The restaurant was shaped like a big bottle, though squatter than a real bottle, and on its cap was a revolving figure of a grinning boy holding a hamburger aloft. One night in midsummer they ran across, breathless with daring, and right away someone leaned out a car window and invited them over, but it was just a boy from high school they didn't like. It made them feel good to be able to ignore him. They went up through the maze of parked and cruising cars to the bright-lit, fly-infested restaurant, their faces pleased and expectant as if they were entering a sacred building that loomed up out of the night to give them what haven and blessing they yearned for. They sat at the counter and crossed their legs at the ankles, their thin shoulders rigid with excitement, and listened to the music that made everything so good: the music was always in the background, like music at a church service; it was something to depend upon.

A boy named Eddie came in to talk with them. He sat backwards on his stool, turning himself jerkily around in semicircles and then stopping and turning back again, and after a while he asked Connie if she would like something to eat. She said she would and so she tapped her friend's arm on her way out—her friend pulled her face up into a brave, droll③ look—and Connie said she would meet her at eleven, across the way. "I just hate to leave her like that," Connie said earnestly, but the boy said that she wouldn't be alone for long. So they went out to his car, and on the way Connie couldn't help but let her eyes wander over the windshields and faces all around her, her face gleaming with a joy that had nothing to do with Eddie or even this place; it might have been the music. She drew her shoulders up and sucked in her breath with the pure pleasure of being alive, and just at that moment she happened to glance at a face just a few feet from hers. It was a boy with shaggy black hair, in a convertible jalopy④ painted gold. He stared at her and then his lips widened into a grin. Connie slit her eyes at him and turned away, but she couldn't help glancing back and there he was, still

---

① duck：躲躲闪闪地走。
② drive-in restaurant：免下车餐馆，顾客可坐在自己的车上点餐、进餐。
③ droll：滑稽可笑的，怪里怪气的。
④ a convertible jalopy：一辆破旧的敞篷汽车。

watching her. He wagged a finger and laughed and said, "Gonna get you, baby," and Connie turned away again without Eddie noticing anything.

She spent three hours with him, at the restaurant where they ate hamburgers and drank Cokes in wax cups that were always sweating①, and then down an alley a mile or so away, and when he left her off at five to eleven only the movie house was still open at the plaza. Her girl friend was there, talking with a boy. When Connie came up, the two girls smiled at each other and Connie said, "How was the movie?" and the girl said, *"You* should know." They rode off with the girl's father, sleepy and pleased, and Connie couldn't help but look back at the darkened shopping plaza with its big empty parking lot and its signs that were faded and ghostly now, and over at the drive-in restaurant where cars were still circling tirelessly. She couldn't hear the music at this distance.

Next morning June asked her how the movie was and Connie said, "So-so."

She and that girl and occasionally another girl went out several times a week, and the rest of the time Connie spent around the house—it was summer vacation—getting in her mother's way and thinking, dreaming about the boys she met. But all the boys fell back and dissolved into a single face that was not even a face but an idea, a feeling, mixed up with the urgent insistent pounding of the music and the humid night air of July. Connie's mother kept dragging her back to the daylight by finding things for her to do or saying suddenly, "What's this about the Pettinger girl?"

And Connie would say nervously, "Oh, her. That dope②." She always drew thick clear lines between herself and such girls, and her mother was simple and kind enough to believe it. Her mother was so simple, Connie thought, that it was maybe cruel to fool her so much. Her mother went scuffling around the house in old bedroom slippers and complained over the telephone to one sister about the other, then the other called up and the two of them complained about the third one. If June's name was mentioned her mother's tone was approving, and if Connie's name was mentioned it was disapproving. This did not really mean she disliked Connie, and actually Connie thought that her mother preferred her to June just because she was prettier, but the two of them kept up a pretense of exasperation, a sense that they were tugging and struggling over something of little value to either of them. Sometimes, over coffee, they were almost friends,

---

① 由于天气炎热，盛着冰镇可乐的蜡质杯外壁一直凝结着水汽。
② dope：傻瓜，笨蛋。与下文出现的 jerk 与 creep 都是口语中侮辱性言词。

but something would come up—some vexation that was like a fly buzzing suddenly around their heads—and their faces went hard with contempt.①

One Sunday Connie got up at eleven—none of them bothered with church—and washed her hair so that it could dry all day long in the sun. Her parents and sister were going to a barbecue at an aunt's house and Connie said no, she wasn't interested, rolling her eyes to let her mother know just what she thought of it. "Stay home alone then," her mother said sharply. Connie sat out back in a lawn chair and watched them drive away, her father quiet and bald, hunched around so that he could back the car out, her mother with a look that was still angry and not at all softened through the windshield, and in the back seat poor old June, all dressed up② as if she didn't know what a barbecue was, with all the running yelling kids and the flies. Connie sat with her eyes closed in the sun, dreaming and dazed with the warmth about her as if this were a kind of love, the caresses of love, and her mind slipped over onto thoughts of the boy she had been with the night before and how nice he had been, how sweet it always was, not the way someone like June would suppose but sweet, gentle, the way it was in movies and promised in songs; and when she opened her eyes she hardly knew where she was, the back yard ran off into weeds and a fence-like line of trees and behind it the sky was perfectly blue and still. The asbestos③ "ranch house" that was now three years old startled her—it looked small. She shook her head as if to get awake.

It was too hot. She went inside the house and turned on the radio to drown out the quiet. She sat on the edge of her bed, barefoot, and listened for an hour and a half to a program called XYZ Sunday Jamboree④, record after record of hard, fast, shrieking songs she sang along with, interspersed by exclamations from "Bobby King": "An' look here, you girls at Napoleon's—Son and Charley want you to pay real close attention to this song coming up!"

And Connie paid close attention herself, bathed in a glow of slow-pulsed joy that seemed to rise mysteriously out of the music itself and lay languidly about the airless little room, breathed in and breathed out with each gentle rise and fall of her chest.

After a while she heard a car coming up the drive. She sat up at once,

---

① 这一段文字精彩地描述了母女之间的微妙关系，母亲面对漂亮女儿的矛盾心情跃然纸上。
② poor old June, all dressed up：姐姐盛装出行，显然与烤肉野餐会的场景不符。
③ asbestos：石棉瓦。
④ jamboree：喧闹的娱乐会，狂欢活动。

startled, because it couldn't be her father so soon. The gravel kept crunching all the way in from the road—the driveway was long—and Connie ran to the window. It was a car she didn't know. It was an open jalopy, painted a bright gold that caught the sunlight opaquely. Her heart began to pound and her fingers snatched at her hair, checking it, and she whispered, "Christ. Christ," wondering how bad she looked. The car came to a stop at the side door and the horn sounded four short taps, as if this were a signal Connie knew.

  She went into the kitchen and approached the door slowly, then hung out the screen door, her bare toes curling down off the step. There were two boys in the car and now she recognized the driver: he had shaggy, shabby black hair that looked crazy as a wig and he was grinning at her.

  "I ain't late, am I?" he said.

  "Who the hell do you think you are?" Connie said.

  "Toldja[①] I'd be out, didn't I?"

  "I don't even know who you are."

  She spoke sullenly, careful to show no interest or pleasure, and he spoke in a fast, bright monotone. Connie looked past him to the other boy, taking her time. He had fair brown hair, with a lock that fell onto his forehead. His sideburns[②] gave him a fierce, embarrassed look, but so far he hadn't even bothered to glance at her. Both boys wore sunglasses. The driver's glasses were metallic and mirrored everything in miniature.

  "You wanta come for a ride?" he said.

  Connie smirked and let her hair fall loose over one shoulder.

  "Don'tcha like my car? New paint job," he said. "Hey."

  "What?"

  "You're cute."

  She pretended to fidget, chasing flies away from the door.

  "Don'tcha believe me, or what?" he said.

  "Look, I don't even know who you are," Connie said in disgust.

  "Hey, Ellie's got a radio, see. Mine broke down." He lifted his friend's arm and showed her the little transistor radio the boy was holding, and now Connie began to hear the music. It was the same program that was playing inside the house.

---

 ① Toldja：应为 Told you，这种拼写体现了讲话人的实际发音，下文例子仍有很多。
 ② sideburns：短络腮胡子。

"Bobby King?" she said.

"I listen to him all the time. I think he's great."

"He's kind of great," Connie said reluctantly.

"Listen, that guy's *great*. He knows where the action is."

Connie blushed a little, because the glasses made it impossible for her to see just what this boy was looking at. She couldn't decide if she liked him or if he was just a jerk, and so she dawdled in the doorway and wouldn't come down or go back inside. She said, "What's all that stuff painted on your car?"

"Can'tcha read it?" He opened the door very carefully, as if he were afraid it might fall off. He slid out just as carefully, planting his feet firmly on the ground, the tiny metallic world in his glasses slowing down like gelatine hardening, and in the midst of it Connie's bright green blouse. "This here is my name, to begin with," he said. ARNOLD FRIEND was written in tarlike black letters on the side, with a drawing of a round, grinning face that reminded Connie of a pumpkin, except it wore sunglasses. "I wanta introduce myself, I'm Arnold Friend and that's my real name and I'm gonna be your friend, honey, and inside the car's Ellie Oscar, he's kinda shy." Ellie brought his transistor radio up to his shoulder and balanced it there. "Now, these numbers are a secret code, honey," Arnold Friend explained. He read off the numbers 33, 19, 17 and raised his eyebrows at her to see what she thought of that, but she didn't think much of it. The left rear fender had been smashed and around it was written, on the gleaming gold background: DONE BY CRAZY WOMAN DRIVER. Connie had to laugh at that. Arnold Friend was pleased at her laughter and looked up at her. "Around the other side's a lot more—you wanta come and see them?"

"No."

"Why not?"

"Why should I?"

"Don'tcha wanta see what's on the car? Don'tcha wanta go for a ride?"

"I don't know."

"Why not?"

"I got things to do."

"Like what?"

"Things."

He laughed as if she had said something funny. He slapped his thighs. He was standing in a strange way, leaning back against the car as if he were balancing himself. He wasn't tall, only an inch or so taller than she would be if she came down to him. Connie liked the way he was dressed, which was the way all of them dressed: tight faded jeans stuffed into black, scuffed boots, a belt that pulled his waist in and showed how lean he was, and a white pull-over shirt that was a little soiled and showed the hard small muscles of his arms and shoulders. He looked as if he probably did hard work, lifting and carrying things. Even his neck looked muscular. And his face was a familiar face, somehow: the jaw and chin and cheeks slightly darkened because he hadn't shaved for a day or two, and the nose long and hawk-like, sniffing as if she were a treat① he was going to gobble up and it was all a joke.

"Connie, you ain't telling the truth. This is your day set aside for a ride with me and you know it," he said, still laughing. The way he straightened and recovered from his fit of laughing showed that it had been all fake.

"How do you know what my name is?" she said suspiciously.

"It's Connie."

"Maybe and maybe not."

"I know my Connie," he said, wagging his finger. Now she remembered him even better, back at the restaurant, and her cheeks warmed at the thought of how she had sucked in her breath just at the moment she passed him—how she must have looked to him. And he had remembered her. "Ellie and I come out here especially for you," he said. "Ellie can sit in back. How about it?"

"Where?"

"Where what?"

"Where're we going?"

He looked at her. He took off the sunglasses and she saw how pale the skin around his eyes was, like holes that were not in shadow but instead in light. His eyes were like chips of broken glass that catch the light in an amiable way. He smiled. It was as if the idea of going for a ride somewhere, to someplace, was a new idea to him.

"Just for a ride, Connie sweetheart."

"I never said my name was Connie," she said.

"But I know what it is. I know your name and all about you, lots of things,"

---

① treat: 美食, 盛宴。

Arnold Friend said. He had not moved yet but stood still leaning back against the side of his jalopy. "I took a special interest in you, such a pretty girl, and found out all about you—like I know your parents and sister are gone somewheres and I know where and how long they're going to be gone, and I know who you were with last night, and your best girl friend's name is Betty. Right?"

He spoke in a simple lilting voice, exactly as if he were reciting the words to a song. His smile assured her that everything was fine. In the car Ellie turned up the volume on his radio and did not bother to look around at them.

"Ellie can sit in the back seat," Arnold Friend said. He indicated his friend with a casual jerk of his chin, as if Ellie did not count and she should not bother with him.

"How'd you find out all that stuff?" Connie said.

"Listen: Betty Schultz and Tony Fitch and Jimmy Pettinger and Nancy Pettinger," he said in a chant. "Raymond Stanley and Bob Hutter—"

"Do you know all those kids?"

"I know everybody."

"Look, you're kidding. You're not from around here."

"Sure."

"But—how come we never saw you before?"

"Sure you saw me before," he said. He looked down at his boots, as if he were a little offended. "You just don't remember."

"I guess I'd remember you," Connie said.

"Yeah?" He looked up at this, beaming. He was pleased. He began to mark time with the music from Ellie's radio, tapping his fists lightly together. Connie looked away from his smile to the car, which was painted so bright it almost hurt her eyes to look at it. She looked at that name, ARNOLD FRIEND. And up at the front fender was an expression that was familiar—MAN THE FLYING SAUCERS. It was an expression kids had used the year before but didn't use this year. She looked at it for a while as if the words meant something to her that she did not yet know.

"What're you thinking about? Huh?" Arnold Friend demanded. "Not worried about your hair blowing around in the car, are you?"

"No."

"Think I maybe can't drive good?"

"How do I know?"

"You're a hard girl to handle. How come?" he said. "Don't you know I'm your friend? Didn't you see me put my sign in the air when you walked by?"

"What sign?"

"My sign." And he drew an X in the air, leaning out toward her. They were maybe ten feet apart. After his hand fell back to his side the X was still in the air, almost visible. Connie let the screen door close and stood perfectly still inside it, listening to the music from her radio and the boy's blend together. She stared at Arnold Friend. He stood there so stiffly relaxed, pretending to be relaxed, with one hand idly on the door handle as if he were keeping himself up that way and had no intention of ever moving again. She recognized most things about him, the tight jeans that showed his thighs and buttocks and the greasy leather boots and the tight shirt, and even that slippery friendly smile of his, that sleepy dreamy smile that all the boys used to get across ideas they didn't want to put into words. She recognized all this and also the singsong way he talked, slightly mocking, kidding, but serious and a little melancholy, and she recognized the way he tapped one fist against the other in homage to the perpetual music behind him. But all these things did not come together.①

She said suddenly, "Hey, how old are you?"

His smile faded. She could see then that he wasn't a kid, he was much older—thirty, maybe more. At this knowledge her heart began to pound faster.

"That's a crazy thing to ask. Can'tcha see I'm your own age?"

"Like hell you are."

"Or maybe a coupla years older. I'm eighteen."

"Eighteen?" she said doubtfully.

He grinned to reassure her and lines appeared at the corners of his mouth. His teeth were big and white. He grinned so broadly his eyes became slits and she saw how thick the lashes were, thick and black as if painted with a black tarlike material. Then, abruptly, he seemed to become embarrassed and looked over his shoulder at Ellie. "*Him*, he's crazy," he said. "Ain't he a riot? He's a nut, a real character." Ellie was still listening to the music. His sunglasses told nothing about what he was thinking. He wore a bright orange shirt unbuttoned halfway to show

---

① But all these things did not come together.：这名陌生男子的着装、作派、言谈举止等一切细节都让康妮感到熟悉，可放在一起却让人感到不太协调。

his chest, which was a pale, bluish chest and not muscular like Arnold Friend's. His shirt collar was turned up all around and the very tips of the collar pointed out past his chin as if they were protecting him. He was pressing the transistor radio up against his ear and sat there in a kind of a daze, right in the sun.

"He's kinda strange," Connie said.

"Hey, she says you're kinda strange! Kinda strange!" Arnold Friend cried. He pounded on the car to get Ellie's attention. Ellie turned for the first time and Connie saw with shock that he wasn't a kid either—he had a fair, hairless face, cheeks reddened slightly as if the veins grew too close to the surface of his skin, the face of a forty-year-old baby. Connie felt a wave of dizziness rise in her at this sight and she stared at him as if waiting for something to change the shock of the moment, make it all right again. Ellie's lips kept shaping words, mumbling along with the words blasting in his ear.

"Maybe you two better go away," Connie said faintly.

"What? How come?" Arnold Friend cried. "We come out here to take you for a ride. It's Sunday." He had the voice of the man on the radio now. It was the same voice, Connie thought. "Don'tcha know it's Sunday all day? And honey, no matter who you were with last night, today you're with Arnold Friend and don't you forget it! Maybe you better step out here," he said, and this last was in a different voice. It was a little flatter, as if the heat was finally getting to him.

"Hey."

"You two better leave."

"We ain't leaving until you come with us."

"Like hell I am—"

"Connie, don't fool around with me. I mean—I mean, don't fool *around*," he said shaking his head. He laughed incredulously. He placed his sunglasses on top of his head, carefully, as if he were indeed wearing a wig, and brought the stems down behind his ears. Connie stared at him, another wave of dizziness and fear rising in her so that for a moment he wasn't even in focus but was just a blur standing there against his gold car, and she had the idea that he had driven up the driveway all right but had come from nowhere before that and belonged nowhere and that everything about him and even about the music that was so familiar to her was only half real.

"If my father comes and sees you—"

"He ain't coming. He's at a barbecue."

"How do you know that?"

"Aunt Tillie's. Right now they're—uh—they're drinking. Sitting around," he said vaguely, squinting as if he were staring all the way to town and over to Aunt Tillie's back yard. Then the vision seemed to get clear and he nodded energetically. "Yeah. Sitting around. There's your sister in a blue dress, huh? And high heels, the poor sad bitch—nothing like you, sweetheart! And your mother's helping some fat woman with the corn, they're cleaning the corn—husking the corn—"

"What fat woman?" Connie cried.

"How do I know what fat woman, I don't know every goddamn fat woman in the world!" Arnold Friend laughed.

"Oh, that's Mrs. Hornsby... Who invited her?" Connie said. She felt a little lightheaded. Her breath was coming quickly.

"She's too fat. I don't like them fat. I like them the way you are, honey," he said, smiling sleepily at her. They stared at each other for a while through the screen door. He said softly, "Now, what you're going to do is this: you're going to come out that door. You're going to sit up front with me and Ellie's going to sit in the back, the hell with Ellie, right? This isn't Ellie's date. You're my date. I'm your lover, honey."

"What? You're crazy—"

"Yes, I'm your lover. You don't know what that is but you will," he said. "I know that too. I know all about you. But look: it's real nice and you couldn't ask for nobody better than me, or more polite. I always keep my word. I'll tell you how it is, I'm always nice at first, the first time. I'll hold you so tight you won't think you have to try to get away or pretend anything because you'll know you can't. And I'll come inside you where it's all secret and you'll give in to me and you'll love me"

"Shut up! You're crazy!" Connie said. She backed away from the door. She put her hands up against her ears as if she'd heard something terrible, something not meant for her. "People don't talk like that, you're crazy," she muttered. Her heart was almost too big now for her chest and its pumping made sweat break out all over her. She looked out to see Arnold Friend pause and then take a step toward the porch, lurching①. He almost fell. But, like a clever drunken man, he managed to catch his balance. He wobbled in his high boots and grabbed hold of

---

① lurch：东倒西歪地走，蹒跚而行。

one of the porch posts.

"Honey?" he said. "You still listening?"

"Get the hell out of here!"

"Be nice, honey. Listen."

"I'm going to call the police—"

He wobbled again and out of the side of his mouth came a fast spat curse, an aside not meant for her to hear. But even this "Christ!" sounded forced. Then he began to smile again. She watched this smile come, awkward as if he were smiling from inside a mask. His whole face was a mask, she thought wildly, tanned down to his throat but then running out as if he had plastered make-up on his face but had forgotten about his throat.

"Honey—? Listen, here's how it is. I always tell the truth and I promise you this: I ain't coming in that house after you."

"You better not! I'm going to call the police if you—if you don't—"

"Honey," he said, talking right through her voice, "honey, I'm not coming in there but you are coming out here. You know why?"

She was panting. The kitchen looked like a place she had never seen before, some room she had run inside but that wasn't good enough, wasn't going to help her. The kitchen window had never had a curtain, after three years, and there were dishes in the sink for her to do—probably—and if you ran your hand across the table you'd probably feel something sticky there.

"You listening, honey? Hey?"

"—going to call the police—"

"Soon as you touch the phone I don't need to keep my promise and can come inside. You won't want that."

She rushed forward and tried to lock the door. Her fingers were shaking. "But why lock it," Arnold Friend said gently, talking right into her face. "It's just a screen door. It's just nothing." One of his boots was at a strange angle, as if his foot wasn't in it. It pointed out to the left, bent at the ankle. "I mean, anybody can break through a screen door and glass and wood and iron or anything else if he needs to, anybody at all, and specially Arnold Friend. If the place got lit up with a fire, honey, you'd come runnin' out into my arms, right into my arms an' safe at home—like you knew I was your lover and'd stopped fooling around. I don't mind a nice shy girl but I don't like no fooling around." Part of those words were spoken with a slight rhythmic lilt, and Connie somehow recognized them—the echo of a song from last year, about a girl rushing into her boy friend's arms and coming home again—

Connie stood barefoot on the linoleum floor, staring at him. "What do you want?" she whispered.

"I want you," he said.

"What?"

"Seen you that night and thought, that's the one, yes sir. I never needed to look anymore."

"But my father's coming back. He's coming to get me. I had to wash my hair first—" She spoke in a dry, rapid voice, hardly raising it for him to hear.

"No, your daddy is not coming and yes, you had to wash your hair and you washed it for me. It's nice and shining and all for me. I thank you sweetheart," he said with a mock bow, but again he almost lost his balance. He had to bend and adjust his boots. Evidently his feet did not go all the way down; the boots must have been stuffed with something so that he would seem taller. Connie stared out at him and behind him at Ellie in the car, who seemed to be looking off toward Connie's right, into nothing. This Ellie said, pulling the words out of the air one after another as if he were just discovering them, "You want me to pull out the phone?"

"Shut your mouth and keep it shut," Arnold Friend said, his face red from bending over or maybe from embarrassment because Connie had seen his boots. "This ain't none of your business."

"What—what are you doing? What do you want?" Connie said. "If I call the police they'll get you, they'll arrest you—"

"Promise was not to come in unless you touch that phone, and I'll keep that promise," he said. He resumed his erect position and tried to force his shoulders back. He sounded like a hero in a movie, declaring something important. But he spoke too loudly and it was as if he were speaking to someone behind Connie. "I ain't made plans for coming in that house where I don't belong but just for you to come out to me, the way you should. Don't you know who I am?"

"You're crazy," she whispered. She backed away from the door but did not want to go into another part of the house, as if this would give him permission to come through the door. "What do you... you're crazy, you..."

"Huh? What're you saying, honey?"

Her eyes darted everywhere in the kitchen. She could not remember what it was, this room.

"This is how it is, honey: you come out and we'll drive away, have a nice ride. But if you don't come out we're gonna wait till your people come home and then they're all going to get it."

"You want that telephone pulled out?" Ellie said. He held the radio away from his ear and grimaced, as if without the radio the air was too much for him.

"I toldja shut up, Ellie," Arnold Friend said, "you're deaf, get a hearing aid, right? Fix yourself up. This little girl's no trouble and's gonna be nice to me, so Ellie keep to yourself, this ain't your date—right? Don't hem in on me, don't hog, don't crush, don't bird dog, don't trail me," he said in a rapid, meaningless voice, as if he were running through all the expressions he'd learned but was no longer sure which of them was in style, then rushing on to new ones, making them up with his eyes closed. "Don't crawl under my fence, don't squeeze in my chipmunk hole, don't sniff my glue, suck my popsicle, keep your own greasy fingers on yourself!"① He shaded his eyes and peered in at Connie, who was backed against the kitchen table. "Don't mind him, honey, he's just a creep. He's a dope. Right? I'm the boy for you and like I said, you come out here nice like a lady and give me your hand, and nobody else gets hurt, I mean, your nice old bald-headed daddy and your mummy and your sister in her high heels. Because listen: why bring them in this?"

"Leave me alone," Connie whispered.

"Hey, you know that old woman down the road, the one with the chickens and stuff—you know her?"

"She's dead!"

"Dead? What? You know her?" Arnold Friend said.

"She's dead—"

"Don't you like her?"

"She's dead—she's—she isn't here any more—"

But don't you like her, I mean, you got something against her? Some grudge or something? Then his voice dipped as if he were conscious of a rudeness. He touched the sunglasses perched up on top of his head as if to make sure they were

---

① Don't crawl under my fence, don't squeeze in my chipmunk hole, don't sniff my glue, suck my popsicle, keep your own greasy fingers on yourself!: 讲话人一口气用了时下流行的一系列俚语，表达"不要干涉我的私事"的意思。

still there. "Now, you be a good girl."

"What are you going to do?"

"Just two things, or maybe three," Arnold Friend said. "But I promise it won't last long and you'll like me the way you get to like people you're close to. You will. It's all over for you here, so come on out. You don't want your people in any trouble, do you?"

She turned and bumped against a chair or something, hurting her leg, but she ran into the back room and picked up the telephone. Something roared in her ear, a tiny roaring, and she was so sick with fear that she could do nothing but listen to it—the telephone was clammy and very heavy and her fingers groped down to the dial but were too weak to touch it. She began to scream into the phone, into the roaring. She cried out, she cried for her mother, she felt her breath start jerking back and forth in her lungs as if it were something Arnold Friend was stabbing her with again and again with no tenderness. A noisy sorrowful wailing rose all about her and she was locked inside it the way she was locked inside this house.

After a while she could hear again. She was sitting on the floor with her wet back against the wall.

Arnold Friend was saying from the door, "That's a good girl. Put the phone back."

She kicked the phone away from her.

"No, honey. Pick it up. Put it back right."

She picked it up and put it back. The dial tone stopped.

"That's a good girl. Now, you come outside."

She was hollow with what had been fear but what was now just an emptiness. All that screaming had blasted it out of her. She sat, one leg cramped under her, and deep inside her brain was something like a pinpoint of light that kept going and would not let her relax. She thought, I'm not going to see my mother again. She thought, I'm not going to sleep in my bed again. Her bright green blouse was all wet.

Arnold Friend said, in a gentle-loud voice that was like a stage voice, "The place where you came from ain't there any more, and where you had in mind to go is cancelled out. This place you are now—inside your daddy's house—is nothing but a cardboard box I can knock down any time. You know that and always did know it. You hear me?"

She thought, I have got to think. I have got to know what to do.

"We'll go out to a nice field, out in the country here where it smells so nice and it's sunny," Arnold Friend said. "I'll have my arms tight around you so you won't need to try to get away and I'll show you what love is like, what it does. The hell with this house! It looks solid all right," he said. He ran a fingernail down the screen and the noise did not make Connie shiver, as it would have the day before. "Now, put your hand on your heart, honey. Feel that? That feels solid too but we know better. Be nice to me, be sweet like you can because what else is there for a girl like you but to be sweet and pretty and give in?—and get away before her people come back?"

She felt her pounding heart. Her hand seemed to enclose it. She thought for the first time in her life that it was nothing that was hers, that belonged to her, but just a pounding, living thing inside this body that wasn't really hers either.

"You don't want them to get hurt," Arnold Friend went on. "Now, get up, honey. Get up all by yourself."

She stood.

"Now, turn this way. That's right. Come over here to me.—Ellie, put that away, didn't I tell you? You dope. You miserable creepy dope," Arnold Friend said. His words were not angry but only part of an incantation①. The incantation was kindly. "Now, come out through the kitchen to me, honey, and let's see a smile, try it, you're a brave, sweet little girl and now they're eating corn and hot dogs cooked to bursting over an outdoor fire, and they don't know one thing about you and never did and honey, you're better than them because not a one of them would have done this for you."

Connie felt the linoleum under her feet; it was cool. She brushed her hair back out of her eyes. Arnold Friend let go of the post tentatively and opened his arms for her, his elbows pointing in toward each other and his wrists limp, to show that this was an embarrassed embrace and a little mocking, he didn't want to make her self-conscious.

She put out her hand against the screen. She watched herself push the door slowly open as if she were back safe somewhere in the other doorway, watching this body and this head of long hair moving out into the sunlight where Arnold Friend waited.

---

① incantation: 咒语。

"My sweet little blue-eyed girl,"① he said in a half-sung sigh that had nothing to do with her brown eyes but was taken up just the same by the vast sunlit reaches of the land behind him and on all sides of him—so much land that Connie had never seen before and did not recognize except to know that she was going to it.

在欧茨已发表的四百多个短篇小说当中,《何去何从》不仅是作者早期最优秀的短篇小说代表作,而且至今一直是多次收入文集并引发争议最多的一篇作品。1985年,该小说被改编成电影《蜜语甜言》(*Smooth Talk*)。作品代表了欧茨典型的爱与暴力主题以及现实主义与象征主义相结合的表现手法。

首先值得关注的是作品的心理现实主义层面。故事取材于美国60年代一个连环杀人案的真实新闻故事。事实上,报刊杂志上的新闻标题常常是欧茨创作灵感的源泉。她说:"我想,正是报纸新闻骷髅般精干的特点吸引了我,这使我觉得有必要给这种简洁而缺乏细节的故事增添血肉。"《何去何从》的灵感来自于亚利桑那州的查尔斯·施米德案:这名23岁的男青年经常驾驶一辆金色的敞篷车出入青少年聚集的场所,多次勾引少女,并杀死了其中三名,后被判谋杀罪,1965至1966年冬季各个新闻杂志上相继出现有关报道。欧茨在小说中从遇害少女的心理角度出发重构了这一诱奸过程,以女性视角重新审视了该事件背后的深层社会心理因素。

另外一个比较突出的特征是作品的象征主义寓言层面。从女性主义的角度来看,作品体现了欧茨对父权社会中女性命运的深切关注,生动地勾勒出从少女到妇人的女性成长经历缩影。15岁的女主人公康妮是美国20世纪60年代一个典型的中产阶级白人少女形象。"不断在背景中响起"的流行乐曲烘托了当时美国社会的流行文化氛围。在弗兰德的人物塑造上淡化了其个性化特点,而更多体现的是时代特征,小说反复强调了大众媒体对其仪表言行的程式化影响。事实上,当弗兰德驾着他那辆金色的篷车来到康妮家门前,带着熟识的口气问独自在家的少女"我没来迟,是吗?",故事增添了一种寓言色彩;但是,情节并没有朝"王子和公主从此过上了幸福的生活"这样的传统童话结局套路发展。康妮逐渐看穿了对方集各种流行文化元素于一体的程式化包装,察觉到表象下暗藏的凶险杀机,于是开始对自身的危急处境产生了忧惧。这名身份诡异、来历不明的男子坚持要她像个"乖女孩"那样从"老爸的房子"里自己走出来,甚至以暴力相威胁。评论家格雷格·约翰逊(Greg Johnson)认为,康妮"在一个男性'朋友'("弗兰德"一词的意译)的操纵下"离开了父亲的家,带着对未来的莫名恐惧走向了"阳光照耀下的一片广阔的"陌生地带,从而完成了从女儿向妇人(情妇/妻子/母亲)的转变,进入了另一个既定的传统女性角色模式,这无异于一种精神死亡。

---

① My sweet little blue-eyed girl:我可爱的蓝眼睛小姑娘。取自于当时的流行歌曲,与康妮的棕色眼睛无关,在一定程度上表现了流行文化对女性的物化倾向。

总之，小说背景的时代文化特色、故事情节的寓意和人物塑造的象征意义都颇具深度和复杂性，值得进行多角度分析。

思考题

1. The story, written in 1966, is a product of its time. In what ways is Connie a typical American adolescent of the 1960s? Is it still relevant? Has teenage culture changed since then?
2. What roles do various members of Connie's family play in her life? Discuss the theme of the house as a metaphor of Connie's identity.
3. How do you interpret Arnold? Why does he dress and conduct himself in that way?
4. Where does Arnold take Connie, and what happens to her? Write your own continuation of the story.
5. Consider the role of each of these elements—society, the parents, and the individual—in this story? Which element is most to blame for Connie's victimization?

推荐作品

Them (1969)
Wonderland (1971)
"Heat" (1991)

参考资料

Bloom, Harold. *Joyce Carol Oates*. New York: Chelsea House Publishers, 1987.

Johnson, Greg. *Joyce Carol Oates: A Study of the Short Fiction*. Boston: Twayne Publishers, 1994.

---. *Understanding Joyce Carol Oates*. Columbia, SC: U of South Carolina P, 1987.

---. *Invisible Writer: A Biography of Joyce Carol Oates*. New York: E. P. Dutton, Inc., 1998.